MUSICAL ALLUSIONS IN THE WORKS OF JAMES JOYCE

MUSICAL ALLUSIONS
IN THE WORKS OF
JAMES JOYCE

EARLY POETRY THROUGH *ULYSSES*

Zack Bowen

State University of New York Press   Albany 1974

For Pat

Published with assistance from
the University Awards Committee
of State University of New York

First Edition

First Published in 1974 by
State University of New York Press
99 Washington Avenue, Albany, New York 12210

Library of Congress Cataloging in Publication Data

Bowen, Zack R
    Musical allusions in the works of James Joyce.
    Bibliography: p.
    1. Joyce, James, 1882–1941—Knowledge—Music.
2. Joyce, James, 1882–1941. Ulysses.   I. Title.
ML80.J75B7   823'.9'12   74-13314
ISBN 0-87395-248-0
ISBN 0-87395-249-9 (microfiche)

CONTENTS

93878

ACKNOWLEDGMENTS

I am deeply grateful to Mabel Worthington, who first interested me in the project and whose constant help, suggestions, additional references, and encouragement have proved to be of invaluable aid, and to Thomas Connolly, whose counsel in the early stages of this manuscript helped shape and define it. I am indebted also to the Research Foundation of the State University of New York and the Graduate Research Office at the State University of New York at Binghamton for subsidizing the research on this project, and to the staffs of the Music Division of the New York Public Library, and the Philadelphia Public Library for their painstaking efforts on my behalf. I am especially indebted for their assistance and kindness to the staffs of the Music Department of the Buffalo and Erie County Public Library and of the Poetry Collection of the Lockwood Memorial Library at the State University of New York at Buffalo. My special thanks go to Joseph Hickerson and especially to Wayne D. Shirley of the Music Division of the Library of Congress for locating hard to find songs, particularly "Seaside Girls," on which I had just about given up hope.

I would like to acknowledge my sincere appreciation to my colleagues, Sheldon Grebstein, Bernard F. Huppé, and John V. Hagopian for reading the manuscript and contributing valuable suggestions. I am also grateful to Maxine Gilgoff for attending to much of the detail work of proofreading quotations and citations. I am especially indebted to Marguerite Harkness for her contributions to this study. Beside providing the initial impetus for some critical ideas central to this work, her counsel in editing and correcting the manuscript proved most valuable.

INTRODUCTION

The importance of music in the works of James Joyce has long been acknowledged by Joycean scholars, though few systematic attempts have been made to deal with the problem. Scholarly references to the music which appears in Joyce's early works are rare, partly because prior to *Ulysses* there are relatively few musical allusions in Joyce's work. Most of the major commentaries on the novel refer to musical allusions in *Ulysses,* but these references are at best occasional mention of specific lines in the narrative and identifications of the songs from which they come. There have been several general treatments of the tonal qualities of *Ulysses* by such musicians as Terrence White, who sees the "Deshil Holles Eamus" passage of the Oxen of the Sun episode as a series of wind-instrument effects; [1] Luigi Dallapiccola, who claims various words and sounds in the Circe episode correspond to a twelve-note scale; [2] and Martin Ross, who envisions all of *Ulysses* as a musical composition rather than a literary work. [3] These studies, while sometimes graced by aesthetic flights of fancy, are of little use to scholars in terms of textual explication. A much more interesting and useful overall musical schema for *Ulysses* is Father Robert Boyle's, *"Ulysses* as Frustrated Sonata Form," [4] in which he admits that his application of the novel to the sonata isn't exactly congruent in all details. He does, however, provide an outline of the book in musical terms, which can be a handy device for introducing the structure of the novel in the classroom. From a practical standpoint another good treatment of the musical techniques of Joyce's prose appears in Frederick Sternfeld's "Poetry and Music—Joyce's *Ulysses."* [5] Sternfeld renders the aural dimensions of the words in a few musical allusions in *Ulysses* by considering the actual musical scores to which they refer.

There are many interpretations of the Sirens chapter of *Ulysses,* some of which will be discussed in the course of this study. Since the chapter deals primarily with music and Joyce's musical technique, these commentaries are of special significance in any work dealing with the topic. In this connection, Lawrence Levin's article, "The Sirens Episode as Music: Joyce's Experiment in Prose Polyphony," [6] is an interesting attempt to deal with the shape and style of the Sirens chapter with reference to music. The early treatments of the Sirens chapter which are especially comprehensive appear in Harry Levin's book, *James Joyce;* [7] Stanley Sultan's "The Sirens at the Ormond Bar: *Ulysses";* [8] Marian Kaplun's "The Search for 'The Song the Sirens Sang': Two Notes on the Sirens of Joyce's *Ulysses";* [9] Walton Litz's *The Art of James Joyce: Method and Design in ULYSSES and FINNEGANS WAKE;* [10] and L. A. G. Strong's *The Sacred River.* [11] Much of the present discussion of the music in the Sirens was originally published in my monograph, "The Bronzegold Sirensong: A Musical Analysis of the Sirens Episode in Joyce's *Ulysses.*" [12]

The burden of identifying actual song references in *Ulysses* was begun also by Strong in his essay, "James Joyce and Vocal Music." [13] Strong's article was followed in its quest for song titles by Joseph Prescott's "Local Allusions in Joyce's *Ulysses*" [14] and "Notes on Joyce's *Ulysses*" [15] and by Vivien Mercier's "James Joyce and an Irish Tradition," [16] Mabel Worthington's "Irish Folk Songs in Joyce's *Ulysses,*" [17] Joseph Duncan's "The Modality of the Audible in Joyce's *Ulysses,*" [18] and William M. Schutte's *Joyce and Shakespeare.* [19]

All these studies identified various song references in the text of *Ulysses.* Schutte was, of course, concerned with Elizabethan song references, while the others confined their activities primarily to Irish songs. In few cases was there much attempt to go beyond the citing of the song and the appropriate passage from *Ulysses.* There was, however, one very excellent commentary which attempted to link thematically the repeated references to a single musical work in *Ulysses.* Vernon Hall's article, "Joyce's Use of Da Ponte and Mozart's *Don Giovanni,*" [20] to which I am indebted in the present study, traces the many references to *Don Giovanni* throughout the novel and demonstrates how the musical work is inextricably bound to the action of the book both thematically and in the mind of the protagonist, Leopold Bloom. The longest treatment to date of music in thematic developments of *Ulysses* as a whole is James Penny Smith's dissertation, "Musical Allusions in James Joyce's *Ulysses.*" [21] Smith deals with song references relating to three major themes of the novel. His study provides valuable insights into *Ulysses* particularly from a variety of operatic sources. All of the studies mentioned, however, from Sternfeld through Smith, were severely limited, and none pretended to be comprehensive in dealing with all the music alluded to in *Ulysses*. The two books that do try to treat all the musical allusions in the novel provide only a list.

The most important work on the music in Joyce is *Song in the Works of James Joyce,* by Matthew Hodgart and Mabel Worthington.[22] In this book Hodgart and Worthington have gone far beyond the musical discoveries of their predecessors and have listed references to over 1000 songs in Joyce's works. The book identifies musical titles with the page and line references to Joyce's work in which the musical allusions appear. No attempt was made by Hodgart and Worthington in their already monumental task to explain the function or significance which the musical references have in the context of the passages in which they are mentioned.

Weldon Thornton's *Allusions in "Ulysses"* [23] was the other major source which has proven exceptionally valuable in compiling this study. Thornton's list includes not only songs and appropriate page and line numbers in *Ulysses,* but occasional short quotations of song lyrics and collections in which the music might be located.

The present study is a natural outgrowth of Hodgart and Worthington's work. Where they merely identified musical titles, I will attempt to fit the musical works to the text, to make them understandable as working, integrated elements in the works considered. In general I have followed Hodgart and Worthington's citations. Where their citation of a song did not seem justified by the text, I have omitted the song. Except when there was compelling reason for calling the reader's attention to differences, I have changed their citation errors and made additions without comment.

During the academic year 1971–2 Mabel Worthington and I were given a grant and other assistance by the State University of New York at Binghamton to study the problem of musical allusions in the works of James Joyce. We agreed that I would cover the earlier works through *Ulysses* and that she would be responsible for *Finnegans Wake*, since we had each already been concentrating in those particular areas. The *Wake* contains three or four times more allusions than all the rest of Joyce's works, so Professor Worthington's job is much longer and of course more complicated. In this study, then, I refer only in passing to *Finnegans Wake,* but treat as completely as I can the earlier works.

Any attempt to go beyond the mere listing of musical titles and to explicate their use in the text of the several works considered presents certain organizational problems. Since this book attempts to be both a definitive annotation of musical allusions and a critical study of the uses of music in Joyce's style, characterization, structure, and theme, it must list all the allusions and comment at length on the ones that relate to the critical issues of the novel. At the same time there has to be more coherence of thematic continuity than would be permitted by an item-by-item listing of the allusion with appropriate text. The organization adopted was a compromise between the two major aims of the book: to comment on every allusion discovered and to present a unified critical study. So, an introductory essay precedes the main body of musical allusions for each of the works considered. Each essay attempts to incorporate in general terms a summary of the ways in which music is used in the particular book under discussion. The main body of the text consists of each passage in the order of its appearance in the text of Joyce's work, followed by the title of the song or songs alluded to in the passage; then remarks, containing all of the scholarly and critical information I feel is germane to the reference. Neither the essays nor the explication of the allusions are complete in themselves but each is intended to inform the other and thus present a complete picture to the reader.

It will, I hope, become increasingly apparent as the study progresses that music provides a new dimension to Joyce's works not immediately available to those readers who lack Joyce's apparent knowledge of Irish folk music, music-hall songs, nursery rhymes, sixteenth-century madrigals, liturgical music, and opera. So careful an author as Joyce places little or no extraneous material in his text, and so the very volume of musical references dictates the significant contribution they make to his works. It is hoped that this book will delineate the method and meaning of that contribution.

POETRY

Joyce's use of musical allusions increases in proportion to the increasing complexity of the later works. In general, not only are there a greater number of musical references in subsequent works, but the significance of the musical images in terms of style, structure, and theme becomes more and more important, until Joyce's last book is in a sense the explanation of the ballad after which it is named. Having said that, we begin with the suite of lyrical poems bearing a musical title and intended to be set to music, as indeed Joyce himself did with several.

Only one major musical allusion pattern appears in *Chamber Music: The Song of Solomon,* which may have existed for Joyce as literature rather than as music, though Bloom's "modulations of voice" in Ithaca indicate that *Solomon* is at least partially sung or chanted in *Ulysses.* The allusion to *Solomon* in four separate poems makes it the most extensively developed allusion source in *Chamber Music.* Not only did it give great allusive dignity to the young poet's love songs in implying their comparison with *The Song of Solomon,* but the meaning and purpose of the biblical fusion of sensual and worshipful into one ambiguous whole suited the mood of Joyce's poems, in which the act of love would take place in the poet's mind in an "enaisled pine forest," and in which the woman would fit the dichotomous roles of lover-destroyer, virgin-temptress, Holy Mother-sex symbol. I have stated elsewhere how the sources of paradox in Joyce's concept of woman found their earliest expression in *Chamber Music* [1] and how the three-way female figure at the end of poem XXXVI is really an expression of the diverse and often paradoxical aspects of woman which Joyce was to embody in all the works to follow. The lover-Mother-Church aspects of Solomon's bride and the ecclesiastical overtones of the sensuality of their love form a natural allusive backdrop for the complex portrait the poet seeks to present. In poem VII *Solomon* references provide the girl with the image of

5

the life-giving fertility force, as well as defining her role as the source of the fall of both man and the persona. In XIII she becomes the fountain of inspiration as well as fertility, in XIV the maternal figure and by extension the Holy Mother Church, and in XVIII the sensual, so that the many-faceted-image pattern of womankind in Joyce's later works really owes something to the ambiguities of *Solomon* in these early delineations of character and theme by Joyce. These ambiguities of the tripartite woman to whom "My love, my love, my love" is addressed in poem XXVI will haunt all of Joyce's subsequent books.

Chamber Music

VII

My love is in a light attire
Among the apple-trees, (p. 15) *

Cf. *The Song of Solomon:* "As the apple tree among the trees of the wood, so is my beloved among the sons" (2:3).

REMARKS: "In the *Solomon* motif, the bride, Israel, brings with her the promise of the fulfillment of God's word. She is the means by which the word will be made whole, the earthly fertility symbol of her lover-God. So it is with the poet's lover: she will be the catalyst, the means and the force giving life to the poet's words. Her ultimate rejection of the poet is the hard but inevitable factor in the poet's development." [2] Here the apple trees also have overtones of the bitterness inherent in the knowledge she will bring to the poet. The *Solomon* passage refers to the apple tree as a symbol of the male lover, but the tree image is further extended in VII to provide a *Genesis* background for the temptress figure and the source of the poet's new knowledge.

XIII

Wind of spices whose song is ever
Epithalamium.

. . . .

Now, wind, of your good courtesy
I pray you go,

And come into her little garden
And sing at her window;
Singing: The bridal wind is blowing
For Love is at his noon: (p. 21)

Cf. *The Song of Solomon:* "Awake, O north wind, and come, thou south;
blow upon my garden, that the spices thereof may flow out. Let my beloved
come into his garden, and eat his pleasant fruits" (4:16).
"A garden inclosed is my sister, my spouse" (4:12).

REMARKS: "The poet of the *Song* sees the wind as his poem, the girl as the
potential life-giver, and the garden as the source of fertility. . . . Not only
will she be brought to fruition by the union; so will the poet-God-Solomon.
The indications are that in XIII the nuptial song is similarly the wind-poem,
the girl the promise of fulfillment, and the garden fertility. So the girl of
Chamber Music, as the sensual aspects of the poems increase, assumes the
fertility role hinted at in Poem VII." [3]

XIV

The night-dew lies
Upon my lips and eyes.

. . . .

I wait by the cedar tree,
My sister, my love.

. . . .

The pale dew lies
Like a veil on my head. (p. 22)

Cf. *The Song of Solomon:* "Open to me, my sister, my love, my dove, my
undefiled: for my head is filled with dew, and my locks with the drops of
the night" (5:2).

REMARKS: " 'In the Vulgate, as in the Douay and King James versions, the
love of Solomon is allegorized as that of Christ for his spouse,' [4] who in the
Douay version is the church and especially the Holy Mother aspects of the
church. Here, then, we get a combination of the mother-Virgin-lover fulfillment theme but with another Joycean subtlety: the poet will assume the
substantive position. He tells her: 'My breast shall be your bed.' As he waits,

The pale dew lies
Like a veil on my head.

In the song of this lover there are overtones of the reversal of the male-female
roles, the active-passive behavior pattern which plays so large a role in *Exiles*
and *Ulysses.* His dew-veiled head further suggests Virgin-mother aspects." [5]

XVIII

His hand is under
Her smooth round breast; (p. 26)

Cf. *The Song of Solomon:* "His left hand is under my head and his right hand doth embrace me" (2:6).

REMARKS: In moving the lover's hand south, Joyce obviously increases the explicit sensuality.

Pomes Penyeach

"Tutto è sciolto" (p. 51)

Cf. *"Tutto è sciolto"*

REMARKS: A very short but beautiful aria in Bellini's *La Sonnambula,* the lines are sung by Elvino after his bride-to-be has been caught sleepwalking in Rudolpho's room. Elvino, not knowing her innocence, upbraids her and then in despair sings the song. Joyce's poem describes the emotions and the situation of the song:

> All is lost now,
> By all hope and joy am I forsaken,
> Nevermore can love awaken
> Past enchantment, no nevermore.

EXILES

Musical allusions play a less significant role in *Exiles* than in any of Joyce's works. The two references to opera which provide the only musical background are both tangential to the action, though even a perfunctory glance at Joyce's notes to the play will sustain the impression that there is not one word or reference in *Exiles* which is not fraught with significance for its author.

Exiles

Richard Rowan *

Cf. "Oh Rowan Tree"

REMARKS: Ruth Bauerle[1] cites as a possible Joycean source for the protagonist's name the song by Lady Caroline Nairne in which "the singer addresses the tree which is entwined 'wi' mony ties, o'hame and infancy.'" Professor Bauerle sees the tree which in the song has the names of the persona and his family engraved on it as being a symbol of Richard Rowan, around whom the other characters revolve. The distance of the persona from the scene of remembered happiness is also cited as being analogous to Rowan's exile. At the risk of seeming even more ingenious I would like to suggest that the names carved on the tree are like the runes on Woton's spear and as such unlock the mysteries of the past to the artist-diviner Richard Rowan. As Bauerle points out the rowan tree is the mountain ash; hence its association with Woton's ash spear and Stephen Dedalus's ashplant-divination rod, so important in both *Portrait* and *Ulysses*. For a fuller discussion of the whole association of the ashplant and the Ring Cycle, see pages 81–82.

He knew I wanted to go to the theatre to hear *Carmen*. (p. 24:24–25)

9

Cf. *Carmen*

REMARKS: Perhaps this opera is mentioned because it is concerned with romance and youth, hence appealing to the romantic boy. It is conceivable that Carmen's self exile from the prevailing society and the love triangle of the opera may have provided the basis for Richard's penchant for exile and love rivalry in his adult life. His father has nurtured these aspects of Richard's nature by providing him with funds to go.

He plays softly in the bass the first bars of Wolfram's song in the last act of "Tannhäuser." (pp. 57–58)

Cf. *"O du mein holder Abendstern"* (The Evening Star)

REMARKS: When Wolfram sings this greeting to the evening star and the departing and presumably dying Elizabeth, he sings as the responsible, God-fearing lover-rival of Tannhäuser, who is a slave to the lust of Venus. Robert, about to consummate a liaison with Bertha, should be singing Tannhäuser's songs instead of the chaste and good Wolfram's. The aria is part of the false picture he presents of himself and his own motivations.

DUBLINERS

In *Dubliners* music becomes increasingly significant both structurally and thematically. As in the later works, music is often used to orchestrate and reiterate existing themes, without really contributing new or vital links or thematic interpretations. An example of such peripheral references is Polly Mooney's song of coquettishness. However, music does become an integral part of the stories in at least two instances. To explain how music works as an organizing agent in *Dubliners,* it is necessary to discuss briefly a prominent narrative thematic pattern in all Joyce's major works: the idea of the simultaneity of existence, or that everyone lives through similar experiences all through life. By this is meant more than merely Jung's collective subconscious or the universality of human experience; rather, that we live every day each other's lives and the lives of everyone who has preceded us.

The usual interpretation of the structure of *Dubliners* divides it into stories of youth, maturity, and public life, with a summary in "The Dead." I have no quarrel with this division, but would add a defining footnote: that all the action is taking place at the same time or at about the same time, and that all of the frustrations and epiphanies are really about the same thing. To this end Joyce, in a manner fairly obvious to the careful reader, inserts objects or references in stories merely to provide similarities to things in other stories, like the yellowing picture of the priest in "Eveline" to suggest the priest of "The Sisters," or the discussion of "the late priest" in "Araby" to suggest the first story, or the remark of Maria's brother Joe to his superior to suggest Farrington. The list is long, culminating in the many hints of similarity in characters and action between "The Dead" and earlier stories. For instance Lily's remark that "the men that is now is all only palaver and what they can get out of you" is strongly reminiscent of "Two Gallants," while Gabriel's coin for her is in some measure an attempt at recognition of the wrong done the slavery in extracting a coin from her in the earlier story. The point is that the links which seemed superficial between the earlier stories assume thematic importance in the last story, and what seemed initially like a number of individual cases of hopelessness and frustration in previous stories is drawn together in a progressively tighter knot in "The Dead," until the final metaphor of the snow stresses the communal existence of all the living and the dead and they become interchangeable, all in fact part of the same existence.

The similarities between Maria and Eveline are not intended, then, to suggest that Maria is Eveline thirty or forty years later, but they are too striking to be passed over lightly. Like Eveline, Maria seems to have elected the unmarried state as a way of life, though she is not above what flirtations she can have, and she is not completely without hope. But like Eveline, Maria decided to take care of her brothers and keep the home together as long as she could, becoming the "proper mother," like her namesake, rather than a real mother. These superficial connections between the two stories set up the more important final connection, which is to *The Bohemian Girl*. When Frank sings to Eveline "about the lass that loves a sailor," he establishes musical connotations for their love. The song has meaning for them, since the words fit their situation. So does *The Bohemian Girl,* the heroine of which is rescued from a life of obscurity with the gypsies to dwell in the marble halls of the royalty to which she really belongs. When Frank takes Eveline to see the operetta, he is in effect showing her the good life. When Maria sings "I Dreamt that I Dwelt" from *The Bohemian Girl,* the way has already been paved by the other similarities for the association of Maria and Eveline. Maria dreams of the same things as Eveline, but sublimates her vision of the suitors who will carry her from Dublin and the world of the laundry and virgin piety. Though Maria is more than an Eveline grown old, their experience is essentially the same: the living death of the caged animal for Eveline and the imminence of literal death, foreshadowed by the lump of clay, as well as living death, for Maria. Their lives encompass the same experience.

The second use of music, as a thematic agent, occurs in "The Dead." Just as the epiphany of the folly and futility forming Jimmy Doyle's existence is heralded with the announcement of the dawn by the artist-musician Villona,[1] so is Gabriel's epiphany precipitated by the artist-musician Bartell D'Arcy as he sings "The Lass of Aughrim." The fact that D'Arcy has a sore throat and cold provides a thematic link between the dead Furey, who lives in the mind of Gretta-Ireland because he exposed his soul and body to life and the elements, and Gabriel and the rest of the Morkans' company, whose galoshes, overcoats, conventions, and vicarious existences protect them from pneumonia and the actual living of life. It is not chance that this most important story of *Dubliners* should also be the most musical or that music should provide the key to the final epiphany. The only difference between the Morkan sisters and the Flynn sisters of the first story is that so far as we know the Flynns have little to offer except clichés, while the Morkans have music to sustain their contact with the past, the only source of life in the story. This is why so much of the conversation centers upon music and performers of the past, upon dead singers who live in memory and music no longer heard. As "The Dead" progresses to the final metaphor, and the connections to other stories make them a part of the final epiphany of death, so do the references to music draw the company closer to the world of the dead, until Aunt Julia in her intricate rendition of "Arrayed for the Bridal" comes closest to living death in the anguish of the persona for the vision of life she witnesses. Thus the scene is set for "The Lass of Aughrim" and its final metaphor of death which becomes explicit in Gretta's story of Michael Furey. The techniques for utilizing the associations of music to further structure and theme are present for the first time in *Dubliners* as well as the narrative pattern of simultaneous existence in which they become operative.

Dubliners

"ARABY"

"Araby" (p. 29, story title) *

* From *Dubliners* by James Joyce. Originally published by B. W. Huebsch, Inc. in 1916. Copyright © 1967 by the Estate of James Joyce. Reprinted by permission of The Viking Press, Inc. (All page references are to the Viking Press edition, 1967.)

Cf. "I'll Sing Thee Songs of Araby"

REMARKS: The title of the story does have a factual basis in the bazaar which took place in Dublin, 14–19 May 1894. But Joyce did know and utilize the Araby song in *Finnegans Wake,* and its lyrics fit completely the courtly love motif upon which the short story is based:

> I'll sing thee songs of Araby,
> And tales of fair Cashmere,
> Wild tales to cheat thee of a sigh,
> Or charm thee to a tear.
> And dreams of delight shall on thee break,
> And rainbow visions rise,
> And all my soul shall strive to wake
> Sweet wonder in thine eyes.
> And all my soul, etc.

The theme of illusions coming to nothing in the boy's epiphany of futility and frustration is suggested in the song by the tentative, dreamlike quality of the tales the persona will render. The boy's "rainbow visions" of Araby come tumbling down as he realizes his own pretensions through the epiphany of frivolousness exhibited by the girl in the booth and her reaction to the small-talking would-be lovers and by the degraded ecclesiastical imagery of the hall.

"EVELINE"

He took her to see *The Bohemian Girl* and she felt elated as she sat in an unaccustomed part of the theatre with him. (p. 39)

Cf. *The Bohemian Girl*

REMARKS: The central action of the opera stems from the abduction of the heroine, Arline, by the gypsies and her subsequent love affair with Thaddeus, a member of the band. Eveline's proposed trip to Buenos Aires, far from her father, parodies the abduction and the long absence of Arline from her father. Thaddeus, a Polish exile, and Frank, most lately from Argentina, are both unknown quantities, but Arline's eventual happiness is not as dependent on willing choice as is Eveline's, and its outcome therefore is much more romantic. For a girl of Eveline's Irish Catholic training, there is little real choice.

People knew that they were courting and, when he sang about the lass that loves a sailor, she always felt pleasantly confused. (p. 39)

Cf. "The Lass That Loves a Sailor"

REMARKS: The song is a very gentlemanly ballad about sailors tippling and offering toasts:

But the standing toast that pleased the most
Was the wind that blows, the ship that goes,
And the lass who loves a sailor.

The lyrics fit the story in several ways. Eveline's *pleasant* feeling of confusion has its parallel in the song: The "ship that goes" has its connotations of the boat on which Eveline and Frank will make their escape from Dublin; and, of course, she is "the lass that loves a sailor."

"AFTER THE RACE"

They proceeded towards it with linked arms, singing *Cadet Roussel* in chorus, stamping their feet at every:
—Ho! Ho! Hohé, vraiment! (p. 47)

Cf. "Cadet Roussel"

REMARKS: The comic song of Cadet Roussel deals with a man who has "arrived" in the sense of having three of everything. The opulence of the song is associated with acquisition and lack of it, a central theme in "After the Race." Jimmy and the elder Doyle have been *acquiring* their way to the top of Dublin's middle class. Jimmy's conspicuous consumption having accrued for them additional dignity, they are trying to go beyond the narrow confines of Dublin to engage in the acquisitions of the continent. Hence "Cadet Roussel," about the man who has three of everything, acts as a sort of musical theme song.

"TWO GALLANTS"

One hand played in the bass the melody of *Silent, O Moyle,* while the other hand careered in the treble after each group of notes. (p. 54)

Cf. "Silent, O Moyle"

REMARKS: The musician's harp, adorned presumably with a carved and nearly naked lady, is used for money-making purposes and seems in the description to resemble an exploited woman giving forth the beauty of the Thomas Moore song to please passers-by. The casual way in which the harp is played is a foreshadowing of the casual way the slavey is to be used by Corley. The song, in which "Lir's lonely daughter/Tells to the night star her tales of woes," reveals the wish of the persona that Erin, still sleeping in darkness, be warmed with the daystar of peace and love. The corruption of Ireland, its slaveys, and its harps by its mercenary gallants insures its darkness in the foreseeable future and leads to the death wish expressed so beautifully in "Silent, O Moyle!" and in "The Dead."

"THE BOARDING HOUSE"

She sang:

> *I'm a . . . naughty girl.*
> *You needn't sham:*
> *You know I am.* (p. 62)

Cf. "I'm a Naughty Girl"

REMARKS: The lyrics of the song fit closely the situation in "The Boarding House":

Stanza I

I'm an imp on mischief bent,
Only feeling quite content
When doing wrong!
When doing wrong!
Sometimes when I've *had* the fun
I repent of what I've done,
But not for long!
But not for long!
On my mistress tricks I play,
Telling her what love should say,
Whispering what love should do;
She believes and does it too!
I'm a naughty girl
You needn't sham;
You know, I am!
Rome is in a whirl,
Because they're all afraid
Of this naughty little maid!

CHORUS:

She's a naughty girl!
We know it well
And mean to tell!
She's a bad one
If we ever had one:
Oh, she's a very very naughty little girl!

Stanza II

At the Roman Clubs, no doubt,
Funny tales you hear about
My goings on!
Your goings on!

If I like to sit and chat,
What can be the harm in that
Though daylight's gone?
Though daylight's gone!
If some youth with manners free
Dares to snatch a kiss from me,
Do I ask him to explain?
No I kiss him back again!

I'm a naughty girl, etc.

The first stanza foreshadows impish Polly's contentment on Doran's bed, as well as her momentary regrets for her wrongdoing. Polly's "mistress," Mrs. Mooney, "The Madame," goes along with unspoken acquiescence in Polly's romance. Meanwhile the boarders in "Rome" all have reason to fear the wiles of this little coquette and her burly brother, Jack, who is so "handy with the mits." In parallels to stanza two, tales about Polly's doings are indeed bruited about as the house begins "to get a certain fame." Finally the seduction is described fairly accurately in stanza two as the song outlines in considerable detail the plot of the story.

"CLAY"

She sang *I Dreamt that I Dwelt,* and when she came to the second verse she sang again:

I dreamt that I dwelt in marble halls
With vassals and serfs at my side
And of all who assembled within those walls
That I was the hope and the pride.
I had riches too great to count, could boast
Of a high ancestral name,
But I also dreamt, which pleased me most,
That you loved me still the same. (p. 106)

Cf. "I Dreamt that I Dwelt"

REMARKS: The verse that Maria fails to sing is as follows:

I dreamt that suitors sought my hand;
That knights on bended knee,
And with vows no maiden heart could withstand,
They pledg'd their faith to me,
And I dreamt that one of the noble host
Came forth my hand to claim;
But I also dreamt, which charm'd me most,
That you lov'd me still the same.

The meaning of Maria's slip in forgetting the words to the second verse (that she sublimates the references to suitors and marriage) is not lost on her sentimental, understanding brother Joe. More importantly in structural terms, the song is from *The Bohemian Girl,* the opera to which Frank took Eveline, who, like Maria, took care of her brothers after her mother's death. Thus, the song reference is part of Joyce's intentional suggestion that in Ireland the Evelines of today become the Marias of tomorrow. Phillips George Davies sees in the forgotten stanza and the song a further imagery of the Death-All Hallows Eve pattern.[2] To do this, however, Davies had to make the marble halls heaven and alter the context of the opera from which it was taken.

"A MOTHER"

One night, when an operatic *artiste* had fallen ill, he had undertaken the part of the king in the opera of *Maritana* at the Queen's Theatre. (p. 142)

Cf. *Maritana*

REMARKS: The unassuming bass, of humble origin and slight, seems an unlikely candidate for the role of Charles II in the opera, but all of the performers in this story are slightly out of place on the stage and seem slightly like caricatures. Only Mrs. Kearney seems completely realistic as she fuses her theatrical ambitions with her less artistic nature and demands cash for Kathleen's appearance.

The poor lady sang *Killarney* in a bodiless gasping voice, with all the old-fashioned mannerisms of intonation and pronunciation which she believed lent elegance to her singing. (p. 147)

Cf. "Killarney"

REMARKS: This song was especially well known and often sung, perhaps because it is not too vocally taxing. The beautiful scenes described in the song form an interesting contrast to Madame Glynn's rendition.

"THE DEAD"

It was that of an old song of Aunt Julia's—*Arrayed for the Bridal.* Her voice, strong and clear in tone, attacked with great spirit the runs which embellish the air and though she sang very rapidly she did not miss even the smallest of the grace notes. (p. 193)

Cf. "Arrayed for the Bridal"

REMARKS: The persona of Aunt Julia's song expresses admiration for the fair bride-to-be:

> Arrayed for the bridal, in beauty behold her,
> A white wreath entwineth a forehead more fair:
> I envy the zephyrs that softly enfold her, enfold her,
> And play with the locks of her beautiful hair.
> May life to her prove full of sunshine and love,
>   full of love, yes! yes! yes!
>
> Who would not love her?
> Sweet star of the morning! shining so bright,
> Earth's circle adorning, fair creature of light!

The song is not easy to sing: it is replete with long and complicated runs, requiring a sophisticated and gifted singer. Aunt Julia's creditable singing job reflects some degree of vocal prowess. The subject matter of the song, the beauty of the bride, and the entrapment inspired in the persona displays the contrast between Aunt Julia and the fair bride, as well as foreshadowing the love motif of Michael Furey, who later will fill the role of the persona of the song, and Gabriel, the about-to-be-humbled groom of bride-Gretta.

One of her pupils had given her a pass for *Mignon*. Of course it was very fine, she said, but it made her think of poor Georgina Burns. (p. 199)

Cf. *Mignon*

REMARKS: The first London production of the opera was in 1870, and probably it appeared in Dublin sometime after that, so that Mary Jane's nostalgic memory of Georgina Burns probably goes back about thirty years.

He told too of how the top gallery of the old Royal used to be packed night after night, of how one night an Italian tenor had sung five encores to *Let Me Like a Soldier Fall,* introducing a high C every time. . . . (p. 199)

Cf. "Yes! Let Me Like a Soldier Fall"

REMARKS: The introduction of the high C would presumably come at the end of Don Caesar's aria, with the Italian tenor, in a gratuitous alteration of the music to please the gallery, transposing the last two notes of the song up an octave since the original score calls for a middle C. But even high C's can get a little redundant.

Why did they never play the grand old operas now, he asked, *Dinorah, Lucrezia Borgia?* Because they could not get the voices to sing them: that was why. (p. 199)

Cf. *Dinorah*
   Lucrezia Borgia

REMARKS: Contrary to Mr. Browne's theory, *Dinorah* probably was not performed in Dublin because the libretto was so absurd and vacuous. However, *Lucrezia Borgia* was exceptionally popular with American audiences in the late nineteenth century and was about the time of Mr. Browne's remarks (1904) being revived for Caruso, whose ability Mr. Browne doubts in the next few lines. The facts seem to disprove Browne's statement that there are no voices around to sing "the grand old operas."

All the guests stood up, glass in hand, and, turning towards the three seated ladies, sang in unison, with Mr Browne as leader:

> *For they are jolly gay fellows,*
> *For they are jolly gay fellows,*
> *For they are jolly gay fellows,*

. . . the singers turned towards one another, as if in melodious conference, while they sang, with emphasis:

> *Unless he tells a lie,*
> *Unless he tells a lie*

Then, turning once more towards their hostesses, they sang:

> *For they are jolly gay fellows,*
> *For they are jolly gay fellows,*
> *For they are jolly gay fellows,*
> *Which nobody can deny.* (p. 205)

Cf. "For He's a Jolly Good Fellow"

REMARKS: In a way the company's affirmation that the Morkans are "jolly gay fellows" fails to sense the imminent presence of the dead, which permeates the nostalgic scene of Dublin gone by, and fails also to realize, despite all the talk of death, that the Morkans' only vestige of life comes from their memories of the dead. Nobody really can "deny" the jollity of the Morkans and Mary Jane without a painful realization of their living death, and the assemblage would brand that "a lie," if anyone told it.

The voice, made plaintive by distance and by the singer's hoarseness, faintly illuminated the cadence of the air with words expressing grief:

> *O, the rain falls on my heavy locks*
> *And the dew wets my skin,*
> *My babe lies cold* . . . . (p. 210)

—Mr D'Arcy, she said, what is the name of that song you were singing?

—It's called *The Lass of Aughrim,* said Mr D'Arcy, but I couldn't remember it properly. Why? Do you know it?

—*The Lass of Aughrim,* she repeated. I couldn't think of the name. (p. 212)

—O, I am thinking about that song, *The Lass of Aughrim.* (p. 218)

—It was a young boy I used to know, she answered, named Michael Furey. He used to sing that song, *The Lass of Aughrim.* (p. 219)

Cf. "The Lass of Aughrim"

REMARKS: Donagh MacDonagh's essay, " 'The Lass of Aughrim' or the Betrayal of James Joyce" [3] includes a comprehensive history of the song and its variations as traced through Child's ballads as well as a thoughtful application of the ballad to "The Dead" as the key to the relation between the story and Joyce's own life particularly the Michael (Sonny) Bodkin affair. The words sung to Joyce by Nora were:

> If you'll be the lass of Aughrim
> As I am taking you mean to be
> Tell me the first token
> That passed between you and me.
>
> O don't you remember
> That night on yon lean hill
> When we both met together
> Which I am sorry now to tell.
>
> The rain falls on my yellow locks
> And the dew it wets my skin;
> My babe lies cold within my arms:
> Lord Gregory let me in. [4]

MacDonagh reconstructs the rest of the song:

> Oh, if you be the lass of Aughrim
> As I suppose you not to be
> Come tell me the last token
> Between you and me.
> Between you and me.
> Oh Gregory, don't you remember
> One night on the hill
> When we swapped rings off each other's hands
> Sorely against my will?
> Mine was of the beaten gold,
> Yours but block tin.[5]

The third stanza, which reminds Gretta of Michael Furey, seems on first glance to be similar to Furey's situation only in the similarity of the rain and the dampness. In the original version, *The Lass of Roch Royal,* however, the banished lass comes to Love Gregory's house in search of her lover and the father of her child. After an interrogation of the lass at the door by Gregory's mother in which the girl answers all the questions correctly, she is turned away and told that Gregory has gone to sea. When he returns he goes looking for her only to find the funeral procession carrying her away to be buried. MacDonagh suggests that the initial rejection of Gretta by Gabriel's mother is analogous to the situation in the ballad. But there is more to the parallel than merely the image of Gretta as the rejected suitor. In Gretta's account of the Furey story she is being sent off to a convent and not allowed to see him. He comes anyway and is destroyed by the rain because he doesn't care to live once Gretta has gone away. If Gretta is in fact the Ireland symbol kept from her ardent young lover by the strictures of the convent and church, as Gregory in the ballad is restrained by his mother, then Gabriel, the unfeeling establishment figure, is all that is left to her. Their marriage is to typify the whole sterility of the *Dubliners* in contrast with Gretta's suggestion that there was fertility in the liaison between her and Furey ("I was great with him at the time"). What vitality is forthcoming in Ireland seems only to come through the dead and the memories and snow which link them to the dead living.

Marguerite Harkness has suggested further that, in another parallel to Gregory's mother in the ballad, Gabriel's dominating, family-dignity-conscious mother, who opposed Gabriel's marriage to Gretta (p. 187), is the source of his inability to feel love and experience emotion as Furey does. Further, in *Ulysses,* the psychological dominance of May Dedalus in the life of her Oedipal son, Stephen, creates a similar inability to love.

> He had caught that haggard look upon her face for a moment
> when she was singing *Arrayed for the Bridal.* (p. 222)

Cf. "Arrayed for the Bridal"

REMARKS: As Gabriel senses Aunt Julia's imminent death, the life wish implicit in her song of the beautiful bride stresses more forcefully her own removal from life and vitality. Yet there is something about the dexterity and beauty of her rendition as well as the genuine sentiment of the Morkans' party that mitigates some of the grimness of the Dublin scene and the rest of the stories. It is true that the characters are all dead and dying, and it is true that in the short stories Ireland lacks even the dubious hope of an artist forging an uncreated conscience for her people; but there is a softening on Joyce's part here of the unrelenting despair of the other stories and an appreciation of the struggles of the Morkans, Gabriel, and the rest to ease the plight of their own captivity. Hence we have the pathetic joy of the party and the balm sought by the characters from the bygone sounds of Parkinson and the Italian tenors. Perhaps Joyce was mellowing by the time he added "The Dead" to *Dubliners:* Gabriel's realization is more complete and humane than the epiphanies of the boy of "Araby," Chandler, or even Mr. Duffy. Even if we have nothing left but the dreams of the persona of "Arrayed for the Bridal," some fragments of the past may still be shored against our ruins, and the community of the dead-living and the living-dead may be endured and some solace taken.

STEPHEN HERO

It is not really legitimate to treat as finished pieces of literature works not intended for publication or not ready for publication. Hence I will confine my few remarks about *Stephen Hero* to whatever might be gleaned by way of a comparison in technique to *Portrait.* Music contributes very little by way of furthering the themes or plot, such as it is, of *Stephen Hero,* but like the narrative technique as a whole the music tends toward obviousness and an open and direct approach to Stephen's mind, an approach infinitely less satisfactory than the indirect inferences and effects on Stephen of the events of *Portrait.* In *Stephen Hero* the narrative pattern, as the narrative pattern of all the third-person stories of *Dubliners,* approaches in style and content the mind of the person discussed. As the language in "Counterparts," for instance, has a "furious" quality about it to duplicate the rage of Farrington,[1] so *Stephen Hero* is composed of a narrative pattern so condescendingly close to the arrogant mind of Stephen that it really intrudes too irritatingly and obviously on what is being said, as for example this description of the president's reaction to one of Stephen's thrusts about morality and literature: "The president far from resenting this hardy statement seemed to bow to its justice."[2] The point is not that there is a certain amount of irony in calling the statement "hardy," but that it is all done so obviously that it calls attention to itself and the author's intention, so that the book becomes "epic" in the terminology of Stephen's aesthetic theory and hence diminished as a prospective work of art. It is essentially the shift in the focus of the narrative voice from a bold embracing of Stephen's mind with all its arrogance in *Stephen Hero* to the much less colored lens of the experiences Stephen considers significant which provides the necessary aesthetic distance and makes for the real work of art in the final novel.

In *Stephen Hero,* then, there are few musical references which need elaborate explication, since, like the narrative pattern in general, they are nearly all used by Stephen to elaborate some point he is trying to make to someone or to himself. So the clown's songs from *Twelfth Night,* "God Save the Queen," "Come Unto These Yellow Sands," and "Washed in the Blood of the Lamb" are all utilized as debating points, and any explanation of them in a volume such as this one is merely to pay homage or derision to Stephen's ingeniousness. But in one case at least there is a reference which does not proceed from the mind of Dedalus, and which in the light of the musical references in *Ulysses* gives us the first glimpse of the sort of problems which are to follow Stephen into his adult life. Father Moran counsels Stephen that he should learn "The Holy City," with which the priest connects humanity and sentiment, to counteract the cold scholasticism of the Gregorian music Stephen knows so well. This is essentially the same advice Stephen's mother gives him in her admonishment that she hopes he will "learn . . . what the heart is and what it feels," [3] the information which Leopold Bloom is so ready and able to dispense in *Ulysses,* also, incidentally, to the tune of "The Holy City." Hence the chief value of the musical references in *Stephen Hero* is, again, to foreshadow the works to follow.

Stephen Hero

In reading through 'Twelfth Night' for the class Father Butt skipped the two songs of the clown without a word and when Stephen, determined on forcing them on his attention, asked very gravely whether they were to be learned by heart or not Father Butt said it was improbable such a question would be on the paper:

—The clown sings these songs for the duke. It was a custom at that time for noblemen to have clowns to sing to them . . . for amusement. (pp. 28-29) *

Cf. Clown's Songs in *Twelfth Night*

REMARKS: The clown sings four songs in *Twelfth Night* and it is not certain which songs Stephen refers to. The only one the clown sings for the duke deals with the adolescent fantasy of death and ignominious burial without a

---

friend to greet "the poor corpse." The song, which matches the duke's melancholy mood, works in the context of the continuing conversation between Stephen and Father Butt about the liberal and useful arts and the language of tradition and literature as opposed to the language of the market place. The conversation, which foreshadows the paper on Ibsen and the aesthetic theory of *Portrait,* deals with Augustine's doctrine of the usefulness or utilitarian value of literature. Stephen's idea of their value probably touches on whether their reason for being is didactic or merely "for amusement" as Father Butt judges them to be. Unlike *Othello,* which Father Butt treats as significant because of its great moral object lessons on jealousy, the clown's songs are insignificant because they are not useful, in the Augustinian sense of the word. Though they may be "for amusement," as Father Butt claims, a case can be made, of course, for any of the songs being integral to the structure, etc. of the play or even for the songs' deserving recognition for their own intrinsic importance, as liberal rather than useful arts. Francis X. Newman has suggested further that Stephen's satiric criterion of the useful aspects of the songs was embodied in his question of whether or not they should be learned by heart, presumably for examination purposes.

> Stephen used to call him 'Bonny Dundee' nonsensically associating . . . his brisk name and his «brisk manners with the sound» of the line:
>
> Come fill up my cup, come fill up my can. (p. 44)

Cf. "Bonnie Dundee"

REMARKS: Dundee, the Jacobite leader, was the subject of this well-known ballad which commemorates the emotional appeal of John Graham of Claverhouse (Viscount Dundee) to the Scottish Lords for their support of the returning James in his bid for the throne. The line Stephen quotes is the opening of the refrain. Aside from the pun on McCann's name, the allusion to Dundee is not very uncomplimentary:

> Bonnie at least he [Dundee] was in out-
> ward form, with the 'long dark curled locks'
> and the 'melancholy haughty countenance'
> which we know by his portraits and by
> Scott's matchless description.[4]

The only really uncomplimentary thing about the name in Ireland was, of course, that Dundee was a royalist. The lines to which Stephen has reference are in the refrain:

> Come fill up my cup, and fill up my can,
> Come saddle my horses and call up my men;
> Unhook the west port, and let us gae free,
> For it's up wi' the bonnets o' Bonnie Dundee.

—But you cannot distinguish one air from another.

—No: I can recognise some airs.

—For instance?

—I can recognise 'God save the Queen.' (p. 51)

Cf. "God Save the Queen"

REMARKS: The Socratic dialogue conducted by Stephen with McCann in which Stephen "riddles . . . [McCann's] theories with agile bullets" shows McCann defending his tone-deafness with the admission that he can only recognise the anthem of the oppressor and that in consequence his life has been so long under the yoke of subservience and his ideas so moulded by that yoke that this is the only tune the tone-deaf man can recognise. The example reenforces the "epical" quality of didacticism which permeates *Stephen Hero*.

Two young men would then be called on for songs in Irish and when it was time for the whole company to break up all would rise and sing the Rallying-Song. (p. 61)

Cf. Rallying-Song

REMARKS: I have not been able to identify the Rallying-Song, presumably some sort of patriotic song, full of objectionable gusto from Stephen's point of view.

He said that one could not expect the people to take kindly to severe music and that the people needed more human religious music than the Gregorian and ended by advising Stephen to learn "The Holy City" by Adams.

—There is a song now, beautiful, full of lovely melody and yet—religious. It has the religious sentiment, a touching «melody, power—soul, in fact.» (p. 66)

Cf. "The Holy City"

REMARKS: The first reference in Joyce's works to this key music from *Ulysses* comes in the form of a suggestion from Father Moran that Stephen might do well to encounter the "human religious" experience, oddly enough from what is essentially a Protestant anthem. The ascribing of "soul" to the music foreshadows the soul of Leopold Bloom and his humanity which hopefully will rub off on Stephen in *Circe* while the gramophone plays "The Holy City" and the "new Bloomusalem" is born. It is entirely possible that Emma might be attracted to Father Moran for other reasons than that he seems to be somewhat coquettish: he might just possess that human religiosity or humanity that Stephen lacks.

He sang her one of the few Irish melodies which he knew "My love she was born in the North Countree." (p. 155)

Cf. "My love she was born in the North Countree" or "The North Country Lass" or "The Oak and the Ash"

REMARKS: I have not yet been able to find the version of this song alluded to in the text, perhaps because it is in Gaelic, but the principal variant, "The Oak and the Ash" doesn't seem to be Irish, the song beginning, "A north country maid up to London had strayed."

The tide was lapping softly . . . by the wall, being at the full, and through the clear air Stephen heard his father's voice like a muffled flute singing a love-song. He made his mother stop to listen and they both leaned on the heavy picture-frames and listened:

> Shall carry my heart to thee
> Shall carry my heart to thee
> And the breath of the balmy night
> Shall carry my heart to thee (p. 160)

Cf. "Winds that blow from the South"

REMARKS: I have not yet been able to locate this song.

You know the song "Come unto these yellow sands?"
—No.
—This is it, said the youth making a graceful anapaestic gesture with each arm. That's the rhythm, do you see? (p. 184)

Cf. "Come unto these yellow sands"

REMARKS: There is nothing in this song from *The Tempest* to suggest that anapestic rhythm that Stephen seems to hear or feel in the song except that the first line might be twisted to contain at least one anapestic foot. Stephen's anapestic gesture might indeed be made by forcing the lines into two-foot gestures which resemble anapests. All the versions of the song examined, including the seventeenth-century one by John Banister, indicate through the values of the notes an iambic metric pattern, so Stephen must either have forced the song, as he has the rest of his experiences, to fit his own aesthetic picture of the world, or merely be mistaken, or not know the text of the song to which he alludes.

When she had gone in he went along the canal bank still in the shadow of the leafless trees, humming to himself the chant of the Good Friday Gospel. (p. 189)

Cf. Chant of the Good Friday Gospel

REMARKS: The chant obviously has been triggered by Stephen's encounter with Emma, in which tender solicitude has seemed to flow from her while he fingered some coins in his pocket. Whether the coins represent his betrayal or his lack of love or giving remains conjectural, but the gospel celebrates the betrayal and the agony of the friendless Christ, the all-loving sacrificer of Himself. It is clear from his remarks following the allusion to the Good Friday chant that love is associated irrevocably in his mind with giving and sacrifice, which he must make as well as Emma if their relationship is ever to achieve any permanence and meaning. His conclusion, however, is, "I will never speak to her again." Immediately following the Good Friday chant reference a whore offers herself to Stephen, a "giving" he could not get from Emma. His coins, fingered while he was talking to Emma, are given to the whore. After her offering herself to him, that solicitation, in terms of giving and Christ's sacrifice, has to Stephen more meaning and love than his relationship with Emma.

Blood will have blood. There are some people in this island who sing a hymn called "Washed in the blood of the Lamb" by way of easing the religious impulse. (p. 190)

Cf. "Washed in the Blood of the Lamb"

REMARKS: Christ's love leads Stephen to muse on the final outcome of the Irish demand for sacrifice. If the Protestants have pushed the blood lust to its natural conclusion in the hymn, Stephen, who occasionally sees himself as Christ, has no desire to pursue giving and loving to any such point in his relations with Emma; hence he will not see her any more.

—What is Bonny Dundee at? (p. 215)

Cf. "Bonny Dundee"

REMARKS: The exhortations of McCann to the sodality for the improvement of that august body reenforce the earlier associations Stephen has made [5] between the Scottish leader and McCann, whose address to the sodality is reminiscent of Dundee's pleas in the song when in the opening line "to the Lords of Convention 'twas Claverhouse spoke."

A PORTRAIT OF THE ARTIST
AS A YOUNG MAN

As a part of the shift in narrative pattern from *Stephen Hero* to *Portrait,* the increasing selectivity of events portrayed in the latter work gives far greater significance to the action. Also, the typical passage from innocence to knowledge of the *Bildungsroman* protagonist is modified in *Portrait* by the perceptions of the young artist. Joyce chose to include in the book only those things that were especially significant to Stephen, so that from the first page of the novel it is really Stephen who is selecting and recreating a work of art out of his own life. If the events seem important to Stephen they are included; if not, they are omitted; and all events are seen from Stephen's perspective. For instance, Father Conmee's reprimand to Father Dolan, originally anticipated in chapter one by Stephen as a sort of divine justice dispensed by an omniscient last-judgment figure with a skull adorning his desk, becomes (if one is to take at face value Mr. Dedalus' report of his later conversation with Father Conmee) the laughing stock of the Clongowes' faculty and his father. But for Father Dolan to have been chastised in so public a place as the Jesuit dining room at dinner time should not be construed as anything less than a serious reprimand, no matter how tactfully it is delivered. In the narrative pattern, we have only to surmise how Stephen took his father's comments, and we extrapolate that his faith in the justice of the occasion was destroyed. But if we go a step further, we will have to argue that Stephen's probable perspective on events did not reveal what they really meant. The fact is that the Dolan affair was at least in part instrumental in Conmee's getting Stephen into Belvedere. The point I am trying to make here is that the selectivity of the events as well as the reason they were selected all bear fully upon Stephen's vision of reality, but to a far less extent on reality itself. Stephen sees his life as a work of art. Through his selection he is in effect the author of the book, creating a work of art out of the events of his own life. Thus, his decision to "recreate life out of life" is the answer to Stephen's search for identity, and this recreation provides the narrative means of Joyce's novel. As the events of Stephen's life as reported in the novel proceed, his selection of the details is more and more modified by the symbol patterns which increasingly suggest themselves to him throughout the book. Thus, the events which began merely as separate meaningful experiences are increasingly formed into patterns through Stephen's artistic propensity to create symbols and see his life as some sort of archetypal-symbolic pattern. The situations of the first few pages are repeated in different guises again and again throughout *Portrait* until at last Stephen begins to define their significance and sees them leading to the final outcome, that is, his projected artistry, martyrdom, exile, and potential entrapments. As the novel progresses, his outlook is formed less by external events than by his divination of them, so that by chapter five his life becomes a struggle to free himself from the tyrannies of imposed circumstances and to give himself control over which choices he will make, in effect to forge the wings of Dedalus with which he shall fly over the entrapping nets.

But his raw material, the dross from which he must forge the uncreated conscience of himself and his race, is still "the foul rag and bone shop" of his own heart and the very Irish as well as universal things that happen to him. Stephen devotes a great deal of energy to identifying the differences between himself and other youngsters, between himself and other Irish nationalists, all because his life is to be unique, as a work of art. So in his denial of accepted national, religious, and moral standards he becomes Satanic in his own mind, just as his exile and suffering for his newly created conscience cause him in his own mind to become analogous with Christ. As Satan he rebels but as Christ he is ripe for betrayal, saving the race, and transubstantiation into art, his saving wine and wafer. The hymn which celebrates all this is Stephen's villanelle, a song about himself and his miraculous transformation by and of himself into the very song which celebrates the transformation, an ultimate blend of life and art.

All of this narrative pattern and symbology is apparent in the musical references of *Portrait* as well as the other image and symbol patterns which emerge with the development of the novel. "Lilly Dale" is Stephen's initial song of youth and innocence, while his early preoccupation with verbal art is manifested in his love for "Dingdong! The Castle Bell!" The adolescent fantasy of martyrdom and early death connected with the latter song is not, however, purged from his mind as he grows older. Rather, as the book draws to a conclusion, it helps form Stephen's final artistic image of himself as martyr. Stephen's distrust of the institutions of both church and state initiated at the Christmas dinner scene manifests itself later in Stephen's identification with the Parnell martyrdom and his refusal to do his Easter duty. The first foreshadowing of that refusal comes at the disruptive Christmas dinner when Mr. Dedalus sings his "Come all ye" about "Roman catholics/That never went to mass."

As Stephen begins to pass from innocence to knowledge in chapter two, he becomes increasingly aware of the incongruities of reality when juxtaposed against the roseate haze of expectation and parental and ecclesiastical euphemism. There are a number of images and experiences which signal that this debunking process is taking place in the boy's mind. The earliest of these incongruities involves the beautiful and idyllic songs of Uncle Charles intoned on the less-than-idyllic platform of the outhouse. As Stephen's respect for parental and spiritual institutions diminishes, he manages to reflect his dissatisfaction through his comparison of the desecrations of his father with those of the priest. This is orchestrated by *The Lily of Killarney* with its plot revolving around mortgages, obligations, and the frustrations of natural desire.

Stephen accompanies his father to Cork, now determined to deny any paternal similarities, or for that matter, any similarities with anyone living. Here is where the theme of the universality of experience that I developed in the introduction to *Dubliners* becomes operative in *Portrait*. Stephen is determined to be unique, or at least to share his existence only with such worthies as Christ, Satan, and Parnell. In the anatomy theater of his father's school he is shocked not so much by the word *Foetus* carved in the desk as by the fact that other youngsters were and are living through similar pubescent experiences. It shocks him "to find in the outer world a trace of what he had deemed till then a brutish and individual malady of his own mind" (p. 90). The recognition that everyone lives through

similar experiences mocks "his bodily weakness and futile enthu-
siasms and . . . [makes] him loathe himself for his own mad and
filthy orgies" (p. 91). Stephen will not admit that he shares common experience with everyone else. His first step is to dissociate
himself from his link to the rest of mankind, his father. While his
father reminisces about the past and his youth, and while com-
parisons are made between Simon and his son by the company of
his father's drinking companions, Stephen removes himself from
any similarity between his life and theirs:

> An abyss of fortune or of temperament sundered him from them.
> His mind seemed older than theirs: it shone coldly on their strifes
> and happiness and regrets like a moon upon a younger earth. No
> life or youth stirred in him as it had stirred in them. He had
> known neither the pleasure of companionship with others nor the
> vigour of rude male health nor filial piety. (pp. 95–96)

This whole sequence of events in which Stephen perceives the
universality of experience and tries to sunder himself from it and
his father is foreshadowed and its significance implied in Mr. Dedalus' rendition of " 'Tis Youth and Folly," where the theme of
escape asserts itself for the first time. If youth and folly like his
father's make young men marry, Stephen will not be young and
filled with folly or share the common experience; hence, he, like
the persona of the song, will "no longer stay."

The intrusions of universal experience occur again in Stephen's
interview with the director at Belvedere, where he hears in the
director's speech "an echo of his own proud musings." Even though
he shares the pride of the Jesuits and their love of the "semblance
of reality and of their distance from it," his religion must have more
life in it than theirs. The ritual of transubstantiation will be his and
the power of recreating life will be his, but as a high priest of art not
the church.

Stephen's denial of common experience must inevitably lead him
to a denial not only of his father and his country, in which everyone
must do the same things—sign peace petitions and shout down plays
which seem detrimental to the image of Irish perfection—but it must
lead him to a denial of his family, whom he was to raise from the
fallen state of poverty to which his father has led them. The sentimentality of his familial attachment is conveyed by his brothers and

sisters singing "Oft in the Stilly Night" and by the hard death of Ellen.

But now Stephen has his own network of defences: his simultaneity of existence will be with Ben Jonson, Aquinas, and comparable figures of the past. His objective correlatives will come from literature like Jonson's song, "I was not wearier where I lay," if satiric from operettas like *The Mikado,* or if serious from grand opera, like *Siegfried.*

In the last chapter music plays a substantial role in the evolving character of himself which Stephen has created. His martyr-savior face as well as his role as artist-creator is developed further through his allusions to the *"Pange lingua"* and *"Vexilla Regis,"* and further refined by his association with Siegfried. I think my explications of the allusions speak amply to this point. The intellectual pretensions of Stephen's aesthetic theory are furthered by his allusion to "Turpin Hero," and his role as romantic bard of antiquities is conveyed also through his renditions of "The Ballad of Agincourt" and "Greensleeves."

The one element of the external world with which he has the most difficulty coping, however, is the temptress, E. C., whom he has endowed with all the aspects of every female who has had significance in his life, his mother, the BVM, Mercedes, the whore, the flower seller, the girl on the beach, the Shan Van Vocht, Davin's pregnant temptress, and all the rest. Her sirensong has all the innocent ingenuousness of "Sweet Rosie O'Grady" and all the overtones of death inherent in "Adieu, farewell earth's bliss." So his struggle is not only to free himself from a nice eligible Irish catholic girl and the encroachments of a Little Chandler existence, it is the titanic struggle of all freedom-loving Siegfrieds everywhere to be liberated from the clutches of their Belles Dames and from the nets with which they entrap unwary Dedaluses. For Stephen the simultaneity of life is vertical, historical, and allusionary, not immediate, mundane, or particularly Irish. And so Stephen prepares to set off, Siegfried-like, to destroy the old order of gods with his sword, Needful, "the lancet of . . . [his] art."

A Portrait of the Artist as a Young Man

> *O, the wild rose blossoms*
> *On the little green place.*

He sang that song. That was his song. (p. 7) *

Cf. "Lilly Dale"

REMARKS: Stephen's song is altered from the original version, the chorus of which follows:

> Oh! Lilly, sweet Lilly, dear Lilly Dale,
> Now the wild rose blossoms o'er her little green grave,
> Neath the trees in the flow'ry vale.

The symbol patterns of the red and the green are, until the Christmas dinner scene, completely compatible in Stephen's mind. Thoughts of death are not present, nor premonitions of discord. The idealistic image of rose blossoms in Ireland or any little green place are no more than a vision of innocence.

Perhaps a wild rose might be like those colours and he remembered the song about the wild rose blossoms on the little green place. (p. 12)

Cf. "Lilly Dale"

REMARKS: The principal narrative structure of *Portrait* consists of a metamorphosis and reshaping of the images introduced at the beginning of the novel. The seeds of discord are sown by introducing the War of the Roses as the basis for the mathematics competition in Stephen's class. The association of roses with English and Irish history begins to reshape the song into an allegory of church-state relations in Ireland and foreshadow the cataclysm of the Christmas dinner scene.

> *Dingdong! The castle bell!*
> *Farewell, my mother!*
> *Bury me in the old churchyard*
> *Beside my eldest brother.*
> *My coffin shall be black,*

> *Six angels at my back,*
> *Two to sing and two to pray*
> *And two to carry my soul away.*

How beautiful and sad that was! How beautiful the words were where they said *Bury me in the old churchyard!* A tremor passed over his body. How sad and how beautiful! He wanted to cry quietly but not for himself: for the words, so beautiful and sad, like music. The bell! The bell! Farewell! O farewell! (p. 24)

Cf. "Dingdong! The Castle Bell"

REMARKS: The song reference explores musically the theme of Stephen as artist, preoccupied with words and sounds, and also introduces the theme of martyrdom which permeates so much of Stephen's thinking throughout the novel.

> *O, come all you Roman catholics*
> *That never went to mass.* (p. 35)

Cf. "Come All You Roman Catholics"

REMARKS: This song is probably one of the class of comic songs in Ireland known as "Come all ye's" which start with the phrase, "Come all ye (you)." The allusion is of course a calculated insult on Mr. Dedalus' part. It is the first foreshadowing of Stephen's refusal to do his Easter duty.

> . . . she had hit a gentleman on the head with her umbrella because he had taken off his hat when the band played *God save the Queen* at the end. (p. 37)

Cf. "God Save the Queen"

REMARKS: Dante Riordan brings fervor to all her causes. The harmony with which she could espouse both religious and nationalistic conventions is the harmony and well-being of Stephen's innocent early childhood, shattered by the collision of the two sources of unquestionable faith, church and state, in the Christmas dinner scene.

> . . . and every morning he hummed contentedly one of his favourite songs: *O, twine me a bower* or *Blue eyes and golden hair* or *The Groves of Blarney* . . . . (p. 60)

Cf. "O Twine Me a Bower"
  "Blue Eyes and Golden Hair"
  "The Groves of Blarney"

REMARKS: These songs of ideal love, beauty, and setting are among the first signs of Stephen's increasing awareness of the blemishes of reality in contrast to the perfections supposed in his innocence. The beauty of the songs can hardly be fully appreciated with Stephen now painfully cognizant of "the reeking outhouse" which provides the incongruous setting for their execution.

> *As Tyson was riding into Jerusalem*
> *He fell and hurt his Alec Kafoozelum.* (p. 81)

Cf. "Kafoozelum"

REMARKS: Boland's song is even more banal than Stephen suspects, since the rhyme of Jerusalem and Kafoozelum was used in a well-known bawdy song and was not even original with Boland.

> He could hear the band playing *The Lily of Killarney* . . . (p. 85)

Cf. *The Lily of Killarney*

REMARKS: The opera involves a mortgage collection by the money lender, Corrigan, who has the poor but virtuous Cregan family in his power. The association in *Portrait* is between the operatic situation and the smiling, well-dressed priest who holds the mortgaged Ireland in his power. The same paternalistic desecration of office has led Stephen to discern the likeness between the priest and his father immediately before the *Killarney* reference. Stephen has already extended his conviction of corruption and perversion of real values to his sire.[1]

> *'Tis youth and folly*
> *Makes young men marry,*
> *So here, my love, I'll*
> *   No longer stay.*
> *What can't be cured, sure,*
> *Must be injured, sure,*
> *   So I'll go to*
> *   Amerikay.*
>
> *My love she's handsome,*
> *My love she's bonny:*
> *She's like good whisky*
> *   When it is new;*
> *But when 'tis old*

> *And growing cold*
> *It fades and dies like*
> *The mountain dew.* (p. 88)

Cf. " 'Tis youth and folly"

REMARKS: The themes of escape will be predominant in the novel, and the theme of youth and old age constitutes a major section of this chapter. The last nets over which Stephen must fly are the temptation of E.C. to hold him in Ireland. During chapter two, Stephen tries to dissociate himself from the follies and exuberances of the youth his father describes, while his father desperately clings to them. It is Stephen who feels old "and growing cold," while his father tenaciously clings to the memories and sensibilities of his young manhood. In cutting himself off from them, Stephen will liberate himself also from the "bonny" E.C. and fly off not to "Amerikay" as the persona of the song, but to Paris.

> . . . I'm sorry to say that they are only as I roved out one fine May morning in the merry month of sweet July. (p. 97)

Cf. "As I roved out. . ."

REMARKS: The nonsense lyrics of the song suggest the nonsensical minds of contemporary legislators to Mr. Dedalus.

> Heron, beside Stephen, began to hum tunelessly.
> *My excellent friend Bombados.* (p. 105)

Cf. "My Excellent Friend Bombados"

REMARKS: I have not located this song.

> The voice of his youngest brother from the farther side of the fireplace began to sing the air *Oft in the Stilly Night.* (p. 163)

Cf. "Oft in the Stilly Night"

REMARKS: This beautiful Thomas Moore song of memories of childhood and departed friends makes the persona "feel like one who treads alone/Some banquet hall deserted/Whose lights are fled." The family from whom Stephen has dissociated himself at considerable cost is perhaps the strongest attachment he has to Ireland and the responsibility of caring for them a burden most difficult to avoid, if he should leave. The pictures of his poverty-stricken brothers and sisters are invariably given in sentimental terms; i.e., in this scene they are seated around the fire singing this lovely sentimental air.

. . . passing a grimy marinedealer's shop beyond the Liffey he would repeat the song by Ben Jonson which begins:

I was not wearier where I lay.

His mind, when wearied of its search for the essence of beauty amid the spectral words of Aristotle or Aquinas, turned often for its pleasure to the dainty songs of the Elizabethans. (p. 176)

Cf. "I was not wearier where I lay"

REMARKS: The entire text of the lines Stephen recites is as follows:

> I was not wearier where I lay
> By frozen Tythons side to night;
> Then I am willing now to stay,
> And be a part of your delight.
>   But I am urged by the Day,
> Against my will, to bid you come away.

The line from Jonson's poem which is echoed in the first line of the villa-nelle may have been one of the sources of the temptress idea in the villanelle. Aurora, having carried off Tythonus from his father's palace, like Stephen's temptress, has had her "will of him," and the language has of course a strong similarity to stanza one of the villanelle. Tythonus' suffering from im-mortality without youth is the sort of living death the phoenix-persona of the villanelle would escape if only the temptress will let him go.

On a cloth untrue
With a twisted cue
And elliptical billiard balls. (p. 192)

Cf. "My Object All Sublime"

REMARKS: Mabel Worthington discusses the significance of the allusion:

> The physics professor, in making a distinction
> between elliptical and ellipsoidal, quotes from
> the song in which the Mikado says that his object
> all sublime is to make the punishment fit the
> crime: the billiard shark must play
>
>   On a cloth untrue . . . .
>
> A minute later, when the professor brings out
> a set of coils, Stephen whispers, "with weary
> humour," "Ask him if he wants a subject for
> electrocution. He can have me." It is likely

> that the quotation from *The Mikado* has led
> Stephen to identify himself with Nanki-Poo,
> the wandering minstrel, who offers to let him-
> self be beheaded by the Lord High Executioner.[2]

Perhaps Aquinas would understand me better than you. He was a poet himself. He wrote a hymn for Maundy Thursday. It begins with the words *Pange lingua gloriosi*. They say it is the highest glory of the hymnal. It is an intricate and soothing hymn. (p. 210)

Cf. *"Pange lingua"*

REMARKS: The mention of this hymn and the next, *Vexilla Regis,* precedes two climactic scenes in the novel: the development of the aesthetic theory and its application in the villanelle. While Aquinas's hymn deals with the transformation of the Word into flesh and the transformation of bread and wine into the Eucharist, Stephen's theory deals with the transformation of experience, in terms of Plato's world of appearances, into the form, the epiphany, or Stephen's *quidditas.* As Christ has transformed the body and blood of his own life into bread and wine, celebrated in *Pange lingua,* so will Stephen "recreate life out of life" by transubstantiating into the villanelle the daily bread of his own life experience. That is why Stephen thinks that Aquinas, the poet of the *Pange lingua* and the author of the *quidditas* concept, would understand him (Stephen) better than Lynch ever could. Like Stephen's own villanelle about transformation "it is an intricate and soothing hymn" and like his own it is a work of art celebrating artistic and hence spiritual creation.

I like it: but there is no hymn that can be put beside that mournful and majestic processional song, the *Vexilla Regis* of Venantius Fortunatus.
    Lynch began to sing softly and solemnly in a deep bass voice:

> *Impleta suntquae concinit*
> *David fideli carmine*
> *Dicendo nationibus*
> *Regnavit a ligno Deus.* (p. 210)

Cf. *"Vexilla Regis"*

REMARKS: The Fortunatus hymn, which Stephen prefers, is a triumphal procession celebrating the agony of Christ and the cross. Its victorious tone celebrates the new life which emerges from Christ's suffering. The stanza Lynch sings, which pleases Stephen so mightily, deals with the triumph:

> The prophecies which David uttered in his
> true song are fulfilled, when he declared

to the nations: "God has reigned from a
tree."

The conclusion of the song celebrates the life-giving qualities of the sacrifice:

Hail, altar, and hail, victim, because
of the glory of the passion. In that
passion life endured death and by dying
gave back life.[3]

In the villanelle Stephen, in his role as priest on the altar celebrating his own martyrdom and transforming it into the "broken cries and mournful lays [which]/Rise in one eucharistic hymn," assumes the role of the martyred Christ and the celebrator of the transformed experience into the new life of the work of art: He the victim, his the sacrifice, his the act of transformation, and his art the new life which will become "the uncreated conscience of his race."

This progress you will see easily in that old English ballad *Turpin Hero* which begins in the first person and ends in the third person. (p. 215)

Cf. "Turpin Hero" ("O Rare Turpin, Hero")

REMARKS: There are a number of versions of the ballad, but only one, brought to my attention by Thomas Connolly, begins in the first person and ends in the third. Joyce was evidently familiar with the song, having sung it at Sheehy's and for the Espositos.[4] Like most other versions of the ballad, "O Rare Turpin, Hero" outlines a meeting with a lawyer:

On Hounslow heath as I rode o'er,
I spied a lawyer riding before;
Kind sir, said I, ar'n't you afraid
Of Turpin, that mischievous blade?
O rare Turpin, hero, O rare Turpin O.

Says Turpin, he'd ne'er find me out. . . .

The transition is from the first person, who is not really identified in stanza one with Turpin, to a discussion of the conversation of Turpin and the lawyer and then Turpin's subsequent adventures. The ballad, which makes a considerable hero of Turpin, who unmasks the hypocrisies of the people he meets on the road and punishes them by robbing them, ends in Turpin's being caught and condemned to die "for stealing a poor dunghill cock."

The ballad could easily be another link between Stephen's aesthetic theory and his own creation of a great transubstantiated work of art from his own life. Turpin begins with himself as the main character of his story, but as it progresses Turpin is refined out of the picture until the ballad deals with another heroic figure who is the creation of the first but has assumed a separate identity of his own, like the dicta of Stephen's aesthetic theory and his own life transubstantiated in his poem and finally in *A Portrait of the Artist as a Young Man*. Further, the picture of Turpin as the bringer of truth and light to the hypocritical forces of respectability parallels Stephen's vision of himself, even down to their respective martyrdom for trivial offenses.

> Then he saw himself sitting at the old piano, striking chords softly from its speckled keys and singing, amid the talk which had risen again in the room, to her who leaned beside the mantelpiece a dainty song of the Elizabethans, a sad and sweet loth to depart, the victory chant of Agincourt, the happy air of Greensleeves. (p. 219)

Cf. "The Ballad of Agincourt"
　　"Greensleeves"

REMARKS: Stephen sings upon the request of E.C. for "one of his curious songs." Aside from the fact that the two songs named are old there seems little "curious" about them. Stephen is probably trying to establish himself with E.C. as a singer of touching ballads of antiquity rather than a singer of popular faddistic songs.

> . . . the kitchengirl in the next house who sang over the clatter of her plates with the drawl of a country singer the first bars of *By Killarney's Lakes and Fells* . . . . (p. 220)

Cf. "Killarney"

REMARKS: Stephen sees the singer of this popular song of Michael Balfe as representing E.C. in her role of the embodiment of the female symbol of Ireland, the temptress in the villanelle who bids Stephen stay on in his native land. The song to that end is about the paradise "in that Eden of the West, Beauty's home, Killarney."

> She had passed through the dusk. And therefore the air was silent save for one soft hiss that fell. And therefore the tongues about him had ceased their babble. Darkness was falling.
>
> *Darkness falls from the air.*
>
> A trembling joy, lambent as a faint light, played like a fairy host around him. But why? Her passage through the darkening

air or the verse with its black vowels and its opening sound, rich and lutelike? (pp. 232–233)
The life of his body, illclad, illfed, louseeaten, made him close his eyelids in a sudden spasm of despair: and in the darkness he saw the brittle bright bodies of lice falling from the air and turning often as they fell. Yes; and it was not darkness that fell from the air. It was brightness.

Brightness falls from the air.

He had not even remembered rightly Nash's line. All the images it had awakened were false. His mind bred vermin. His thoughts were lice born of the sweat of sloth. (p. 234)

Cf. "Adieu, farewell earth's bliss"

REMARKS: As Stephen forms a metaphor of darkness around E.C.'s image and the darkness of the hour, he first misquotes a line from Nashe's famous song about the encroachments of death. The temptations of this temptress of the villanelle is toward a living death in Ireland, the snake's hiss and the ensuing silence paying homage to her attractions. But in one of several passages that involve Stephen's becoming aware that his symbols and metaphors do not accurately reflect events as they are, he shifts his symbols to his own poverty, the lice and their brightness which falls from the air. Not that Nashe's line is any less appropriate for Stephen, but now quoted properly the interpretation of the lines is to the bright bodies of the lice and the desolation of his own position. To attribute brightness to lice bodies might of course be an equal distortion of reality, but it does fit Stephen's shifting mood.[5]

The birdcall from *Siegfried* whistled softly followed them from the steps of the porch. Cranly turned: and Dixon, who had whistled, called out: —Where are you fellows off to? (p. 237)

Cf. *Siegfried*

REMARKS: The young, arrogant, all-conquering Siegfried hears the birdcall in the opera just before he meets the dragon, Fafner. Hoping to attract a companion after he hears the call, Siegfried fashions a reed and then blows his hunting horn. But instead of an ally, the predestined enemy, Fafner, emerges from the cave. It is entirely possible that the birdcall in *Portrait* is the prelude in Siegfried-Stephen's mind to his verbal engagement with Fafner-Cranly, the guardian of the Nibelung-Irish treasure of respectability. Immediately following the Siegfried reference, Stephen confesses his refusal to make his Easter duty and declares his independence, ready to brave the onslaught of the forces of righteousness in the form of Cranly's arguments.

Behind a hedge of laurel a light glimmered in the window of a kitchen and the voice of a servant was heard singing as she sharpened knives. She sang, in short broken bars, *Rosie O'Grady*. (p. 244)

Cf. "Sweet Rosie O'Grady"

REMARKS: The slavey's song of love, marriage, and the mundane things of life prompts Cranly's remarks in Latin *"Mulier cantat,"* whereupon both he and Stephen go into a revery about the "figure of woman as she appears in the liturgy of the church" and the chanting of the passion by a woman. The jump from the slavey's "Rosie O'Grady" to the chanting of the passion by a female singer and the female figure of church liturgy is, of course, the kind of association and symbol-making Stephen has been engaged in all through the novel. The slavey, the choir girl, the virgin, the temptress are all one and the same, "consubstantial," as Stephen will decide in *Ulysses.* Interestingly enough, it is Cranly, with his compassion and understanding of women, who makes the association in which Stephen concurs.

They went on together, Cranly repeating in strongly stressed rhythm the end of the refrain:

> *And when we are married,*
> *O, how happy we'll be*
> *For I love sweet Rosie O'Grady*
> *And Rosie O'Grady loves me.* (p. 244)

Cf. "Sweet Rosie O'Grady"

REMARKS: After Cranly finished the lines from the song, returning the drift of thought to earthly things, he continues,

> —There's real poetry for you . . . . There's
> real love . .
> Do you consider that poetry?
> Or do you know what the words mean?
> —I want to see Rosie first, said Stephen. (pp. 244–45).

Cranly here is testing the otherworldliness of Stephen. Certainly Stephen can rhapsodize over the symbolism of the church woman, but can he love someone who is just a girl like Rosie O'Grady: can he understand mundane human emotions like love: or must all be an abstraction? This is the question Cranly is to repeat several times during their prolonged interview, finally asking if Stephen is capable of love. Stephen's reply is evasive. It suggests that for him as well as the symbolic woman there may be lust as we have seen through *Portrait,* and there may be abstract devotion: but those things "the heart feels," as his mother says, have as yet evaded him. Hence the sentimentality of the song has no meaning for him; only the symbol of the liturgical woman the song calls forth.

Alas, poor William!

I was once at a diorama in Rotunda. At the end were pictures of big nobs. Among them William Ewart Gladstone, just then dead. Orchestra played *O, Willie, we have missed you.*

A race of clodhoppers! (p. 249)

Cf. "Oh! Willie, We Have Missed You"

REMARKS: The song sung for Gladstone, whose death in 1898 occurred several years before Stephen's diary recollection, is triggered by Blake's line to William Bond and the Irish tendency to sentimentalize over departed leaders, even British oppressors. Stephen is about to leave Ireland, and E.C. has not passed to or from the library so that he can see her. She—and by extension Ireland—can rhapsodize and play sentimental songs for a British statesman, but not for him, her unsung forger of the uncreated conscience of the race. Foster's song about how Willie is eagerly awaited by all, including "the little ones," increases Stephen's own anguish about his lacking E.C.'s love and hence that of all the rest of Ireland.

I go to encounter for the millionth time the reality of experience and to forge in the smithy of my soul the uncreated conscience of my race. (pp. 252–253)

Cf. Wagner's Ring Cycle

REMARKS: Matthew J.C. Hodgart has suggested [6] that Stephen has in mind here Siegfried's forging of the sword, *Needful.* We have already heard the birdcall and warning to Siegfried (p. 237), which could conceivably have sparked Stephen's identification of himself as a Siegfried figure. Further, it is clear that in *Ulysses* Stephen sees himself as Siegfried when with his ashplant-sword he breaks the chandelier in Bella Cohen's. The parallels between Stephen and Siegfried are close: both are arrogant and prideful, both see themselves as unconquerable and as the sole hope for the survival of the world. Both are out to destroy the old order of gods. Stephen will challenge the order apparent in *Dubliners* through his sword of conscience. Siegfried's destruction of the spear of Woton, which embodies all the old covenants, runes, and mysteries of the universe, parallels Stephen's attempt to destroy the mysteries, runes, superstitions, folklore, and covenants which dominate the hearts and minds of the Irish race. Both are on guard against betrayal and treachery which seek to destroy them, and finally both have forged a weapon to ward off their enemies and bring peace and a state of superior existence to themselves and their people.

ULYSSES

Ulysses * not only contains a far greater number of musical allusions than any of its predecessors, but also illustrates the far more varied use Joyce made of music to develop the style, characterization, mood, structure, and themes of his novel. I will deal with approximately seven hundred allusions to various musical works in *Ulysses,* yet I am certain that many more remain undiscovered. Many of these allusions appear to have little bearing on the major themes of the novel, but even these are part of the panorama of stylistic devices Joyce uses throughout his incredibly varied book.

Joyce often employs musical references not for their intrinsically musical connotations, but for the fact that musical titles and lyrics are familiar and can be used in the same manner as any body of cultural allusions, such as the Bible, literary titles and situations, myth, etc. On the simplest stylistic level, song titles which are also names of well-known people, such as "The Man Who Broke the Bank at Monte Carlo," "The Bowld Sojer Boy," "The Colleen Bawn," and *The Lily of Killarney,* swell the lists of persons in the giganticized narration of Cyclops and in the crowds in the hallucinatory passages of Circe. Joyce also employs music to underscore points in the narrative and to add weight to the statements of characters as they spontaneously evoke musical allusions in their thoughts or discussion. Like literary allusions, the broad concepts, histories, and connotations of the songs evoked, when seen in detail, assist in explaining, delineating, and emphasizing the points made by the characters in the text, so that, for instance, Bloom's reference to an "Alice Ben Bolt topic" (624), immediately calls up a musical picture of a sailor's return after a number of years to find his wife dead and things greatly altered. This sort of allusion operates throughout the novel to reiterate and stress the topics under discussion.

At other times in the text, however, song references are used as music as well as a source of literary reference. There are many instances where the characters actually sing either aloud or to themselves, the music to which they allude. Joyce signals this with such devices as hyphens in words where they normally wouldn't appear. For instance, *la-amp* from "The Young May Moon" is mentally sung by Bloom on two notes, as the music demands, as is the word *co-ome* in *"M'appari."* At other times the narrator informs us that characters are in fact singing the words as, for instance, the music makers in the Ormond Bar.

Stylistically, however, music has its most profound impact in the Sirens episode. The character of the third-person narration changes drastically in the chapter: the manner in which the activities are described acquires an emphasis on sound devices that are more poetic and hence musical than they are prosaic. Following is a partial list of poetic-musical devices with examples of each:

Assonance: Mr Leopold Bloom envisaged candlestick melodeon oozing maggoty blowbags. (290:19–21)

Phrase repetition: Bald Pat who is bothered mitred the napkins. Pat is a waiter hard of his hearing. Pat is a waiter who waits while you wait. Hee hee hee hee. He waits while you wait. Hee hee. A waiter is he. Hee hee hee hee. He waits while you wait. While you wait if you wait he will wait while you wait. Hee hee hee hee. Hoh. Wait while you wait. (280:36–41)

Alliteration: Corncrake croaker: belly like a poisoned pup. (277:28)
On the smooth jutting beerpull laid Lydia hand lightly, plumply, leave it to my hands. (286:18–19)

Onomatopoeia: To pour o'er sluices pouring gushes. Flood, gush, flow, joygush, tupthrop. (247:38–40)

In addition to the prosodic devices used above there are in the Sirens many attempts at duplicating types of musical intonation, such as a staccato or a sustained effect:

Staccato: Miss Douce, Miss Lydia, did not believe: Miss Kennedy, Mina, did not believe: George Lidwell, no: Miss Dou did not: the first, the first: gent with the tank: believe, no, no: did not, Miss Kenn: Lidlydiawell: the tank. (278:1-4)

Sustained: . . . all soaring all around about the all, the endlessnessnessness . . . . (276:4-5)

Similarly, the sounds of things like snapping garters, shuffling boots, and clacking clocks play a dominant role in Sirens, a chapter of sounds as well as music. Though all of these devices occur throughout the book, the narration of the Sirens chapter consists principally of these techniques, as opposed to their occasional use in other chapters.

A second principal role of music in *Ulysses* is to further the delineation of character and personality by means of stream-of-conscious thought and dialogue. One song often triggers an association with another, as with Bloom's light melody, "Sing a Song of Sixpence," leading to the light strains of Ponchielli's "Dance of the Hours," and characterizing for him the pleasant aspects of the morning defecation. Often music indicates or sets the tone of a character's thinking. Bloom's irreverent and comic thoughts during the obsequies for Dignam are often accompanied by light or comic songs such as "The Bugaboo" and "Who Killed Cock Robin?" which spring full blown from his mind, or such rollicking songs as "Has Anybody Here Seen Kelly?" which is overheard during the funeral procession.

Nearly every aspect of Bloom's personality is reenforced or described somewhere in the book in musical terms. His hedonism manifests itself with reference to such activities as making love on one's death bed, which he describes by alluding to Edgardo's aria in *Lucia,* "Thou Hast Spread Thy Wings to Heaven." His irreverence for institutions such as the Crown is expressed in his comic renditions of songs like "God Save the King." His fatalism comes through in his reference to "Every Bullet Has Its Billet." His masochistic feelings appear in his repeated references to *"Là ci darem"* and "Doran's Ass," his Jewishness with *"Shema Israel"* and *"Hatikvah,"* and his sense of the ludicrousness of decorum with "O Mary Lost the Pin of Her Drawers." Moreover, his opinions on most matters, such as war and politics, are reenforced with references to music. In the Sirens episode Bloom is concerned with music *per se.* Following are some of the aspects he considers: origins (278), definition (278), effects (280, 281), the physiology of perception (282), sounds and instruments (282, 284), and production (278–285, 289).

Stephen's thoughts and personality are likewise heavily characterized by music. The songs in which he is interested, like sixteenth-century canting music or obscure German Renaissance music, delineate his predilection for the remote and the esoteric. Stephen's references to Shakespearean songs parallel his affinity for Elizabethan drama and are tied in as well with his labyrinthine rationalizations for his own failures and psychological shortcomings. Stephen's guilt feelings manifest themselves in his riddle, "The Cock Crew," which plays a major role in defining his guilt about his mother, on the religious as well as the Oedipal level.

Stephen's bawdy cast of mind is apparent in his reference to the canting songs, and his sarcasm in characterizing people he considers beneath him is augmented by musical allusions, such as his use of "The Rocky Road to Dublin" to disparage Deasy's pretentions about ancestral involvement in Ireland's struggle for independence.

Musical allusion often provides the vehicle of conscious thought association, taking Bloom smoothly from one subject to another. Stephen's stream-of-conscious musical allusions are ancillary in that he forces them into the predisposed direction he wants his thoughts to travel, but Bloom's thoughts seem to follow any random pattern which is suggested by the music or other more externally oriented things. In other words, most of the time Stephen has a notion where his thoughts are going, and he uses musical and other allusions to further the image pattern he has preshaped in his mind, while Bloom is more flexible, letting his mind and thought pattern wander, and reacting to whatever he hears or sees. For this reason the pattern of Bloom's thought is easier to ascertain and his musical stream-of-consciousness allusions seem to follow more easily from what precedes. Initially for most of Bloom's musical references there is not nearly as much thematic significance in terms of the novel as there is for Stephen's. Rather the thematic importance of the music grows with Bloom's body of experience during the day, so that as his thoughts are united with Stephen's in Circe they become more thematically meaningful for the rest of the novel.

Stephen, on the other hand, as we have seen in *Portrait,* tries not to think an unimportant thought, so that his stream-of-consciousness allusions, musical and otherwise, tend to bear thematically on the action of the novel from his first lines. His life is still a work of art, while, in the early chapters at least, Bloom makes few pretensions to artistic significance in his life, with the possible exception of envying kindly Mr. Beaufoy his two and six and thinking that he himself might indeed capitalize upon the artistry of his own experiences. This is, of course, a parody of Stephen's mental set as well as one of the later bases of their consubstantiality.

Molly's songs, on the other hand, are appropriate to a mental outlook which is fairly uncomplicated, romantic, and sensual. The recurring motives of anticipation of a coming love affair, and of love affairs about to be consummated and already consummated are punctuated in her mind with remarkably similar songs of love, such as "Love's Old Sweet Song," "Waiting," "In Old Madrid," and "Shall I Wear a White Rose or Shall I Wear a Red?" Molly's role as Virgin is developed in her religious renditions, like her solo in the *Stabat Mater,* and her temptress role is delineated in "The Young May Moon."

Two characters who are distinguished by their constant use of musical clichés are the citizen, whose whole patriotic being is one long slogan, and Simon Dedalus, whose ideas always seem to come out in the form of aphorisms, particularly musical ones. The citizen relies naturally on the vast stock of Irish nationalistic music, much of which seems to provide the primary synapses in his train of thought.

Other characters' personalities are also defined or suggested by musical allusion. For instance, Mulligan's mocking, blasphemous attitude is articulated in his "Ballad of Joking Jesus" and his *joie de vivre* in his rendition of Fergus's song, which in the Oedipal context of his thought pattern acts as a depressing reference for Stephen. Mr. Deasy's Orange connections are manifested in Stephen's mind by Stephen's linking Deasy with "Croppies Lie Down," a vehement Orange ballad, and Boylan's triumphal entrance into the Ormond is orchestrated with "See the Conquering Hero Comes." Other characters are similarly known by the musical company they keep.

The third major function of music is to set the mood or tone of whole passages and scenes in *Ulysses.* In Hades, for instance, the funereal mood is set with reference to songs dealing with death, such as the "Dead March" from *Saul,* but the somber overtones are relieved with the light, comic strains of "Has Anybody Here Seen

Kelly?" Songs like "I Never Nursed a Dear Gazelle" supplement Bloom's depressed frame of mind. Scenes are characterized with music, as for instance, "The Boys of Wexford" sets a martial tone for the conquering British soldiers, Carr and Compton; the "Hallelujah Chorus" gives Bloom's triumphal processions in Circe an even greater attitude of aggrandizement; and Rakoczy's March heralds the ascension of Bloom in Cyclops. His hopeless attitude at the low point of his day, the four o'clock hour of assignation, is described in terms of the aria "All Is Lost Now."

All the instances where music sets or reenforces tone or mood are far too numerous to mention, but major examples include the shift in tone of Sirens from sentiment in the early part of the episode to militancy and drinking in the latter part, as songs of love give way to songs of war and booze. The common theme running through many of those songs and the linking motive of the chapter is betrayal.

It is difficult to ascertain where mood leaves off and structure begins, but clearly music plays a large part in each. One such borderline case involves the orchestration of Paddy Dignam's funeral procession. During the carriage trip, another last ride, celebrated in the dirge "The Pauper's Drive," occurs to Bloom. Dignam's death is linked by Bloom's thought patterns and by the circumstances of the cemetery trip to Bloom's father's death and the death of a child whose hearse passes them on the way to the cemetery. All are linked by references to "The Pauper's Drive," which broadens in context to provide a consubstantial umbrella under which all the dead may lie.

But the most obvious and significant use of music in the structure of *Ulysses* occurs in the Sirens episode, where the author's apparent intent was to bring about a blend of literature and music, and Joyce's method of effecting this union occasions the major differences in critical opinion about the Sirens chapter. Many musical forms have been used to describe the chapter,[1] the predominant ones being the fugue and the leitmotif. The fugal idea was given some impetus by Stuart Gilbert, when he described the "Technic" in his schema for the Sirens chapter as being *"fuga per canonem."* According to Gilbert the chapter is not only a fugue but a fugue with invariable, congruent repetitions of theme! Though there are in the chapter many repetitions, both musical and verbal, nothing is ever repeated in exactly the same manner. A canon is "a polyphonic composition in which all the parts have the same melody throughout, although starting at different points. The canon is the strictest species of imitation." [2] Gilbert describes the fugal *Subject* as "obviously the Sirens' song: the *Answer*, Mr. Bloom's entry and monologue; Boylan . . . the countersubject"; and the *Episodes*, or *Divertimenti*, the songs by Mr. Dedalus and Ben Dollard.[3] It is not clear whether Gilbert means that they are all singing the same song or strictly imitating one another.

Gilbert does not, however, completely overlook in his musical classifications the significance of the first two pages of the chapter, which clearly constitute an overture. If the chapter were fugal, it would probably not begin with an overture. Of all the commentators on the music in *Ulysses*, only Harry Levin seems to take issue with Gilbert on the *fuga per canonem* question. Levin's conclusion is that "the Siren episode should not be expected to stand on its form alone, any more than any chapter in any novel." [4]

Walton Litz, who agrees with Gilbert on the question of the fugal arrangement of the Sirens chapter, reiterates also Gilbert's references to the Wagnerian leitmotifs [5] (i.e., the representation of the acting personalities, of typical situations, and of recurrent ideas by musical motif). No one has ever explained the function of the leitmotif in *Ulysses*, though the parallel is not difficult to see. This characteristic in the Sirens episode occurs in the repeated metonymical phrases such as "Bronze by Gold" for Miss Douce's and Miss Kennedy's heads and "Jingle jingle jaunted jingling" for Boylan's carriage and hence for Boylan. Another sort of leitmotif in the Sirens which has received scant critical mention is the use of musical themes such as the *Rose of Castille* for Molly, "The Bloom Is on the Rye" for Bloom, and " 'Tis the Last Rose of Summer," *"M'appari,"* and "Goodbye, Sweetheart, Goodbye," for various aspects of the relationship between Molly and Bloom. These will subsequently be discussed in detail, but for the purpose of the present discussion I will only point out that bits and snatches of the songs are used repeatedly to suggest circumstances or characters as they will appear throughout the episode. The piecing together of these main leitmotifs comprises the overture to the chapter. These themes are linked with brief bits of third-person narrative description gleaned from the body of the episode. Other critics—Sultan, Litz, Strong, and Levin—also agree that the first two pages of the episode comprise the overture.

The contention of Sultan that the overture is parallel to the overture from the opera *Martha* is, I feel, incorrect.[6] There are several types of overture. The overture to the Siren's chapter is a medley composed of sixty-seven theme and description motifs from the entire chapter, clearly different in form as well as content from the overture to Flotow's *Martha,* which contains only two significant motifs from the rest of the opera. Though abundant parallels between *Ulysses* and *Martha* are present—and will be discussed subsequently—they are merely part of all the musical references in the overture and the chapter. Furthermore, there is no plot similarity between *Martha* and the Sirens episode. Lionel in *Martha* has Lady Harriet begging for forgiveness; a situation into which Bloom never manages to maneuver Molly either in the chapter or elsewhere in the novel.

" 'Tis the Last Rose of Summer" and *"M'appari,"* the two songs from *Martha* mentioned in *Ulysses,* are referred to four times in the Siren's overture, which contains twenty-one references to eleven songs; and they are mentioned thirty-two times in the entire chapter, which contains one hundred fifty-eight references to forty-seven songs.[7] In sum, though the importance of this opera must not be underrated, it does not provide the model for the structure of the overture or the entire chapter musically, numerically, or thematically.

The main body of the chapter encompasses five principal songs. Three, "Goodbye, Sweetheart, Goodbye," "All Is Lost Now," and "When First I Saw that Form Endearing," deal with the loss or leave-taking of a lover. The song "Love and War" indicates a synthesis and transition from the love songs which predominate in the earlier parts of the chapter to the patriotic ballads of the latter part. Mabel Worthington has suggested to me that the entire chapter might be built around the principles of love and war, although much music, especially Irish music, has one or the other of the two topics for its dominant themes. Present in most of the chapter, however, is a sense of the pathos of both lonely, betrayed Bloom, and, through the song "The Croppy Boy," the betrayed country. The chapter does not appear to be a light or comic opera, as its overture might suggest, for it seems to have no happy resolution, or, for that matter, no resolution at all, but rather combines in its conclusion the elements of physiology, love, patriotism, and religion in their magnificently pathetic and humorously naturalistic proportions.

If the chapter is not composed along fugal lines, neither is it an opera. The fundamental operatic plot elements of the Sirens episode existed long before the chapter started, and their resolution does not take place in this chapter, despite Sultan's view that the Sirens chapter is the dramatic climax and turning point of *Ulysses*. The themes of the chapter are as general as life itself and can be perceived only in the broadest possible terms. Just as the novel can never be tied exclusively to the rigorous formula of the *Odyssey,* the signs of the zodiac, or the mass, neither can the Sirens chapter be limited to one musical form exclusively. The number and type of songs included in the chapter substantiate this contention. The music ranges from the simplicity of "Home Sweet Home" to the complexities of Liszt's "Hungarian Rhapsodies," from the pious strains of *"Quis est homo?"* to the bawdy lyrics of "O Mary Lost the Pin of Her Drawers," and from the militancy of "The Boys of Wexford" to the tranquility of " 'Tis the Last Rose of Summer." If anything, the Sirens chapter is a medley or chronicle of the musical themes of *Ulysses,* just as the overture was a medley of themes for the chapter, a sort of musical microcosm of the book and its conflicts.

Just as the line between mood and structure is nearly impossible to draw, so too the demarcation between structure and theme. In my opinion the structure of *Ulysses* hinges upon its main theme, which like that of Joyce's earlier work is, simply, consubstantiality.[8] Before discussing the use of music *per se* in developing this central theme of themes, it might be useful to delineate the scope and meaning of the communal-existence motif in the novel. The twist that the simultaneity of being takes on in structure, narrative, and theme of *Ulysses* is a great deal more complicated than in any of the other of Joyce's works, including *Finnegans Wake,* for *Ulysses* is a great deal less frank in its admission that the novel deals predominantly with the reconciliation of opposites. In *Ulysses* as in the *Wake,* the dozen or so principal themes are embellished with scores of variations and variations on variations.

The major theme of reconciliation of father and son encompasses at least eight principal variations in character and nearly as many with the same characters in different roles. So we can list among many more the significant relationships between Shakespeare and Hamlet, Shakespeare and Hamnet, Reuben J. Dodd and son, God and Christ, Joseph and Christ, Bloom and Rudy, Bloom and his father, Bloom and his grandfather, Simon and Stephen, Patrick Dignam and Patrick, Jr., Odysseus and Telemachus, and the false father and the croppy boy. All of these reflect merely the major aspects of the father-son relationship between Bloom and Stephen. The minor variations, including the father-son themes from at least six operas brought in to bolster and broaden the major spiritual and physical aspects of the two principal characters of *Ulysses,* provide the father-son relationship with dimensions which approach complete communality on both historical and immediately present levels. In order to achieve this reconciliation Joyce proceeds from such traditional antagonisms of father and son as the Oedipal theme, but also from the widely divergent ways of thinking of the two major characters. The narrative methods, however, remains constant, with the exception of the subheads in Aeolus, from the first chapter through Wandering Rocks. Not until Sirens does the basic style of the narration change drastically. That the character of the narration seems to change in these early chapters is due to the basic difference between the streams of consciousness of Stephen and Bloom. Stephen's life and thought are conducted on an historical, abstract level, Bloom's on an immediate, literal level.

Stephen provides what Eliot calls in "Tradition and the Individual Talent," the historical sense:

> . . . the historical sense involves a perception, not only of the pastness of the past, but of its presence; the historical sense compels a man to write not merely with his own generation in his bones, but with a feeling that the whole of the literature of Europe from Homer and within it the whole of the literature of his own country has a simultaneous existence and composes a simultaneous order. This historical sense, which is a sense of the timeless as well as of the temporal and of the timeless and of the temporal together, is what makes a writer traditional. And it is at the same time what makes a writer most acutely conscious of his place in time, of his own contemporaneity.[9]

Stephen's mind brings into historical-literary-vertical perspective the major themes, such as rivalry, nationalism, etc., by couching them in terms of such figures as the heresiarchs, Lessing, and Shake-speare, as well as in terms of Renaissance music and the canting academy of the sixteenth and seventeenth centuries. Bloom's mind, preoccupied with his physical being and its surroundings, brings a sense of the here and now, of immediacy, to the overall perspective of the novel. His body of musical reference consists of popular music-hall songs, nursery rhymes, and his wife's solos. Bloom's salvation for Ireland lies, like Faust's, in physical improvements for the country rather than improvements to its conscience. The po-tential for the communality of Bloom and Stephen lies in their con-viction that they need the completeness they both lack. But the basis of their complete identification is again that in essence they are living each others' lives. I am certain, though I can't begin to prove it here, that all of Bloom's experiences throughout the day have, in broad thematic terms, their parallel in Stephen's experiences. Cer-tainly their symbol systems, their conscious rationalizations and re-flections, as divergent as they are, ultimately produce the same major themes in their lives. For instance, the rivalry motive encompasses Molly and Milly, Bloom and Boylan, Stephen and Buck, Stephen and Simon, Bloom and Simon, Shakespeare Sr. and Jr., and hence Stephen and Bloom. All of these relationships subtly inform each other and hence the relationship of the two protagonists.

Both Bloom and Stephen in fact develop congruent themes of their identification. This motif of motifs is developed independently in Bloom's mind through parallax and Molly's question about me-tempsychosis, and in Stephen's thought through his ecclesiastical theme of consubstantiation and transubstantiation and through his Hamlet motif.

The metempsychosis theme, or as Bloom glosses the word, the transmigration of souls, is the passing of souls at death from one body to another. The soul of one individual is reincarnated in an-other body or form. It is Molly, the presider over penumbra urina-tions and the great fusion producer, who asks Bloom about this body-and-soul-reshuffling term, and the theme never leaves his mind for long during June 16th. The reincarnation metaphor is another variation of the communal sharing of essence, or being.

Bloom's second major variation on the communality motif is his preoccupation with the term parallax. In his initial reference to this physical phenomenon, Bloom links it with the metempsychosis motif:

> Fascinating little book that is of sir Robert Ball's. Parallax. I never exactly understood. There's a priest. Could ask him. Par it's Greek: parallel, parallax. Met him pikehoses she called it till I told her about the transmigration. O rocks! (154:5-9)

The phenomenon of parallax occurs when one holds his thumb up at arm's length before his eyes and concentrates on a farther distant object. The thumb comes up as two thumbs or a double image. Conversely, when the eyes are focused on the thumb, the far distant object becomes two. So parallax provides a basis in physics for the consubstantiality of father and son. The image of one becoming two and vice versa with every shift of focus is, in effect, a working model in physics for the spiritual consubstantiation theory. That there are ecclesiastical overtones to the theory is suggested by Bloom's thought that he should ask a priest about the meaning of the term.

The second major meaning of parallax, and the one developed in Ball's little book, concerns how the movements of stars and the workings of the universe may be deduced by sightings of the celestial bodies from various positions on earth or from the same position over a period of time. The point here is that the metempsychic process is comprehended in this aspect of the parallax motif. So the relationship between Bloom and Stephen is universalized into the communality of all things.

Stephen's modifications on the theme include first his variations on the transubstantiation-consubstantiation doctrines. Theologically, as the father and son are distinct as persons but are really one in the same nature, consubstantial, so analogously are Bloom and Stephen, and it is their communality of experience which makes them seem so. As many critics have noted, the transubstantiation doctrine is manifested most obviously in the partaking of the cocoa by Bloom and Stephen in Ithaca, after which they assume each other's identities, becoming Stoom and Blephen.

In my remarks throughout this study I assume this identification, similarity, or common identity between Bloom and Stephen. They live through similar experiences, they think about the same things, and in fact in Circe share the same hallucinations and subconscious.

By the same token, two more dissimilar people one is not likely to discover. Stephen is erudite, historical, classical, and obtuse in his approach to life, while Bloom is literal, empirical, pedestrian, and practical in his view of things and the events in his existence. But this is a classical definition of the term "consubstantiality." Two things or people are the same, but at the same time completely different. In this sense Bloom and Stephen represent a sort of ultimate consubstantiality.

Further, my assertion that Bloom and Stephen are of the same essential nature does not imply that they will be physically united under the same roof throughout life. When Bloom offers Stephen the hospitality of his home and the services of his wife and himself, Stephen undeniably rejects him. They will never live together as father and son or even as tenant and landlord. Their temperaments and inclinations are as night and day. At the same time a union of a different sort has taken place, and by the end of Ithaca, Stoom and Blephen have passed into each other's beings and minds forever, and that union, and their recognition of that union, is unequivocal.

Stephen's second motif of motifs is, of course, the Hamlet pattern, in which Hamlet Sr. and Jr. are one and the same because they both share a common existence with their creator, Shakespeare, whose own life all three have been metempsychically living. This is the burden of Stephen's argument in Skylla and Charybdis, but the main direction of his thesis lies in the unfaithfulness of Ann Hathaway and subsequently of Gertrude. Stephen's conclusion that Shakespeare and the Hamlets are all one in the same necessitates their all being cuckolded by the same woman, the temptress-mother-wife. That all of this will apply directly to Stephen and Bloom is hinted at early in *Ulysses* with Bloom's recitation of Hamlet Sr.'s lines and Stephen's "Hamlet" hat and quotations and song allusions from the play. It is then built upon in succeeding episodes until the transubstantiating moment in Circe before the mirror. For the son the rivalry is initially with the father for the affections of the mother, but as another rival, Claudius, intervenes, father and son are amalgamated in the role of cuckold and allied against their mutual rival. That Stephen feels a bit more than filial affection for his mother has long been the contention of Ruth Von Phul. Few other critics have recognized the importance, or even existence, of the Oedipal theme in *Ulysses*, but it is not hard to find substantial numbers of passages supporting this contention (e.g., pp. 9, 47–48). However, the theme is only a tangential variation on the shared existence motif.

The common identity of Bloom and Stephen emerges in Circe when they look in the mirror and both see the reflection of Shakespeare's face under the sign of the cuckold.

LYNCH

(*Points*). The mirror up to nature. (*He laughs.*) Hu hu hu hu hu hu.

(*Stephen and Bloom gaze in the mirror. The face of William Shakespeare, beardless, appears there, rigid in facial paralysis, crowned by the reflection of the reindeer antlered hatrack in the hall.*) (567:14–20).

From this and the violent dance immediately following arises the specter of May Goulding Dedalus talking of a line from Fergus's song, "love's bitter mystery," and Stephen's implication in it. Consequently the Shakespeare motif becomes much more than a reconciliation of father and son; it encompasses and amalgamates their identity.

Just as characters share common identities and experiences, so themes become interchangeable, intertwined, and hence consubstantial. For instance, the Moses-Elijah theme, a political variation on the search of the Irish for a leader to liberate them from the yoke of British domination, also works as a variation of the father-son motive. The motif is too complicated to develop at any length here, because it involves Stephen and Bloom not only as Moses and Elijah, but as most of the other prophets and, of course, Christ. In an article by Roderick Davis on the Moses theme, there is one paragraph of startling perception which bears on my argument:

Both Stephen and Bloom can be identified with Moses because Joyce so identified himself and they both are also Joyce. This strange algebraic equation is worked out in the library scene. There, Hamlet-Stephen is able to be "reading the book of himself" only because Shakespeare-Joyce has written it—has written himself into it, appearing as both Bloom (Ghost-Father) and Stephen (Son). Through associations and parallels drawn between Moses-Bloom, Moses the Proto-Jew, and Stephen the Protomartyr, the metempsychic conclusion is being anticipated when "Jewgreek is

greekjew," "The son consubstantial with the father," and "Blephen
. . . Stoom." Joyce, the "jew jesuit," is here too, in all of what is
"the book of himself." [10]

While I am not ready to endorse the autobiographical aspect in
Davis' idea, he seems perfectly correct in his assumption that the
theme hinges for its being on the "metempsychic" combination of
characters. The point is that so does everything else in *Ulysses*.

Music does much to develop the communality of circumstances as
well as characters, as time after time a song is used in connection
with one experience of a character only to appear later in an analogous experience with other characters. For instance, most of the
music alluded to in various aspects of Molly's affair with Blazes
recurs in other circumstances. *"M'appari,"* for example, is alluded to
in connection with Martha Clifford and Bloom, and "Seaside Girls,"
first identified with Molly's seductiveness and Boylan, becomes a
song linking, directly by its lyrics and later indirectly by its associations, the temptations evoked by all women. Almost the entire
catalogue of love songs associated with Molly and the theme of love
are used in other situations to suggest their consubstantiality.

To conclude this discussion of the role of music in theme and the
consubstantiality motifs I would like to survey several relevant
episodes briefly in order to point out other important examples.

In Hades, Bloom links the worlds of the dead and the living, not
as in "The Dead" by the snow metaphor with its spiritual overtones,
but by his direct earthly images of making love in graveyards, or
working out various positions on and against tombstones, of the
caretaker's wedding night, of the obese "gray alive" of the rats whose
life is lived in direct communality with the dead, of the maggots'
swirling lifelike through the heads of the temptress seaside girls.
Coupled with these are a plethora of allusions to light comic songs,
like "Three Women to Every Man," "Poor Old Robinson Crusoe,"
and "Who Killed Cock Robin?" used in connection with various
aspects of death. The most important song reference in this consubstantiality motif in Hades is, however, "The Pauper's Drive," discussed earlier, which links all the dead in one communal non-
existence.

Sirens utilizes music to suggest communality as the musical allusions denoting similar circumstances crisscross in a welter of songs reconciling in the word *Siopold* such diverse characters as Lionel from the opera *Martha,* Simon Dedalus, and Leopold Bloom. The overture, a distillation of the chapter into musical-type motives, provides the same collective function, combining characters and themes into one cohesive whole. The most important song reference in this respect is "The Croppy Boy," which provides still another variation on the father-son motive. Allusions to the song establish the identification of Stephen with the blind piano-tuner and their joint consubstantiality with the croppy boy. We hear the complete croppy-boy song in Sirens, and at the end of the episode the tuner comes back to retrieve his tuning fork in the Ormond, entering to the words and motif of the song and becoming the croppy boy: "Tap. A youth entered a lonely Ormond hall" (290:32). Stephen and the croppy boy have already been identified as counterparts overtly through their epithet "you bitch's bastard." Stephen prefigures the blind piano-tuner when he closes his eyes and taps his way along Sandymount Strand with his ashplant divination rod in the Proteus episode.

As Stephen tries to escape the ineluctable modality of the visible by closing his eyes, so Bloom lives through the same experience. Having helped the blind piano-tuner across Dawson Street, in a father-surrogate act, Bloom begins to contemplate the nature of the world outside the modality of the visible, as he lives through the same experience as Stephen by trying to feel the color of his navel under his pants and shirt. Thus is Bloom established not only as a father figure for the piano-tuner and hence for Stephen and the croppy boy, but they have all lived through the same experience. What this all leads to in terms of the father image for Bloom and Stephen is that through the croppy-boy allusion we develop the false-father motif.

The croppy boy comes to confess to a priest who turns out to be a false father, a British yeoman captain, who, hearing of the croppy boy's loyalty to Ireland above the king of England, orders him taken away to prison where he is subsequently hanged. The croppy boy's chief sin, that he forgot to pray for his mother's rest, is reminiscent of what produces Stephen's agenbite of inwit. As Bloom proves to be a true father to the piano-tuner, so he will through the consubstantiality of their beings become a real father to Stephen, whose false father, Simon, has condemned both Stephen and his *fidus Achates,* Mulligan.

The "Croppy Boy" ramifications extend far beyond the father-son motif, however, into the betrayal motif as well as political and social themes, which connect them with other themes in an incredibly complicated mesh of motifs, all inextricably intertwined, as the communality of existence becomes the reality of theme and hence narrative pattern of the book.

Stephen's Oedipal guilt, associated with his riddle, "The Cock Crew," in Nestor and made explicit through his reference to "My Grief on the Sea" in Proteus, finally comes to the fore in Circe. His attempts to break away from the tyranny of Oedipal guilt are culminated in musical terms in Circe by his assumption of Siegfried's role as he tries to shatter the old rule of conscience. But a new order does dawn in Circe through the great amalgamation of the two protagonists and the transubstantiation of the old order into the new. The song "The Holy City" heralds this magnificent transformation of all things into the new millennium and provides the metaphor for conversion of Dublin-Jerusalem into a new age, a reincarnated "Holy City," under the guidance of the Messiah, Moses-Christ-Suffering Servant-Ben-Bloom Elijah, who sees a new Bloomusalem of consubstantiality arise out of the ashes and human wreckage of Mabbot Street.

In the postorgasmic depression of Eumaeus, Stephen and Bloom find their common meeting ground of shared experience in music and go off like sweet Peggy and her lover in the song to be married by Father Maher. The deadly, disparate periodicity of the style, and the clichés which form most of the narrative conjunctions reflect not only the tired quality of the day, but the lack of communication and the opposed natures of the two men who cannot communicate. But their reconciliation is expressed, however tentatively, in their musical interest, and Ithaca finds them trying to effect a more positive consubstantiation in comparing the Hebrew language, handwriting, and music with the Celtic. The ritual cocoa serving, complete with Molly's cream, the mutual identification of Bloom and Stephen in the ballad of "Little Harry Hughes," and the penumbra urination which closes their meeting, are all overt, physical signs that at last even though Stephen rejects Bloom and leaves, some sort of union has been effected.

Thus when the "Little Harry Hughes" ballad is sung the comment and appositives are especially interesting:

Condense Stephen's commentary.

One of all, the least of all, is the victim predestined. Once by inadvertence, twice by design he challenges his destiny. It comes when he is abandoned and challenges him reluctant and, as an apparition of hope and youth holds him unresisting. It leads him to a strange habitation, to a secret infidel apartment, and there, implacable, immolates him, consenting.

Why was the host (victim predestined) sad?

He wished that a tale of a deed should be told of a deed not by him should by him not be told.

Why was the host (reluctant, unresisting) still?

In accordance with the law of the conservation of energy. (692: 1–12)

The Jew's daughter who will perform the potential destruction on Harry-Stephen-Bloom is both daughter and mother and Molly and Milly. Bloom and Stephen share the billing or title of victim predestined. It may be that Stephen's warning is as much for Bloom as for himself and a realization of their consubstantial status.

Stephen and Bloom share the victim role as well as the role of victimizer and cuckold: Stephen in the Oedipal pattern and Bloom in his marriage. And finally since the identities of all the characters have now become interchangeable, Bloom is victimized by Stephen, who leaves, denying him the son of whom he had dreamed. Stephen is victimized by Bloom, who would once again impose the nets of family identification over which Stephen has been trying to fly.

So it is up to Molly, the great earth figure, to confirm the community of existence by linking all men, her lovers, into one great stream-of-consciousness soliloquy. Molly's love affairs are punctuated by constant allusions to the same songs, as the lovers lose their differentiation from each other. The reason that all the "he's" from Mulvey to Boylan have no antecedents is that they are all one and that one is, among everybody else who is living the unique existence, Leopold Bloom, the Here Comes Everybody of *Ulysses.*

Having said that, we see that all the other themes of *Ulysses,* with their attendant musical motives become intertwined. The themes of politics, infidelity and betrayal, social betterment and the Near East-promised land are all associated with each other and all have their consubstantial musical motives which orchestrate, define, and re-enforce. The burden of that explication must be borne by the individual critiques of the allusions in the following text with only the outlines described here.

Music, then, plays a significant role in *Ulysses.* While it initiates few new themes or actions, and while nothing in the plot or themes of the novel depends for its existence on song or musical allusion alone, references to music appear in connection with every theme, action, or major character in the novel. Music reenforces the major motives of *Ulysses* and establishes and maintains links between these motives. It operates in the style and narrative pattern of the book as well as in the structure of major scenes, and it predominates in all these areas in the Sirens episode. Music is too important an ingredient in the development of this complex novel to have received as little critical attention as it has. I hope that this study will, in part, remedy that neglect.

1. Telemachus

He held the bowl aloft and intoned:
    —*Introibo ad altare Dei.* (3:4–5)

Cf. Ordinary of the Mass

REMARKS: Although the *Introibo* is not sung, and should not therefore be technically included in a book of musical allusions, it is intoned and musical notation exists, as for example at the Mass on Corpus Christi day. Hence it appears as one of the references here.

Mulligan's starting the book with the beginning of the Mass has occasioned much scholarly comment about the parallels between *Ulysses* and the Mass. My own theory is that Buck in the beginning parodies Stephen's role of priest in *Portrait,* the transubstantiator or recreator of life (art) out of life (the history of Stephen's life). *Ulysses* provides in Bloom the ultimate parody not only of Odysseus but everything Stephen seems to be, so that in the end all characters and events become one and interchangeable, the ultimate transubstantiation and the center of the Mass.

Palefaces: they hold their ribs with laughter, one clasping another, O, I shall expire! Break the news to her gently, Aubrey! I shall die! (7:22–24)

Cf. "Break the News to Mother"

REMARKS: In the first extended stream-of-consciousness passage in the book, Stephen includes a reference to Charles K. Harris's exceptionally popular American ballad. In the song a dying young soldier exhorts his companions to:

> Just break the news to mother,
> She knows how dear I love her,
> And tell her not to wait for me,
> For I'm not coming home;
> Just say there is no other
> Can take the place of mother;
> Then kiss her dear sweet lips for me,
> And break the news to her.

In Stephen's memory the rowdy exclamations of the students at Kempthorpe's ragging strike an ironic tone as his own exile and the pain of his refusal to submit to his mother's dying entreaties is satirically reversed. In the song the persona's love for his mother introduces another aspect of Stephen's relationship with his own mother. Stephen never overtly admits his love because it has Oedipal overtones which he refuses to acknowledge, but which come back to haunt him in his agenbite of inwit. Stanza two of the song contains further implications for Stephen:

> From afar a noted general had witnessed this brave
>   deed.
> "Who saved our flag? Speak up lads; 'twas noble,
>   brave, indeed!"
> "There he lies, sir," said the captain, "he's
>   sinking very fast,"
> Then slowly turned away to hide a tear.
> The general, in a moment, knelt down beside the
>   boy;
> Then gave a cry that touch'd all hearts that day.
> "It's my son, my brave, young hero; I thought you
>   safe at home."
> "Forgive me, Father for I ran away."

Another major motif of *Ulysses* introduced here is the reconciliation of father and son. Like the boy of the song, Stephen has attempted to sever the parental bonds and is haunted by thoughts and memories of his mother and his inability to be reconciled with her. So, the song introduces and links the themes of May's death and Stephen's guilt and separation from his father.

> *And no more turn aside and brood*
> *Upon love's bitter mystery*
> *For Fergus rules the brazen cars.*   7.5

Woodshadows floated silently by through the morning peace from the stairhead seaward where he gazed. Inshore and farther out the mirror of water whitened, spurned by lightshod hurrying feet. White breast of the dim sea. The twining stresses, two by two. A hand plucking the harpstrings merging their twining chords. Wavewhite wedded words shimmering on the dim tide. (9:22–31)

Cf. "Who Goes With Fergus?"

REMARKS: Mulligan's lines are from the second stanza of the song from *The Countess Cathleen.*

> *Who will go drive with Fergus now,*
> *And pierce the deep wood's woven shade,*
> *And dance upon the level shore?*
> *Young man, lift up your russet brow,*
> *And lift up your tender eyelids, maid,*
> *And brood on hopes and fear no more.*
>
> *And no more turn aside and brood*
> *Upon love's bitter mystery;*
> *For Fergus rules the brazen cars,*
> *And rules the shadows of the wood,*
> *And the white breast of the dim sea*
> *And all dishevelled wandering stars.*[1]

Fergus, the son of Roigh, gave up his claim to the throne in favor of his half brother, Conchobar, and spent the rest of his life feasting, fighting, and hunting. The life Fergus promises in the song is one free from care and struggle, a life of escape, which, pleasant as it sounds, may be merely a sirensong to Stephen, coming as it does from the arch-rival, Mulligan. In the agonizing rivalry between Stephen and Buck, felt so keenly by Dedalus and tacitly acknowledged by Mulligan, such an invitation to take life easy can only be construed by the artist-sans-works as an attempt to seduce him into a life of indolent and unwary defeat. Even Mulligan, however, cannot realize how deeply responsive a chord he has struck in Stephen's mind, as the words trigger still another response in the following line.

A cloud began to cover the sun slowly, shadowing the bay in deeper green. It lay behind him, a bowl of bitter waters. Fergus' song: I sang it alone in the house, holding down the long dark chords.

Her door was open: she wanted to hear my music. Silent with awe and pity I went to her bedside. She was crying in her wretched bed. For those words, Stephen: love's bitter mystery.

Where now? (9:32–39)

Cf. "Who Goes With Fergus?"

REMARKS: The green bowl of the bitter waters of Dublin Bay is associated with May's bowl of green bile and the green thoughts of jealousy as the agenbite of inwit takes on Oedipal overtones. The bitterness of her love and life with Simon is part of the bile as well as Stephen's rejection of his father-rival. Also, as Thornton points out, the bowl-of-bitter-waters allusion appears in chapter five of Numbers, noting that it is connected with the test for adultery. Hence the love's bitter mystery upon which she and Stephen brood is in part unacknowledged and Oedipal.[2]

Her secrets: old feather fans, tasselled dancecards, powdered with musk, a gaud of amber beads in her locked drawer. A bird-cage hung in the sunny window of her house when she was a girl. She heard old Royce sing in the pantomime of Turko the terrible and laughed with others when he sang:

I am the boy
That can enjoy
Invisibility. (9:40–10:6)

Cf. *Turko the Terrible* or *Sinbad the Sailor*

REMARKS: Thornton explains that Old Royce's song "I am the boy" is from a pantomime ballet, *Turko the Terrible,* the title role of which was later revived in *Sinbad the Sailor.*[3] The reference is one of the earliest of the overt links between the experiences of Bloom and Stephen. Turko, who will occupy Bloom's thought a number of times during the day, is closely allied with the whole Near Eastern motif, which runs throughout the novel. Bloom, Molly, Ireland, and Stephen's mother are always looking to the East, the land of mystery, for salvation and a happy issue out of their afflictions. Stephen realizes that this is only a musky dream, folded away in sunless depositories with the other hopes and dreams of the unobtainable. Despite the futility of his mother's aspirations and despite her erroneous choice of a husband, Stephen is unable to shake the subconscious guilt of his love and rejection of her and the church. This memory and the passage from the song pay homage to her faded sensuality and link it with his own childish fantasies. Once he could identify with the boy who enjoyed invisibility, but now the modality of the visible as well as his guilt is inescapable, as Stephen's thoughts turn to his present dreams in which her coming to him, still with sensual overtones, is filled with horror and death.

Phantasmal mirth, folded away: muskperfumed.
And no more turn aside and brood
Folded away in the memory of nature with her toys. (10:7–9)

Cf. "Who Goes With Fergus?'

REMARKS: Now as the echo of Mulligan's rendition of the song crosses Stephen's mind it seems a warning to forget his mother, to put his love for her, her smells, her secrets out of his mind, to avoid the pangs of conscience, and to go with Fergus, but her specter keeps pulling him back.

He flung up his hands and tramped down the stone stairs, singing out of tune with a Cockney accent:

> *O, won't we have a merry time*
> *Drinking whisky, beer and wine,*
> *On coronation,*
> *Coronation day?*
> *O, won't we have a merry time*
> *On coronation day?* (11:8–15)

Cf. "De Golden Wedding"

REMARKS: Mulligan's version of the chorus combines his enthusiasm for booze with a snide cockney parody of Haines' English background, this last in part to placate Stephen who resents the Englishman's usurpation of the tower for which Stephen has paid the rent.

Mother Grogan was, one imagines, a kinswoman of Mary Ann. (13:11–12)

> —*For old Mary Ann*
> *She doesn't care a damn,*
> *But, hising up her petticoats. . .* (13:20–23)

Cf. "McGilligan's Daughter Mary Ann"

REMARKS: Joseph Crofts' version of the song, which is the one I have located, contains none of Mulligan's lyrics. Mabel Worthington has identified a bawdy variant, however, with the concluding line, "She pisses like a man!" Mary Ann and Mother Grogan, linked through their kidneys, possibly foreshadow Molly in her urinary function as fertility goddess and in her role as figure of Ireland.

He passed it along the table towards the old woman, saying:
—Ask nothing more of me, sweet. All I can give you I give.

Stephen laid the coin in her uneager hand.

—We'll owe twopence, he said.

—Time enough, sir, she said, taking the coin. Time enough. Good morning, sir.

She curtseyed and went out, followed by Buck Mulligan's tender chant:

> —*Heart of my heart, were it more,*
> *More would be laid at your feet.* (15:19–28)

Cf. "Ask Nothing More of Me Sweet"

REMARKS: Swinburne's poem was set to music by Theophile Marzials:

> Ask nothing more of me, Sweet
> All I can give you I give
> Heart of my heart, were it more,
> More would be laid at your feet
> Love that would help you to live,
> Song that would spur you to soar
> Ask nothing more of me, Sweet,
> Ask nothing more, nothing more.

Mulligan's mock protestations of love for the old milk woman are little more than a taunt of the Ireland she represents. Mulligan, in Stephen's opinion, takes her milk, shortchanges her, and then taunts her with mock wooing. J. P. Smith has some interesting observations on the political motivations of Mulligan and Stephen:

> The playful allusions to song . . . are truly indicative of Mulligan's mocking attitude towards his country and her defender. It might seem that he and Stephen share the same contempt for the country, but they are really opposites in their views of Ireland. Stephen rejects the claims of a priest-ridden Catholic Ireland which will keep him from his flight, but ultimately he loves the country he tries to reject. He simply wishes that Ireland could be a greater and freer country. Buck is content with the country and his plans to Hellenize Ireland can hardly be considered seriously.[4]

Hurry out to your school kip and bring us back some money. Today the bards must drink and junket. Ireland expects that every man this day will do his duty. (15:30–33)

Cf. "The Death of Nelson"

REMARKS: The last sentence is, of course, a paraphrase of Nelson's famous line, then currently on everyone's lips because of the popular song. The song depicts the dying Nelson urging his men to do battle for England. Mulligan's substitution of Ireland for England is a sort of slur on the Irish, whose duty—according to Mulligan—is not bravery but providing their drinking cronies with funds for booze. The allusion is meant to further the aura of Mulligan's irreverence toward many of the institutions Stephen is seriously concerned about.

—Billy Pitt had them built, Buck Mulligan said, when the French were on the sea. But ours is the *omphalos*. (17:36–37)

Cf. "The Shan Van Vocht"

REMARKS: Mulligan alludes to the opening line of the widely known song, the first stanza of which follows:

> . . . The French are on the sea,
> Says the Shan Van Vocht;
> The French are on the sea,
> Says the Shan Van Vocht:
> . . . the French are in the Bay,
> They'll be here without delay,
> And the Orange will decay,
> Says the Shan Van Vocht.

The link between the Shan Van Vocht (Gaelic for "The Poor Old Woman"), Ireland, and the milk woman is apparent enough; however, Mulligan's reference to the tower as the *omphalos* serves to tie it in with Stephen's mother. Later Stephen will explicitly associate tower, navel, umbilicus, heritage, and universal experience (37:41–38:5). Even as *Ulysses* opens Stephen is desperately trying to break the umbilical cord that links him to his country, mother, and heritage. The pattern of Stephen's attempts to free himself from universal experience, so apparent in *Portrait,* are still operative. Hence his decision not to return to the tower or meet Buck at the tavern. The relationship between tower, mother, and Ireland, established by Mulligan through the song, is an additional link in this chain of association.

Stephen's attempts to escape from the omphalos, the mother, and the Irish national cause all become intertwined with the additional connotation the song provides: that help is on the way. Like the French, who are on the sea coming to save Ireland, Stephen's link to humanity, Leopold Bloom, is abroad to bring an end to Ireland's bondage to England and Stephen's bondage to the agenbite of inwit, his Oedipal complex, and the world of Simon Dedalus.

—*I'm the queerest young fellow that ever you heard.*
My mother's a jew, my father's a bird.
With Joseph the joiner I cannot agree,
So here's to disciples and Calvary. (19:3–6)

—If anyone thinks that I amn't divine
He'll get no free drinks when I'm making the wine
But have to drink water and wish it were plain
That I make when the wine becomes water again. (19:8–11)

—Goodbye, now, goodbye. Write down all I said
And tell Tom, Dick and Harry I rose from the dead.
What's bred in the bone cannot fail me to fly
And Olivet's breezy . . . Goodbye, now, goodbye. (19:16–19)

Cf. "Ballad of Joking Jesus"

REMARKS: Joyce has presented slightly modified words to stanzas 1, 2, and 9 of Oliver St. John Gogarty's "The Song of the Cheerful (but slightly sarcastic) Jesus."[5] Mulligan is not merely irreverent, however. His disbelief and mockery characterize for Stephen his essentially destructive character. His song mocks the symbolic parallels Stephen has drawn between himself and Christ. Stephen's homage to his father, the old artificer, Dedalus, is mocked in stanza one, his doctrine of the transubstantiation of art in two, and his flight over the nets in three. When Mulligan mocks standard symbols such as Christ, he mocks Stephen, who has transformed them into his own being and for his own use.

—We oughtn't to laugh, I suppose. He's rather blasphemous. I'm not a believer, that is to say. Still his gaiety takes the harm out of it somehow, doesn't it? What did he call it? Joseph the Joiner?

—The ballad of Joking Jesus, Stephen answered. . .

—You're not a believer, are you? Haines asked. I mean, a believer in the narrow sense of the word. Creation from nothing and miracles and a personal God.

—There's only one sense of the word, it seems to me, Stephen said. (19:26–37)

Cf. "Ballad of Joking Jesus"

REMARKS: Haines's idea that Mulligan's gaiety takes the harm out of his disbelief is completely alien to the Jesuitical mind of Stephen. It is precisely the lack of commitment and the lightness with which Mulligan regards country, mother, and church that is the cardinal sin. For Stephen, there are no halfway commitments. To rail out in opposition is one thing, to mock another. His own allegiances are not to Christ, but to himself as artist, and Mulligan's offense not to Christianity but, by the extension of Stephen's symbol pattern, to himself, as it was when Mulligan said *"O, it's only Dedalus whose **mother*** *is beastly dead"* (8:19–20). As Mulligan the mocking anarchist would scorn Christ, so he scorns the Christ-like creator, Stephen. And it seems to Stephen all through Telemachus that it is the Mulligans who gain the favor of Ireland while they attempt to destroy her.

2. Nestor

Riddle me, riddle me, randy ro.
My father gave me seeds to sow. (26:19–20)

Cf. "Riddle me, riddle me"

REMARKS: The full text of this first riddle is as follows:

> Riddle me, riddle me, randy-bow,
> My father gave me seed to sow,
> The seed was black and the ground was white.
> Riddle me that and I'll give you a pipe (variant: pint).
> —Writing a letter.

Thornton sees Stephen's omission of the last two lines as significant: "Probably he does so here because the riddle and its solution remind him of his failure to justify himself as an author." [1] However, the riddle was triggered by Talbot's quotation from "Lycidas" and Stephen's subsequent thoughts of Christ, so it follows that Stephen's thoughts encompassed only the first two lines, which are the only ones appropriate to the biblical Father-Son theme. In a broader context, however, the riddle suggests more than Thornton has commented upon. The lines dealing with the blackness of the seed and the whiteness of the ground are suppressed not only because they have connotations of Stephen's inability to write, but because they have Oedipal-sexual connotations of Stephen's guilt regarding his mother. His seeds, bequeathed by his father, have come to no fruition either in writing or in the physical sense because Stephen has been emasculated by love for his mother, the white ground of the mother-virgin. So his connection with the mainstream of existence, his father's legacy of seeds, has been dissolved and must be replaced with a new father figure, Bloom, and Bloom's seeds, which are currently being wasted in masturbation. The Oedipal connotations of the riddle are strengthened when the rhyme triggers the second riddle of guilt in Stephen's mind.

The cock crew
The sky was blue:
The bells in heaven
Were striking eleven.

Tis time for this poor soul
To go to heaven. (26:33–38)

—The fox burying his grandmother under a hollybush. (27:8)

She was no more: the trembling skeleton of a twig burnt in the fire, an odour of rosewood and wetted ashes. She had saved him from being trampled under foot and had gone, scarcely having been. A poor soul gone to heaven: and on a heath beneath winking stars a fox, red reek of rapine in his fur, with merciless bright eyes scraped in the earth, listened, scraped up the earth, listened, scraped and scraped. (27:40–28:5)

Cf. "The Cock Crew"

REMARKS: As is obvious from the passage the riddle becomes for Stephen a riddle of his own guilt concerning his mother's death and his answer, the burying of his deed under a hollybush. The original riddle, reprinted in Thornton, is as follows:

> Riddle me riddle me right:
> What did I see last night?
> The wind blew
> The cock crew,
> The bells of heaven
> Struck eleven
> Tis time for my poor *sowl* to go to heaven. Answer:
The fox burying his mother under a holly tree.[2]

The words *riddle me* form the preliminary association with the preceding riddle. But the context is widened through the use of the fox burying not only a mother figure but also the guilt of his associations with her. It is easy for Stephen to transfer generations and substitute grandmother for mother, because it fits so well the central Shakespeare theme upon which he seems to be positing his life. If Shakespeare is grandfather and father, as well as son, why shouldn't the fox's mother be his grandmother? Further, in Webster's *The White Devil*, Cornelia says: *"But keep the wolf far thence, that's foe to men,/ For with his nails he'll dig them up agen."*[3] Eliot gives these lines a new twist in *The Waste Land:* "Oh keep the dog far hence, that's friend to men,/ Or with his nails he'll dig it up again."[4] The Webster lines indicate the cruelty of exposing the body and soul to the slings and arrows of outrageous fortune, hence the wolf as enemy. The point in Eliot is that though the dog in a friendly manner tries to resurrect us, man is better off forgetting, for winter at least keeps us warm in forgetful snow, and there is less pain in not being aware of our plight. Stephen's version has overtones of each. The fox burying his grandmother is Stephen's attempt to sublimate his Oedipal and religious memories and guilt by relegating them to the subconscious. Perhaps Stephen's rapine-reeking fox is not so much struggling to bury his misdeeds as to uncover them. Subconscious guilt keeps struggling to the surface through the fox association, both here and in Circe where the fox is pursued by Simon Dedalus leading an entire assembly of huntsmen.

Croppies lie down. (31:26)

Cf. "Croppies Lie Down"

REMARKS: Stephen's association of Deasy with what he believes to be the worst of the Orange causes concludes with his association of Deasy with the vitriolic Orange ballad. The first stanza sufficiently indicates the sentiments of the ballad:

> We soldiers of Erin, so proud of the name,
> We'll raise upon rebels and Frenchmen our fame;
> We'll fight to the last in the honest old cause,
> And guard our religion, our freedom and laws;
> We'll fight for our country, our King, and his crown,
> And make all the traitors and croppies lie down.[5]

—I have rebel blood in me too, Mr Deasy said. On the spindle side. But I am descended from sir John Blackwood who voted for the union. We are all Irish, all kings' sons.

—Alas, Stephen said.

—*Per vias rectas,* Mr Deasy said firmly, was his motto. He voted for it and put on his topboots to ride to Dublin from the Ards of Down to do so.

> *Lal the ral the ra*
> *The rocky road to Dublin.*

A gruff squire on horseback with shiny topboots. Soft day, sir John. Soft day, your honour . . . Day . . . Day . . . Two topboots jog dangling on to Dublin. Lal the ral the ra, lal the ral the raddy. (31:28–40)

Cf. "The Rocky Road to Dublin"

REMARKS: Stephen manifests his impatience with Deasy's rebel and loyalist pretensions by associating his ancestor with the comic hero of the ballad. In the song the persona has mended his new footwear and left his home for Dublin, as has Sir John. The persona, however, upon reaching Dublin embarks on a boat for England where he immediately gets into a brawl with the English:

> The boys of Liverpool, when we safely landed,
> Called myself a fool, I could no longer stand it;

Blood began to boil, temper I was losin'
Poor ould Erin's isle they began abusin',
"Hurrah my soul," sez I, my shillelagh I let fly;
Some Galway boys were by, saw I was a hobble in,
They with a loud hurray, they joined in the affray,
We quickly cleared the way, for the rocky road to Dublin.

Stephen's comparison of Sir John with the militant Irishman in the song is another manifestation of his disgust with Deasy whose Orange ancestry is hard enough to take without his claiming rebel blood to boot.

3. Proteus

The drunken little costdrawer and his brother, the cornet player. Highly respectable gondoliers. (38:34–35)

Cf. Don Alhambra's first song in *The Gondoliers*

REMARKS: Thornton correctly identifies the song from Gilbert and Sullivan, but suggests that Simon's reference is connected with the cornet player in another part of the operetta.[1] It is much more direct than that. The "highly respectable gondolier" referred to in the song is a drunkard who is in such a perpetual state of inebriation that he can't tell which of the two boys he raised is his son and which a royal stripling left to his charge. Simon's comments deal with the Goulding drinking habits. Also the song is one of a series of references involving lost sons and the invariable discovery of their true paternity and families. The relevance to the father-son motif of *Ulysses* is obvious.[2]

All'erta!

He drones bars of Ferrando's *aria de* [sic][3] *sortita*. The grandest number, Stephen, in the whole opera. (39:27–29)

Cf. *"Aria di Sortita"*

REMARKS: "On guard," Ferrando's warning, which begins *Il Trovatore*, is an admonishment to the guards to look alert because the count may be abroad. That the count in the opera finally kills his own brother may bear on Simon's relation with Richie. Stephen's remembered conversation is almost identical with what Richie says and whistles to Bloom later in the Ormond, except that the tune on the latter occasion significantly is "All Is Lost Now." Therefore it is probable that Ferrando's warning here should also be taken seriously by both the reader and Stephen. There are a number of parallels between the opera and those themes of *Ulysses* linking Bloom and Stephen. The fratricide ties in vaguely with Simon's character assassination of his brother-in-law and also with Hamlet senior and Claudius, upon which much of the Stephen-

Bloom-Simon relationship is thematically posited. Also, as with *The Gondoliers*, the opera involves a case of confused paternity and a search for the real family relationship. Garzia di Luna, captured by a gypsy witch as a child and supposed dead by his brother, the count, is raised by the gypsy's daughter and the count finally kills him, knowing him only as an enemy knight and rival for the affections of the fair Leonora. The secret of Garzia's real identity is not discovered until in vengeance his witch-mother or false mother gleefully reveals all.[4] The parallels to *Ulysses* are to Stephen's search for his identity, to his conscience-ridden picture of May's lust for vengeance, to Bloom's discovery of kinship with Stephen, and to the murder of little Harry Hughes, which is pivotal in the Bloom-Stephen motif.

—Mother dying come home father.
The aunt thinks you killed your mother. That's why she won't.

> *Then here's a health to Mulligan's aunt*
> *And I'll tell you the reason why.*
> *She always kept things decent in*
> *The Hannigan* [sic] *famileye.*

His feet marched in sudden proud rhythm over the sand furrows, along by the boulders of the south wall. (42:15-23)

Cf. "Mathew Hanigan's Aunt"

REMARKS: As Stephen remembers Mulligan's remark about his aunt's dislike of Stephen, he manifests his scorn of her again by making her the brunt of a song as he did Mr. Deasy. Stephen sings a slightly altered version of the opening lines of the chorus to this lively comic song about a domineering old woman who runs the Hanigan [sic] household smoothly but with an iron hand. The last stanza indicates the mixed feelings of the Hanigan family toward her:

> Oh, 'tis often we'd praise her up,
>   We'd laud her to the sky,
> We'd all discant on Hanigan's Aunt,
>   And hope she never would die
> But still, I'd like to add—
>   If Hanigan isn't about—
> That when we plant Mat Hanigan's Aunt,
>   We won't be too put out.

The song serves to free Stephen momentarily from his sense of dejection regarding the disillusionment of his less than successful Paris sojourn.

How the head centre got away, authentic version. Got up as a young bride, man, veil orangeblossoms, drove out the road to Malahide. (43:25-27)

Cf. "The Bridal of Malahide"

REMARKS: Egan's version of the escape of James Stephens, the head centre, from Ireland, includes both an apocryphal bride disguise as well as the established fact of his leaving along the Malahide Road. Perhaps the bridal-disguise story was prompted by Egan's association of the Malahide Road with the poem in which the groom goes off to war immediately after his marriage.

I taught him to sing. *The boys of Kilkenny are stout roaring blades.* Know that old lay? I taught Patrice that. Old Kilkenny: saint Canice, Strongbow's castle on the Nore. Goes like this. *O, O.* He takes me, Napper Tandy, by the hand.

> *O, O the boys of*
> *Kilkenny . . .*

Weak wasting hand on mine. They have forgotten Kevin Egan, not he them. Remembering thee, O Sion. (44:1–9)

Cf. "The Boys of Kilkenny"
"The Wearing of the Green"

REMARKS: The first stanza of the song which Egan taught Patrice to sing begins with a rollicking tribute to the good life in Kilkenny:

> Oh, the boys of Kilkenny are stout roving blades
> And whenever they meet with nice little maids
> They'll kiss them and coax them and spend their
>   money free,
> And of all the towns in Ireland, Kilkenny for me
> And of all, . . .

The last lines of the song, however, are much closer to Egan's exiled position:

> For 'tis there I'd have sweethearts but here
>   I have none.
> For 'tis there I'd . . . .

As he starts to sing his nostalgic song for Stephen, Stephen associates him with another exile, hungry for Irish company and news:

> I met with Napper Tandy
>   And he tuk me by the hand,
> And he said "how's poor ould Ireland
>   And how does she stand?"
> She's the most distressful country,
>   That ever you have seen;
> They're hanging men and women there
>   For wearing of the green.

But to Stephen the suffering country of the song is also ungrateful for her suffering servant, Egan. While the exile still remembers his home, the old distressful country in forgetting him, her would-be savior, has demonstrated her fickleness again, as in the preceding scene with the old milk woman, and in the future she will scorn her potential emancipator, Dedalus, the artist-priest.

> Danevikings, torcs of tomahawks aglitter on their breasts when Malachi wore the collar of gold. (45:12–13)

Cf. "Let Erin Remember the Days of Old"

REMARKS: Stephen's reference is to the first stanza of Thomas Moore's song of pre-English Ireland:

> Let Erin remember the days of old,
> Ere her faithless sons betrayed her;
> When Malachi wore the collar of gold,
> Which he won from the proud invader;
> When her kings with standards of green unfurled,
> Led the Red Branch Knights to danger;
> Ere the em'rald gem of the western world
> Was set in the crown of a stranger.

The song suits Stephen's train of thought. Having speculated on the faithfulness of the country, Stephen's thoughts turn to the glorious time before betrayals. The song refers to Malachi, a tenth-century monarch of Ireland, and his defeat of two Danish champions, whom he encountered successively hand to hand, taking a collar from the neck of one and carrying off the sword of the other as trophies of his victory.

> Something he buried there, his grandmother. He rooted in the sand, dabbling, delving and stopped to listen to the air, scraped up the sand again with a fury of his claws, soon ceasing, a pard, a panther, got in spouse-breach, vulturing the dead. (46:40–47:3)

Cf. "The Cock Crew"

REMARKS: A number of images begin to merge in Stephen's mind as he thinks of his inability to save either the drowned man in Dublin Bay or his mother (46:3–5). Tatters, the cocklepickers' dog, intrudes upon Stephen's thoughts and is included in them. First Tatters's search along the beach takes on overtones of Stephen's search through the ineluctable modality of the visible and the past history represented by the seaspawn on the beach and the times "when Malachi wore the collar of gold." Stephen thinks, "Looking for something lost in a past life" (46:8). Then as the dog digs, Stephen sees him as the fox of his riddle of the subconscious. Juxtaposed against this, in the next lines Stephen recalls his dream-premonition of his coming meeting with Bloom in Circe. The point is that the riddle has become a leitmotif for Stephen's Oedipal guilt and his need for a reconciliation with the father, and

Bloom serves to fulfill that need; hence the placing of the premonition here, immediately after the riddle reference.

... the ruffian and his strolling mort. (47:13)

... bing awast, to Romeville. (47:16)

Buss her, wap in rogue's rum lingo, for, O, my dimber wapping dell. (47:19–20)

> *White thy fambles, red thy fan*
> *And thy quarrons dainty is.*
> *Couch a hogshead with me then.*
> *In the darkmans clip and kiss.* (47:23–26)

Call away let him: *thy quarrons dainty is.* Language no whit worse than his. Monkwords, marybeads jabber on their girdles: roguewords ... (47:28–30)

Cf. "The Rogue's Delight in Praise of His Stroling Mort"

REMARKS: The cocklepickers Stephen sees on the beach become in his mind analogous to sixteenth- and seventeenth-century gypsies. His speculations on their relationship take on sexual overtones as the woman becomes lover, then whore. The words Stephen quotes refer to a sixteenth- or seventeenth-century canting song collected by Richard Head in *The Canting Academy*.[5] Stephen refers to phrases from the title and the second and last of the seven stanzas of the song. The words to the appropriate stanzas appear on the left and Head's translation on the right:

1. Doxy oh! Thy Glaziers shine	1. My honey chuck, byth' Mass I swear,
As Glymmar by the Salomon,	Thine eyes do shine than fire more clear,
No Gentry Mort hath prats like thine	No silken Girl hath thighs like thine,
No Cove e're wap'd with such a one.	No doe was ever buck'd like mine.
2. White thy fambles, red thy gan,	2. Thy hand is white and red thy lip,
And thy quarrons dainty is,	Thy dainty body I will clip.
Couch a hogshead with me than,	Let's down to sleep our selves then lay,
In the Darkmans clip and kiss.	Hug in the dark and kiss and play.
7. Bing awast to Rome-vile then	7. Therefore to *London* let us hie
O my dimber wapping Dell,	O thou my sweet bewitching eye,
Wee'l heave a booth and dock agen	There wee'l rob and kiss pell-mell,
Then trining scape and all is well.	Escaping Tyburn all is well.[6]

While there seems little in the scene to titilate Stephen, the couple triggers the fairly crude if antiquated song and brings on Stephen some guilt pangs and a reference to Aquinas's doctrine of the pleasure of sinful thought without desire. But Thomas's ancient words become, like the call of the male cocklepicker and the Rogue in the song, the "roguewords" of sensuality to Stephen.

A side-eye at my Hamlet hat. (47:33)

Cf. Ophelia's Song (*Hamlet,* IV. v. 23–26)

REMARKS: As the female cocklepicker glances at Stephen, he equates her, through a *Hamlet* reference, to Ophelia, whose songs in madness reflect the sensuality she repressed when she was sane. Having established the sensual theme in the previous canting-song reference, Stephen extends it to *Hamlet* and Ophelia. Later in the passage through two other allusions to the play, he further broadens Ophelia's sensuality to Gertrude and thence to his own mother ("Bridebed, childbed, bed of death, ghostcandled" [47:40–48:1]). Here Stephen becomes for the first time in his own mind a Hamlet figure, with all the overtones of Oedipal sensuality implied in both the play and in May's relationship with Stephen. As Bloom's thoughts return again and again to his wife, so Stephen's eventually return to his ever present female figure, May Dedalus, and the guilt of his sensual association deepens. Stephen's need to be reconciled with a father figure in the Oedipal rivalry as well as the spiritual sense becomes more apparent as the day and his association patterns continue.

> He comes, pale vampire, through storm his eyes, his bat sails bloodying the sea, mouth to her mouth's kiss.
>
> Here. Put a pin in that chap, will you? My tablets. Mouth to her kiss. No. Must be two of em. Glue 'em well. Mouth to her mouth's kiss.
>
> His lips lipped and mouthed fleshless lips of air: mouth to her womb. Oomb, allwombing tomb. (48:1–8)

Cf. "My Grief on the Sea"

REMARKS: Stephen continues the *Hamlet* associations as his mother's ghost figure becomes fused with the ghost figure of Hamlet senior, but with a new wrinkle. The father becomes the lover as overtones of Douglas Hyde's song are blended in the associative pattern. The mouth-to-mouth reference is from the last stanza of the song, which deals with a girl "abandoned, forsaken" with her "grief" and "trouble" by her lover, who presumably has died. As the girl mourns, her lover's ghost returns in the last stanza to pick up where he left off:

> And my love came behind me—
> He came from the South;
> His breast to my bosom,
> His mouth to my mouth.

Stephen's reference to tablets alludes to Hamlet's promise to the ghost that
he will wipe away from the tables of his mind "all trivial and fond records"
of his youth and concern it only with his father's commandment, thoughts of
his mother, a "most pernicious woman," and the "smiling, damned villain."
What he will set down are villainy and lack of conscience as he muses on
Claudius, "My tables—meet it is I set it down/ That one may smile, and
smile, and be a villain." But then Stephen begins to assume the lover's role in
the song and the father-lover's in *Hamlet* as he tries to kiss the lips of mother-
womb and tomb. The womb-tomb association occurs in Shakespeare (*Romeo
and Juliet,* II, iii, 9–10) and as Thornton points out [7] is more to the point in
Blake:

> The Door of Death I open found
> And the Worm Weaving in the Ground:
> Thou'rt my Mother from the Womb,
> Wife, Sister, Daughter to the Tomb,
> Weaving to Dreams the Sexual strife
> And weeping over the Web of Life.[8]

As Stephen reaches to kiss the womb of his life's beginning and the sexual
strife of his youth, he, like the ghost figure of his father-Hamlet, reaches to
appease "love's bitter mystery," which haunts his conscience and leads him to
seek the father figure. As Hamlet junior he must punish the "damned
villain" usurper, himself, for coveting the father's rightful prize. Hence the
agenbite of inwit. The passage just discussed is the most graphic exposure yet
of Stephen's problems regarding his mother and father.

Why not endless till the farthest star? Darkly they are there behind this light, darkness shining in the brightness, delta of Cas-
siopeia, worlds. Me sits there with his augur's rod of ash, in
borrowed sandals, by day beside a livid sea, unbeheld, in violet
night walking beneath a reign of uncouth stars. (48:16–21)

Cf. *Das Rheingold*
Ophelia's Song (*Hamlet* IV. v. 23–26)

REMARKS: Stephen's ashplant, his "rod of augury" since *Portrait,* now is
linked with the order of the universe in the beginning of a complicated series
of allusions to Wagner's ring cycle. The spear with which Woton-Stephen, in
his father's role, rules, is the source of all the covenants, runes, and symbols
which govern the universe. It is the rod upon which Stephen has depended
for divination and symbol interpretation all through *Portrait* and the early

part of *Ulysses* and which he will finally break with his sword, Needful, in his role as Siegfried in Circe. The point of the present reference to the augur's rod is that as he bends to write on a scrap of paper his universe is still that of Woton's divination. The augur's rod, his spear of Woton, is still intact as he borrows his existence from runes of the old order, all Stephen's allusionary sources. At the same time he is trying to escape the ineluctable modality of the visible, the actual world of the here and now. His sandals, a *Hamlet* reference by way of Ophelia (the allusion is to IV, v. 25–26; "By his cockle hat and staff/ And his sandal shoon"), with all the Oedipal connotations pointed out earlier,[9] are, like the rest of his existence, more borrowed than real.

Who ever anywhere will read these written words? Signs on a white field. (48:24–25)

Cf. "Riddle me, riddle me"

REMARKS: This reference, one of the lines hitherto suppressed from Stephen's first riddle, connects his own writing with the answer to the riddle and recalls the Oedipal associations of the earlier passage.[10] This is the reason for his subsequent references to the "darkness" of his words and "Our soul, shamewounded by our sins. . . ," etc.

And no more turn aside and brood. (49:16)

Cf. "Who Goes with Fergus?"

REMARKS: Stephen's sensuality and desire for escape converge in the song reference. His peace of mind would return if Stephen could turn no more aside and brood upon the bitter mysteries of love associated with May,[11] or if he could accept Mulligan's invitation [12], . . . but he can't. In the next line he continues his brooding.

. . . hising up their petticoats . . . (49:36)

Cf. "McGilligan's Daughter Mary Ann"

REMARKS: See earlier discussion above.[13]

Five fathoms out there. Full fathom five thy father lies. (50:4)

A seachange this, brown eyes saltblue. (50:19)

Cf. Ariel's Song (*Tempest*, I, ii, 397–403)

REMARKS: The lines from Ariel's song are as follows:

> Full fathom five thy father lies,
> Of his bones are coral made,

> Those are pearls that were his eyes:
> Nothing of him that doth fade
> But doth suffer a sea change
> Into something rich and strange.
> Sea nymphs hourly ring his knell.

The reference is significant in the father-son motif. Ferdinand, like Stephen, is searching for his father. Neither Stephen's nor Ferdinand's father is dead, but though alive they have been the disseminators of falsehood and disparagers of truth. Ferdinand and Stephen are both destined to meet men, who, although not their biological fathers, possess a wisdom and understanding that the younger men need and that their real fathers cannot give them. Ferdinand will achieve understanding, satisfaction, and happiness at the hands of Prospero, and Stephen will, hopefully, achieve a certain understanding of humanity, a resolution of his agenbite of inwit, and perhaps equanimity from Bloom. At least it is these things for which Stephen searches at the present moment. The false songs heard by Ferdinand and Stephen in this early segment of their stories betoken their delusions, needs, and similarities to each other.

The "seachange" referred to by Stephen is undergone by Ferdinand's supposedly drowned father in Ariel's song. When at the end of the play Alonso is rediscovered by Ferdinand, the father will indeed be changed into something better by the wisdom of Prospero. So too Simon will be changed in Stephen's eyes after Stephen solves his Oedipal problem and learns the wisdom of humanity from Simon's consubstantial counterpart, Bloom. At any rate, that Stephen looks and yearns for a transformed father figure is apparent in his analogy between himself and Ferdinand.

> Come. I thirst. Clouding over. No black clouds anywhere, are there? Thunderstorm. Allbright he falls, proud lightning of the intellect, *Lucifer, dico, qui nescit occasum.* No. My cockle hat and staff and his my sandal shoon. Where? To evening lands. Evening will find itself. (50:23–27)

Cf. Ophelia's Song (*Hamlet*, IV, v, 23–26)

REMARKS: In rapid succession Stephen places himself in the position of Christ, Satan, and, through Ophelia's Song, Hamlet. The sensual aspects of the Ophelia-Gertrude-Hamlet association have already been discussed.[14] First Stephen quotes from Christ's words on the cross. Then the cockle hat and staff of the song are traditional pilgrim, Christian symbols. Stephen's shoes were given to him by Mulligan, with his Satanic connotations, and Stephen becomes Hamlet-Oedipus through Ophelia's reference, which is really about her lover. So the reference combines all three symbol patterns which have been operating in Stephen's mind.

Tuesday will be the longest day. Of all the glad new year, mother, the rum tum tiddledy tum. Lawn Tennyson, gentleman poet. *Già*. For the old hag with the yellow teeth. (50:30–33)

Cf. "Call Me Early Mother Dear"

REMARKS: Stephen's reference is to the third line of the first stanza, quoted here in its entirety:

> You must wake and call me early, call me early, mother dear;
> To-morrow'll be the happiest time of all the glad New-year;
> Of all the glad New-year, mother, the maddest merriest day;
> For I'm to be Queen o' the May, mother, I'm to be Queen o' the May.

Stephen's *rum tum's* fill out the end of verse three, ". . . the maddest merriest day." The association here is between the longest day of the year and the May-day celebration alluded to in the poem. The persona of the poem, as later stanzas develop, is a flighty, selfish young woman who cares little for her spurned, heartbroken lover or anything other than the all-encompassing fact that on the morrow she will be queen of the May. The persona is then associated with the old hag, who in the light of earlier associations (*Ulysses* p. 20) [15] could be either Victoria or the Shan Van Vocht. Stephen, like the lowly rhymster, Tennyson, serves the "crazy queen, old and jealous" and the other who wants him "for odd jobs."

4. Calypso

Wander through awned streets. Turbaned faces going by. Dark caves of carpet shops, big man, Turko the terrible, seated cross-legged smoking a coiled pipe. Cries of sellers in the streets. (57: 20–23)

Cf. *Turko the Terrible* or *Sinbad the Sailor*

REMARKS: See earlier explication of Turko.[1] The symbol patterns for Bloom and Stephen begin to merge early in Bloom's first chapter. He like Stephen is a wanderer. The pilgrim theme blends in Bloom's thoughts with the Near Eastern motif, associated with Molly's stay on Gibraltar, and finally leads, as it does in "Araby," to the association of the Near East with some utopian way out of all their afflictions, a nirvana, a promised land. For Bloom the Near East and Turko are associated with Molly, for Stephen the pantomime or ballet with May Dedalus. As the two become merged through the day the all-encompassing female figure of Molly will blend the separate aspects of the motif into one in her soliloquy. For now, it provides the first overt connection of the novel between the two and their thoughts.

Brats' clamour. Windows open. Fresh air helps memory. Or a lilt. Ahbeesee defeegee kelomen opeecue rustyouvee double you. Boys are they? (58:33–36)

Cf. "ABC Song"

REMARKS: Bloom passes by St. Joseph's National School, where the sounds of the classes are filtering out through the window. While he speculates on how the fresh air might aid the boys' memory he thinks of another memory aid to learning the alphabet, the simple ABC song which most children are taught. As Bloom seeks to improvise and improve the song we have one of the curious little turns of mind that characterize him. Instead of the normal ABC lyrics usually sung to the tune of "Twinkle, Twinkle Little Star," [2] Bloom tries to make words out of the letters. Joyce gives us a phonetic spelling for Bloom's new lyrics:

O, please, Mr Policeman, I'm lost in the wood. (60:3–4)

Cf. "O Please Mr. Policeman, I'm Lost in the Wood"

REMARKS: Hodgart and Worthington list this as a music-hall song, but I have not been able to locate it.

Blazes Boylan's seaside girls. (62:36)

Cf. "Seaside Girls"

REMARKS: Bloom tears open his letter from his daughter Milly and scans it quickly, at first misreading, "Blazes Boylan's seaside girls" for Milly's statement, ". . . he sings Boylan's (I was on the pop of writing Blazes Boylan's) song about those seaside girls" (66:14–15). This is the first reference to the song to which Milly alludes in her letter and which is to become one of the major musical motifs of the novel. The song has, according to Milly, been written by a man named Boylan, whom, Milly confides in her letter, she has almost confused with Blazes Boylan. Later when Bloom rereads Milly's letter in detail he will see that she is not referring to Blazes Boylan as the author; however the initial association of Blazes with the song becomes irrevocably planted in Bloom's stream of consciousness. The song is not historically identified with any Boylan so far as I have been able to make out. "Seaside Girls" was written and composed by Harry B. Norris and published in London by Frank Dean and Co. in 1899. It was endorsed and sung by Miss Vesta Tilley, who is associated with it in *Finnegans Wake*.[3] But it was popular at the turn of the century in music-hall circles.

Perhaps because of its association with Boylan, the song takes on sensual overtones, providing Bloom with Boylan as the first link between the consubstantiality of his wife and his daughter and all the temptresses and sirens who are a part of his existence and whose combined associations Joyce utilizes so fully in the mother-daughter aspects of *Finnegans Wake*.

> *O, Milly Bloom, you are my darling.*
> *You are my looking glass from night to morning.*
> *I'd rather have you without a farthing*
> *Than Katey Keogh with her ass and garden.* (63:1-4)

Cf. "Oh Thady Brady, you are my darlin'"

REMARKS: Bloom's song is an amended version of a song by Samuel Lover. The appropriate quatrain of Lover (as quoted by Thornton) is as follows:

> Oh Thady Brady you are my darlin,
> You are my looking-glass from night till morning
> I love you better without one fardin
> Than Brian Gallagher wid house and garden.[4]

Bloom begins here to equate Molly with Milly in terms not only of their characteristics, but also of his need and love for them. As Stephen and Bloom will be blended together by the end of the novel, so Molly and Milly will merge as sirens, sex symbols, and all the other paraphernalia associated with the composite female image.

> —Who was the letter from? he asked.
> Bold hand. Marion.
> —O, Boylan, she said. He's bringing the programme.
> —What are you singing?
> —*La ci darem* with J. C. Doyle, she said, and *Love's Old Sweet Song*. (63:27-32)

Cf. "*Là ci darem*"
"Love's Old Sweet Song"

REMARKS: Boylan's letter arranging for an afternoon audience with Molly also arrives in the morning mail, and Bloom, aware that the meeting will end in love-making, questions Molly about the envelope, which she has stuffed under the pillow. These two songs are destined to play major roles in Bloom's mind throughout the day, "*Là ci darem,*" recurring eight times more throughout the novel, and "Love's Old Sweet Song" eleven times. "*Là ci darem la mano*" (Give Me Thy Hand), a duet sung by Giovanni and the not-too-reluctant Zerlina, forms part of the *Don Giovanni* motif in *Ulysses*.

The Don importunes Zerlina to go away with him, "With Joy [his] . . . life to bless." Zerlina's feeble refusals:

> I would and yet I would not,
> I dare not give assent,
> Alas! I know I should not,
> Too late I may repent . . .

are answered by the insistent Giovanni:

> Come then, come then!
> Give me thy hand, oh fairest!
> Whisper a gentle 'yes.'
> With Joy my life thou'lt bless.

This is more than enough persuasion for the susceptible Zerlina. She answers "I come" and they sing the following together:

> With thee, with thee, my treasure,
> This life is naught but pleasure,
> My heart is fondly thine!

The melody, one of the most haunting, light, and lyrical in the whole opera, is one with which Bloom is familiar, as later references will indicate. Though Molly is to sing this duet with J. C. Doyle, it becomes in Bloom's mind symbolic of the liaison of Boylan and Molly. As Giovanni has lured the almost willing Zerlina, so Boylan will succeed with Molly. If Blazes is the amorous Don, and Molly is Zerlina, then Bloom must assume the role of the jealous and avenging Masetto. As Vernon Hall points out,[5] however, Bloom's role in the *Don Giovanni* motif changes from the jealous husband to the Don in his relationship with Martha Clifford.

"Love's Old Sweet Song," the other piece which Molly will sing on Boylan's program, tends to reenforce the image of the Boylan-Molly intimacy and is destined also to recur many times through the rest of the book, each time with the overtones of Molly's promiscuity.

Voglio e non vorrei. Wonder if she pronounces that right: *voglio.* (64:4–5)

Cf. *"Là ci darem"*

REMARKS: Hall notes the significance of Bloom's alteration of Zerlina's original statement in the duet:

Bloom's mind is sometimes able to push unpleasant thoughts away and concentrate on unemotional details. So, here, when he thinks of the first lines Molly-Zerlina sings, his thoughts run, *"Voglio e non vorrei.* Wonder if she pronounces that right: *voglio."* Obviously it is more pleasant to think of pronunciation than of what the words mean. But even here he unconsciously betrays himself; the correct reading is "Vorrei e non vorrei (I should like to, yet I shouldn't)." Zerlina uses the conditional, "vorrei." Alas, there is so little of the conditional in Molly's coming betrayal that Bloom thinks of her as using the plain indicative "voglio (I want to)." [6]

Hello, Illustration. Fierce Italian with carriagewhip. Must be Ruby pride of the on the floor naked. Sheet kindly lent. (64:26–28)

Cf. "Lead Kindly Light"

REMARKS: The last could be a parody of the hymn. The "ee" sounds in "lead" and "sheet" are similar, as are the "l" sounds in "lead" and "lent." Bloom's incongruous association of the hymn and the semipornographic novel is typical of his sense of the ridiculous. He treats his wife's taste for lurid literature patronizingly; but as the parody on the hymn indicates, he senses the banality of cheap novels. The blasphemous connotations of associating the sensual illustration with the hymn indicates also the skeptical eye with which Bloom views organized religion. When heard from nude, outstretched Ruby's point of view, the words to the hymn take on a double meaning:

> Lead, kindly light,
> Amid th' encircling gloom,
> Lead thou me on.
> The Night is dark,
> And I am far from home.

On the other hand, as Bloom's mood changes, the hymn, with its overtones of death, helps provide a serious, quasi-religious vehicle of association which leads Bloom from his lighter, half-satirical humor, to speculations on death and life after death.

There is a young student comes here some evenings named Bannon his cousins or something are big swells he sings Boylan's (I was on the pop of writing Blazes Boylan's) song about those seaside girls. (66:12–15)

Cf. "Seaside Girls"

REMARKS: After Bloom's initial misreading of the statement,[7] this correction serves in Bloom's subconscious only to reenforce his association of the song with Boylan and sex. The seaside-girls song will occur many times again during the day and will become intimately linked to Bloom's images of Boylan's and Bloom's own "Don Giovannism."

No, nothing has happened. Of course it might. Wait in any case till it does. (66:36–38)

Cf. *Don Giovanni*

REMARKS: As Hall points out, Milly's prospective but imminent affair with the young student now forces her into the Donna Anna role in the *Don Giovanni* theme and recasts Bloom as the outraged father, the Commendatore.[8] In the opera the Commendatore intervenes as the Don attempts to force himself on the Commendatore's daughter. The Don kills the older man, whose ghost later leads Giovanni to his retribution. Unlike the Commendatore, however, Bloom will resign himself to "wait in any case till it [Milly's seduction] does [happen]." The *Don Giovanni* motif serves again as a central agent blending Bloom and Boylan, Molly and Milly through their correspondences at various times to the several characters in the opera.

On the *Erin's King* that day round the Kish. Damned old tub pitching about. Not a bit funky. Her pale blue scarf loose in the wind with her hair.

> *All dimpled cheeks and curls,*
> *Your head it simply swirls.*

Seaside girls. Torn envelope. Hands stuck in his trousers' pockets, jarvey off for the day, singing. Friend of the family. Swurls, he says. Pier with lamps, summer evening, band,

> *Those girls, those girls,*
> *Those lovely seaside girls*

Milly too. Young kisses: the first. Far away now past. Mrs Marion. Reading lying back now, counting the strands of her hair, smiling, braiding. (67:2–15)

Cf. "Seaside Girls"

REMARKS: Bloom evidently knows the whole song, but imperfectly. He misquotes slightly the words of the chorus, but refers to both first and third stanzas in this passage. The text of this important song should be quoted in full:

> Down at Margate looking very charming you are sure to meet,
>   Those girls, dear girls, those lovely seaside girls,
> With sticks they steer and promenade the pier to give the boys
>   a treat,
> In pique silks and lace, they tip you quite a playful wink.
> It always is the case you seldom stop to think,
> You fall in love of course upon the spot,
> But not with one girl always with the lot.

Chorus:

    Those girls, those girls, those lovely seaside girls,

    All dimples smiles and curls, your head it simply whirls,

    They look all right, complexions pink and white,

    They've diamond rings and dainty feet,

    Golden hair from Regent Street,

Lace and grace and lots of face those pretty little seaside girls.

There's Maud and Clara, Gwendoline and Sarah where do they
      come from?

    Those girls, dear girls, those lovely seaside girls,

In bloomers smart, they captivate the heart, when cycling down
the prom.

    At wheels and heels and hose, you must not look 'tis under-
    stood,

But ev'ry Johnnie knows, it does your eyesight good,

The boys observe the latest thing in socks,

They learn the time by looking at the *clocks*.

When you go to do a little boating just for fun you take,

    Those girls, dear girls, those lovely seaside girls,

They all say "we so dearly love the sea" their way on board they
    make

    The wind begins to blow each girl remarks "how rough to-
    day."

"It's lovely don't you know," and then they sneak away.

And as the yacht keeps rolling with the tide,

You'll notice hanging o'er the vessel's side.

Chorus:

    Those girls, those girls, those lovely seaside girls,

    All dimples smiles and curls, each head it simply whirls,

    They look a sight, complexions green and white,

    Their hats fly off and at your feet,

    Falls golden hair from Regent Street,

    Rouge and puffs, slip down the cuffs of pretty little seaside
    girls.[9]

Bloom's thoughts about the song are immediately stimulated by Milly's resistance to seasickness, which in stanza three finally subdues the seaside girls.
After a reflection on Boylan and his relation to the song, and a compounding
of the error substituting *swirls* for *whirls,* Bloom returns to the seaside girls
in their more alluring sirenesque pose, promenading the pier in stanza one. In
their role as temptress, women become one: "You fall in love of course on
the spot,/ But not with one girl always the lot." This is the main burden
of the "Seaside Girls" references, which are so liberally distributed through-

out the book. While, as we have seen, the song has become identified with Boylan, the connotations are far broader than merely his affair with temptress-seaside girl Molly: through stanza one she includes all women as temptress figures. The song is the musical embodiment of the union of all girls in the temptress image. In stanza two "ev'ry Johnnie" looks and "knows." The universality of the female attraction, which critics have been wont to accord only to Molly in this novel, is expanded by Bloom to include all temptations by all women. This is the reason he broadens Molly's attractions immediately after the song reference to include Milly, ending the passage with a universal statement about all women and their charms:

> A soft qualm regret, flowed down his backbone, increasing. Will happen, yes. Prevent. Useless: can't move. Girl's sweet light lips. Will happen too. He felt the flowing qualm spread over him. Useless to move now. Lips kissed, kissing kissed. Full gluey woman's lips. (67:16–20)

So Molly and Milly blend into one in this passage, as all women become part and parcel of the same thing, living through each other's lives the unity of common experience.

The union of Molly and Milly is further underscored in Bloom's mind by his inability to do anything about either situation. As Masetto in *Don Giovanni*, Bloom has given up hope of taking action in the case of Molly-Zerlina, and as the Commendatore he is unable to stop Milly's impending seduction. The opera augments the consubstantial motif of the previous reference and implies that some of the physical associations with Molly are transferred in an Electra pattern to Milly, a mother-daughter motif which figures prominently in the *Wake*.

Incidental to musical references, but linked in the general consubstantial pattern, the similarity between this passage and Stephen's description of his mother—womb, tomb—and Jocasta can hardly be accidental. Both Stephen and Bloom are primarily concerned with lips. Stephen thinks: "Mouth to her kiss. No. Must be two of em. Glue 'em well. Mouth to her mouth's kiss. His lips lipped and mouthed fleshless lips of air: mouth to her womb" (48:4–8); and Bloom: "Girl's sweet light lips. . . . Lips kissed, kissing kissed. Full gluey woman's lips." (67:17–20). As Stephen's confused sexuality is indicated in his passage about his mother's lips, so Bloom's sexuality and his confusion of father-lover roles is indicated through his passage about Molly-Milly's lips.[10]

> Perhaps hanging clothes out to dry. The maid was in the garden. (68:6–7)

> Before sitting down he peered through a chink up at the next-door window. The king was in his counting house. Nobody. (68: 34–36)

Cf. "Sing a Song of Sixpence"

REMARKS: The nursery rhyme, invoked by the thoughts of the maid next door, runs through Bloom's mind all during the defecation episode. Bloom's allusions are to the following two stanzas:

> The King was in the counting house,
> Counting out his money,
> The Queen was in the Parlor
> Eating bread and honey.

> The maid was in the garden
> Hanging out the clothes,
> Down came a black bird
> And pecked off her nose.

The pleasure that Bloom derives from the physical functions is underscored by the cheerfulness of the tune. The transformation of Bloom from servile, breakfast-bearing slavery to king is accomplished through one of the simple pleasures of even the poor and graphically spelled out in the song.

Morning after the bazaar dance when May's band played Ponchielli's dance of the hours. Explain that morning hours, noon, then evening coming on, then night hours. Washing her teeth. That was the first night. Her head dancing. Her fansticks clicking. Is that Boylan well off? He has money. Why? I noticed he had a good smell off his breath dancing. No use humming then. Allude to it. Strange kind of music that last night. The mirror was in shadow. She rubbed her handglass briskly on her woollen vest against her full wagging bub. Peering into it. Lines in her eyes. It wouldn't pan out somehow.

Evening hours, girls in grey gauze. Night hours then black with daggers and eyemasks. Poetical idea pink, then golden, then grey, then black. Still true to life also. Day, then the night. (69:27–41)

Cf. "Dance of the Hours"

REMARKS: The pleasant aspects of Bloom's defecation are incongruously and playfully underscored throughout the scene as the light music of "Sing a Song" gives way to Ponchielli's "Dance of the Hours." The tripping melody of "Sing a Song" modulates in Bloom's thought to the similar tripping melody of Ponchielli. The dance with its minuetlike quality brings Molly, Boylan, and the bazaar dance at which the lovers met into Bloom's consciousness. The music underlies Bloom's thoughts throughout the entire passage. Moreover, the passage of the hours in the dance symbolizes "the eternal struggle between the powers of darkness and light." [11] The point is that the struggle between Bloom and Boylan over Molly takes on here cosmic, *Finnegans Wake*-like overtones.

In the passage we get the first hint that Bloom-Ulysses will not be conquered by the suitors and that his patience as well as his equanimity will win in the end. As the hours of the dance advance from night and dawn to the next night, only Bloom understands and is willing to accept the passage of time and the cyclical nature of things, including Molly's passions.

But in the passage Bloom is thinking of the actual music in terms of background as well as the theme of his relations with Molly. And the music is gay, airy, and light, hardly that of a downtrodden, conquered cuckold.

> *Heigho! Heigho!*
> *Heigho! Heigho!*
> *Heigho! Heigho!*

Quarter to. There again: the overtone following through the air, third.

Poor Dignam! (70:11–16)

Cf. Tone pattern of Westminster Chimes

REMARKS: As the bells of St. George's Church toll a quarter of the hour, we have the information before Bloom does. It takes Bloom longer to hear the chimes than it does the reader to read them because large chimes following the Westminster tonal pattern allow several seconds for the overtones of each musical phrase to die out before the next phrase begins. Each phrase is equal to a quarter of an hour, with the low pitched gongs tolling the hour at the end of four tonal patterns. Hence Bloom's interpretation of their literal significance. The passage of Ponchielli's hours from morning through dark now leads to dusky death in Bloom's associative pattern as the thematic meaning of the chimes merges with John Donne's admonishment, "Do not ask for whom the bell tolls," and Bloom answers, "Poor Dignam."

5. Lotus Eaters

Paradise and the peri. (74:30)

Cf. *Lalla Rookh*

REMARKS: "Paradise and the Peri" is the title of section two of Moore's cantata. "The peri, in Persian mythology, are creatures descended from the fallen angels and excluded from paradise until their penance is done." [1] M'Coy, to whom Bloom is talking, provides an ongoing penance for him, while Bloom is once again denied the paradise of a woman's exposed leg, prompting Bloom's association of the Moore lines.

Mrs Marion Bloom. Not up yet. Queen was in her bedroom eating bread and. No book. Blackened court cards laid along her thigh by sevens. Dark lady and fair man. Cat furry black ball. Torn strip of envelope. (75:14–17)

Cf. "Sing a Song of Sixpence"

REMARKS: Just as Bloom was king in his outhouse-counting house, Molly, in her bed-parlor, is still the queen of stanza two of Bloom's royal "Sing a Song of Sixpence" family. As queen, Molly must have a *court,* and the word in the above passage takes on a double meaning. First Molly has laid out the cards in sevens for a game of solitaire. These constitute a *court.* Next it is Boylan who is responsible for organizing the trip which M'Coy has asked about, and Boylan's envelope, arranging an appointment, ostensibly to discuss the program, contains a *court* card or a card paying *court* to the all-too-receptive queen. The song provides the stream-of-consciousness link to the next, centrally thematic reference.

> *Love's*
> *Old*
> *Sweet*
> *Song*
> *Comes lo-ve's old . . .*

—It's a kind of tour, don't you see? Mr Bloom said thoughtfully *Sweet song.* There's a committee formed. Part shares and part profits. (75:18–25)

Cf. "Love's Old Sweet Song"

REMARKS: The word *court* and Boylan's torn envelope open for Bloom a whole association of significance in "Love's Old Sweet Song." The song becomes the theme of the impending assignation:

> Once in the dear dead days beyond recall,
> When on the world the mist began to fall,
> Out of the dreams that rose in happy throng
> Low in our hearts love sang an old sweet song;
> And in the dusk where fell the firelight gleam,
> Softly it wove itself into our dream.
>
> Just a song at twilight, when the lights are low,
> And the flick'ring shadows softly come and go,
> Tho' the heart be weary, sad the day and long,
> Still to us at twilight comes
> Love's old song, comes Love's old, sweet song.

That Bloom is mentally singing the song rather than merely thinking of the words is apparent in the line "comes lo-ve's old . . ." which is a part of the last line of the refrain. In the song the last "love's" though a one syllable word, is sung on two notes; hence Joyce indicates the musical interval with a hyphen. The "dear dead days" and perennially falling mists and rising dreams provide the song and the affair between Molly and Boylan with an archetypal aura. Love's old sweet song has been sung before by Molly, as the all-encompassing female principle, from Gibraltar to Eccles Street, and Bloom in this wider sense is perfectly correct in thinking, "As easy stop the sea." (273:4)

Bloom might very well be describing to M'Coy his marriage as he discusses the financial arrangements of the concert tour. He links sharing the wealth with the Boylan affair by interspersing the theme of the illicit liaison with the leitmotif of "Love's Old Sweet Song."

He drew the letter from his pocket and folded it into the newspaper he carried. Might just walk into her here. The lane is safer.

He passed the cabman's shelter. Curious the life of drifting cabbies, all weathers, all places, time or setdown, no will of their own. *Voglio e non.* Like to give them an odd cigarette. Sociable. Shout a few flying syllables as they pass. He hummed:

> *La ci darem la mano*
> *La la lala la la* (77:10–18)

Cf. "*Là ci darem*"

REMARKS: The thought that the cabmen are at the command of anyone with a fare and have no will of their own suggests to Bloom the line from "*Là ci darem*," "*Voglio e non*" (I want to, yet not). The line from the song then combines with Martha's letter to suggest to Bloom a new role for himself in the *Don Giovanni* motif. This time the "*Voglio e non*" is sung in Bloom's thoughts by Martha-Zerlina, and Bloom is the dashing, lady-killing Don pleading rakishly for his love as he begins the duet. The tense is still altered in the line from the song [2] indicating that when Bloom is in this jaunty mood Martha seems just as willing for him as Molly is for Blazes. Once again the song links Bloom and Blazes as consubstantial in the structure of the novel, as their leitmotifs blend to suit their ever-changing roles.

Flat Dublin voices bawled in his head. Those two sluts that night in the Coombe, linked together in the rain.

> *O, Mary lost the pin of her drawers.*
> *She didn't know what to do*
> *To keep it up*
> *To keep it up.*

It? Them. Such a bad headache. Has her roses probably. Or sitting all day typing. Eyefocus bad for stomach nerves. What perfume does your wife use? Now could you make out a thing like that?

To keep it up.

Martha, Mary. I saw that picture somewhere I forget now old master or faked for money. He is sitting in their house, talking. Mysterious. Also the two sluts in the Coombe would listen.

To keep it up. (78:36–79:10)

Cf. "O Mary Lost the Pin of Her Drawers"

REMARKS: The "It? Them" after the song is an indication of Bloom's literal mind as he worries about the pronoun-antecedent agreement in the song. The agreement error is part of the associative pattern between the song and Martha's letter, in which there is a subject-verb agreement error ("patience are" [78:8]). He seems to overlook the bawdy ambiguity in the ballad of *it* possibly referring to the sex act or male organ. References to this song will occur five more times in the book, serving in Bloom's mind throughout the day as an antithesis to purity, wholesomeness, and pomp. In Bloom's mood it adds an undercurrent of roguish impropriety to his love affair with Martha.

Martha's romantic question about Molly's perfume strikes the practical-minded Bloom as being incongruous, since the adulterous nature of the whole business is all too apparent to him. The association of the song and the sluts in the Coombe affirms this. The naivete of Martha and her concern with what to Bloom seems unimportant reminds him of a picture of Christ talking to Mary and Martha, the sisters of Lazarus. The story involving the sisters is related in *Luke* 10:38–42. It seems to Bloom that Martha Clifford, like the biblical Martha, has placed her values on trivia rather than on the essentials, i.e., the physical aspects of their liaison. In *John* 11:2 Martha's sister is identified with the Mary who dried Jesus' feet with her hair and consequently Mary Magdalene, a reformed prostitute. If Mary would listen to Jesus' word, so too, Bloom thinks, would the sluts in Coombe. This chain of thought brings Bloom back full cycle to the last line of their bawdy song: *"To keep it up."*

The priest bent down to put it into her mouth, murmuring all the time. Latin. The next one. Shut your eyes and open your mouth. (80:32–34)

Cf. "Open your mouth . . ."

REMARKS: Bloom speculates on the Latin and irreverently likens the priest's words to the traditional nursery rhyme of patient mothers spoonfeeding their hesitant children at meal time:

> Open your mouth
> And close your eyes

> And I'll give you something
> To make you wise.

To Bloom, whose disposition is predominantly secular, the ecclesiastical business of communion and the mass has little more significance than Mother Goose.

Look at them. Now I bet it makes them feel happy. Lollipop. It does. Yes, bread of angels it's called. There's a big idea behind it, kind of kingdom of God is within you feel. First communicants. Hokypoky penny a lump. (81:4–8)

Cf. "Hokey Pokey"

REMARKS: The quotation has more connotations than the mere nursery rhyme suggests. "Hokey Pokey" is a nursery rhyme with a great many variations, the most popular of which follows:

> Hokey, pokey, whisky thum,
> How d'you like potatoes done?
> Boiled in whisky, boiled in rum,
> Says the King of the Cannibal Islands.

The expectant communicants kneeling at the rail in anticipation of the host are to Bloom very like children waiting for their potatoes. The rhyme suggests also a happy family atmosphere of togetherness, which Bloom so longs for but can't find at home or in the church.

The *Oxford Dictionary of Nursery Rhymes* tells us of "Hokey Pokey":

. . . the lines are evidently a somewhat rationalized memory of the chorus of a popular comic song "The King of the Cannibal Islands" written about 1830 by A. W. Humphreys and "Sung by him with great applause at the London Concerts." [3]

Versions of this song were published also in 1845, 1888, 1889, and 1917, so that Joyce may well have heard it. The verse follows:

> Oh, have you heard the news of late,
> About a mighty King so great?
> If you have not, 'tis in my pate—
> The King of the Cannibal Islands.
> He was so tall—near six feet six,
> He had a head like Mister Nick's,
> His palace was like Dirty Dick's,
> 'Twas built of mud for want of bricks,
> And his name was Poonoo wingkewang,
> Flibeedee-flobeedee-buskeebang;
> And a lot of the Indians swore they'd hang,
> The King of the Cannibal Islands.

It is impossible to know if Bloom had the nursery rhyme or the song "The King of the Cannibal Islands" in mind. He has, however, already referred to the cannibalism of the communion idea: "eating bits of a corpse why the cannibals cotton to it" (80:37–38). If he is thinking of the Cannibal Islands song, the cannibal connotations in the transubstantiated communion wafer and the associations between the King and Christ in the verse of the song would provide Bloom with an even more blasphemous set of incongruities.

> Blind faith. Safe in the arms of kingdom come. Lulls all pain. Wake this time next year. (81:14–15)

Cf. "Safe in the Arms of Jesus"

REMARKS: The words of the Protestant hymn seem appropriate to the sleeping parishioner who prompts Bloom's thought:

> Safe in the arms of Jesus,
> Safe on his gentle breast,
> There by his love o'er shaded
> Sweetly my soul shall rest.

Bloom uses the reference with a touch of envy for the old man's peace, and with irony as an extension of the childlike quality of the believers that he has already satirized in the preceding nursery rhymes.

> Suppose he lost the pin of his. He wouldn't know what to do to. (81:18–19)

Cf. "O Mary Lost the Pin of Her Drawers"

REMARKS: The reference is another instance of Bloom's using the bawdy ballad to provide a base foil to debunk what he considers a sham. Subconsciously, by associating the priest and the dirty song. Bloom seeks to degrade the former.

> Molly was in fine voice that day, the *Stabat Mater* of Rossini. Father Bernard Vaughan's sermon first. Christ or Pilate? Christ, but don't keep us all night over it. Music they wanted. Footdrill stopped. Could hear a pin drop. I told her to pitch her voice against that corner. I could feel the thrill in the air, the full, the people looking up:
> *Quis est homo!* (82:8–15)

Cf. "*Quis est homo?*"

REMARKS: Although Hodgart and Worthington attribute *"Quis est homo"* to Mercadante, the work Bloom refers to is in fact a duet for two sopranos in the *Stabat Mater*. When Bloom says, "Footdrill stopped. Could hear a pin drop," he is probably referring to the pause which follows the series of sixteenth and thirty-second notes in the introduction to the first soprano part, which Molly must have been singing. There is a series of chromatic progressions (Bloom's "footdrill"), a dominant chord, a pause, and the opening measure of Molly's solo. Bloom's memory in this case is extremely accurate:

Rossini's music sets off a brief association of other religious music in Bloom's mind, but in the subsequent allusions, his taste and knowledge are not as acute as in his memory of Molly's duet.

Some of that old sacred music is splendid. Mercadante: seven last words. (82:16–17)

Cf. *Seven Last Words of Christ*

REMARKS: Mercadante's *Seven Last Words,* a Lenten oratorio, held some attraction for the uninitiated and evidently much for Bloom. It does not compare in excellence with Rossini and is seldom performed now by choirs which can afford to rent anything else.

Mozart's twelfth mass: the *Gloria* in that. (82:17)

Cf. *Twelfth Mass* of Mozart

REMARKS: Bloom probably was betrayed into inaccuracy in this citation. Worthington and Hodgart point out that there was and still is an immensely popular spurious work put out by the Novello Publishing Company which is called the "Twelfth Mass of Mozart" and is frequently known as "The Gloria." The Novello publication is not from Mozart's "Twelfth Mass" at all. Worthington and Hodgart tells us the following:

> Koechel puts it [the spurious work] in an appendix and designates it K. Anh. 232. The true Twelfth Mass is K. 262.[4]

However, Bloom cannot be condemned for his taste, because his error would probably have been the rule rather than the exception in 1904.

> College sports today I see. He eyed the horseshoe poster over the gate of college park: cyclist doubled up like a cod in a pot. Damn bad ad. (86: 17–20)

Cf. "Johnny I Hardly Knew Ye"

REMARKS: The penultimate lines of stanzas four and five of the ballad, "Like a cod, you're doubled up head and tail," and "You'd have to be put in a bowl to beg," combine to produce Bloom's phrase.

That the cyclist is likened to the cod in a pot carries with it for Bloom the implications not only of the cyclist's ridiculous posture, but of the song also. In the ballad, Johnny, who has gone off to war, returns broken and disfigured to his waiting wife and family. The not overly tactful wife in stanzas four and five outlines for the returning Johnny her tribulations and his infirmities:

> It grieved my heart to see you sail,
>   Hurroo! Hurroo!
> It grieved my heart to see you sail,
>   Hurroo! Hurroo!
> It grieved my heart to see you sail,
> Tho' from my heart you took leg bail
> Like a cod, you're doubled up head and tail.
> Och! Johnny, I hardly knew ye!
>
> You haven't an arm and you haven't a leg,
>   Hurroo! Hurroo!
> You haven't an arm and you haven't a leg,
>   Hurroo! Hurroo!
> You haven't an arm and you haven't a leg.
> You're an eyeless, boneless, chickenless egg,
> You'd have to be put in a bowl to beg.
> Och! Johnny, I hardly knew ye!

The position of the cyclist evokes in Bloom visions of the cripple in the song. To one who sells and designs ads, as Bloom does, a poster which produces this kind of image to advertise a sporting event is a "damn bad ad." The song precedes and foreshadows Bloom's vision of himself stretched out at full length in the baths, not as "an eyeless, boneless, chickenless egg," but as the source of all fertilization, as the "pale Galilean" and the "father of thousands," returning to the womb not as the fetus bicycler but as the great seed bearer and the father of his race.

And the skulls we were acracking when M'Carthy took the floor . . . (86:30–31)

Cf. "When McCarthy Took the Flure at Inniscorthy"

REMARKS: The song, prompted by thoughts of cricket matches, Captain Buller's breaking a window, and the drunken ruffians at the Donneybrook fair, extols a brawler named McCarthy: "When they gurgled all the whiskey, faith, a desperate row arose./McCarthy sure he levelled them, he fought them to a close. . ." The brawlers Bloom envisions are signified in his mind by the terrible McCarthy:

> And the sticks they went whacking
> And the skulls, faith they were cracking,
> When McCarthy took the flure in Enniscorthy.[5]

6. Hades

Slop about in slipperslappers for fear he'd wake. (87:18–19)

Cf. "Old Mother Slipperslapper" or "The Fox"

REMARKS: The slipperslappers may be a reference to the song in which the fox steals a goose and rouses an old lady out of bed. The reference is to stanza four:

> Then old mother slipperslapper jumped out of bed
> And out of the window popped her head,
> Crying, "John, John, John the grey goose is gone
> And the fox is away to his den-oh."

In the passage under consideration mother slipperslapper is a surrogate for Ireland as well as all of womankind and the women who prepare the bodies for burial in Ireland. The woman peering from behind her blind triggers the association. Bella Cohen is later linked to old mother slipperslapper by Zoe, but the lady in the song seems here to have been merely used as a cliché for an aroused and wary old woman.

They waited still, their knees jogging, till they had turned and were passing along the tramtracks. Tritonville road. Quicker. The wheels rattled rolling over the cobbled causeway and the crazy glasses shook rattling in the doorframes. (87:34–37)

Cf. "The Pauper's Drive"

REMARKS: Joyce describes the scene in terms which sound roughly analogous to the chorus of this popular dirge, usually arranged for a male group. The song, which provides the background music for much of the chapter, is worth quoting in full:

> There's a grim one-horse hearse in a jolly round trot;
> To the churchyard a pauper is going, I wot:
> The road it is rough, and the hearse has no springs,
> And hark to the dirge which the sad driver sings:
> "Rattle his bones over the stones:
> He's only a pauper whom nobody owns!"
>
> Oh, where are the mourners? alas! there are none:
> He has left not a gap in the world, now he's gone;
> Not a tear in the eye of child, woman, or man,
> To the grave with his carcass as fast as you can.
> "Rattle his bones over the stones:
> He's only a pauper whom nobody owns!" . . .
>
> What a jolting, and creaking, and plashing, and din;
> The whip how it cracks! and the wheels how they spin!
> How the dirt, right and left, o'er the hedges is hurled!
> The pauper at length makes a noise in the world!
> "Rattle his bones over the stones:
> He's only a pauper whom nobody owns!"
>
> Poor pauper defunct! he has made some approach
> To gentility, now that he's stretched in a coach!
> He's taking a drive in his carriage at last,
> But it will not be long, if he goes on so fast.
> "Rattle his bones over the stones;
> He's only a pauper whom nobody owns."
>
> But a truce to this strain; for my soul it is sad
> To think that a heart, in humanity clad,
> Should make, like the brute, such a desolate end,
> And depart from the light, without leaving a friend!
> "Bear soft his bones over the stones;
> Though a pauper, he's one whom his Maker yet owns!"
>
> You bumpkins! who stare at your brother conveyed—
> Behold what respect to a cloddy is paid!
> And be joyful to think, when by death you're laid low,
> You've a chance to the grave like a gemman to go!
> "Rattle his bones over the stones;
> He's only a pauper whom nobody owns!"

During the chapter the song with its desolate unison chorus chant reappears in Bloom's mind as the embodiment of the harsh truth of Dignam's death, which is antithetical to the euphemisms and conventional platitudes of the mourners.

Wait till you hear him, Simon, on Ben Dollard's singing of *The Croppy Boy.*

—Immense, Martin Cunningham said pompously. *His singing of that simple ballad, Martin, is the most trenchant rendering I ever heard in the whole course of my experience.* (90:41–91:5)

Cf. "The Croppy Boy"

REMARKS: Kernan, having been relatively unaffected by his spiritual, allegorical journey in "Grace," presumably is qualified to pass on the celestial voice of Dollard singing this song of priestly or fatherly betrayal. As we will see later in Hades, Kernan still holds his Protestant biases. These remarks serve to foreshadow the rendering of this key ballad in the Sirens section.[1]

Could I go to see *Leah* tonight, I wonder. I said I. Or the *Lily of Killarney?* Elster Grimes Opera company. Big powerful change. Wet bright bills for next week. *Fun on the Bristol.* Martin Cunningham could work a pass for the Gaiety. Have to stand a drink or two. As broad as it's long.

He's coming in the afternoon. Her songs. (92:5–11)

Cf. *Lily of Killarney*
　　Fun on the Bristol

REMARKS: *Leah* is a play starring Mrs. Bandman Palmer and the *Lily of Killarney* an opera which involves the ruin of the innocent "Colleen Bawn" by a Don Giovanni-Leporello combination with whom, in turn, Bloom associates Blazes Boylan. The operatic association combines with the title of the forthcoming musical *Fun on the Bristol* to produce the subsequent Boylan reference ("He's coming in the afternoon. Her songs") as Bloom thinks of Boylan's prospective fun on the jingling bedstead. In addition, J. P. Smith points out that there is a marriage reconciliation in the opera which parallels the action of *Ulysses.*[2] Hardress Cregan is secretly married to Eily, the Colleen Bawn, but forced to court Ann, a local heiress. The husband and wife are reunited at the end, though each has had a rival for the spouse's affections. This is the first of seven references to the opera in *Ulysses.* The happy conclusion of the opera tends, then, to give added weight to the argument that the novel ends in a successful reconciliation between Leopold and Molly.

Tweedy, crown solicitor for Waterford. Has that silk hat ever
since. Relics of old decency. Mourning too. Terrible comedown,
poor wretch! Kicked about like snuff at a wake. (93:19–22)

Cf. "The Hat Me Father Wore"

REMARKS: The song Bloom alludes to here is about an Irish expatriate who
wears his father's silk hat on St. Patrick's Day and not about a down-and-
outer; however, the association of the proud, ancient silk hats links the old
man's plight with the nostalgia of the chorus:

> It's old, but it's beautiful, the best was ever seen,
> 'Twas worn for more than ninety years in that little isle so green.
> From my father's great ancestors it descended, galore;
> It's a relic of old decency, the hat me father wore!

Bloom's reference, "Relics of old decency," a part of the last line of the
chorus, embodies the spirit of the song. The allusion introduces a rationale
for the hat theme, a major motif in Joyce's works since "Grace," where the
tumbled hat of Kernan in the beginning is replaced by the decorous hats of
the entire congregation at the Gardiner Street Church at the end. The hat
motif continues to operate through *Ulysses* as a surrogate for how people re-
gard themselves, beginning with Stephen's Hamlet hat in the Proteus episode. Later in Hades we will see Bloom, that thorn in the side of the decorous
and pompously proper, act as a sort of conscience of his race when he calls
John Henry Menton's attention to the dent in his hat. Finally it is Bloom who
restores dignity and respect to Parnell by returning his hat during the time of
Parnell's public trials and accusations. Bloom himself contrasts Parnell's dignity on that occasion with Menton's lack of it in Glasnevin. The point here
is that in the hat sequence Bloom takes on the role of the creator of the
uncreated conscience of his race. Stephen in his Hamlet hat has much to
learn about his own mission from Bloom-Hamlet Senior. The song, then,
spells out the meaning of the hat sequence and thematically provides the
background of dignity and Irish history and tradition which become symbolized in that sequence.

. . . humming: *voglio e non vorrei*. No: *vorrei e non*. Looking at
the tips of her hairs to see if they are split. *Mi trema un poco il*.
Beautiful on that *tre* her voice is: weeping tone. A thrust, A
throstle. There is a word throstle that expressed that. (93:25–29)

Cf. "*Là ci darem*"

REMARKS: Hall discusses Bloom's placing *vorrei* correctly in the conditional
tense here and his attitude at the moment:

> Bloom has found the right word, at last. It is *vorrei* not *voglio,* but he still
> finds a substitute for thinking about Blazes and Molly by thinking of the

tone of Molly's voice—a substitute as good as thinking of pronunciation if he wants to avoid thinking about what the words signify.[3]

Rattle his bones. Over the stones. Only a pauper. Nobody owns. 96:12–13)

Cf. "The Pauper's Drive"

REMARKS: These unison lines from the chorus are meant to sound like a crier's lament as the carriage winds its way through the streets, much like the cries of the dead-cart carriers during the London plagues. This time the song is not meant for Dignam but the dead child whose hearse comes galloping by. For Bloom, who sees no hope of a second life and little ultimate reward in the first, the song has the effect of reducing the dead to the common denominator of hopelessness.

Lord, she must have looked a sight that night, Dedalus told me he was in there. Drunk about the place and capering with Martin's umbrella:

> —And they call me the jewel of Asia.
> Of Asia,
> The geisha.

He looked away from me. (96:37–97:1)

Cf. "The Jewel of Asia"

REMARKS: Mrs. Cunningham's song relates a typical *Madame Butterfly* story:

> A small Japanese
> Once sat at her ease
> In a garden cool and shady,
> When a foreigner gay
> Who was passing that way
> Said, "May I come in, young lady?"
> So she open'd her gate,
> And I blush to relate
> That he taught Japan's fair daughter
> To flirt and to kiss
> Like the little white Miss
> Who lives o'er the western water!
> He call'd her the jewel of Asia, of Asia, of Asia,
> But she was the Queen of the Geisha, the Geisha, the Geisha;
> So she laugh'd, "Though you're ready today, sir,
> To flirt when I flutter my fan,
> Tomorrow you'll go on your way, sir,
> Forgetting the girl of Japan!"

But when he came back (Alas! and alack!)
To that garden cool and shady,
The foreigner bold
Was decidedly cold,
And talk'd of an English lady.
With his heart in a whirl
For the little white girl,
He declared how much he miss'd her,
And forgot, if you please,
His poor Japanese
For he never even kiss'd her!
But she was the jewel of Asia, of Asia, of Asia,
The beautiful Queen of the Geisha, the Geisha, the Geisha,
And she laugh'd "It is just as they say, sir—
You love for as long as you can!
A month, or a week, or a day, sir,
Will do for a girl of Japan!"

Mrs. Cunningham switches the lyrics from the third to the first person, revealing her need for affection, but also reviving in Bloom's mind the love and faithlessness motif which he is trying so desperately to forget. The song in a way parodies the relationship between Bloom and Molly. While the "foreigner gay" description fits Leopold, Molly by the time of the episode on Howth was not entirely inexperienced in affairs of the heart or flesh. Further, while Molly's heart may indeed have remained constant, Bloom's never strayed too far in the direction of Martha, Josie, or any other "little white girl," and the Blooms' relationship is as permanent as the relationship in the song is ephemeral. While there may be Geisha-like overtones in Molly's services to Boylan and the others, it is comical to picture her as sweetly acquiescent, servile, or resigned to her fate. Since Mrs. Cunningham sings the song, it has some bearing on the unsatisfactory relationships of the Cunninghams and therefore on Bloom through the identification of both Bloom and Cunningham with Shakespeare, all of whose wives were a considerable source of anguish to their spouses. The point of Mrs. Cunningham's singing the song is that she is as deluded as Molly is about her blameless, devoted role in life. Where fantasy stops and reality begins seems difficult to ascertain for either of the women. So the song provides a number of variations on the marital relationship of the Blooms and introduces additional nuances in the faithlessness pattern.

He knows [about my father's death]. Rattle his bones. (97:1)
No more pain. Wake no more. Nobody owns.
The carriage rattled swiftly along Blessington street. Over the stones. (97:9-11)

Cf. "The Pauper's Drive"

REMARKS: The first quotation involves Cunningham's knowledge of the suicide of Bloom's father. The reference to the song this time is for the father, and Cunningham, in his role as Shakespeare-creator, provides a sort of omniscience about the father-son motif. The line acts as an invocation to the whole association of thoughts surrounding the father's death. This passage ends with two phrases from Virag's last letter to his son and a phrase from the song, which constitutes a musical benediction for Bloom's father.

The last passage quoted above, which pulls together the combination of the narrator's line describing the progress of the carriage and the phrase from the "Pauper's Drive" in Bloom's stream of consciousness, serves to complete the circle. As Joyce reenforces each aspect of Bloom's day with variations on a central theme in each chapter, so Bloom relates various aspects of what he sees. The dead which comprise the Hades chapter are given in Bloom's mind a kind of unity through background orchestration. As Dignam's carriages begin their journey to the cemetery, we hear from the narrator the first echoes of "The Pauper's Drive." The song occurs again, this time in Bloom's stream of consciousness, when the child's body is carried past. Again the song recurs to Bloom in connection with his father, and then comes back full cycle to Dignam's hearse in the chorus reference, "Over the stones," on page 97.

In the last several pages, the story of Reuben J. Dodd's son's attempt at suicide has been related, then the child's casket rolls by, and the child's death reminds Bloom of Rudy. Immediately after, Shakespeare is alluded to, then Bloom's father's suicide. Clearly the father-son theme is linked here with life and death. All the themes come under the umbrella of "The Pauper's Drive." The death of the innocent child in the beginning of life, the suicide of Virag with its concomitant shame, and the death of Dignam are all equalized in Bloom's mind by the great leveler, symbolized by the recurring, plaintive, unromantic, matter-of-fact strains of the dirge: "Rattle his bones over the stones/He's only a pauper whom nobody owns."

As they turned into Berkeley street a streetorgan near the Basin sent over and after them a rollicking rattling song of the halls. Has anybody here seen Kelly? Kay ee double ell wy. Dead march from *Saul*. He's as bad as old antonio. He left me on my ownio. Pirouette! The *Mater Misericordiae*. Eccles street. My house down there. Big place. Ward for incurables there. Very encouraging. Our Lady's Hospice for the dying. Deadhouse handy underneath. Where old Mrs Riordan died. They look terrible the women. Her feeding cup and rubbing her mouth with the spoon. Then the screen round her bed for her to die. Nice young student that was dressed that bite the bee gave me. He's gone over to the lying-in hospital they told me. From one extreme to the other. (97:18–30)

Cf. "Has Anybody Here Seen Kelly?" or "Oh, Oh, Antonio"
    "Dead March from *Saul*"

REMARKS: As Bloom hears the melody of "Has Anybody Here Seen Kelly?"
he supplies the lyrics to the song himself. He interrupts the chorus, however,
to refer to the "Dead March" from *Saul,* which is a slow, stately procession,
quite the antithesis of the rollicking music-hall song of the streetorgan.
Bloom's remark is an attempt to demonstrate with a musical allusion the
irony of the lively "Has Anybody Here Seen Kelly?" accompanying a funeral.
He further emphasizes the irony by mentally providing a lighthearted, twirling pirouette as choreography for the streetorgan song.

Underlying the passage and the music is the theme of the continual cycle
of life. Even in a funeral procession life goes on. The incongruity of the
quick of "Kelly" and the dead of *Saul* is linked in Bloom's mind with the
death of Mrs. Riordan in the Mater Misericordiae Hospital and the medical
student who worked there and is now delivering babies at the lying-in hospital. Joyce's view that all men live consubstantial lives is broadened to include
the dead as well as the living.[4]

For Liverpool probably. Roast beef for old England. They buy up all the juicy ones. (97:41–98:1)

Cf. "The Roast Beef of Old England"

REMARKS: The allusion to roast beef for old England could have a double
significance if Bloom were aware of its origins in the song. Written in the
early part of the eighteenth century, the lyrics complain about the spineless-
ness of what then was contemporary England. Following are stanzas 1, 2,
4, and 6 of the song:

> When mighty roast beef was the Englishman's food,
> It ennobled our hearts, and enriched our blood,
> Our soldiers were brave and our courtiers were good.
>   Oh, the roast beef of Old England!
>   And oh, for old England's roast beef!

> But since we have learn'd from effeminate France
> To eat their ragouts as well as to dance,
> We are fed up with nothing but vain complaisance:
>   Oh, the roast beef, etc.

> When good Queen Elizabeth sat on the throne,
> Ere coffee and tea, and such slip-slops were known,
> The world was in terror if e'en she did frown:
>   Oh, the roast beef, etc.

> Oh, then we had stomachs to eat and to fight,
> And when wrongs were cooking, to set ourselves right;

But now we're a—h'm—I could, but good night:
        Oh, the roast beef, etc.

Bloom might well use the song reference ironically. It was a popular bone of contention that Ireland was being drained of its cattle and natural resources, so that the use of Irish beef to ennoble the hearts and enrich the blood of Englishmen, as the song declares, constitutes an obvious irony to any Irishman, especially since the song indicates (stanza 4) that there is a correlation between the oppressive, imperialistic tendencies of the English and the beef they eat.

Aboard of the *Bugabu*. (99:11)

Cf. "Aboard of the Bugaboo"

REMARKS: The song is about a ludicrous turf-laden ship to which the captain sets fire as he smokes in his bed. In a series of misadventures, the helmsman fails to put out the fire when the captain calls, because he is asleep at the wheel. The turf catches fire 15,000 miles from land, and ". . . a thousand sods of turf and fifty thousand men smothered in the Bugaboo." The line which Bloom remembers is from the last line of the first stanza, ". . . on board of the Bugaboo." The voyage of the barge "from the midland bogs" seems to have little in common with the voyage of the Bugaboo except the similarity of their cargoes.

—Though lost to sight, Mr Dedalus said, to memory dear. (99:31)

Cf. "Though Lost to Sight to Memory Dear"

REMARKS: The song begins:

        Though lost to sight, to memory dear
        Thou ever will remain;
        One only hope my heart can cheer,—
        The hope to meet again.

Thornton tells us the song title was a cliché often carved on tombstones, mortuary cards, etc., so it is impossible to know whether the song was the impetus for the popularity of the phrase or the other way around.[5] At any rate, it is another example of one of the chief characteristics of Simon Dedalus, his thinking in and use of hackneyed clichés as vehicles of thought and speech.

—A great blow to the poor wife, Mr Kernan added.
—Indeed yes, Mr Bloom agreed.
Has the laugh at him now.

He looked down at the boots he had blacked and polished.
She had outlived him, lost her husband. More dead for her than
for me. One must outlive the other. Wise men say. There are more
women than men in the world. Condole with her. Your terrible
loss. I hope you'll soon follow him. (102:4–11)

Cf. "Three Women to Every Man"

REMARKS: It is apparent that Bloom, for the moment at least, is not in the
most sympathetic state of mind toward Mrs. Dignam's bereavement. The note
of levity in his thought is reenforced by the context of the song, from which
come the words, "Wise men say. There are more women than men in the
world." The alternate title of the song is "Why Can't Every Man Have
Three Wives?" The last words of the verse and the chorus are:

> Soon as a maiden gets married, you know,
> She wants at once to be "boss" of the show;
> I think tho' perhaps my opinion is small,
> She ought to feel lucky she's married at all.

> Chorus:
> Wise men say there are more women than men in the world
> That's how some girls are single all their lives.

That Bloom is thinking of the music as well as the words is indicated by the
period Joyce puts in after the word *say*. This is a facsimile reproduction of
the four beat pause on that word in the music:

There is more than merely the male-chauvinist image of Bloom in the passage.
The song reference is surrounded by the traditional burial clichés of Kernan
and the rest. Bloom is at least honest with himself and not really without
compassion. Still if there are more women than men in the world, why is it
that Molly needs to take so many lovers, and why can't he at least have his
quota? More immediately to the point the song represents Bloom's natural
aversion to affectation and the shows that accompany such traditional events
as funerals. It is merely one of a series of allusions reflecting his stream-of-
conscious irreverence on predominantly solemn occasions.

How are all in Cork's own town? (102:23)

Cf. "Cork's Own Town"

REMARKS: Though the title phrase of the song is not to be found in the
lyrics, the title itself was popular enough to be a cliché and hence appropriate

for use by Simon Dedalus, whose propensity to think and talk in clichés has already been established.[6]

A server, bearing a brass bucket with something in it, came out through a door. The whitesmocked priest came after him tidying his stole with one hand, balancing with the other a little book against his toad's belly. Who'll read the book? I, said the rook. (103:20–24)

Cf. "Who Killed Cock Robin?"

REMARKS: The last two sentences of the passage, both in Bloom's stream of consciousness, are from the fifth stanza of the song, which deals with Cock Robin's death and funeral. The Sparrow, Fly, Bull, Owl, Rook, and Dove all have functions to perform in the death and burial of Cock Robin. In the fifth verse, the Rook volunteers to perform the job of the priest at Dignam's funeral:

> Who'll be the parson?
> I, said the Rook,
> With my bell and book,
> I'll be the parson.

The immediate association between the song and the scene is triggered by the priest's book. Further, the priest's toadlike appearance suggests an animal burial. The analogy between Cock Robin's funeral festivities and Dignam's is just the sort Bloom would draw. The effect again is to emphasize Bloom's irreverence at the proceedings. His mood is so uncongenial to the solemn surroundings that he is on the point of bursting into song: "The ree the ra the ree the ra the roo. Lord, I mustn't lilt here." (104:39–40)

That's the first sign when the hairs come out grey and temper getting cross. Silver threads among the grey. Fancy being his wife. Wonder how he had the gumption to propose to any girl. Come out and live in the graveyard. Dangle that before her. (107:40–108:2)

Cf. "Silver Threads Among the Gold"

REMARKS: The "siliver threads" allusion is to a song sung by one aging lover to another. The song is an attempt to romanticize the creeping paralysis of age and death:

> Darling I am growing old,
> Silver threads among the gold,
> Shine upon my brow today,

Life is fading fast away;
But, my darling you will be, . . .
Always young and fair to me.

Bloom's predominantly unromantic, literal mind takes one of the curious twists that often characterize him. The silver hairs of O'Connell's beard are not among the gold, but among the grey, and the cemetery seems to Bloom, incongruously enough, an appropriate place to rhapsodize about eternal youth. The song acts as an associative vehicle opening a whole new avenue of thought about graveyard love-making.

> But they must breed a devil of a lot of maggots. Soil must be simply swirling with them. Your head it simply swurls. Those pretty little seaside gurls. (109:3–5)

Cf. "Seaside Girls"

REMARKS: Bloom persists in his misquotation here to further the theme, if not the exact words, of the song. We have already seen [7] how the "Seaside Girls" has become a major theme of the communality of existence. A great deal of the burden of Bloom's stream-of-conscious thought in the cemetery has been precisely to that end, to link the living and the dead into one communal existence; hence, all the scenes of love-making in graveyards that he conjures up and the other life-in-death images which provide most of the substance of his stream of consciousness. Here he is linking the world of the bodies of the dead with the swirling life of the maggots which feed on them. The song, with its connotations of communality, strengthen his life-in-death and death-in-life idea.

> *O, poor Robinson Crusoe,*
> *How could you possibly do so?* (109:38–39)

Cf. "Poor Old Robinson Crusoe"

REMARKS: Bloom slightly alters the lyrics to the nursery rhyme:

Poor old Robinson Crusoe!
Poor old Robinson Crusoe!
They made him a coat,
Of an old nanny goat,
    I wonder how they could do so! . . .

Bloom's line follows a stream-of-consciousness passage about how only men and ants bury their dead. He mistakenly has Friday burying Crusoe. Altering the lines from the nursery rhyme to fit a death situation provide Bloom with another comic variation on the death theme.

Feel no more. (110:33)

Cf. "Fear No More the Heat of the Sun"

REMARKS: Bloom's phrase suggests the song from *Cymbeline*, IV, ii, the lines
of which certainly fit the tenor of Bloom's thoughts:

> Fear no more the heat o' th' sun,
> Nor the furious winter's rages;
> Thou thy worldly task hast done,
> Home art gone, ta'en thy wages.
> Golden lads and girls all must,
> As chimney-sweepers, come to dust.

The reference underscores again Bloom's view of the finality of death and
its curious juxtaposition with the things of life.

Devil in that picture of sinner's death showing him a woman.
Dying to embrace her in his shirt. Last act of *Lucia*. *Shall I nevermore behold thee?* Bam! expires. Gone at last. People talk about
you a bit: forget you. Don't forget to pray for him. Remember
him in your prayers. (110:42–111:4)

Cf. "Shall I Nevermore Behold Thee"

REMARKS: The aria that Bloom refers to here is undoubtedly *"Tu che a Dio
spiegasti l'ali"* ("Thou Hast Spread Thy Wings to Heaven"). I have been unable to locate any English translation which uses the words, "Shall I never
more behold thee," though the words exactly fit the music of the first line
as well as the situation in Edgardo's well-known aria from Act III of *Lucia
di Lammermoor*. The picture of a last temptation triggers Bloom's association with the third act of the opera, where Edgardo, feeling lost and betrayed by Lucia, comes to the graveyard to kill himself. He sings:

> To earth I bid a last farewell,
> The tomb will soon close o'er me,
> Friendless, unwept and unbelov'd,
> No ray of hope before me.
> Ah! Tears, that are balm for misery,
> Ne'er will be shed for me.
> Forget, forget a heart betray'd,
> Forget the grave that hides me . . .

Edgardo is informed that Lucia, with his name on her lips, is dying. He is
moved to these recitative lines:

> Naught shall longer now restrain me,
> Once again I will behold her
> I will see her, unhand me. . . .

Bide-the-Bent, entering, informs Edgardo of Lucia's death and Edgardo decides to kill himself in any case:

> Thou hast spread thy wings to heaven,
> Oh thou spirit, pure and tender,
> From on high, 'mid starry splendor,
> Look down in pity, look in pity and forgive.
> Tho' by mortals doom'd to sever,
> Ours a love that cannot perish,
> Thee alone on earth alone I cherish,
> Reft of thee, reft of thee I will not live.

It is to this aria that Bloom refers in his allusion to the opera. The chorus, under the tenor obbligato, is praying for the suicidal Edgardo:

> Heavenly mercy, oh forgive . . .
> Oh heaven, in mercy, forgive . . .

The picture in Bloom's memory of the temptation of a woman for a dying sinner is associated with Edgardo's desire to embrace Lucia in his last moments. His admonishment of the chorus to forget him corresponds to Bloom's thinking, ". . . [people] forget you," and finally the prayers of the chorus as Edgardo dies are analogous to Bloom's thoughts. ("Don't forget to pray for him. Remember him in your prayers.")

The last act of *Lucia* in its mixture of sex and anguish, finally culminating in irrevocable death, is representative of one aspect of Bloom's philosophy. Life for him is, at least in part, a hedonistic gratification of the sensual; and death, following so closely, is the final spiritless void, shorn of immortality either through memory in this world or eternal spiritual life in the next. The music of Edgardo's transition from passion to nothing becomes the last song of Paddy Dignam and the great company of the dead which he and Edgardo have joined.

—Charley, Hynes said writing. I know. He was on the *Freeman* once.

So he was before he got the job in the morgue under Louis Byrne. Good idea a postmortem for doctors. Find out what they imagine they know. He died of a Tuesday. Got the run. Levanted with the cash of a few ads. Charley, you're my darling. That was why he asked me to. (111:37–112:1)

Cf. "Charlie Is My Darling"

REMARKS: Charley M'Coy's brashness reminds Bloom of the popular ballad:

> Oh! Charlie is my darling,
> My darling, my darling,
> Oh! Charlie is my darling,
> The young Chevalier.

There are two possible explanations for Bloom's reference to the song. The first is that Bloom merely associates ironically the first name of M'Coy, who has made off with some *Freeman* advertising money, with the darling of the song title and chorus. The second explanation is perhaps a bit more ingenious, but certainly within the realm of possibility: the Charlie of the song is "Bonnie Prince Charlie," the Stuart pretender to the English throne, who organized the Highlanders into a nearly successful revolt in 1745. The Stuarts were after the throne in the same way that M'Coy was after the *Freeman* funds. As Charley M'Coy was banished from the *Freeman,* so the Pretender was banished from England, and neither dared show his face. Bloom sees the connection immediately after the song reference ("Charley, you're my darling. That [because he didn't want to show his face] was why he asked me to [put his name in]"). Prince Charlie was banished to France under Louis XV, while Charley M'Coy was banished to the morgue under Louis Byrne. The overall similarity between Prince Charles and Charley M'Coy, then, may well have evoked the song in Bloom's stream of consciousness.

Where has he disappeared to? Not a sign. Well of all the. Has anybody here seen? Kay ee double ell. Become invisible. Good Lord, what became of him? (112:13–15)

Cf. "Has Anybody Here Seen Kelly?"

REMARKS: Most of the versions of the song relate the search for Kelly or Antonio by a lady of leisure who brought him along only to be abandoned by him for someone else.[8] The stranger in the mackintosh, like Kelly, has disappeared. He will reappear several times in the novel, but always mysteriously. Bloom, like Kelly's girl, is to worry about the man off and on all day.

Mr Bloom walked unheeded along his grove by saddened angels, crosses, broken pillars, family vaults, stone hopes praying with upcast eyes, old Ireland's hearts and hands. (113:3–5)

Cf. "Old Ireland's Hearts and Hands"

REMARKS: The figures "praying with upcast eyes" on the tombstones combine with the Irish patriotism of the preceding discourse on Parnell to remind Bloom of the Irish nostalgic song "Old Ireland's Hearts and Hands." The song, "sung with immense success" by Madame Marie Roze and Miss Bess Craig,[9] is a sentimental song of Erin sung by an expatriate who yearns for his native country:

> O Erin, home of lovely scenes,
>   O land of love and song!
> In joy once more my fond heart leans

On thee, so true and strong;
For like a restless bird I've strayed,
    And oft on far-off strands,
I dreamed of "love-knots" years have made
    With Ireland's hearts and hands.

Chorus:
O sweetheart Erin! good old land!
    Tho' near or far I stray,
I love them all, thy heart and hand,
    I love thy shamrock spray;
Old Ireland's hearts and hands!
    Old Ireland's hearts and hands!
O sweetheart Erin! good old land!
    I love thy hearts and hands.

The veneration of the dead Parnell, the dead country, and all of the departed souls is not, however, for Bloom. His next remarks, in the light of the patriotic aspects of the song he has just quoted, can be applied as well to the dead country as to Mr. O'Connell's charges: "More sensible to spend the money on some charity for the living" (113:5–6). As the prospective savior of his country, Bloom wastes little time on the traditional Irish occupation of feeding entirely on memory for whatever vitality life holds. Bloom's schemes, social and otherwise, for the salvation of the country lie in the economic improvement of the Irish in his own time and in the future. This is perhaps one of the principal differences between him and Stephen, who looks not to the present or future, but principally to the past for his *raison d'etre*, and for whom salvation of the race lies not in the physical, but the spiritual. But it is in the parallax and reconciliation of the opposites that the real salvation of the novel lies. Nowhere else is that reconciliation of opposites so apparent as when life is blended with death in Hades.

7. Aeolus

Our Saviour: beardframed oval face: talking in the dusk Mary, Martha. Steered by an umbrella sword to the footlights: Mario the tenor.

—Or like Mario, Mr Bloom said.

—Yes, Red Murray agreed. But Mario was said to be the picture of Our Saviour.

Jesus Mario with rougy cheeks, doublet and spindle legs. Hand on his heart. In *Martha*.

Co-ome thou lost one,
Co-ome thou dear one. (117:28–37)

Cf. *"M'appari"*

REMARKS: The last words are from *"M'appari,"* the popular tenor solo in Act III of the opera *Martha*. The song will assume an extremely important role later in the novel. Bloom, in the present passage, has not only the words to *"M'appari"* in mind, but also the music itself. Joyce has placed hyphens in the first word of each quoted line, indicating for the reader the intervals between the two notes which the tenor spans in each phrase during the closing lines of the solo.

CO - OME THOU LOST ONE, CO-OME THOU DEAR ONE.

The words of the song which Bloom quotes are not those of Jesus calling to a lost sinner, as the passage above might imply, but of Lionel crying out for his lost love. The Christ image is connected to the song ironically by Bloom, who uses the music as a means of providing a slightly blasphemous double meaning to Mario's performance. The associations among Jesus, Mario, Lionel, who sings the song in the opera, and Bloom begin here, with the linking of Jesus and Lionel in Bloom's mind through Mario's rendition of the song. Allusions to the song will become especially significant in the Sirens chapter.

I could ask him perhaps about how to pronounce that *voglio*. But then if he didn't know only make it awkward for him. Better not. (120:34–36)

Cf. *"Là ci darem"*

REMARKS: Bloom is still very much concerned with *Don Giovanni* and *"Là ci darem"* with all their adulterous connotations.[1] The reference may have been suggested by the previous reference to *"M'appari,"* from the opera *Martha*. "Martha" is linked in *Ulysses* to the adultery theme, with which *"Là ci darem"* is so closely associated. According to Vernon Hall:

Voglio is still on his mind as a symbol of Molly's willingness even though he has already reminded himself it is not in her song.[2]

It is interesting to note that though Hall's thesis seems to be true (i.e., that there are subconscious reasons for Bloom's changing Molly's conditional *vorrei*, "I would like to," to the present indicative *voglio*, "I want to"), Bloom is still unable to pronounce the word, even though he shows some technical knowledge of Italian by being able to translate the verb in two tenses. The song, however, serves to remind us once again of the impending Molly-Boylan assignation.

He stayed in his walk to watch a typesetter neatly distributing type. Reads it backwards first. Quickly he does it. Must require some practice that. mangiD, kcirtaP. Poor papa with his hagadah book, reading backwards with his finger to me. Pessach. Next year in Jerusalem. Dear, O dear! All that long business about that brought us out of the land of Egypt and into the house of bondage *alleluia. Shema Israel Adonai Elohenu.* No, that's the other. Then the twelve brothers, Jacob's sons. And then the lamb and the cat and the dog and the stick and the water and the butcher and then the angel of death kills the butcher and he kills the ox and the dog kills the cat. Sounds a bit silly till you come to look into it well. Justice it means but it's everybody eating everyone else. That's what life is after all. How quickly he does that job. Practice makes perfect. Seems to see with his fingers. (122: 17–31)

Cf. *"Shema Israel"*
    "Krias Shema"
    "Chad Gadya"

REMARKS: This passage is of particular interest both for its music and for Bloom's views on the Judaic liturgy involved. Looking at the type in reverse order in the form, Bloom is reminded of Jewish prayer books, which start on the last page and read from back to front. Bloom's father's *Hagadah* is the book that is read during passover or Pessach. The words "next year in Jerusalem" are very like the phrase used as the Matzoth is uncovered and the ceremonial plate is lifted at the beginning of the service:

This year we are here; next year we shall be in the land of Israel.

The phrase is used also at the conclusion of the *Hagadah.* A large part of the particular ceremony toward which Bloom's thoughts are directed deals with the plight of the Jews under Ramses II and their exodus from Egypt. "Next year in Jerusalem" is the eternal promise to the Jewish people of their return. Bloom is perfectly right about the words in italics, *"alleluia. Shema Israel Adonai Elohenu"* (Hear oh Israel, the Lord our God), not being in the *Hagadah* ("No, that's the other"). These are the words of *"Krias Shema,"* sung in the morning and evening prayers. From Bloom's initial mistake of placing the song in the *Hagadah,* his long dissociation from the liturgy becomes apparent.

The phrase "then the twelve brothers, Jacob's sons" is also an inaccurate recollection of part of the *Hagadah.* In the "First Day of Omer" section, a childlike counting prayer is recited, with each number holding a special significance. The section Bloom refers to is, "Who knows twelve? I know twelve. Twelve are the tribes of Israel."

That he had learned his religious lessons very well as a boy is also apparent from Bloom's memory of the symbolic last part of the *Hagadah*, the song *"Chad Gadya"*:

One kid, one kid that father bought for two zuzim. One kid, one kid.

And the cat came and ate the kid that father bought for two zuzim. One kid, one kid.

And the dog came and bit the cat that ate the kid that father bought for two zuzim. One kid, one kid.

And the stick came and beat the dog that bit the cat that ate the kid that father bought for two zuzim. One kid, one kid.

And the fire came and burned the stick that beat the dog that bit the cat that ate the kid that father bought for two zuzim. One kid, one kid.

And the water came and quenched the fire that burned the stick that beat the dog that bit the cat that ate the kid that father bought for two zuzim. One kid, one kid.

And the ox came and drank the water that quenched the fire that burned the stick that beat the dog that bit the cat that ate the kid that father bought for two zuzim. One kid, one kid.

And the slaughterer came and slaughtered the ox that drank the water that quenched the fire that burned the stick that beat the dog that bit the cat that ate the kid that father bought for two zuzim. One kid, one kid.

And the Angel of Death came and slew the slaughterer that slaughtered the ox that drank the water that quenched the fire that burned the stick that beat the dog that bit the cat that ate the kid that father bought for two zuzim. One kid, one kid.

And the Holy One, blessed is He, came and killed the Angel of Death that slew the slaughterer that slaughtered the ox that drank the water that quenched the fire that burned the stick that beat the dog that bit the cat that ate the kid that father bought for two zuzim. One kid, one kid.

Bloom in his enumeration, "And then the lamb. . .," has left out only the fire and the ox. Hodgart and Worthington, in giving the song reference for this as the "House that Jack Built," were not completely in error,[3] for the analogy is used in an explanation of the song in a reliable version of *Passover Hagadah*:

One of the most gripping of songs retained by Jewish tradition is the Chad Gadya recited at the conclusion of the Seder service. Though it is a simple nursery rhyme like "The House That Jack Built," it has come to illustrate in allegorical fashion the fate of the people of Israel, who, persecuted by the nations of old, still survive whereas their persecutors perished. The Assyrian *cat*, the Babylonian *dog*, the Persian *fire*, the Roman *waters*, the Saracen *ox*, the crusading *slaughterers*, have all met their fate. Every anti-Jewish *angel of death* will be likewise punished, it is our belief, by the principle of *jus talionis*. The most *Holy One* will surely in time release Israel, the *one only kid*, which was spiritualized by the teachings of the *two*—Moses and Aaron. The Jew always remembers that though he is the Chad Gadya in chains, he can never be slaughtered.[4]

The section containing Bloom's references to Semitic liturgy and music is extremely significant, for it reveals not only some of the background for his opinions on Christianity, but also the fact that he had a detailed knowledge of a relatively little used section of the ritual. From this background, then, may very well spring Bloom's sense of survival and his view of the world.

Bloom's survival instinct and his plans for the regeneration of his country, the basis for his eventual role as Moses and the saviour of Ireland, undergo considerable development in this episode. As Roderick Davis points out, however,[5] Bloom alone as Moses cannot bring Ireland into the New Bloomusalem; rather, it will have to be a combination of the consubstantial Bloom and Stephen, a reconciliation of opposites in mutual, all-pervasive transubstantiation. At any rate, these passages dealing witih Bloom's Semitic background and practicality of mind serve to establish his connection with the Moses figure developed later in the episode.

ERIN, GREEN GEM OF THE SILVER SEA (123:17)

Cf. "Let Erin Remember the Days of Old"
   "When Erin First Rose"

REMARKS: Hodgart and Worthington list the allusion as being to Moore's first stanza which ends, "Ere the emerald gem of the western world/Was set in the crown of a stranger." Thornton, however, lists "When Erin First Rose," the first stanza of which begins: "When Erin first rose from the dark swelling flood,/God bless'd the green island and saw it was good." Thornton also lists the headline as possibly a reference to "John of Gaunt's description of England" as "this precious stone set in the silver sea" in *Richard II*, II, i, 46.[6] At any rate the reference seems to have little outside the obvious half-comical connotations.

> Rather upsets a man's day a funeral does. He has influence they say. Old Chatterton, the vice-chancellor, is his granduncle or his greatgranduncle. Close on ninety they say. Subleader for his death written this long time perhaps. Living to spite them. Might go first himself. Johnny, make room for your uncle. The right honourable Hedges Eyre Chatterton. Daresay he writes him an odd shaky cheque or two on gale days. Windfall when he kicks out. Alleluia. (124:10–17)

Cf. "Tommy Make Room for Your Uncle"

REMARKS: The associative thought pattern in which the song operates is especially interesting here. Ned's ability to take off a day whenever he wishes is, according to Bloom, probably attributable to the influence of his relative, Hedges Eyre Chatterton. Bloom is not quite sure how Ned and Chatterton are related. The ambiguity of this relationship is for Bloom like that between Fred Jones and a little boy named Tommy, whose widowed mother is being wooed on a train by the rakish Fred, in the half-spoken, half-sung comic music-hall song. Amorous Fred is separated from the widow on the train by Tommy. Part of the dialogue and chorus are as follows:

Yes, the confounded young urchin caused me a great deal of pain, and sorrow, and the Widow his Mother introduced me to him as his Uncle? Fred Jones was never an Uncle before, and will never be again, not if he knows it—and the whole of the journey the Mother said to the boy—

> Tommy make room for your Uncle,
> There's a little dear,
> Tommy make room for your Uncle,
> I want him to sit here
> You know Mamma has got a *bun,*
> And that she'll give to you,
> So don't annoy, there's a good boy,
> Make room for your Uncle do . . .

In his association of Ned and Chatterton with Tommy and Fred, Bloom misquotes the first line of the chorus, confusing "Johnny" with "Tommy" ("Johnny make room for your uncle"). Ned, who, Bloom speculates, has had his uncle's death notice written for some time, stands, like Tommy, to profit by the nephew-uncle relationship. Tommy's profit will be a bun, while Ned stands to inherit a sizeable windfall. Ned's good fortune leads to Bloom's speculation and allusion to the song.

We are the boys of Wexford
Who fought with heart and hand. (129:13-14)

Cf. "The Boys of Wexford"

REMARKS: The song, an extremely popular ballad of the resistance, is meant to be ironically contrasted with the relatively unsavory Irish characters who are present in the office discussing the bombastic piece on Ireland's virtues which Lambert had been reading from the paper. Bloom hears the newspaper boys singing the first two lines of the chorus, the rest of which is:

> To burst in twain the galling chain,
> And free our native land.

On one level the reader might merely compare the heroism of the boys of Wexford with the antiheroes of the *Telegraph* office. On another level, the analogy between the two groups becomes even more pronounced if we examine the song in more detail. It is not the stirring chorus which is of primary interest on this level, but the contrast between the noble motivations of the boys of Wexford and the reason for their being defeated so often. The cause of these defeats is outlined in stanzas 3 and 4:

We bravely fought and conquered,
At Ross, and Wexford town;
And, if we failed to keep them,
'Twas drink that brought us down.
We had no drink beside us,
On Tubber'neering's day,
Depending on the long bright pike,
And well it worked its way.
  We are the boys, etc.

My curse upon all drinking,
It made our hearts full sore,
For bravery won each battle,
But drink lost evermore;
And if for want of leaders,
We lost at Vinegar Hill,
We're ready for another fight,
And love our country still!
  We are the boys, etc.

The irony of the Wexford patriots' alcoholic failures lies in the fact that no lesson has been learned from their defeats or songs, for the boys that sing them today will be tomorrow's frequenters of the Dublin bars. By the time Bloom hears the song, Simon Dedalus and Ned Lambert have left for a brief libation; Miles Crawford is already slightly intoxicated; and Professor Mac-Hugh and O'Molloy will presently be leaving with Stephen for the nearest bar. The saviors of Ireland, the gentlemen of the press, are losing their battle for old Erin just as the boys of Wexford did, and for some of the same reasons!

He declaimed in song, pointing sternly at professor MacHugh:
  'Twas rank and fame that tempted thee,
  'Twas empire charmed thy heart. (130:26–29)

Cf. " 'Twas Rank and Fame That Tempted Thee"

REMARKS: As Bloom exits from the newspaper office, he has been established musically by the tune of the mocking newsboys' "Boys of Wexford" as the savior of Ireland or at least the Moses who will lead the Irish out of bondage. Now Joyce proceeds to set up a series of false saviours in the orators, the newsmen, and the ineffectual fault-finding false priest, Stephen. As the episode begins to mount to the climax of John F. Taylor's speech, which clearly reveals the relationship of the Messianic tradition and the Jewish nation and Ireland, the various conquering nations are catalogued along with their betrayers.

" 'Twas Rank and Fame" introduces the list since it is a song of betrayal, of playing off the affections of a devoted lover for position and power. In Ireland, at least, with every Messiah there is a Judas. The song serves to link betrayal to empire and thus to Ireland, the conquered nation, as Crawford's mention of empire and betrayal begins the string of empire references with the Roman empire, then the Greek, and finally the Egyptian and their slaves, the Jews. The obvious association here lies between the Jews in their bondage to the Egyptians and the Irish in their bondage to the English. The Messianic theme is a long standing one in Irish literature. The song, from Balfe's *Rose of Castille,* triggers Lenehan's riddle in the following reference.

—. . . What opera resembles a railway line? (132:3)
—*The Rose of Castille.* See the wheeze? Rows of cast steel. (134: 19)

Cf. *The Rose of Castille*

REMARKS: The opera is a cycle of false disguises and betrayal as my remarks on " 'Twas Rank and Fame," a song from the opera, indicate. The work is destined to play a major role in the explication of the relationship between Bloom and Molly and as a revelation of Bloom's character. Briefly the plot is that Elvira, the Queen of Leon, is to be married to the brother of the King of Castille. Elvira, under the impression that the brother, Don Sebastian, has disguised himself as a muleteer, disguises herself as a peasant to meet the muleteer. There is a cast of fumbling conspirators who attempt to use the queen to serve their own ends. Assuming her to be a peasant girl, they re-disguise her as the queen. In the end she is happily united with the muleteer, who turns out to be not Don Sebastian but the King of Castille himself! J. P. Smith has an excellent commentary upon the thematic parallels and meaning of the opera as it pertains to *Ulysses.*[7] The opera with its disguises and its interchange of characters presents another variation upon the major Joycean theme that everyone is living everyone else's life. Smith's application of the opera to the Bloom marriage will be discussed elsewhere, but some points he introduces can be elaborated here. Smith is right in seeing Bloom as Don Florio, one of the ridiculous and inept conspirators, trying to seize the throne of Castille.[8] However, the point to be made, in the present context of this episode of nationalism and Messianic figures to liberate Ireland, is the same idea presented in the patriotic song, "The Boys of Wexford," that even the newsboys think of Bloom as anything but a hero.

He comes and he goes from the newspaper office, an object of scorn for editor and newsboy alike, and unnoticed by Stephen Dedalus. At present he is forced into the role of Don Florio, the bungling conspirator, but the stage has already been set for him to be the Moses figure of the Promised Land-wasteland of Dublin described by Stephen in the parable of the plums. In the mouth of Lenehan, one of the betrayers of "Two Gallants," the allusion to false identity embodied in the operatic reference will remain always in riddle form, for his world is a world of falsity and disguise, and if Bloom does become the leader of Ireland, few Irish will know it.

> *On swift sail flaming*
> *From storm and south*
> *He comes, pale vampire,*
> *Mouth to my mouth.*

—Good day, Stephen, the professor said, coming to peer over their shoulders. Foot and mouth? Are you turned . . . ? (132: 12–17)

Cf. "My Grief on the Sea"

REMARKS: We have already examined the Oedipal overtones to the song in the allusion in Proteus.[9] Stephen's alteration of Hyde's original lyrics makes the dead lover a vampire, a theme hinted at in *Chamber Music*,[10] pressing his mouth to hers. Hyde's version is much less sinister.[11] The quotation is an interesting display of the stream-of-consciousness associative pattern. Stephen's stanza, partially in ridicule of the imminent approach of Professor MacHugh from the rear, is prompted in part by his ghost-Oedipal image of his mother [12] and partly by Deasy's letter about foot-and-mouth disease in cattle. He uses the allusion as a satiric defense mechanism to protect himself against involvement with other people, living and dead.

Would anyone wish that mouth for her kiss? How do you know? Why did you write it then?

RHYMES AND REASONS

Mouth, south. Is the mouth south someway? Or the south a mouth? Must be some. South, pout, out, shout, drouth. Rhymes: two men dressed the same, looking the same, two by two.

> . . . .*la tua pace*
> . . . .*che parlar ti piace*
> . . *mentrechè il vento, come fa, si tace.*

He saw them three by three, approaching girls, in green, in rose, in russet, entwining, *per l'aer perso* in mauve, in purple, *quella pacifica oriafiamma,* in gold of oriflamme, *di rimirar fe piu ardenti.* But I old men, penitent, leadenfooted, underdarkneath the night: mouth south: tomb womb.

—Speak up for yourself Mr. O'Madden Burke said. (138:16–31)

Cf. "My Grief on the Sea"

REMARKS: This song is destined again to bear the burden of Stephen's Oedipal guilt. As Crawford rattles on, his mouth twitching, Stephen wonders why he wrote such a set of lyrics. Clearly here Stephen is back again trying to figure out his own motivations in the Oedipal lines. His confusion over the rhyme of mouth and south and why that particular rhyme is used may be related to Leopold Bloom's remark, "Good job it wasn't farther south" (83:37), meaning toward the direction of his crotch. This of course brings us right back to sex, as do the rhymes about Paolo and Francesca which Stephen uses as examples. As the terza rima stanzas appear in threes so do the seaside temptress figures, now linked with May and the Virgin-mother through Dante's lines in "Paradiso" as he gazes up at Mary. Stephen stops his "Inferno" quotation just short of the admission of the lovers' involvement:

> Love, which in gentlest hearts will soonest bloom
> seized my lover with passion for that sweet body
> from which I was torn unshriven to my doom.

> Love, which permits no loved one not to love,
> took me so strongly with delight in him
> that we are one in Hell, as we were above.

> Love led us to one death. In the depths of
> Hell Caina waits for him who took our lives.[13]

Stephen's fear of May's ghost warning him of hell in Circe may very well have its origin and antecedent in these lines.

The other aspect of the quotation above is the consubstantiality motif embodied in the similarities of the rhyming words described as "two men dressed the same, looking the same, two by two." The point here is that they are all the vampire, along with Hamlet senior and junior, who "feeds" on the earth mother, May-Molly-Gertrude, who links and implicates them all by birth in the womb and death in the tomb.

. . . your Cork legs are running away with you. (139:2)

Cf. "The Cork Leg"

REMARKS: The reference is a good example of how Joyce lets his characters use musical allusions as contemporary metaphors to punctuate their speech. The reference is to a song of the early nineteenth century, about a miser who broke his leg kicking out a poor suppliant relative, had his leg amputated, and was awarded a cork leg which would not stop running once it was screwed on. It killed the old man running, but his skeleton is destined to go on through the years still tied to the running leg. The moral intended by O'Molloy is that one should not be carried away by one's own rhetoric and become the victim of a verbal "cork leg." Thematically the story in the song is linked to that ghoulish perception of May Dedalus that festers in Stephen's mind. The image of being tied forever to an ever-running leg has Freudian overtones of Stephen's agenbite of inwit and the Oedipal furies which pursue him.

Out for the waxies' Dargle. (147:30–31)

Cf. "Waxies' Dargle"

REMARKS: Joseph Prescott says the term *waxies' Dargle* refers to an annual shoemaker's picnic that was held in the glen of the river Dargle,[14] but Mabel Worthington has uncovered a song by that name. Dominic Behan writes of the song:

> This song is as old as the River Dargle itself. Sir Walter took the dargle for a common noun because he had heard the song and he thought Dargle was a kind of beano. Waxies were everybody and anybody who thought enough of drink to go and get it—they'd be called "the Chelsea set" or "beatniks" nowadays.[15]

Clearly the allusion is intended to characterize the two old women of Stephen's tale as heavy drinkers.

VIRGILIAN, SAYS PEDAGOGUE. SOPHOMORE PLUMPS FOR OLD MAN MOSES (149:20–22)

Cf. "Old Man Moses"

REMARKS: When Professor MacHugh suggests a Virgilian title for Stephen's parable of the plums, Stephen rejects it in favor of a title on the Moses-bondage theme. All of this takes place under the above subhead. It is significant that Stephen is the one to tie the Moses-Jewish theme of Aeolus into the salvation of Dublin. Taylor's speech links Moses-Bloom to Stephen, the writer-forger of consciences through Moses' descending from the mount bearing the tables of the law. The implication is that the saving of Ireland will require a consubstantial combination of the two characters—neither one of whom in Aeolus has a chance of doing much. Stephen's satiric, misunderstood parable is less likely to raise the enthusiasm of those in the newspaper office than the promise of a few free drinks in a nearby pub. And the song alluded to in the subhead suggests and summarizes Bloom's ineffectual position during Aeolus in the eyes of those who are to be led from bondage.

The song is about a degraded flower salesman with a red nose who spends his time smelling flowers while he is alive, and when he dies spends eternity smelling the roots. The flippant tone of the headline is further augmented by the levity of the song and its debased protagonist. And so the chapter concludes with its image of a sterile country, with a neurotic conscience, and a debased saviour. There is indeed a long way to go this June 16th.

8. Lestrygonians

Lozenge and comfit manufacturer to His Majesty the King. God. Save. Our. Sitting on his throne, sucking red jujubes white. (151: 3-5)

Cf. "God Save the King"

REMARKS: Probably Bloom is thinking in the last reference about the lyrics to the anthem, rather than merely repeating the traditional words of British subjects. The periods after each word are Joyce's way of indicating a pause after each, since the slow cadence of the song usually begins with the first three notes emphasized and accentuated. Secondly, if Bloom were thinking of the usual spoken line, he would have been more disposed to say, "God Save *the* King," instead of *our* king, which is the form the first line of the anthem takes. The reference is used here satirically, as Bloom pictures the king sucking candy, a pose incongruous with the majesty of the music and its subject. Bloom's Irish mind is far from awed by British royalty or their endorsements.

Heart to heart talks.
Bloo. . . Me? No.
Blood of the Lamb.
His slow feet walked him riverward, reading. Are you saved? All are washed in the blood of lamb. God wants blood victim. Birth, hymen, martyr, war, foundation of a building, sacrifice, kidney burn offering druid's altars. Elijah is coming. Dr John Alexander Dowie, restorer of the church in Zion, is coming.

Is coming! Is coming!! Is coming!!!
All heartily welcome. (151:9-19)

Cf. "Washed in the Blood of the Lamb"

REMARKS: Hodgart and Worthington have cited this spiritual as a song reference, but the thesis that it is the song that Bloom is reading or thinking about is at best a tenuous one. The line, "All are washed in the blood of the lamb," does not originate in Bloom's mind, but is what he reads from the throwaway. The line has its origin in *Revelations* (7:14):

> And he said to me, These are they which came out
> of great tribulation, and have washed their robes,
> and made them white in the blood of the Lamb.

This quotation is often used in truncated form by the more fundamentalist ministers. The spiritual "Washed in the Blood of the Lamb," or "Oh, Redeemed," was also well known in the late nineteenth century.

Although you see me going along so,
Washed in the blood of the Lamb,
I have my trials here below,
Washed in the blood of the Lamb.

Chorus:
O redeemed, redeemed,
I'm washed in the blood of the Lamb,
O redeemed, redeemed,
I'm washed in the blood of the Lamb.

We will never know for certain whether Bloom had in mind the song or merely the words from the pamphlet, though the spiritual could have been a part of his mental image of Dowie's revival meeting.

Gave her that song *Winds that blow from the south.* (156:8–9)

Cf. "Winds that Blow from the South"

REMARKS: No one has yet been able to locate this song.

Professor Goodwin linking her in front. Shaky on his pins, poor old sot. His farewell concerts. Positively last appearance on any stage. May be for months and may be for never. (156:15–18)

Cf. "Kathleen Mavourneen"

REMARKS: The phrase, "May be for months and may be for never," is a deliberate, sarcastic misquotation of "it may be for years and it may be for ever" from the penultimate lines of the song. Usually a baritone solo, "Kathleen Mavourneen" would not have been sung by Molly. Rather, Bloom sees the song lyrics as appropriate to Goodwin's retirement from the stage. Following are the first stanza and chorus of the song:

Kathleen Mavourneen, the gray dawn is breaking,
The horn of the hunter is heard on the hill;
The lark from her light wing the bright dew is shaking;
Kathleen Mavourneen, what! slumb'ring still?
Kathleen Mavourneen, what! slumb'ring still?
Or hast thou forgotten how soon we must sever?
Oh! hast thou forgotten this day we must part?

It may be for years, and it may be for ever;
Then why are thou silent, thou voice of my heart?
It may be for years, and it may be for ever;
Then why art thou silent, Kathleen Mavourneen?

Bloom substitutes old Goodwin's threatened superannuation for the departure of the lover in the song. Each performance of Goodwin's is repeatedly announced as his last; but Bloom, in rearranging the words of the song, implies that Goodwin's retirement is for months, not years, and may be "for never" instead of permanently.

—O dear me, Mrs Breen said, I hope it wasn't any near relation. May as well get her sympathy.

—Dignam, Mr Bloom said. An old friend of mine. He died quite suddenly, poor fellow, Heart trouble, I believe. Funeral was this morning.

> *Your funeral's tomorrow*
> *While you're coming through the rye.*
> *Diddlediddle dumdum*
> *Diddlediddle* . . . (157:4–13)

Cf. "His Funeral Is Tomorrow"
   "Comin' Through the Rye"

REMARKS: In this passage Bloom's fusion of the two songs, which differ widely, provides a transition in his thinking. When Mrs. Breen asks about Bloom's funeral clothes, he is still relatively lighthearted and even a bit cynical about Dignam's death. This blithe feeling gives rise to the first line of his little tune, "Your funeral's tomorrow . . . ," which is an approximation of the title of a light, comic music-hall song relating the story of an obstreperous drunk who engaged in an argument in a bar:

> I will sing of Mike the "turk":
> Mike, one day, got tight,
> And he roam's around the block, dying for a fight!
> Mickey said to me, he would put me on the fire!
> And because I said he'd not, he call'd me a liar!

> And his funeral's tomorrow, my poor heart aches with sorrow;
> I hit him once, that's all; then he heard the angels call,
> And we're going to plant him tomorrow!

Bloom applies this line as the first in the song "Comin' Through the Rye." That Bloom is singing or humming "Comin' Through the Rye" to himself is indicated by the italics and the fact that the lyrics and "diddles" fit the tune of the song:

YOUR FU-NER-ALS TO-MOR-ROW WHILE YOUR COMIN THROUGH THE RYE.

DIO-DLE DID-DLE DUM-DUM-DIDDLE DIDDLE . . . . .

We have already seen Bloom as the great amalgamator of the living and the dead in Hades. Now again death is greeted with comic overtones. Presumably the link between the songs lies in the lyrics of the funeral song being joined with the first lines of "Comin' Through the Rye," "When a body meets a body. . . ."

The transition from cynicism and jocularity in the first song to pensive reminiscence in the second denotes a shifting of gears in Bloom's mind, as Mrs. Breen starts to become sadly thoughtful and he, sympathizing with her, senses her dejected state and tries to change the subject. Bloom can't stay with the dead for long, because his sentiments are predominantly with the living. He wants to avoid useless nostalgia in his conversation with Mrs. Breen, but he can't help remembering that the shabby, worn, changed woman he is speaking to was his girl friend in better days.

It is only natural to frame the story picture of Mrs. Breen in the setting of the plaintive, yet hopeful strains of "Comin' Through the Rye":

> If a body meet a body,
> Comin' thro' the Rye,
> If a body kiss a body,
> Need a body cry?

The spirit and atmosphere of the song underlie Bloom's whole encounter with Mrs. Breen, providing the melancholy orchestration which characterizes their meeting.

> Twilightsleep idea: queen Victoria was given that. Nine she had. A good layer. Old woman that lived in a shoe she had so many children. (161:28–30)

Cf. "There Was an Old Woman Who Lived in a Shoe"

Remarks: Victoria is associated here with the old woman in the nursery rhyme who solves her maternal problems in a traditional manner:

> There was an old woman who lived in a shoe,
> She had so many children she didn't know what to do;

> She gave them some broth, without any bread,
> She whipp'd them all round, and put them to bed.

The old woman's vigorous solution of her problem probably forms the basis of both Bloom's impatience with the lack of a solution to the poverty of large Irish families and his own answer to the problem, giving children a stipend at birth from tax revenues, the money to be saved and compounded as they aged.

> After their feed with a good load of fat soup under their belts. Policeman's lot is oft a happy one. They split up into groups and scattered, saluting towards their beats. Let out to graze. Best moment to attack one in pudding time. A punch in his dinner. (162:21–25)

Cf. "A Policeman's Lot Is Not a Happy One"

REMARKS: The comic effect of the stuffed policemen emerging after their meal strikes Bloom as being fully in keeping with the comic spirit of Gilbert and Sullivan's *Pirates of Penzance*. In the passage above, he slightly alters the title of the song. His substitution of *oft* for *not* is appropriate in terms of the well-fed constables he is watching. Though the words of the chorus, "When constabulary duty's to be done/ A policeman's lot is not a happy one," may be perfectly true, the many off-duty activities of the portly constables seem to Bloom to demand the modification of *not* to *oft*, especially in semi-starved Ireland. J. P. Smith expands the allusion of music to encompass the whole plot of the operetta. He then proceeds to fit that into the father-son motif of *Ulysses*,[1] but I don't think the expansion is warranted here merely by what Bloom says, since there is nothing in the quotation which remotely deals with the theme.

> They did right to put him up over a urinal: meeting of the waters. Ought to be places for women. Running into cakeshops. Settle my hat straight. *There is not in this wide world a vallee.* Great song of Julia Morkan's. Kept her voice up to the very last. Pupil of Michael Balfe's wasn't she? (162:29–34)

Cf. "The Meeting of the Waters"

REMARKS: The meaning of Bloom's remarks can be arrived at only through his song reference. Because Moore wrote "The Meeting of the Waters," it is proper that his statue adorn the top of a urinal. The song strikes Bloom as being appropriate men's-room music.

After a brief tangent on the need for women's toilets, Bloom comes back to the song, singing the first line to himself: *"There is not in this wide world a vallee* [so sweet]. . . ." Here Joyce pushes the joke a little further by making us think of the lyrics of the song as well as the title. Only when the entire song is heard as the description of women's genitals or a water closet can the full incongruity of the double or triple meaning be appreciated:

> There is not in the wide world a valley so sweet,
> As that vale in whose bosom the bright waters meet;
> Oh! the last rays of feeling and life must depart,
> Ere the bloom of that valley shall fade from my heart,
> Ere the bloom of that valley shall fade from my heart.
>
> Yet it was not that Nature had shed o'er the scene,
> Her purest of crystal and brightest of green;
> T'was not her soft magic of streamlet or hill,
> Oh! no it was something more exquisite still,
> Oh! no it was something more exquisite still.

The song leads Bloom to think of the singer who was associated with it. Joyce did not intend a wholly unflattering association here. Julia Morkan was sympathetically enough treated in "The Dead" and now in death she takes on Michael Furey overtones by presiding ironically over the urination-fertility image in Bloom's mind.

Police whistle in my ears still. All skedaddled. Why he fixed on me. Give me in charge. Right here it began.
—Up the Boers!
—Three cheers for De Wet!
—We'll hang Joe Chamberlain on a sourapple tree. (163:8–12)

Cf. "We'll Hang Jeff Davis to a Sour Apple Tree"

REMARKS: In this scene, the well-known parody of the "Battle Hymn of the Republic," "We'll Hang Jeff Davis to a Sour Apple Tree," has been altered by the yelling students to "we'll hang Joe Chamberlain on a sour apple tree." Thornton explains that Joseph Chamberlain was wrongfully blamed for the aggressive act that precipitated the Boer War. "After the war he went to South Africa to try to effect a reconciliation with the Boers. He was granted an honorary degree of L.L.D. by Trinity College, Dublin, on December 18, 1899, at which time a group of students demonstrated against him and against the Boer War." [2] Hence the song reference, with its political overtones of the hatred of the Confederate leader, Jefferson Davis, links Bloom and the students with another time and country—one more example of the simultaneity of existence and the reliving of history which is a major theme of the novel.

Silly billies: mob of young cubs yelling their guts out. Vinegar hill. The Butter exchange band. Few years' time half of them magistrates and civil servants. War comes on: into the army helterskelter: same fellows used to whether on the scaffold high. (163:13-17)

Cf. "The Boys of Wexford"

"God Save Ireland"

REMARKS: Vinegar Hill, immortalized in the song, "The Boys of Wexford," is where the Wexford boys suffered one of their many defeats.[3] As Bloom focuses his attention on war and Irish politics, he recalls a line, ". . . whether on the scaffold high," from the very well-known song about the Manchester Martyrs, Allen, Larkin, and O'Brien, who were captured in a successful attempt to rescue the Fenian military leaders, Kelly and Deasy, in 1867. The song, the epitome of Irish militant martyr songs "was for fifty years Ireland's unofficial national anthem."[4] The first stanza and chorus are as follows:

> High upon the gallows tree swung the noble-hearted three,
> By the vengeful tyrant stricken in their bloom;
> But they met him face to face, with the spirit of their race,
> And they went with souls undaunted to their doom.
>
> Chorus:
> "God save Ireland!" said the heroes;
> "God save Ireland!" said they all.
> "Whether on the scaffold high
> Or the battlefield we die,
> Oh! what matter when for Ireland dear we fall?"

With the two songs, then, the order and meaning of Bloom's thoughts in the passage become clear. He visualizes the shouting boys becoming warriors, returning to civilian life as magistrates and civil servants, and then going back to the army for the next uprising. The ease with which the Irish shift from violent nationalists to cooperative civil servants and conquered people, here commented on by Bloom, has long disturbed Stephen Dedalus. As their thoughts run in parallel channels, like Stephen, Bloom proceeds from this phenomenon to an immediate association with the betrayal motif.

Because several of Ireland's martyrs were betrayed by informers, Bloom's associative pattern goes from martyrs to informers, thence to government men and plain-clothes men trying to pry secrets loose from servants. This pattern leads him to envision a typical interrogation of a maid by a masquerading plain-clothes man.

—Are those yours, Mary?

—I don't wear such things . . . Stop or I'll tell the missus on you. Out half the night.

—There are great times coming, Mary. Wait till you see.

—Ah, get along with your great times coming. (163:30-34)

Cf. "There's a Good Time Coming"

REMARKS: As Bloom's thoughts turn to the imagined scene between the policeman and the maid, the patriotism of the preceding paragraph and the flirtation with Mary are blended in the song about the end of war and the ensuring good time of eternal grace:

> There's a good time coming, boys,
> A good time coming,
> There's a good time coming, boys,
> Wait a little longer.
> We may not live to see the day,
> But earth shall glisten in the ray
> Of the good time coming,
> Cannon balls may aid the truth,
> But thought's a weapon stronger;
> We'll win our battle by its aid,
> Wait a little longer. Oh!
> There's a good time coming,
> A good time coming,
> There's a good time coming, boys,
> Wait a little longer.

Arthur Griffith is a squareheaded fellow but he has no go in him for the mob. Want to gas about our lovely land. Gammon and spinach. Dublin Bakery Company's tearoom. Debating societies. (163:42–164:4)

Cf. "A Frog He Would a Wooing Go"

REMARKS: Griffith is a contemporary politician who will not descend to the mob. Griffith needs to get out on the stump and woo the voters with the usual rhetoric about their lovely land, like a frog wooing his mate—hence the significance of the "gammon and spinach" quotation. The words are part of the refrain of the sixteenth-century English ballad:

> A frog he would a wooing go,
> Heigh ho! said Rowly,
> A frog he would a wooing go,
> Whether his mother would let him or no,
> With a Rowly powly, gammon, and spinach,
> Heigho! said Anthony Rowly.

Griffith's attempts at mixing with the people could, in Bloom's thoughts, begin in suitable forums with traditional subjects, which of course are all too appropriate to the cave of the winds at the newspaper office.

Since I fed the birds five minutes. Three hundred kicked the bucket. Other three hundred born, washing the blood off, all are washed in the blood of the lamb, bawling maaaaaa. (164:22–25)

Cf. "Washed in the Blood of the Lamb"

REMARKS: Bloom, in thinking of the birth rate and linking the dead and newborn infants through the blood of the Lamb, Jesus of Dowie's sermon, provides his own version of Stephen's telephone trunk line of naval cords connecting everyone in one great image of common descent.

And there he is too. Now that's really a coincidence: second-time. Coming events cast their shadows before. (165:30–31)

Cf. "Lochiel's Warning"

REMARKS: The song alluded to by Bloom is from a poem by Thomas Campbell. The Wizard attempts to dissuade Lochiel Donald Cameron from taking up arms for Charles the Pretender, telling Lochiel, ". . . coming events cast their shadows before." Lochiel is the name of the Clan Cameron. Bloom's allusion was probably prompted as much by Russell's allusion to "a Scotch accent" as by the portent of A.E.'s appearance after Bloom had been thinking of him in conjunction with Lizzie Twigg's letter. The coincidence of the themes and thoughts crisscrossing is of course not any more accidental than it looks to Bloom. Lizzie Twigg is not the girl with A.E., though Bloom thinks it might be, but one who works in the *Irish Times* office with Russell.[5] But the navel cords of all intertwine in consubstantiality as Bloom has advertised for a "smart lady typist to aid gentleman in literary work" (160:11–12). He did not effect a liaison with Lizzie Twigg, who goes with Russell, but as a result of the ad Bloom does engage in an amorous correspondence with Martha Clifford, who will later be identified with Molly through "*M'appari*" from the opera *Martha* in Sirens, and also with May Dedalus, whose husband, "heartbroken" at her death, sings the song. Finally Stephen, who has also lost his Oedipal love will get from Bloom a new smart young lady to aid him in his literary work, Molly, whose final soliloquy details exactly how she will be of aid in his literary as well as physical endeavors. All of this prompts Bloom (on the page following the quoted passage) to try to achieve parallax. We have already seen in the introduction how the consubstantiality motif is outlined in Bloom's parallax motif,[6] and the connection here is far from mere coincidence.

Wait. The full moon was the night we were Sunday fortnight exactly there is a new moon. Walking down by the Tolka. Not bad for a Fairview moon. She was huming: The young May moon she's beaming, love. He other side of her. Elbow, arm. He.

Glowworm's la-amp is gleaming, love. Touch. Fingers. Asking.
Answer. Yes.

Stop. Stop. If it was it was. Must. (167:19–25)

Cf. "The Young May Moon"

REMARKS: The words to Molly's song, "The Young May Moon," are slightly
misquoted, but the melody which Molly sings is not altered.

Bloom substitutes *she's* for *is* but accurately describes *la-amp* as having a
hyphen. The one-syllable word is sung on two notes, and again Joyce indicates with a hyphen the interval between the two notes:

THE   GLOW - WORMS LAMP IS   GLEAM - ING, LOVE,

Boylan is presumably the "he" on the other side of Molly attempting inti-
macies even in the cuckolded spouse's presence. In this situation the words,
with which all three parties are undoubtedly familiar, take on a double
meaning:

> The young May moon is beaming, love,
> The glowworm's lamp is gleaming, love,
> How sweet to rove thro' Morna's grove,
> When the drowsy world is dreaming, love!
> Then awake! the heav'ns look bright, my dear,
> 'Tis never too late for delight, my dear,
> And the best of all ways to lengthen our days,
> Is to steal a few hours from the night, my dear.

The implications of the gleaming "glowworm's lamp," the sweetness of
roaming through "Morna's grove/When the drowsy world is dreaming,"
and the admonishment that "it's never too late for delight" could not have
escaped any of the three. Molly, by humming the song, is making an affirma-
tive response to Boylan's questioning fingers. Bloom, who also knows the
song and realizes its significance, guesses what is going on, but in his fatalistic way feels that he could have done nothing to prevent it. ("If it was it
was. Must.")

Broth of a boy. Dion Boucicault business with his harvestmoon
face in a poky bonnet. Three Purty Maids from School. How time
flies eh? Showing long red pantaloons under his skirts. (167:36–
39)

Cf. "Three Little Maids from School"

REMARKS: The song, from Gilbert and Sullivan's *The Mikado*, is sung to dainty, tripping music by Yum-Yum, Peep-Bo, and Pitti-Sing, relating their innocent, girlish status:

> Three little maids, who, all unwary,
> Come from a ladies' seminary,
> Freed from its genius tutelary,
> Three little maids from school,
> Three little maids from school!

The performance of the song by a male would have conveyed a primitive sort of humor to the Old Harp Theatre audience, which Bloom describes next.

> Drinkers, drinking, laughed spluttering, their drink against their breath. More power, Pat. Coarse red: fun for drunkards: guffaw and smoke. Take off that white hat. His parboiled eyes. Where is he now? Beggar somewhere. The harp that once did starve us all. (167:39–168:1)

Cf. "The Harp That Once Through Tara's Halls"

REMARKS: Bob Doran, whose drunken figure started the whole associational train of the passage, is merely following in the footsteps of tradition. There were the same crude drunks at Pat Kinsella's Harp Theatre as there are on Bloomsday. As he speculates on Kinsella's present condition, Bloom recalls and paraphrases the title of the Thomas Moore song of former days. Bloom's version, "The harp that once did starve us all," has its obvious association with the Harp Theatre, which eventually starved out Kinsella. There is, however, still another important association between the song and the context of Bloom's thoughts. This can be seen in the words to the first stanza:

> The harp that once through Tara's halls
> The soul of music shed,
> Now hangs as mute on Tara's walls
> As if that soul were fled,
> So sleeps the pride of former days,
> So glory's thrill is o'er,
> And hearts that once beat high for praise,
> Now feel that pulse no more.

The days of "glory's thrill" which the song describes seem better in retrospect in the song than they do to Bloom. His changing the words *through Tara's halls* to *did starve us all* indicates his sentiment about the false "pride of former days" which many Irishmen use as a rationalization for not making more of their own lives. It is the song of the vanished past and the image of those bygone days of the fun-loving drunkards in the Harp Theatre which prompt Bloom to recall his own feelings in that happier, younger time in his marriage, as again music provides the vehicle for the stream-of-conscious thought pattern.

> He passed, dallying, the windows of Brown Thomas, silk mercers. Cascades of ribbons. Flimsy China silks. A tilted urn poured from its mouth a flood of bloodhued poplin: lustrous blood. The huguenots brought that here. *La causa è santa!* Tara tara. Great chorus that. Tara. Must be washed in rainwater. Meyerbeer. Tara: bom bom bom. (168:17–22)

Cf. *The Huguenots*
  "La causa è santa"
  "Washed in the Blood of the Lamb"

REMARKS: The title of Meyerbeer's opera *The Huguenots* brings into Bloom's consciousness the third-act sextet, *"La causa è santa"* (The cause is sacred), which he mistakenly calls a chorus. The association between the sacred cause and the bloodhued poplin brings about a recollection of "Washed in the Blood of the Lamb" from the religious pamphlet handed to Bloom in the beginning of the chapter. Bloom's thought, "Must be washed in rainwater," combines aspects of the biblical quotation,[7] *La causa è santa,* and the bloody-appearing poplin in Thomas's window.

Hodgart and Worthington have attempted to associate the "Tara: bom bom bom" in the above passage with "Ta Ra Ra Boom De Ay," "At Trinity Church I Met My Doom," and "Bom, Bom, Bom! Zim, Zim, Zim!" However, Bloom, here, is merely singing the second line of *"La Causa,"* which is the title phrase. "Tara: bom bom bom" corresponds exactly to the staccato dotted eighth and sixteenth notes of the line, *"La causa è santa,"* sung by Cosse (the second tenor) and Retz (the first bass) in the song:

TA RA BOM BOM BOM

TA RA BOM BOM BOM

John Howard Parnell example the provost of Trinity every mother's son don't talk of your provosts and provost of Trinity

women and children, cabmen, priests, parsons, fieldmarshals, arch-
bishops. . . . After you with our incorporated drinkingcup. Like
sir Philip Crampton's fountain. Rub off the microbes with your
handkerchief. Next chap rubs on a new batch with his. Father
O'Flynn would make hares of them all. (170:29-32, 35-39)

Cf. "Father O'Flynn"

REMARKS: The communal kitchen idea, with people from all stations of life
feeding at the same trough, leads Bloom to speculate on those stations of life
which would be represented. Both John Howard Parnell and the Provost of
Trinity would have to eat there. The phrase "provost of Trinity" reminds
Bloom of some of the lyrics in the second stanza of the song, "Father
O'Flynn":

> Stanza 2:
> Don't talk of your Provost and Fellows of Trinity,
> Famous forever at Greek and Latinity,
> Faix and the divils and all at Divinity,
> Father O'Flynn'd make hares of them all!
> Come, I venture to give ye my word,
> Never the likes of his logic was heard,
> Down from mythology into thayology
> Troth and conchology if he'd the call.
>
> Chorus:
> Here's a health to you, Father O'Flynn,
> Slainte and slainte and slainte again,
> Pow'rfulest preacher, and tinderest teacher,
> And kindliest creature in ould Donegal! . . .

Bloom changes the first line of stanza two, using *provost* for *Fellows* in his
reference. The variation is natural, since he is trying to superimpose the
associational phrase, "provost of Trinity," on the song.

The idea of a communal food supply carries with it the idea of a communal set of utensils, which remind Bloom of the single drinking cup at
Sir Philip Crampton's fountain. That cup takes on ecclesiastical connotations, probably through the communion chalice, and Bloom returns full cycle
to "Father O'Flynn." The idea of the song, that the kindly parish priest is as
good or better than the faculty of Trinity College at erudite subjects, underlies the whole democratic equalization of various classes of people in Bloom's
communal kitchen.

Davy Byrne came forward from the hindbar in tuckstitched
shirtsleeves, cleaning his lips with two wipes of his napkin. Her-
ring's blush. Whose smile upon each feature plays with such and
such replete. (173:22-25)

Cf. "In Happy Moments Day by Day"

REMARKS: Bloom refers to the following passage from Don Jose's song in *Maritana:*

> Though anxious eyes upon us gaze,
> And hearts with fondness beat,
> Whose smile upon each feature plays
> With truthfulness replete. . . .

Bloom's changing the truthfulness of the smile in the song to "such and such" indicates his doubt about the veracity of Flynn's stories.

He hummed, prolonging in solemn echo, the closes of the bars:

> *Don Giovanni, a cenar teco*
> *M'invitasti.* (179:33–36)

—*A cenar teco.*
What does that *teco* mean? Tonight perhaps.

> *Don Giovanni, thou hast me invited*
> *To come to supper tonight,*
> *The rum the rumdum.*

Doesn't go properly. (180:6–11)

Cf. Commendatore's lines, *Don Giovanni,* V, iii

REMARKS: The hour of Molly's tryst with Boylan is approaching, and all through lunch thoughts of his wife and her sensuality plague Bloom. As he leaves the pub, the thought of food combines with Molly's adultery motif to bring to his mind *Don Giovanni* and the avenging Commendatore's famous last-act acceptance of the Don's invitation to supper.

"The rum the rumdum" is Bloom's rhythmically and syllabically correct equivalent of the last two measures of the ghost's opening address to Giovanni, ". . . *e son venuto*":

THE RUM THE RUM-DUM
E SON VEN-U—TO

Hodgart and Worthington cite the passage in the opera as an aria, but it is only a brief, though extremely important, recitative. Hall says of the passage:

> Bloom knows some Italian. He mistranslates "teco" but gets the rest right. But once again it is not the words, as he pretends, that really concern him, it is their context.[8]

In the opera the ghost of the Commendatore has come to take Giovanni to hell to avenge his daughter's insult and his own death. It is difficult to know whether the association of Boylan with the Don and Bloom with the Commendatore ever rises to the conscious level here, though it plays an exceptionally important part in the passage.

> Tour the south then. What about English watering places? Brighton, Margate. Piers by moonlight. Her voice floating out. Those lovely seaside girls. (180:19–21)

Cf. "Seaside Girls"

REMARKS: Thoughts of "Seaside Girls" replace *Don Giovanni,* but as we have seen,[9] this song too is related to Bloom's preoccupation with the affair between Molly and Blazes. Can Bloom as the avenging Commendatore exact justice from Don Boylan? Hall attempts to answer this in his description of Bloom's near encounter with Blazes at the end of the chapter:

> Then he sees Boylan passing on the street. Far from being the *Commendatore* who grasps Don Giovanni's hand and pulls him down to Hell, Bloom's heart quops softly, he rushes into the Museum so as not to be seen, exclaiming "My heart!" (180). Instead of the stone avenger have we not the new womanly man who like another Zerlina signs the equivalent of her "Mi trema un poco il cor"? [10]

But now Bloom is ready to play for the first time the role of the avenger, of punisher for the wrongs done him. If he still thinks it is as hopeless as his earlier resignation indicated, there is still time to rid the house spiritually if not physically of the suitors. He has been sustained in the body through the Gorgonzola and Burgundy and in the mind through the image of his triumph with Molly on the Hill of Howth. Now he thinks he is ready to conquer and avenge, as, fortified, he emerges in the role of the Commendatore. But he is routed almost immediately. For Bloom the time is not yet ripe. To conquer he needs to effect the liaison with Stephen. He is unfulfilled, a half man, without a son. That is why either he or Molly "could never like it after Rudy died." As Stephen needs Bloom for the fulfillment of identification with humanity so Bloom needs Stephen. Given the aid and consubstantial identification with his son, Bloom-Ulysses will work metempsychically with Stephen-Telemachus to defeat the world's usurpers, the Mulligans, Boylans, and Lynches.

The opera emerges as one more of the vehicles of consubstantiality in Bloom's assumption of all the major roles at one time or another in the book. Though Bloom fails now, by the Penelope episode, he, united with Stephen, through equanimity and endurance will subsume everyone else including all the suitors into himself, the all-encompassing "he" of Molly's soliloquy.

While Margate and the piers suggest stanza one of "Seaside Girls" and hence the song to Bloom,[11] this allusion acts also in its communal sense to enable Bloom to change roles in the opera *Don Giovanni* and go from the cuckolded Masetto to the avenging Commendatore, as all roles become one and Bloom lives through one set of experiences, life style, and role after another. Hence all themes converge into one communality, including the novel's ultimate consubstantiality between the two protagonists.

> Hello, placard. Mirus bazaar. His excellency the lord lieutenant. Sixteenth today it is. In aid of funds for Mercer's hospital. *The Messiah* was first given for that. Yes Handel. (183:5–7)

Cf. *The Messiah*

REMARKS: Bloom's thoughts of Jews and the placard announcing the Mirus bazaar have combined here to bring to Bloom's mind a performance of *The Messiah*. It is to the strains of *The Messiah* that Boylan appears ironically on the scene. Beside the immediate ironic connotations of Boylan as the Messiah, there is also the idea of meekness and turning the other cheek associated with Christ and the oratorio, which provide a contrast to the vengeance of *Don Giovanni*. Perhaps here the negative in the revenge motif Hall ascribes to *Don Giovanni* is counterbalanced, as the negative value of the Jews' slaying of Christ is balanced, by the positive value of Christian suffering, both of which are inherent in *The Messiah*.

Bloom's conquering will not be that of the vengeful Commendatore, but later his identification with the Messiah in Cyclops will give a further key to precisely the sort of conquering he will accomplish. If Boylan comes on to the strains of *The Messiah*, it must not be forgotten that Bloom also exits to this theme, for in the consubstantial motif everyone is living everyone else's life and Bloom's own sexual triumphs are part of Boylan's. So the Messiah role will fit both Bloom and Boylan, and the conquering hero image will result as much from equanimity and submission as from prowess between the sheets.

9. Skylla and Charybdis

—Have you found those six brave medicals, John Eglinton asked with elder's gall, to write *Paradise Lost* at your dictation? *The Sorrows of Satan* he calls it.

Smile. Smile Cranly's smile.

> *First he tickled her*
> *Then he patted her*
> *Then he passed the female catheter.*
> *For he was a medical*
> *Jolly old medi . . .*

—I feel you would need one more for *Hamlet.* (184:20–29)

Cf. "Jolly Old Medical"

REMARKS: I have not been able to locate the original song alluded to here. However, the passage serves to reestablish the Stephen-Satan parallel begun in *Portrait* and, through the bawdy lyrics of the song, to set the lewd tone of the sexual promiscuity motif which will dominate Stephen's *Hamlet* theory.

Green twinkling stone. An emerald set in the ring of the sea. (186:35–36)

Cf. *"Chushla-ma-Chree"* ("Pulse of My Heart")
"Let Erin Remember the Days of Old"

REMARKS: The "emerald set . . ." is from John Curran's song which begins,

> Dear Erin, how sweetly thy green bosom rises,
> An emerald set in the ring of the sea. . . .[1]

The reference is to the cigarette case from which Haines offered Stephen a cigarette in Telemachus (19:38–20:4). The allusion is prompted by Haines's mention of Best. An additional association may be to the lines "Ere the emerald gem of the Western world/Was set in the crown of a stranger." Here the combined references link Haines with the usurper figure and the English, with whom Stephen has consistently identified him in Telemachus and thereafter. The link here is between the rivalry motif and the political motif. Stephen has assumed an unaccustomed servility in accepting the cigarette from the usurper and now reflects on his subservient position.

HAMLET
ou
LE DISTRAIT
Pièce de Shakespeare . . .

—*Pièce de Shakespeare,* don't you know. It's so French, the French point of view. *Hamlet ou . . .*

—The absentminded beggar, Stephen ended. (187:15–18, 20–22)

Cf. "The Absent-Minded Beggar"

REMARKS: Here Stephen goes to the heart of the meaning of his Shakespeare theory and the underlying theme of consubstantiality in the novel. The chorus of the song is:

> Duke's son, cook's son, son of a hundred kings,
> (Fifty thousand horse and foot going to Table Bay). . . .

The communality of all the men in the army being lumped into one "absentminded beggar" is precisely the communality of the creator Shakespeare and the Hamlets, senior and junior, in the play. The metaphor will then work in the metempsychic relationship between Bloom and Stephen in the father-son motif of *Ulysses* and in the community of all characters living each other's lives throughout all of Joyce's works. This song becomes one of the leitmotifs of communal existence in the book. Its overt link here with *Hamlet* solidifies the tie between the *Hamlet* and the general consubstantiality themes in *Ulysses*.

There are in addition further links between the song and the *Hamlet* motif: the song refers to a less-than-perfect soldier who has gone off to fight for his country and who has left many obligations behind. The populace is urged to contribute toward relieving them:

> When you've shouted "Rule Britannia," when you've sung
>   "God Save the Queen,"
> When you've finished killing Kruger with your mouth,
> Will you kindly drop a shilling in my little tambourine,
> For a gentleman, in "khaki," ordered South?
> He's an absent-minded beggar and his weaknesses are great,
> But we and Paul must take him as we find him.
> He is out on active service, wiping something off a slate,
> And he's left a lot o'little things behind him!
> Duke's son, cook's son, son of a hundred kings
> (Fifty thousand horse and foot going to Table Bay!)
> Each of 'em doing his country's work—and who's
>   to look after their things?
> Pass the hat, for your credit's sake, and pay, pay, pay!

Hamlet is, according to the French, a bit more than merely absentminded; however, Stephen's analogy of Hamlet and the beggar is still convincing enough to occasion some mirth from Eglinton. Both Hamlet and the beggar have left a mess at home while they were off to foreign lands. But Stephen sees himself as connected with Hamlet and so he must feel there is also a similarity between himself and the absentminded beggar. The beggar is doing his country's work while Stephen is the forger of the uncreated conscience of his race. In the reference is buried the theme which Stephen has expounded in so dramatic a fashion in the Telemachus episode: the gratitude or ingratitude of one's country. Stephen and the absentminded beggar should stand high in their country's esteem and be acknowledged. The theme continues to lurk just beneath the surface of Stephen's thoughts.

I paid my way. I paid my way.

Steady on. He's from beyant Boyne water. The northeast corner. You owe it. (189:33–35)

Cf. "The Boyne Water"

REMARKS: Deasy's Orange line regarding the evils of indebtedness prompts Stephen to associate his Protestant leanings and subsequent feeling of the evils of owing money with those of Russell. The Irish folksong describes the crossing of the Boyne River under Protestant King William and the subsequent defeat of the Catholics on the other side. Stephen's allusion is, then, to the fact that Russell is a Protestant.

John Eglinton looked in the tangled glowworm of his lamp.
—The world believes that Shakespeare made a mistake, he said, and got out of it as quickly and as best he could. (190:17-20)

Cf. "The Young May Moon"

REMARKS: Eglinton's lamp with its twisted wrought iron base is described in terms of the lyrics of the song associated by both Bloom (167:19-24) and Molly (740:9-13) with the Boylan assignation. The early overtures of the seducer are accompanied by the strains of the song, as are Eglinton's overtures of reason. Here also we are struck by the fact that Shakespeare and Bloom are linked by the author in the juxtaposition of Molly's song of lust with Shakespeare's cuckoldry, one reference directly linked by order of appearance with the other. Heretofore Stephen has provided the link between his situation and *Hamlet,* but its analogy to Bloom's situation with Molly is first made here.

He carried a memory in his wallet as he trudged to Romeville whistling *The girl I left behind me.* (190:42-191:1)

Cf. "The Rogue's Delight in Praise of His Stroling Mort"
   "The Girl I Left Behind Me"

REMARKS: Stephen peppers his narrative with Elizabethan allusions to add a tone of scholarly credibility to his farfetched theories. The allusion to Romeville is again a reference to the seventeenth-century canting song, "The Rogue's Delight in Praise of His Stroling Mort." [2] Stephen links this song with Samuel Lover's "The Girl I Left Behind Me," a song of sad parting, as its title implies. Like Stephen's theories, the juxtaposing of the songs represents a *fin de siècle* attitude superimposed on sixteenth-century events. Stephen through his narration provides what Eliot calls the "historical sense" by making events of the past contemporary. Stephen brings this community of time not only to his own existence, as the Skylla and Charybdis argument does, but to the lives of all the characters, *Ulysses* and the city of Dublin. One method of conferring this immediacy upon the past is through Stephen's juxtaposing these songs of past and present. In the present references Stephen is utilizing the allusion pattern he has previously associated with the cocklepickers through the song: seeing the woman as midwife, lover, then whore (*Ulysses,* p. 47).[3] Here Shakespeare's—and consequently Hamlet's—thought patterns regarding Ann Hathaway are projected as parallel, finally concluding with his reluctant parting from an unfaithful wife. In the *Hamlet* situation the parting is due to death, but in Shakespeare's and Bloom's cases merely leaving Stratford or Eccles Street will suffice.

If others have their will Ann hath a way. By cock, she was to blame. She put the comether on him, sweet and twentysix. The greyeyed goddess who bends over the boy Adonis, stooping to conquer, as prologue to the swelling act, is a boldfaced Stratford wench who tumbles in a cornfield a lover younger than herself. (191:13–18)

Cf. Ophelia's song, *Hamlet,* IV, v, 60–62
   Clown's song, *Twelfth Night,* II, iii, 52.

REMARKS: Although the direct allusion may be to *Venus and Adonis,* there are references also to Ophelia's song, the clown's song in *Twelfth Night,* two sonnets, *Macbeth,* and a Goldsmith play. William M. Schutte glosses the allusions:

He begins with a pun, "If others have their will Ann hath a way," a reflection of familiar lines in Sonnets 135 and 143. "By cock, she was to blame" is adapted from one of Ophelia's suggestive songs:

> Young men will do't if they come to't.
> By cock, they are to blame. (IV. v. 60–1)

"Sweet and twenty-six" in the next sentence is adapted from the Clown's well known song in *Twelfth Night* (II. iii. 52). The "greyeyed goddess who bends over the boy" (*Venus,* l. 140) stoops, like Goldsmith's Miss Hardcastle, to conquer, but the "swelling act" to which she stoops is not that which Macbeth had in mind when he said:

> Two truths are told,
> As happy prologues to the swelling act
> Of the imperial theme. (I. iii. 128)

In the final clause of the sentence, Stephen returns to Ophelia's song:

> Quoth she, "Before you tumbled me,
> You promised me to wed." (IV. v. 62–3)

Thus in five lines Stephen has put together three short sentences using references to the sonnets, *Twelfth Night, Venus and Adonis, Macbeth,* and *Hamlet* (two); and for good measure he has tossed in the title of the Goldsmith play.[4]

The point of Stephen's inclusion of the allusion to the older woman-lover is, of course, to rehearse his by now well-established Oedipal complex in the impending comparison of himself and Hamlet. The older-woman syndrome makes it unmistakable that Shakespeare's play is to be regarded in a Freudian light. There is a reversal of sexual roles in several of the allusions: Venus and Adonis, Shakespeare and Hathaway, all of which lead to Bloom's role reversal made explicit later in Circe.

—Ryefield, Mr Best said brightly, gladly, raising his new book, gladly brightly.

He murmured then with blonde delight for all:

> *Between the acres of the rye*
> *These pretty countryfolk would lie.* (191:21–25)

Cf. The Pages' song from *As You Like It*, V, iii, 23–26

REMARKS: Mr. Best's song comes from the second stanza:

> Between the acres of the rye,
>   With a hey, and a ho, and a hey nonino,
> These pretty country folks would lie,
>   In spring time, &c.

Mr. Best climbs on Stephen's allusive bandwagon as he changes Stephen's cornfield to a rye field to correspond to the song in *As You Like It*. However, the significance seems to be only to show Mr. Best's effort to cap Stephen's allusion.

Peter Piper pecked a peck of pick of peck of pickled pepper. (191:34)

Cf. "Peter Piper"

REMARKS: Stephen's exposition is interrupted by talk of a meeting of Dublin's occult-arty crowd. Stephen, who is not invited, satirizes various members of the group with the same mental device that Bloom so often uses: by making them the brunt of nursery rhymes. Thus through the narrative method Joyce further establishes the communality of Stephen and Bloom.

The faithful hermetists await the light, ripe for chelaship, ring-roundabout him. (191:40–41)

Cf. "Ring a-ring o' Roses"

REMARKS: See comments on "Peter Piper" above.

Hesouls, shesouls, shoals of souls. (192:3–4)

Cf. "She sells sea shells by the seashore"

REMARKS: The "Peter Piper" comments also operate for this reference, but in addition the souls of those with whom the hermeticists are communicating might indeed contain not only the drowned man of the Telemachea, but, by extension, Stephen's mother, drowned in a sea-green, snot-green bowl of bile and the whole agenbite of inwit motif.

Cordelia. *Cordoglio.* Lir's loneliest daughter. (192:36)

Cf. "Silent, O Moyle"

REMARKS: The reference is to the third line of Moore's "Silent, O'Moyle":

> While murmuring mournfully, Lir's lonely daughter
> Tells to the night star her tale of woes.

Fionnuala, the daughter of Lir, was, like Cordelia, an exile. She was doomed to wander in the form of a swan over certain lakes and rivers in Ireland until the coming of Christianity and the sound of the first Mass-bell was to signal her release. The reference Stephen makes, however, seems to have little significance beyond the similarity in sound to the *Lear* situation.

Christfox in leather trews, hiding, a runaway in blighted treeforks from hue and cry. Knowing no vixen, walking lonely in the chase. Women he won to him, tender people, a whore of Babylon, ladies of justices, bully tapsters' wives. Fox and geese. And in New Place a slack dishonoured body that once was comely, once as sweet, as fresh as cinnamon, now her leaves falling, all, bare, frighted of the narrow grave and unforgiven. (193:20–26)

Cf. Forty-second Psalm
　"Fair Maid's Beauty Will Soon Fade Away"
　"The Cock Crew"

REMARKS: Schutte glosses the musical references in the passage:

Here Stephen is thinking; he is not performing for the librarians. The picture of Shakespeare, the runaway "walking lonely in the chase," seems to reflect the opening of David's forty-second psalm in the version of Nahum Tate and Nicholas Brady—Irishmen both—which was published late in the seventeenth century:

> As pants the hart for cooling streams
> When heated in the chase. . . .

In thinking of the women Shakespeare won to him, Stephen certainly has in mind Mrs. Davenant of Oxford the bully tapster's wife, whose possible relations with Shakespeare are referred to by Brandes, Lee, and Harris. The "whore of Babylon" may well be a reflection of Harris' comment that "Shakespeare's 'universal sympathy'—to quote Coleridge—did not include the plainly-clad tub-thumper who dared to accuse him to his face of serving the Babylonish Whore."

Most interesting, however, is the reference to the fading away of Ann's comeliness. In describing the process, Stephen echoes the words of an old Irish song which he may well have sung. It is called "Fair Maidens' Beauty Will Soon Fade Away." The first two stanzas describe the singer's beloved, how fair she is; he and she are "the happiest pair in the north counterie." In the last stanza there is a change in mood:

> My love is as sweet as the cinnamon tree;
> She clings to me as close as the bark to the tree:
> But the leaves they will wither and the roots will decay,
> And fair maidens' beauty will soon fade away.

To this song Stephen naturally turns for words to describe the inevitable change in the Ann Hathaway who "put the comether on" her Will (189). She was "once as sweet, as fresh as cinnamon"; but "now her leaves [are] falling, all, bare." [5]

Stephen in this passage is under no constraint to impress the library crowd with his virtuoso performance is Shakespeare, because it is in his own thought. Thus he is able to fall back upon a song reference from his own mundane Irish folklore background as allusive material with which to interpret his own thoughts. What Schutte does not seem to realize is the real significance of the passage, which lies in Stephen's conjunction between himself and his riddle of the fox and the hollybush, a major metaphor for his Oedipal complex and his guilt. Here is the vital link between that subliminal body of allusion and the Hamlet-Oedipal theme. When Stephen is asked if he thinks Ann was not "faithful to the poet," the basis for his own "affair" with his mother is posited. Stephen's reply is that there must be a breakup before the reconciliation. The mention of the poet includes his idea of himself as both the creator, Shakespeare, as well as his creations, Hamlet senior and junior, who are both manifestations of the poet himself. So Stephen has been cuckolded by his own mother in the Oedipal theme both with himself and with his father. As we have seen in *Portrait,* Stephen's life, like Shakespeare's, is his work of art transubstantiated. Thus, by showing how Shakespeare recreates life (art) out of life (the events of his own history), Skylla and Charybdis provides the aesthetic rationale for my explanation of the narrative structure of *Portrait* as well as *Ulysses.*

Stephen in the passage under consideration is first Christfox, a dual image of the martyred figure including the Parnell-lover figure and the Oedipally stricken fox burying the sensuality of his mother under the hollybush. Hench the Freudian treeforks are blighted and he is metaphorically castrated, "Knowing no vixen." As Christ, Parnell, and the fox, Stephen has won women but the specter of his mother haunts him and un-mans him, limiting his sensual and artistic fertility. Thus he spells out again his need for a reconciliation with the father figure, who will work on a literal level to connect Stephen with the human race from whom he has severed himself and on a figurative level to provide the basis for Stephen's artistry and his mission to the heathen, unconscienced Irish. The Circe episode will combine the Christfox image, which will be identified directly with Stephen, and the image of Bloom as hero and lady-killer. The above passage combines both these references in a foreshadowing of the ultimate consubstantiation of Stephen and Bloom in the later episode.

> *How many miles to Dublin?*
> *Three score and ten, sir.*
> *Will we be there by candlelight?* (195:25-27)

Cf. "How Many Miles to Babylon?"

REMARKS: To meet the rising objections of Eglinton, Stephen again resorts in his stream of consciousness to a nursery rhyme. The rhyme Stephen quotes from has only one stanza:

> How many miles to Babylon?
> Three score miles and ten.
> Can I get there by candle-light?
> Yes and back again.
> If your heels are nimble and light,
> You may get there by candle-light.[6]

The reference again provides an opportunity for Stephen to rationalize away in sarcasm objections to his theory, which he knows is weak. If he can proceed along the theory on the nimble and light heels of allusion, he may yet get through relatively unscathed by his critics.

> . . . he will never be a victor in his own eyes after nor play victoriously the game of laugh and lie down. (196:28-29)

Cf. "The Art of Loving"

REMARKS: The allusion is to an Elizabethan song of potential cuckoldry and the unfaithfulness of woman:

> She'l smile, and she'l frown
> She'l laugh and lie down,
> At every turn you must tend her.[7]

> Assumed dongiovannism will not save him. (196:29-30)

Cf. *Don Giovanni*

REMARKS: Here Stephen broadens the Hamlet-Oedipus-Shakespeare cuckoldry motif, all this emanating from his stream-of-consciousness patterns, to include one of the major themes of the Molly-Blazes relationship and the thematic motif which runs through so much of Bloom's mind during the day, the operatic theme of *Don Giovanni*. Vernon Hall sees the parallel:

> Stephen contends that Shakespeare was seduced by an older woman and then made a cuckold. This is the key to Shakespeare's character. . . . This comment of Stephen's throws light on poor Leopold's love affairs. Shakespeare the cuckold; Bloom the cuckold. Assumed dongiovannism. A key, not to Shakespeare, but to the actions of our modern Ulysses.[8]

The expanded Stephen-Hamlet-Shakespeare-Bloom-father-son-cuckoldry motif will be unmistakably drawn together in the Circe chapter when in the only instance of its kind Bloom and Stephen share an hallucination (pp. 567–68). Bloom has just had an hallucination in which he witnessed Molly and Blazes in the act of copulating. He and Stephen both look in the mirror and see the reflection of Shakespeare framed under the horns of the cuckold, thus completing the pattern.

Every day we must do homage to her. *Life of life, thy lips enkindle.* (201:6–7)

Cf. "Life of Life! thy lips enkindle"

REMARKS: Shelley's line exactly describes the inveterate statue gazer, Leopold Bloom:

> Life of life! thy lips enkindle
>   With their love the breath between them;
> And thy smiles before they dwindle
>   Make the cold air fire; then screen them
> In those looks, where whoso gazes
> Faints, entangled in their mazes.

Bloom, who ducked into the library to avoid Blazes, emerges as fainting to Mulligan because of Bloom's being carried away by the beauty of the goddesses and their lips which surround more than one orifice in which he displays interest. The song continues with the double entendres of Bloom and his quest becoming funnier as the stanzas progress:

> Child of Light! thy limbs are burning
>   Through the vest which seems to hide them;
> As the radiant lines of morning
>   Through the clouds ere they divide them;
> And this atmosphere divinest
> Shrouds thee wheresoe'er thou shinest.
>
> Fair are others; none beholds thee,
>   But thy voice sounds low and tender
> Like the fairest, for it folds thee
>   From the sight, that liquid splendour,
> And all feel, yet see thee never,
> As I feel now, lost for ever!
>
> Lamp of Earth! where'er thou movest
>   Its dim shapes are clad with brightness,
> And the souls of whom thou lovest
> Walk upon the winds with lightness,

Till they fail, as I am failing,
Dizzy, lost, yet unbewailing! [9]

The reference is one of Mulligan's funniest.

—Pretty countryfolk had few chattels then, John Eglinton observed . . . (203:32–33).

Cf. The page's song from *As You Like It,* V, iii, 17–34

REMARKS: As Stephen shifts his defence to Shakespeare's will, Eglinton presses him further, belying Stephen's betrayal version of the Shakespeare-Hathaway love by using another reference to Mr. Best's allusion from the song of idyllic love and the spring.

Acushla machree! It's destroyed we are from this day! (205: 27–28)

Cf. *"Acushla Machree"*

REMARKS: Mulligan's execration at Stephen's mention of Aquinas includes a brief keening, a rune, and a reference to *"Acushla Machree,"* another Ireland surrogate. The rivalry motif comes into play here as Mulligan uses his wit to undermine Stephen's theories and art.

Shy, deny thy kindred, the unco guid. (206:36)

Cf. "The *Unco' Guid"*

REMARKS: Under attack from all sides, Stephen hears Eglinton's argument that Falstaff fails to fit into Shakespeare's allegedly autobiographical scheme and indulges himself in a little spiteful invective. The reference is to a Burns song, "The *Unco' Guid"* (The rigidly righteous). The first quatrain indicates the poet's spleen as he charges the *unco' guid:*

O ye wha are sae guid yoursel,
Sae pious and sae holy,
Ye've nought to do but mark and tell
Your neebour's fauts and folly!

Stephen through the song reference mentally expresses some of his own indignation at the righteous-sounding Eglinton.

(*Piano, diminuendo.*)

*Then outspoke medical Dick
To his comrade medical Davy* . . . (209:17–19)

Cf. "Medical Dick and Medical Davy"

REMARKS: The song is used here by Mulligan to reiterate the bawdy tone of the cuckoldry motif which is central to Stephen's argument and the chapter.

> In *Cymbeline*, in *Othello* he is bawd and cuckold. He acts and is acted on. Lover of an ideal or a perversion, like José he kills the real Carmen. (212:31–33)

Cf. *Carmen*

REMARKS: His argument coming to a conclusion, Stephen now summarizes his position by seeing Shakespeare in all his characters. The reference to *Carmen* is of course to José's passion for a Carmen who never would be faithful and to whose desertion with the bullfighter, Escamillo, José reacts by stabbing her. The allusion is another classic case of betrayal and infidelity to bolster Stephen's analogy to Shakespeare and also the parallel to the Shakespeare-father-cuckold, Leopold Bloom, consubstantial father, son, lover, cuckold, creator, HCE.

> If you like the epilogue look long on it: prosperous Prospero, the good man rewarded, Lizzie, grandpa's lump of love, and nuncle Richie, the bad man taken off by poetic justice to the place where the bad niggers go. (213:9–13)

Cf. "Old Uncle Ned"

REMARKS: The allusion to Foster's song refers to the lines,

> Dere's no more hard work for poor old Ned.
> He's gone where de good niggers go.[10]

The phrase "Grandpa's lump of love," is a paraphrase of Simon Dedalus's "Crissie, papa's little lump of dung." (88:18–19) The words "nuncle Richie" had also been used before to describe Crissie's father, Stephen's maternal uncle, Richie Goulding. So Shakespeare's Lizzie (presumably Elizabeth of Henry VIII), nuncle of Lear, and Richard III are all part not only of the playwright's life, but also Stephen's. By connecting his father with Hamlet senior and Richie Goulding with Claudius, Stephen in his summary projects himself into the Hamlet junior role, this time with his own family as the antecedents for the metaphoric action, to complete this round robin of association in which everybody lives everyone else's lives and metaphors in history and literature. To associate them both with Foster's Uncle Ned puts a universality upon the image that is all transcendent, setting up Stephen's clearest statement of the communality motive in Joyce's work:

We walk through ourselves, meeting robbers, ghosts, giants, old men, young men, wives, widows, brothers-in-love. But always meeting our-selves. (213: 18–20)

Puck Mulligan, panamahelmeted, went step by step, iambing, trolling:

John Eglinton, my jo, John.
Why won't you wed a wife?

He sputtered to the air:
—O, the chinless Chinaman! Chin Chon Eg Lin Ton. (215: 26–31)

Cf. "John Anderson, My Jo"
  "Chin Chin Chinaman"

REMARKS: At the conclusion of Stephen's dissertation, Mulligan pulls him out of the library and toward a pub, chanting as the concluding musical references in the chapter two snide parodies of well-known songs in derision of Eglinton. Both references cast aspersions on Eglinton's manhood. The first is, of course, from Burns's "John Anderson, My Jo" and the second, "Chin Chin Chinaman," from a light opera called *The Geisha*. The references seem to have no deeper significance than providing a means of derisive commen-tary for Mulligan.

10. Wandering Rocks

The Malahide road was quiet. It pleased Father Conmee, road and name. The joybells were ringing in gay Malahide. Lord Talbot de Malahide, immediate hereditary lord admiral of Mala-hide and the seas adjoining. Then came the call to arms and she was maid, wife and widow in one day. Those were old-worldish days, loyal times in joyous townlands, old times in the barony. (223:15–21)

Cf. "The Bridal of Malahide"

REMARKS: The first stanza of the song reflects the gay attitude of the day and a wedding which is to take place:

The joy-bells are ringing
  In gay Malahide,
The fresh wind is singing
  Along the sea-side:
The maids are assembling

> With garlands of flowers,
> And the harpstrings are trembling
> In all the glad bowers.

Father Conmee goes on to describe the rest of the song: the summons of the groom to arms at the end of the ceremony and the bride's widowhood on her marriage day. The song leads Father Conmee to speculate on the histories of the various families who once occupied what are now Jesuit houses, on tyrannical acts and betrayals, and on himself as priest officiating at an historic, noble wedding ceremony. Here the song reference originally appears in Conmee's mind as a reflection of his pleasant frame of mind, but soon becomes the vehicle of association to the past and his own priestly fancies.

> . . . he growled unamiably
> —*For England* . . . (225:19–20)
> . . . halted and growled:
> —*home and beauty.* (225:22–23)
> He halted and growled angrily:
> —*For England* . . . (225:30–31)
> . . . bayed deeply:
> —*home and beauty.* (225:36–37)

Cf. "The Death of Nelson"

REMARKS: The onelegged sailor of the episode orchestrates his begging with the strains of the refrain of this very popular patriotic ballad. The sailor evidently wishes to imply that he, like Nelson, has given his all or at least one appendage for England, a patriotic theme that would not stir the patriotism of the average Dubliner. Neither does the narrator's description of the sailor's tone of voice suggest a humble, contrite soul which had asked like Nelson in the song little more than to sacrifice for his country. Part of the last stanza, in which the sailor's lines are included, is as follows:

> "Now long enough I've lived!
> In honor's cause my life is pass'd,
> In honor's cause I fall at last,
> For England, home and beauty,
> For England, home, and beauty."

The conjunction between the sailor's loss of a limb and Nelson's supreme sacrifice for his country, while it hasn't done much to improve the sailor's disposition, certainly nets him a coin from Molly's "plump bare generous arm."

The lines from the song are the thing for old salts, both wounded and whole, to quote, since later we hear the sailor in the cabman's shelter call forth the same words in describing the sacrifice he and his wife have been making during his seven years' absence on the high seas. Thus the song acts here, later in the episode, and in Eumaeus as a leitmotif refrain.[1]

> —There he is, Lenehan said.
> —Wonder what he is buying, M'Coy said, glancing behind.
> —*Leopoldo or the Bloom is on the Rye,* Lenehan said. (233: 29-31)

Cf. "When the Bloom Is on the Rye"

REMARKS: In sarcastically suggesting the title of the book Bloom is buying, Lenehan suggests the title of Bloom's leitmotif song for the next chapter, Sirens. June 16th is just about the time of the year when "the bloom is on the rye." The song is indeed an appropriate appositive for the hero of the Bloomsday Odyssey and a fitting leitmotif for the upcoming musical extravaganza in Sirens.

> We started singing glees and duets: *Lo, the early beam of morning.* (234:27-28)

Cf. "Lo, the Early Beam of Morning"

REMARKS: The song, which Lenehan, Molly, and the jaunting-car crowd were singing as he was made the beneficiary of her considerable pulchritudinous charms while Poldy sat on the other side of the car all unaware, deals appropriately with duplicity. Thornton glosses the allusion:

"Lo, the early beam of morning" is a quartet which occurs just before the finale of act I of Edward Fitzball and Michael William Balfe's opera *The Siege of Rochelle* (1835). It begins, "Lo! the early beam of morning softly chides our longer stay; hark! the matin bells are chiming, Daughter, we must hence away." The quartet is sung by Father Azino, Clara, the servant Michel, and his wife Marcella, and it expresses Clara's need to flee from Rochelle if she is to remain safe and undetected.[2]

> They rose in dark and evil days. Fine poem that is: Ingram. They were gentlemen. Ben Dollard does sing that ballad touchingly. Masterly rendition.
>
> *At the siege of Ross did my father fall.* (241:12-16)

Cf. "The Memory of the Dead"
  "The Croppy Boy"

REMARKS: Kernan has his ballads slightly mixed up. He begins by quoting a line from stanza four of "The Memory of the Dead":

> They rose in dark and evil days
> To right their native land;
> They kindled here a living blaze
> That nothing shall withstand.
> Alas! that might can vanquish right—
> They fell and passed away;
> But true men, like you, men,
> Are plenty here today.

It is appropriate that Kernan be the first to allude to that patriotic drinking ballad which is to be mentioned so prominently in Sirens, since Kernan's problem since "Grace" has long been alcohol. While Ben Dollard undoubtedly has sung the song many times, Kernan's reference to a touching rendition is hardly appropriate for a lusty song of drink and war, and Kernan follows his comments on Dollard's rendition by quoting from stanza five of "The Croppy Boy," a major musical reference in the Sirens chapter, and a song that Dollard does sing so touchingly as to bring barmaids nearly to tears. Though Kernan is mistaken, the error works structurally, as do the references to the blind stripling, to Bloom's leitmotif, and all the Blazes and Molly references in the chapter, to anticipate the all-important action in Sirens. This action is foreshadowed not only in the narrative sense, as Boylan's buying fruit in anticipation of the liaison, but also in a stylistic sense in anticipating the performance of music as one of the major narrative devices, as well as the crucial pattern of musical references which comprise the body of Sirens. As the ringing of the hoofs of the viceregal's carriage horses dissolves into the jingle of Blazes' jaunting cart bells in Sirens, so do these references fore-shadow the great wealth of sound leitmotifs so central to Sirens.

The onelegged sailor growled at the area of 14 Nelson street:
—*England expects* . . . (248:37–38)

Cf. "The Death of Nelson"

REMARKS: By the time the beggar has reached Nelson street he is growling out another part of his song, this rendition a segment of the refrain for the first two stanzas. The words in the song are the famous quotation of Nelson at Trafalgar:

> "England expects that every man
> This day will do his duty."

Here the sailor's song acts as one of the numerous leitmotifs giving the im-pression of the simultaneity of action or everything taking place at once in the episode. By utilizing a theme or literally musical motif from the be-ginning of the episode at this point toward the end of the chapter, the nar-rative pattern suggests a compression of events into one immediate whole. This happens with other recurring scenes and events, but here it is used in its Wagnerian purity to suggest through structure the universality of events and themes in a given work. Translating them into music, no matter how degraded the parody, raises them from a literal level and places them in the allusionary context of an art form that exists in time and therefore suggests more forcefully the simultaneity of action, a time relationship. Also the recurrent leitmotif of a musical form foreshadows the predominant device of Sirens, just as the viceregal's carriage linking the chorus of characters at the end of Wandering Rocks carries over the structural aspects of the community of the characters during the episode.

By the provost's wall came jauntily Blazes Boylan, stepping in tan shoes and socks with skyblue clocks to the refrain of *My girl's a Yorkshire girl.*

Blazes Boylan presented to the leaders' skyblue frontlets and high action a skyblue tie, a widebrimmed straw hat at a rakish angle and a suit of indigo serge. His hands in his jacket pockets forgot to salute but he offered to the three ladies the bold admiration of his eyes and the red flower between his lips. As they drove along Nassau street His Excellency drew the attention of his bowing consort to the programme of music which was being discoursed in College park. Unseen brazen highland laddies blared and drumthumped after the *cortège:*

> *But though she's a factory lass*
> *And wears no fancy clothes.*
> *Baraabum.*
> *Yet I've a sort of a*
> *Yorkshire relish for*
> *My little Yorkshire rose.*
> *Baraabum.* (253:41–254:18)

Cf. "My Girl's a Yorkshire Girl"

REMARKS: The associations of the song and its juxtaposition with Blazes Boylan here suggest another major musical allusion pattern on the theme of the Blazes-Molly assignation. It is worth quoting the song in full to appreciate all of its ties to the situation in *Ulysses:*

> Two young fellows were talking about
> Their girls, girls, girls
> Sweethearts they left behind
> Sweethearts for whom they pined
> One said, "My little shy little lass
> Has a waist so trim and small

Grey are her eyes so bright,
But best of all

Chorus:
My girl's a Yorkshire girl,
Yorkshire through and through
My girl's a Yorkshire girl,
Eh! by gum she's a champion!
Though she's a factory lass,
And wears no fancy clothes,
I've a sort of Yorkshire Relish
For my little Yorkshire Rose." . . .

When the first finished singing in praise
Of Rose, Rose, Rose,
Poor Number Two looked vexed,
Saying in tones perplexed,
"*My* lass works in a factory too,
And *also* has eyes of grey
Her name is Rose as well,
And strange, strange to say"

To a cottage, in Yorkshire they hied
To Rose, Rose, Rose
Meaning to make it clear
Which was the boy most dear
Rose, their Rose didn't answer the bell,
But her husband did instead
Loudly he sang to them
As off, off they fled.

The parallels with Molly's situation are obvious, though her retinue of lovers is not limited to two. As Blazes prepares to hie himself to her house, there will be no husband there to run off the ardent lover, at least no husband in person. But we learn later that Poldy may indeed have been there in spirit, as indeed he is in Sirens. The "unconquered hero" of Sirens may very well rout the suitors as his namesake did, but not so much through force, like Homer's Odysseus, but with his equanimity. I think that this song is one of the very first indications that a battle indeed is taking place, that its climax will come in Sirens, and that Bloom will emerge as the ultimate recipient of Molly's "Yes." For it is to her husband that our Penelope turns again and again in her soliloquy; and as Bloom sails off to sleep with Sinbad the Sailor, etc., it is he who, through his all-conquering humanity and equanimity, has emerged the victor. And as the subtitle of "My Girl's a Yorkshire Girl" indicates about the woman-lover-sex symbol, "Eh! By Gum, She's a Champion!" Blazes may be on his way to possess the field at four o'clock, which is what the Sirens is about, but if he tills it, his seed never reaches the spot where fertility reigns. By dint of perseverance and presence, as in the Yorkshire Girl song, the ultimate battle will be won by the one most able to survive and meet life on its own terms—Leopold Bloom.

11. Sirens

Since all song references in the overture occur in the body of the episode, they will be listed merely by title following the appropriate quotation from the overture, and remarks will be deferred until the songs appear later in the chapter.[1]

Blue bloom is on the . . . (256:6)

Cf. "When the Bloom Is on the Rye"

. . . rose of Castille. (256:8)

Cf. *The Rose of Castille*

Trilling, trilling: Idolores. (256:9)

Cf. "The Shade of the Palm"

The bright stars fade. (256:13)

Cf. "Goodbye, Sweetheart, Goodbye"

O rose! . . . Castille. (256:13–14)

Cf. *The Rose of Castille*

The morn is breaking. (256:14)

Cf. "Goodbye, Sweetheart, Goodbye"

I could. . . . Not leave thee. . . . Sweetheart, goodbye! (256:17, 18–19)

Cf. "Goodbye, Sweetheart, Goodbye"

When love absorbs. War! War! (256:21)

Cf. "Love and War"

Lost. . . . All is lost now. (256:24)

Cf. *"Tutto è sciolto"*

When first he saw. Alas! (256:26)

Cf. *"M'appari"*

Martha! Come! (256:29)

Cf. *"M'appari"*

So lonely blooming. (256:34)

Cf. "'Tis the Last Rose of Summer"

Liszt's rhapsodies. (256:38)

Cf. Liszt's Hungarian Rhapsodies

Naminedamine. All gone. All fallen. (257:4)
Amen! He gnashed in fury. (257:6)
Pray for him! Pray, good people! (257:12)

Cf. "The Croppy Boy"

Last rose Castille of summer left bloom . . . alone. (257:15)

Cf. *The Rose of Castille*
   "'Tis the Last Rose of Summer"

True men. . . . Like you men. Will lift your tschink with tschunk. (257:17–18)

Cf. "The Memory of the Dead"

End of the Overture

I looked so simple in the cradle they christened me simple Simon. (261:19–20)

Cf. "Simple Simon"

REMARKS: There seems little more to Dedalus's remarks than what appears on the surface: that he is the most simple of males and that therefore he is tempted by Miss Douce.

Gaily Miss Douce polished a tumbler, trilling:
—*O, Idolores, queen of the eastern seas!* (261:38–39)

Cf. "The Shade of the Palm"

REMARKS: This song from *Floradora* recurs throughout the chapter and is, in a sense, both Blooom's and Boylan's song. The words of the song, part of which Miss Douce misquotes, are especially significant when taken in their entirety:

Stanza 1:
There is a garden fair
Set in an Eastern sea,
There is a maid keeping her tryst with me
In the shade of the palm,
With a lover's delight,
Where 'tis ever the golden day,
Or a silvery night;
How can I leave her alone in this dream of sweet Arcadia—
How can I part from her for lands away?
In this valley of Eden,
Fairest isle of the sea,
Oh, my beloved, bid me to stay
In this fair land of Eden,
Bid me beloved to stay.

Stanza 2:
There is an island fair,
Girt by a Western sea;
Dearest, 'tis there
One day thou'lt go with me.
'Neath the glorious moon
Hand in hand we will roam,
Hear the nightingale song of June,
In the dear Land of Home!
There, dearest heart, will the past but seem an idle vision
Nought but a dream that fadeth fast away,
And the songs we were singing, in Elysian vales
Seem but a carol of yesterday.
Happy songs we were singing,
Songs of a bygone day.

Chorus:
Oh Idolores Queen of the Eastern seas!
Fair one of Eden, look to the West for me!
My star will be shining, love, when you're in the moonlight calm,
So be waiting for me by the Eastern sea in the shade of the shelt'ring
    palm . . .

Molly is, of course, Idolores of the eastern sea. She has, through Bloom's many references to her eastern features and complexion, and her Moorish background, become synonymous with the East. The first stanza belongs to Boylan with its assurances of a tryst, as he wanders while his Dolores waits in the shade of the jingling bedstead.

Stanza two, especially in the latter part, is more applicable to Bloom with its echoes of former days of love and happier times. The "idle vision" of former love which sustains Bloom so much through his present trial "seems but a carol of yesterday," and the "happy songs. . . , songs of a bygone day." This note of pathos on which the song closes is a dominant one in the chapter. The musical reference here is, in some measure, purposefully ambiguous and is intended to convey a mood rather than a plot synopsis with exact correlations to the characters and situation. The song, which occurs repeatedly throughout the chapter, represents its first musical variation on the issue of Molly's promiscuity and gives us the first and most important of all the Sirensongs sung in the Ormond during the episode.

Mr Bloom reached Essex bridge. Yes, Mr Bloom crossed bridge of Yessex. To Martha I must write. Buy paper. Daly's. Girl there civil. Bloom. Old Bloom. Blue Bloom is on the rye. (261:41–262:2)

Cf. "When the Bloom Is on the Rye"

REMARKS: Ironically this song speaks also of a coming meeting, though the one in the song seems entirely honorable since it contains also a proposal of marriage.

> My pretty Jane, my pretty Jane!
> Ah! never, never look so shy,
> But meet me, meet me in the ev'ning,
> When the bloom is on the rye.
>
> The Spring is waning fast, my love,
> The corn is in the ear,
> The summer nights are coming, love,
> The moon shines bright and clear;
> Then pretty Jane, my dearest Jane,
> Ah! never look so shy,
> But meet me, meet me in the ev'ning,
> When the bloom is on the rye.
>
> But name the day, the wedding day,
> And I will buy the ring,
> The lads and maids in favors white,
> And village bells shall ring.

> The Spring is waning fast, my love,
> Etc.

While the song contains a reference to a proposed rendezvous and is appropriate to Bloom's thoughts of writing to Martha Clifford, its primary function is to act as a theme or leitmotif to introduce the presence of Bloom throughout the chapter. (Lenehan has already introduced the song as Bloom's leitmotif in Wandering Rocks.)

. . . that minstrel boy of the wild wet west who is known by the euphonious appellation of the O'Madden Burke. (263:3–4)

Cf. "The Minstrel Boy"
   "The Men of the West"

REMARKS: Lenehan in his role of professional jester and entertainer for drinks builds all his descriptions with oratorical flourishes. So O'Madden Burke becomes a combination first of Thomas Moore's "Minstrel Boy," the heroic child who sets off to war with "his father's sword . . . girded on,/ And his wild harp slung behind him," only to be found "in the ranks of death"; and second of the gallant "Men of the West," celebrated in the following lyrics:

> I give you the gallant old West, boys
> Where rallied our bravest and best:
> When Ireland lay broken and bleeding;
> Hurrah for the men of the West!

This is the first of several instances during Sirens where Lenehan puts music to allusive use to aggrandize or give stature to various characters and events. Later in Cyclops this will be a device of the third-person narrator in the giganticising passages. In Sirens the musical buildups are provided by Lenehan to enhance his introductions of names and characters.

—*The bright stars fade . . .*
A voiceless song sang from within, singing:
— *. . . the morn is breaking.*
A duodene of birdnotes chirruped bright treble answer under sensitive hands. Brightly the keys, all twinkling, linked, all harpsichording, called to a voice to sing the strain of dewy morn, of youth, of love's leavetaking, life's, love's morn.
—*The dewdrops pearl . . .* (264:19–26)
—*And I from thee . . .* (265:3)
—*. . . to Flora's lips did hie.* (266:17)

—*I could not leave thee . . .* (266:23)
—*. . . Sweetheart, goodbye!*
—I'm off, said Boylan with impatience. (267:8–9)

Cf. "Goodbye, Sweetheart, Goodbye" [2]

REMARKS: As Boylan approaches the bar the opening strains of "Goodbye, Sweetheart, Goodbye" are heard. His stay in the Ormond will end with the conclusion of this song, which is being played, presumably by Simon Dedalus, during the entirety of Boylan's brief visit to the bar. Joyce indicates the significance of the song by quoting the lyrics to both stanzas, although the lyrics themselves are not being sung since the music is merely being played on the piano. The complete words to the song are as follows:

> The bright stars fade, the morn is breaking,
> The dewdrops pearl each bud and leaf,
> And I from thee my leave am taking,
> With bliss too brief, with bliss, with bliss too brief.
> How sinks my heart with fond alarms,
> The tear is hiding in mine eye,
> For time doth tear me from thine arms,
> Goodbye, sweetheart, goodbye,
> Goodbye, sweetheart, goodbye,
> For time doth tear me from thine arms,
> Goodbye, sweetheart, goodbye.
>
> The sun is up, the lark is soaring,
> Loud swells the song of chanticleer,
> The lev'ret bounds o'er earth's soft flow'ring,
> Yet I am here, yet I, yet I am here.
> For since night's gems from heav'n do fade,
> And morn to floral lips doth hie,
> I could not leave thee though I said
> Goodbye, sweetheart, goodbye,
> Goodbye, sweetheart, goodbye,
> I could not leave thee though I said
> Goodbye, sweetheart, goodbye.

When the phrase *"to Flora's lips did hie"* appears in the text, we cannot assume that the disparity between it and the correct phrase in stanza two, "to floral lips doth hie," is due to Bloom's incorrect memory or his tendency to misquote. The lyrics are printed in italics and do not come to us through Bloom's thoughts. Further, the lyrics are not being sung here; Joyce is representing the notes with the lyrics that accompany them and the incorrect quotation is therefore the narrator's. This gives rise to some speculation about how many other times this has happened, only to be attributed to Bloom's poor memory. The mistake does call to our attention the assignation of Molly and Blazes, *floral* having to do with *flower* and hence Bloom (Bloom is referred to as Don Poldo de la Flora in Molly's soliloquy), as Blazes hies to Molly's lips. The song is reversed in a nice Joycean irony as the persona takes leave of a lover. It is the morn which enters to floral lips. But in this crisscrossed theme jumble, Blazes takes leave of the other lovers, not his, and flies to the lips of Mrs. Henry Flower-Leopold Bloom.

Though Bloom is present in the dining room for part of the song and has undoubtedly heard some of the rest from the street in front of the hotel, "Goodbye, Sweetheart, Goodbye" starts with Boylan's entrance and concludes with his exit. There is, however, more significance to the song than a mere leitmotif for Boylan, such as "When the Bloom Is on the Rye" is for Bloom. "Goodbye, Sweetheart, Goodbye" presents the typically Joycean comic irony of the friendly natives in the Ormond bidding goodbye to assignation-bound Boylan as the latter goes off for an afternoon of cuckoldry. Boylan seems to have been waiting impatiently for the end of the song to begin his amorous adventure, for at its conclusion he immediately starts to leave.

> —But look this way, he said, rose of Castille. . . .
> She rose and closed her reading, rose of Castille. (264:28, 30)

Cf. *The Rose of Castille*

REMARKS: While "Goodbye, Sweetheart, Goodbye" is the predominant theme for the Boylan segment, several melodies play a contrapuntal background. J. P. Smith makes an especially good case for the parallels between the opera and the Bloom marital situation:

> The opera is set in Spain, recalling Molly's days in Gibraltar; . . .
>
> Still more interesting are some of the parallels between Molly and Elvira, Bloom and Manuel and Don Florio. During the first act of the opera, the two lovers, disguised as a peasant girl and a muleteer, sing their duet, which emphasizes Elvira's domination and Manuel's subservience. A similar relationship is dramatized in the Circe episode during which Bloom imagines himself subjected to all sorts of foul treatment at the hands of Bella and dominated by Molly. This characteristic relationship is the foundation of the opera's plot: Elvira is a Queen fully able to manage her own affairs and to control the scheming men who surround her. In a very real sense, it is she who decides to marry Manuel, much as Molly decided to marry Bloom ("got him to propose to me"). . . .
>
> In still other ways, Molly is recalled by the opera. At the point in the last act when Elvira finally accepts Manuel as her husband, she begins an aria suitable for Molly at the end of *Ulysses:*

> > Oh joyous, happy day!
> > Since Hymen consecrates
> > The comedy we play,
> > Uniting our blest fates.

Molly is scarcely joyous over the state of her relationship with Bloom, but both women accept life as comedy.

Although none of the three conspirators in the opera is very dangerous, clearly Don Florio is the most fumbling of all, and in several aspects more than a little resembles Leopold Bloom. In the second act, assigned the job of guarding the supposed-peasant girl, who is to impersonate the Queen, Don Florio is eluded by the clever Elvira. When Florio makes his entrance he wonders what his fate will be, "the tortures of the Inquisition or the pleasures of decapitation?" Later, there is a buffo duet between Don Pedro, another conspirator, and Don Florio, in which the latter is described as an ass. Here Florio is trying to keep the other conspirators from learning that he has allowed the girl to escape. Later, as Florio approaches, the Queen's confidante, Carmen, describes him in this way:

> Don Florio, one of our greatest foes, but not one to be much dreaded; were he a type of the conspiracy, I think I could answer for its suppression myself.

This passage and all those in which Florio appears as conspirator are paralleled in the Circe episode when Bloom imagines himself in numerous potentially dangerous, but ineffectual positions. And like the Bloom of the Circe episode, Florio sings of the future and success even as his plans are collapsing around him. The entire conspiracy eventually falls apart, but not before Don Florio is trapped into marriage by Carmen as he fumblingly attempts to learn from her the identity of the peasant Rose of Castille.

All of these operatic allusions work, like the more fully explicated *Don Giovanni* references, to reinforce the possibility of a happy continuance of the Bloom marriage.[3]

The point of the passage from Sirens is that Miss Douce in assuming the role of temptress becomes a Molly-surrogate once again. She has already been identified with Molly through "The Shade of the Palm" and now the identification is reenforced through Balfe's opera. Also, as we have seen,[4] the opera is linked thematically with Joyce's structural theme that everyone is living everyone else's life. So the opera and the cross-identification of Molly with Miss Douce is a wedding of the two themes, as the motifs become more and more intertwined in the novel.

—See the conquering hero comes. (264:39)

Cf. "See the Conquering Hero Comes"

REMARKS: The reference is to the stately chorus in Handel's *Judas Maccabeus*. The music furnishes a properly majestic tone for conqueror Boylan to make his entrance:

Sports prepare, the laurels bring.
Songs of triumph to him sing,
See, the conqu'ring hero comes,
Sound the trumpets, beat the drums.

See the godlike youth advance,
Breathe the flute and lead the dance;
Myrtle wreaths and roses twine
To deck the hero's brow divine.
See, the conqu'ring hero comes,
Sound the trumpets, beat the drums.

Once again Lenehan uses hyperbole in his role as court jester and all 'round drink cager. Even if Boylan is the conquering hero we are told that Bloom is not the vanquished: "Between the car and window, warily walking, went Bloom, unconquered hero" (264:40–41). Though Bloom may be cuckolded in the afternoon, he still is not conquered in a far larger sense. Bloom accepts the world, accepts life, and doesn't try to change it. While Boylan's theme music here is triumphant and pompous, Bloom's ("When the Bloom Is on the Rye"), in contrast, is sentimental and quiet.

> Lenehan still drank and grinned at his tilted ale and at Miss Douce's lips that all but hummed, not shut, the oceansong her lips had trilled. Idolores. The eastern seas. . . . Fair one of Egypt teased and sorted in the till and hummed and handed coins in change. Look to the west. A clack. For me. (265:37–39, 266:2–4)

Cf. "The Shade of the Palm"

REMARKS: Miss Douce's musical admonishment of Boylan to "Look to the west . . . for me" is from the chorus of "The Shade of the Palm." [5] Hodgart and Worthington do not cite "The Shade of the Palm" as the musical source for the passage, but an Irish patriotic song, "The Men of the West." [6] They probably had in mind the similarity of the passage "Look to the west" and a line from stanza one of the war song, "And looked for revenge to the west." Clearly Miss Douce, who is in the process of using all of her seductive charms on Boylan, does not. Secondly, this interpretation of the passage does not take into consideration the words, "For me," as the "Shade of the Palm" reference does. There is an interesting paradox here as Molly has always been identified with the East as in stanza one of the song. The shift from East to West takes Molly away from Gibraltar and the Near East and places her in Ireland, and, metaphorically, nearer death, as the similarity of places accompanies the communality of people.

The bag of Goulding, Collis, Ward led Bloom by ryebloom flowered tables. (266:10–11)

Cf. "When the Bloom Is on the Rye"

REMARKS: The last countertheme in the "Goodbye, Sweetheart, Goodbye" section is Bloom's leitmotif as he and Goulding find a table in the dining room. The association of "rye" and "Bloom" is of course an ingenious, though easily recognizable, variation of the song, used, in the tradition of Wagner, to herald the entrance on the scene of the protagonist.

—Love and war, Ben, Mr Dedalus said. (268:4)

Cf. "Love and War"

REMARKS: Dedalus asks Dollard to sing the popular song, which is really not a solo but a duet.

He wandered back to the bar to the lost chord pipe. (268:28)

Cf. "The Lost Chord"

REMARKS: Simon's pipe is compared to a fife ("He blew through the flue two husky fifenotes" [261:31]) and the note production is fairly close to that of a pipe organ; hence the allusion to the song, which begins, "Seated one day at the organ/I was weary and ill at ease. . . ." Thus the pipe has graduated in size to an organ.

—She was a daughter of . . .
—Daughter of the regiment. (269:19–20)

Cf. *La Figlia del Reggimento* (*The Daughter of the Regiment*)

REMARKS: According to Thornton, Donizetti's opera was announced in the Dublin newspaper on 16 June 1904 to be performed the following night.[7] The opera itself seems to bear little on the Bloom marital situation. Marie, the heroine, is in fact adopted informally and raised by the regiment, and this bears obviously on Molly's situation with Major Tweedy's regiment. But there the parallels seem to end, and the reference seems, like most of Dedalus's musical allusions, to contain little more than surface connotations.

. . . My Irish Molly, O. (269:26)

Cf. "My Irish Molly O"

REMARKS: I have uncovered several songs with the above title. Hodgart and Worthington cite the Jerome-Schwartz version,[8] which is dated 1905, but there are several more which predate Bloomsday and which could conceivably be the song Simon has in mind. However, like the above allusion, the reference in each case seems not to go beyond a surface allusion to title.

> . . . Idolores, a queen, Dolores, silent. (269:31–32)

Cf. "The Shade of the Palm"

REMARKS: Like previous references to the song, the description of Miss Douce as Idolores links her again to Molly and reenforces the association by juxtaposing the allusion and the discussion of Molly's background.

> Over their voices Dollard bassooned attack, booming over bombarding chords:
> —*When love absorbs my ardent soul* . . .
> Roll of Bensoulbenjamin rolled to the quivery loveshivery roofpanes.
> —War! War! cried Father Cowley. You're the warrior.
> —So I am, Ben Warrior laughed. I was thinking of your landlord. Love or money. (270:3–10)
> —. . . . . *my ardent soul*
> *I care not foror the morrow.* (270:29–30)
> Love and war someone is. (270:31–32)

Cf. "Love and War"

REMARKS: The song is a duet for tenor and bass. The tenor is the "lover" and the bass the "warrior":

> Lover (Tenor):
> While Love absorbs my ardent soul,
> I think not of the morrow;
> Beneath his sway years swiftly roll,
> True lovers banish sorrow,
> True lovers banish sorrow;
> By softest kisses, warm'd to blisses,
> Lovers banish sorrow,
> By softest kisses, warm'd to blisses,
> Lovers banish sorrow . . .

> Soldier (Bass):
> While War absorbs my ardent soul,
> I think not of the morrow;
> Beneath his sway years swiftly roll,
> True Soldiers banish sorrow;

By cannon's rattle, rous'd to battle,
Soldiers banish sorrow,
By cannon's rattle, rous'd to battle,
Soldiers banish sorrow . . .

Together:
Since Mars lov'd Venus, Venus Mars,
Let's blend love's wounds with battle's scars, . . .
And call in Bacchus all divine, . . .
To cure both pains with rosy wine,
To cure both pains with rosy, rosy wine.
And thus, beneath his social sway,
We'll sing and laugh the hours away . . .

Dollard's singing "When Love absorbs my ardent soul," the tenor part, prompts Cowley's admonishment to sing about war, the bass's part, and is probably the reason that Ben stops singing. According to the narrator, Ben's voice was booming on what should be a soft passage which crescendos slightly up to the word "soul." The last few notes, however, being in the upper tenor register, are pretty high, and Dollard provides the usual bass answer to high notes, increased volume:

The second line of the base part is a variation of "I think not of the morrow." Here it is not at all certain whether the lines are being sung, or whether Joyce is just describing the musical accompaniment, as he did in "Goodbye, Sweetheart, Goodbye," by means of the lyrics. Bloom, who knows Dollard's voice well, does not know who is performing. If Bloom hears the piano only, then the variation must again be laid to Joyce. While the author's recollection of the lyrics may not be especially good, his musical phraseology is better. He indicates the three eighth notes and the interval of a sixth between the last two, all on the word *for*, by adding, instead of a dash this time, another syllable on the word (see music above).

The preoccupations of the characters who participate in the Sirens chapter are certainly with love and war, and these are reflected in the songs which provide the musical accompaniment. Like the lover and warrior in the duet, the boys in the Ormond Bar decide musically to "blend love's wounds with battle's scars,/And call in Bacchus all divine/To cure both pains with rosy wine/ . . . [and] sing and laugh the hours away." With Dollard's brief solo begins the barroom concert, which in song will relate the major themes and conflicts of the chapter.

Jiggedy jingle jaunty jaunty.

Only the harp. Lovely gold glowering light. Girl touched it. Poop of a lovely. Gravy's rather good fit for a. Golden ship. Erin. The harp that once or twice. Cool hands. Ben Howth, the rhododendrons. We are their harps. I. He. Old. Young. (271: 17–21)

Cf. "The Harp That Once Through Tara's Halls"

REMARKS: Bloom's reverie is punctuated by the sound of Boylan's cart as he proceeds toward Molly's. Thoughts of Molly's snore and the lovely harpist put Bloom in a mood of nostalgic dejection. He meditates on how men are played upon like harps by women, associating the harp with the song "The Harp That Once Through Tara's Halls" as he thinks, "The harp that once or twice." The song is a combination of sentimentality over the glories of former days and patriotic indignation:

> The harp that once through Tara's halls
> The soul of music shed,
> Now hangs as mute on Tara's walls
> As if that soul were fled,
> So sleeps the pride of former days,
> So glory's thrill is o'er,
> And hearts that once beat high for praise,
> Now feel that pulse no more.

"The pride of former days" and "glory's thrill," which the song refers to and which occurred for Bloom in Ben Howth's rhododendrons, are indeed gone for him. The song reference serves only to deepen Bloom's resignation about his, Boylan's, or any man's ability to control the eternal surge of woman's will. ("We are their harps. I. He. Old. Young.")

—*M'appari,* Simon, Father Cowley said.

Down stage he strode some paces, grave, tall in affliction, his long arms outheld. Hoarsely the apple of his throat hoarsed softly. Softly he sang to a dusty seascape there: *A Last Farewell.* A headland, a ship, a sail upon the billows. Farewell. A lovely girl, her veil awave upon the wind upon the headland, wind around her.

Cowley sang:

—*M'appari tutt amor:*

Il mio sguardo l'incontr . . .

She waved, unhearing Cowley, her veil to one departing, dear one, to wind, love, speeding sail, return. (271:25–36)

Cf. *"M'appari"*

"A Last Farewell"

REMARKS: Cowley urges Simon Dedalus to sing *"M'appari"* from Flotow's *Martha,* pressing his request by beginning the song in Italian. Simon, at first heedless of the petition, sings "A Last Farewell," the words of which are described by the narrator in terms of the sea, ships, sails, and winds of the painted backdrop behind the stage. "A Last Farewell" ("Epilogue" by Grieg) may well be a final Sirens' song for the departed Boylan. Though the song is indeed one of parting, it involves parting from this world to the next. A relatively brief segment of the lyrics will demonstrate the tenor of the song:

> Farewell, base world, thy sins oppress me,
> With footsteps fleet I haste away,
> Where foes or friends no more distress me;
> My spirit's higher call obey.

If this song is to be sung for or by Boylan, the intention is purely ironic. The seascape, one of the Sirens motifs of the chapter, hangs on the stage behind the piano. The song is one of the "farewells" attending Boylan's departure from the Ormond and marking the low point of Bloom's day, the four o'clock hour of assignation. In a sense Bloom's lover-Siren bids him and his memories of triumphs gone by a fond farewell for her current lover, and in the ignominy of cuckoldry and defeat, Bloom fashions a new life for himself with letters to Martha Clifford and with the potential for a new son, the Stephen-piano tuner-Croppy Boy, of Sirens.

—Ah, sure my dancing days are done, Ben . . . Well . . . (271:38)

Cf. "Johnny, I Hardly Knew Ye"

REMARKS: Simon, still reticent, replies to the requests for his rendition of *"M'appari"* with Simonesque, cliché-riddled modesty. The words are from the third stanza of the antiwar song:

> Where are the legs with which you run?
> Hurroo! Hurroo!
> Where are the legs with which you run?
> Hurroo! Hurroo!
> Where are the legs with which you run
> When you went to carry a gun?
> *Indeed your dancing days are done!* [Italics mine]
> Faith, Johnny I hardly knew ye.

Simon's false modesty belies his still excellent tenor voice to which his subsequent rendition of *"M'appari"* will attest. Neither of the father figures, Bloom or Simon, has yet to throw in the sponge.

Mr Dedalus laid his pipe to rest beside the tuningfork and, sitting, touched the obedient keys.

—No, Simon, Father Cowley turned. Play it in the original. One flat.

The keys, obedient, rose higher, told, faltered, confessed, confused. (271:39–272:2)

Cf. *"M'appari"*

REMARKS: Simon starts to play the song in a lower, easier-to-sing key, but Cowley admonishes him to play the song in the original key of one flat (F major). *"Ach! so fromm. . . ,"* the original version of *"M'appari"* in Flotow's opera, is written in F major. The version of the song which Simon will eventually sing ("Come Back, Martha! Ah Return Love," words by Charles Jeffreys, arranged by Charles W. Glover) [9] is in two sharps (D major), a minor third below the original key. Finally Cowley sits down to play the accompaniment himself.

Most beautiful tenor air ever written, Richie said: *Sonnambula.* He heard Joe Maas sing that one night. (272:9–10). . . . Never would Richie forget that night. As long as he lived, never. (272:24–25)

Cf. *"Tutto è sciolto"*

REMARKS: Richie's recital of Joe Maas's rendition of the brief aria from *La Sonnambula* follows his usual ecstasy over operatic renditions he has heard. These ravings bear out the accuracy of Stephen's memory in Proteus about his uncle's musical passions.

Backache he. Bright's bright eye. Next item on the programme. Paying the piper. Pills, pounded bread, worth a guinea a box. Stave it off awhile. Sings too: *Down among the dead men.* Appropriate. Kidney pie. Sweets to the. Not making much hand of it. Best value in. Characteristic of him. Power. Particular about his drink. (272:14–19)

Cf. "Down Among the Dead Men"

REMARKS: According to Bloom, Richie's singing "Down Among the Dead Men" is appropriate both to his state of poor health and the cause of his condition. "Bright's bright eye" could refer to Bright's disease, a liver ailment which Bloom attributes to booze. "Down Among the Dead Men" is an old English drinking song which reminds us that after death there is no more drinking:

Here's a health to the king, and a lasting peace,
To faction an end, to wealth increase.
Come, let's drink it while we have breath,
For there's no drinking after death.
And he that will this health deny,
Down among the dead men,
Down among the dead men,
Down, down, down, down,
Down among the dead men let him lie.

The song, tying together the elements of Richie's condition, disease, death, and drink, is the major associative link in Bloom's stream-of-consciousness diagnosis.

—Which air is that? asked Leopold Bloom.
—*All is lost now.*
Richie cocked his lips apout. A low incipient note sweet banshee murmured all. A thrush. A throstle. His breath, birdsweet, good teeth he's proud of, fluted with plaintive woe. Is lost. Rich sound. Two notes in one there. Blackbird I heard in the hawthorn valley. Taking my motives he twined and turned them. All most too new call is lost in all. Echo. How sweet the answer. How is that done? All lost now. Mournful he whistled. Fall, surrender, lost.
(272:31–40)

Cf. *"Tutto è sciolto"*
"How Sweet the Answer Echo Makes"

REMARKS: "All is lost now" is a phrase of which Joyce was very fond, having written a poem by that name. Elvino's aria *"Tutto è sciolto"* in Act II of *La Sonnambula,* is one of deepest despair:

All is lost now,
By all hope and joy am I forsaken,
Nevermore can love awaken
Past enchantment, no, nevermore.

Richie is, of course, whistling the air to Bloom. The third person narration in the passage is bound almost inextricably to Bloom's stream of consciousness and the first line of the song. Richie's whistling is compared to a bird's call. The first "low incipient note," murmuring the word *all* from the song is the dotted half note of the first measure of the solo:

After the description of the tone of Richie's whistle and Bloom's speculations on his teeth, the "is lost" is Richie's continuation of the musical phrase.

Bloom's thoughts are directed next to Richie's dual note production and its similarity to that of a blackbird that once whistled a contrapuntal duet with Bloom. As Leopold whistled, he fancied the bird took his musical motives and made variations on them. The blackbird's echo of Bloom's melody brings to mind the word *Echo,* which is the subtitle of a lovely Thomas Moore song, "How Sweet the Answer Echo Makes," the words of which follow:

> How sweet the answer Echo makes
> To music at night,
> When rous'd by lute or horn, she wakes,
> She starting wakes,
> And far away, o'er lawns and lakes,
> Goes answering light!
>
> Yet Love hath echoes truer far,
> And far more sweet,
> Than e'er beneath the moonlight's star,
> The moonlight's star,
> Of horn, or lute, or soft guitar,
> The songs repeat.
>
> 'Tis when the sigh, in youth sincere,
> And only then—
> The sigh that's breath'd for one to hear,
> For one to hear,
> Is by that one, that only Dear,
> Breath'd back again!

"How sweet the answer . . ." is a song of love which must be reciprocated and sincere to have meaning. The love of Leopold and Molly, having lost its youth, sincerity, and reciprocity is lost; all is lost. The Moore song combines, then, with *"Tutto è sciolto"* to reiterate and reflect Bloom's unhappy position and frame of mind.

Bloom turns his attention to the operatic context of *"Tutto è sciolto,"* trying to place it in the action of *La Sonnambula.* In the opera, Amina, betrothed to Elvino, sleepwalks into another man's room at an inn, dreaming that she is coming to Elvino. Rodolfo, the other man, considerately leaves the room with the girl asleep on his bed, but Lisa, who is also in love with Elvino, brings him in to point out his fiancée sleeping on Rodolfo's bed. Elvino denounces the sleepwalking Amina, and his subsequent misery prompts the aria "All Is Lost Now."

Bloom bent leopold ear, turning a fringe of doyley down under the vase. Order. Yes, I remember. Lovely air. In sleep she went to him. Innocence in the moon. Still hold her back. Brave, don't know their danger. Call name. Touch water. Jingle jaunty. Too late. She longed to go. That's why. Woman. As easy stop the sea. Yes: all is lost.

—A beautiful air, said Bloom lost Leopold. I know it well.

Never in all his life had Richie Goulding.

He knows it well too. Or he feels. Still harping on his daughter. Wise child that knows her father, Dedalus said. Me?

Bloom askance over liverless saw. Face of the all is lost. Rollicking Richie once. (272:41–273:10)

Cf. *"Tutto è sciolto"*

REMARKS: Leopold-Elvino, remembering the story, converts the situation to his own. Bloom's recollection of the opera is fairly close to the original up to the mention of the Boylan motif ("Jingle jaunty"). From there Amina's motives become confused with Molly's and the resulting generalizations are about all of womankind. Bloom, who feels that the drives of women are as easily stopped as the motion of the sea, sees Boylan's assignation as the inescapable outcome of the id. For Bloom-Elvino, "Yes: all is lost." As the parallel between Bloom and Elvino is further underscored in the next few lines by the reference to Bloom as "lost Leopold," the irony of his following statement to Richie becomes increasingly apparent. Bloom's description of Richie's face as being the "face of the all is lost," Richie's pride over the girl he thinks, perhaps erroneously, to be his daughter, and his speculation that Richie *too,* penniless and in poor health, knows that all is lost provide ample evidence that Bloom thinks of his own situation as being analogous to Richie-Elvino's.

—I have no money but if you will lend me your attention I shall endeavor to sing to you of a heart bowed down. (273:23–24)

Cf. "The Heart Bowed Down"

REMARKS: Bloom's thoughts are turned by the piano, playing the introduction to *"M'appari."* Simon, using another musical cliché, finally consents to sing the tenor aria. In Sirens Simon, the great cliché quoter, obligingly shifts his range of well-known aphorisms to musical references, which, if no less worn than those in Hades, fit the reference pattern of the musical barroom. "The Heart Bowed Down," a very popular ballad from Balfe's *Bohemian Girl,* is a song of despair and the weight of woe. The despondent heart of the song can seek refuge only, as Bloom does, in memory, which is "the only friend/That grief can call its own." The song reference provides a musical allusion to despairing love and an additional link between Flotow's song and Bloom's dilemma, as Joyce piles up piece after piece of music reiterating the theme of lost love.

> The harping chords of prelude closed. A chord longdrawn, expectant drew a voice away.
> —*When first I saw that form endearing.* (273:28–30)

Cf. "*M'appari*"

REMARKS: The prelude ends, and Simon begins to sing. Much has been said about the parallels between the opera *Martha* and Bloom's situation,[10] and indeed there is some similarity. It must be remembered, however, that the resemblance between Lionel's situation in *Martha* and Bloom's in *Ulysses* is marked only in their songs of despair.

Briefly, the context surrounding "*M'appari*" in *Martha* is that Lady Harriet, a maid of honor to Queen Anne, for a lark assumes the name Martha and goes to a fair where she hires herself out as a servant to Lionel and Plunkett, two well-to-do farmers. Lionel falls in love with Martha but is left alone and pining when she makes her escape from the farm. His mood of dejection prompts the aria.

Like the circumstances of Elvino in *La Sonnambula,* who sings a Bloom-like song of despair, the context of Lionel's situation is very different from Bloom's. Elvino made a mistake about the innocence of his fiancée, but for Bloom there is no mistake. Lionel has been duped, but certainly not cuckolded, as Leopold is. But all three will eventually see a satisfactory issue out of their afflictions, Elvino and Lionel through happy reconciliations, Bloom through equanimity. It is, therefore, in the passionate cries of outraged and despondent love of the three protagonists that the correspondence of their situations chiefly lies.

The opera *Martha* was written originally in German, and the aria was entitled "*Ach! so fromm, ach so traut.*" Cowley's version (271:33–4) was in Italian, and Simon Dedalus will sing the aria in English. The complete text of Charles Jeffreys's English version, which Simon sings, is as follows:

> When first I saw that form endearing;
> Sorrow from me seem'd to depart:
> Each graceful look, each word so cheering
> Charm'd my eye and won my heart.
> Full of hope, and all delighted,

None could feel more blest than I;
All on Earth I then could wish for
Was near her to live and die:
But alas! 'twas idle dreaming,
And the dream too soon hath flown;
Not one ray of hope is gleaming;
I am lost, yet I am lost for she is gone.
When first I saw that form endearing
Sorrow from me seem'd to depart!
Each graceful look, each word so cheering
Charm'd my eye and won my heart.
Martha, Martha, I am sighing
I am weeping still; for thee;
Come thou lost one,
Come thou dear one,
Thou alone can'st comfort me:
Ah Martha return! Come to me!

Bloom recognizes that the words Simon sings are not the ones that normally go with Flotow's melody when he says, "Singing wrong words" (274:24–25).

The significance of the song in relating Lionel in the opera to Leopold should not be understated. Bloom in the role of Lionel, upon being forsaken by Martha, enters to sing *"M'appari,"* so that the song becomes Bloom's at this, the hour of Molly and Blazes' assignation and Leopold's disconsolation.

—*When first I saw that form endearing.*
Richie turned.
—Si Dedalus' voice, he said.
Braintipped, cheek touched with flame, they listened feeling that flow endearing flow over skin limbs human heart soul spine. . . .

—*Sorrow from me seemed to depart.*
Through the hush of air a voice sang to them, low, not rain, not leaves in murmur, like no voice of strings of reeds or whatdoyoucallthem dulcimers, touching their still ears with words, still hearts of their each his remembered lives. Good, good to hear: sorrow from them each seemed to from both depart when first they heard. When first they saw, lost Richie, Poldy, mercy of beauty, heard from a person wouldn't expect it in the least, her first merciful lovesoft oftloved word. (273:30–35, 273:39–274:5)

Cf. *"M'appari"*

REMARKS: Here Joyce begins to use an unusual procedure in linking music with the text and Bloom's dilemma. The textual material immediately following each line Simon sings of *"M'appari"* relates thematically, symbolically, or descriptively to that line. The technique parallels the headlines in the Aeolus chapter, but the material here is far more significant in terms of the overall action of the novel. The first line serves to awaken the sensibilities of the listeners as they let that "form endearing" "endearing flow" over them.

The music, beautiful in its commiseration, lifts momentarily the pall of sorrow which hangs over the two diners. The sorrow which seemed to depart from anguished Lionel in *Martha* appears also to depart from equally troubled Leopold and Richie, as each makes the associations of the music to his own life. This of course means Bloom will think immediately of the association of the song to Molly, and later Martha. Worthy of special note in the passage is the comment that Bloom would never have expected to hear of his marital situation or any comfort from Simon Dedalus. But as themes crisscross and intertwine it is Simon paradoxically who brings comfort and mercy to his scorned father-rival and his detested brother-in-law. In fact in raising Bloom from his lost-love depression as expressed in the Bellini aria, Simon provides one of the means, through the power of music on the psyche, for Bloom to emerge the "unconquered hero" of Sirens and the day.

> Love that is singing: love's old sweet song. Bloom unwound slowly the elastic band of his packet. Love's old sweet *sonnez la* gold. (274:6–8)

Cf. "Love's Old Sweet Song"

REMARKS: The song *"M'appari"* turns Bloom's thoughts to the first of six songs which provide a background counterpoint to Simon's solo, "Love's Old Sweet Song." That Bloom associates *"M'appari"* with himself becomes increasingly apparent from the context of the words of "Love's Old Sweet Song," a song about the nostalgia and permanence of love's memories, a theme especially obvious in the second stanza:

> Even today we hear Love's song of yore,
> Deep in our hearts it dwells forever more;
> Footsteps may falter, weary grow the way,
> Still we can hear it at the close of day;
> So till the end, when life's dim shadows fall,
> Low will be found the sweetest song of all.

We have learned in the Calypso and Lotus Eaters episodes that the old sweet song which was once sung in the hearts of Molly and Leopold has become the new song of Molly and Blazes, for this is one of the songs Molly will sing on their tour in Belfast. In the Lotus Eaters episode Bloom has made the identification between the song and his wife's adultery with Boylan, so that using the song title to describe *"M'appari"* merely extends the connotations of "Love's Old Sweet Song" to Lionel's lament. Bloom has broadened the overall implications of "Love's Old Sweet Song" by joining its connotations of his and Molly's happy past with its connotations of the adulterous present. In "Love's old sweet *sonnez la* gold," Bloom has blended a parody of Lenehan's statement, *"Sonnez la cloche,"* made as Miss Douce snaps her garter, with both the song and the rubber band around the writing paper and envelope for Martha Clifford's letter. By associating the garter snapping and the rubber band, Bloom is attempting to bury the thoughts of Molly and Blazes behind thoughts of his own roguish affair with Martha. The music can still be a song of love for Martha and him. By this devious rationalization Bloom psychologically prepares himself for the next line of *"M'appari."*

—*Full of hope and all delighted* . . .

Tenors get women by the score. Increase their flow. Throw flower at his feet when will we meet? My head it simply. Jingle all delighted. He can't sing for tall hats. Your head it simply swurls. Perfumed for him. What perfume does your wife? I want to know. Jing. Stop. Knock. Last look at mirror always before she answers the door. The hall. There? How do you? I do well. There? What? Or? Phila of cachous, kissing comfits, in her satchel. Yes? Hands felt for the opulent. (274:11–19)

Cf. *"M'appari"*
    "Seaside Girls"

REMARKS: No matter how he tries to think of something else Bloom's thoughts invariably return to Molly and Blazes. The line "full of hope and all delighted" leads to a reflection on the attraction of tenors for women, who seem to lose their heads. This is immediately related by Bloom to "my head it simply [whirls]" from "Seaside Girls," a song which has been alluded to a number of times in earlier chapters [11] and which is inextricably linked in Bloom's mind with Boylan and with the consubstantial existence theme. Hence Boylan's affair with Molly is directly tied with his own through the allusion to "Seaside Girls" which acts as the linking or combining element. So Molly's perfume for Boylan leads to Martha's question for Bloom. All of this underscores the universality of *"M'appari,"* a love song for Boylan, Molly, Bloom, and Martha, all changing roles and becoming cunsubstantial as the themes crisscross and interrelate.

The words "jingle all delighted" combine the metonymical sound of Boylan's cart with the line of *"M'appari"* which Simon has just sung, directly associating Boylan and his delight with the song. This leads to Bloom's speculation that Boylan can't sing for tall hats and that Molly, in liking him, shows that her head is swirling. But so is Bloom's for Martha, since as the song says, "You fall in love . . . not with one girl always the lot." Molly's being perfumed for Boylan leads Bloom back to Martha's letter; but his thoughts return immediately to Blazes, Molly, the afternoon meeting, and the inevitable seduction. In the end it might be Bloom's as well as Boylan's hands which are full, and both who are "all delighted."

> —But alas, 'twas idle dreaming . . .
> Glorious tone he has still. Cork air softer also their brogue. Silly man! Could have made oceans of money. Singing wrong words. Wore out his wife: now sings. . . . Drink. Nerves overstrung. Must be abstemious to sing. (274:22–25, 27–28)

Cf. "M'appari"

REMARKS: As the next line of "M'appari" brings Lionel back to earth, so do Bloom's thoughts return to the more commonplace speculations of Simon's glorious tone, reduced circumstanes, and intemperance. However, Bloom is aroused and unable to repress thoughts of Molly and Blazes' love-making. As the music progresses, the sensual aspects of it overwhelm Bloom, and it becomes no longer music, but the act of love which Molly and Blazes are carrying out:

> Tenderness it welled: slow, swelling. Full it
> throbbed. That's the chat. Ha, give! Take! Throb,
> a throb, a pulsing proud erect.
> Words? Music? No: it's what's behind.
> Bloom looped, unlooped, noded, disnoded.
> Bloom. Flood of warm jimjam lickitup secretness
> flowed to flow in music out, in desire, dark to
> lick flow, invading. Tipping her tepping her
> tapping her topping her. Tup. Pores to dilate
> dilating. Tup. The joy the feel the warm the. Tup.
> To pour o'er sluices pouring gushes. Flood, gush,
> flow, joygush, tupthrop. Now! Language of love.
> (274:30–40)

When Bloom asks himself if it is the music which is driving him to his disquieting thoughts, his answer, "No: it's what's behind," indicates his appreciation of the symbolism and irony underlying the song and furnishes additional evidence that he sees some of his own dilemma in the music. The sensual effect of the music does inflame his imagination, however, as the next lines in the passage prove. The excited undercurrent of Bloom's thoughts in the passage grows to orgasmic proportions as the musical background builds in intensity.

—. . . *ray of hope* . . .

Beaming. Lydia for Lidwell squeak scarcely hear so ladylike the muse unsqueaked a ray of hope.

Martha it is. Coincidence. Just going to write. Lionel's song. Lovely name you have. Can't write. Accept my little pres. Play on her heartstrings pursestrings too. She's a. I called you naughty boy. Still the name: Martha. How strange! Today. (274:41–275:6)

Cf. "*M'appari*"

REMARKS: As Miss Douce offers a quiet ray of hope to solicitor George Lidwell, Bloom makes the subconscious association between the words "ray of hope" from the solo and Martha Clifford, his "ray of hope." He then makes the conscious association between Martha and the opera title and identifies Simon's solo as Lionel's aria. From this point on the song becomes Lionel's song, and Bloom is frequently called "Lionel-Leopold." As the song goes on the narrator describes the return of the opening selection of "*M'appari*" with its attending similarity in lyrics.

The voice of Lionel returned, weaker but unwearied. It sang again to Richie Poldy Lydia Lidwell also sang to Pat open mouth ear waiting, to wait. How first he saw that form endearing, how sorrow seemed to part, how look, form, word charmed him Gould Lidwell, won Pat Bloom's heart. (275:7–11)

Cf. "*M'appari*"

REMARKS: As Simon-Lionel sadly remembers the graceful glances of Martha in the song, Bloom remembers his first meeting with Molly, when first he saw her "form endearing," and the music begins to blend all the listeners into one. Completing the essential communality of their experience, Richie Goulding and George Lidwell become Lionel or "him" and Leopold Bloom is amalgamated with Pat the waiter.

—*Each graceful look* . . .

First night when first I saw her at Mat Dillon's in Terenure. Yellow, black lace she wore. Musical chairs. We two the last. Fate. After her. Fate. Round and round slow. Quick round. We two. All looked. Halt. Down she sat. All ousted looked. Lips laughing. Yellow knees.

—*Charmed my eye* . . .

Singing. *Waiting* she sang. I turned her music. Full voice of perfume of what perfume does your lilactrees. Bosom I saw, both full, throat warbling. First I saw. She thanked me. Why did she me? Fate. Spanishy eyes. Under a peartree alone patio this hour in old Madrid one side in shadow Dolores shedolores. At me. Luring. Ah, alluring. (275:16–28)

Cf. *"M'appari"*
  "Waiting"
  "In Old Madrid"
  "The Shade of the Palm"

REMARKS: Here the parallels between the words of *"M'appari"* ("Each graceful look . . . charmed my eye . . .") and Bloom's thoughts of his first look at Molly and her Spanishy eyes are readily apparent. Some of the other musical allusions in the passage are not quite so obvious, however. "Waiting," Molly's song of that first night, is, appropriately, the song of a maid standing in a meadow listening to the nightingales as she awaits her lover. Through the novel the song becomes a motif of the perpetually ready temptress. We will discover in Penelope that Molly uses the song to identify herself as Siren. As the present passage indicates, "Waiting" has Molly's intended effect on Bloom.

The paragraph containing the reference to "Waiting" is a very interesting jumble of themes, songs, and memories in Bloom's mind. As he turned Molly's pages that night, he could smell her perfume, the lilac-scented bath water Martha asked about. ("Full voice of perfume of what perfume does your lilac trees.") Hence her figure combines with Martha's in a consubstantial moment. As Bloom remembers Molly's bosom, Lionel's words ("When first I saw . . .") blend in with his own thoughts. ("Bosom I saw, both full, throat warbling. First I saw.") Bloom wonders why she thanked him for turning the pages and decides it must be fate. ("She thanked me. Why did she me? Fate.") Bloom's associative pattern moves from fate, kismet, to the East and thence to Spain and Molly's Spanishy eyes. He combines Dolores, the girl of the East, waiting in the song "The Shade of the Palm" (now a pear tree), with the waiting girl with dark eyes in the song "In Old Madrid." ("Spanishy eyes. Under a peartree alone patio in this hour in old Madrid one side in shadow Dolores shedolores.") The song "In Old Madrid" is about a dark-eyed waiting lover, as the following excerpts will show:

Stanza 1:
Long years ago, in old Madrid,
Where softly sighs of love the light guitar,
Two sparkling eyes a lattice hid,
Two eyes as darkly bright as love's own star!
There on the casement ledge, when day was o'er,
A tiny hand was lightly laid;

A face look'd out, as from the river shore,
There stole a tender serenade! . . .

Stanza 2:
Far, far away from old Madrid,
Her lover fell, long years ago, for Spain;
A convent veil those sweet eyes hid;
And all the vows that love had sigh'd were vain!
But still, between the dusk and night, 'tis said,
Her white hand opes the lattice wide,
The faint sweet echo of that serenade
Floats weirdly o'er the misty tide! . . .

Molly's eyes, the eyes of the waiting girl of "In Old Madrid" and the waiting "Dolores" of "The Shade of the Palm," were that first night on him—Bloom—alluring, luring him. ("At me. Luring. Ah, alluring.") For the moment, in Bloom's thought it is he, not Blazes, who will have the four-o'clock rendezvous (". . . alone patio this hour . . . one side in shadow. Dolores shedolores"), as all music, themes, and identities become interchangeable.

—Martha! Ah, Martha!
   Quitting all languor Lionel cried in grief, in cry of passion dominant to love to return with deepening yet with rising chords of harmony. In cry of Lionel loneliness that she should know, must Martha feel. For only her he waited. Where? Here there try there here all try where. Somewhere. (275:29–34)

Cf. "*M'appari*"

REMARKS: As the forsaken Bloom's thoughts build to a crescendo, so do the forsaken Lionel's. The identification between Lionel and Leopold becomes complete as they both call out for their loves. In the cries of the anguished Lionel, there are parallels to Bloom's relations with both Molly and Martha Clifford. Joyce makes full use of the ambiguity inherent in these cross references to the women to reflect the two issues on Bloom's mind throughout the chapter. Molly, at this hour, is the lost one to whom Lionel-Leopold addresses his plaintive notes, but Lionel's song is sung to Martha, and it is Martha to whom Leopold appeals for deliverance from the ignominy of cuckoldry. In the inclusion of both themes in one song Joyce points up the interdependent relationship between them.

Co-me, thou lost one!
Co-me, thou dear one! (275:35–36)

Cf. *"M'appari"*

REMARKS: Lionel's final anguished entreaties serve a double purpose: to increase Leopold's sense of isolation from his wife, and concurrently to kindle his need for Martha's affection. This becomes obvious in the next lines of Bloom's stream of consciousness: "Alone. One love. One hope. One comfort me. Martha, chestnote, return" (275:37–38). The two *co-me*'s in the above passage from the song are meant to coincide with the third intervals in the music.

CO-OME THOU LOST ONE, CO-OME THOU DEAR ONE.

—*Come!*

It soared, a bird, it held its flight, a swift pure cry, soar silver orb it leaped serene, speeding, sustained, to come, don't spin it out too long long breath he breath long life, soaring high, high resplendent, aflame, crowned, high in the effulgence symbolistic, high, of the ethereal bosom, high, of the high vast irradiation everywhere all soaring all around about the all, the endlessnessnessness . . .

—*To me!* (275:39–276:6)

Cf. *"M'appari"*

REMARKS: The note that Joyce pictures so enthusiastically is the high B flat

COME! TO ME!

The length and content of the description between *"Come!"* and *"To me!"* indicate the duration of the pause as well as the quality of Simon's high B flat as the note combines with the lyrics and description to give the passage overtones of an orgasm.

As if to reenforce the idea that the song is Bloom's, Joyce calls the singer "Siopold" (276:7), a combination of Simon, Lionel, and Leopold,[12] and, while the admiring listeners compliment "Lionel-Simon," we are told, "But Bloom sang dumb" (276:35); i.e., Bloom's love song has provoked no applause, for it was sung unvoiced and unheard. Yet the final word in blending the three into one is the final statement of consubstantial resolve. The music has provided the unifying element in the communality of Bloom and Lionel in loneliness and strangely enough linked Bloom and Simon in the bands of communality which will provide a later basis for their interchangeability as consubstantial father figures.

Richie, admiring, descanted on that man's glorious voice. He remembered one night long ago. Never forget that night. Si sang *'Twas rank and fame:* in Ned Lambert's 'twas. Good God he never heard in all his life a note like that he never did *then false one we had better part* so clear so God he never heard *since love lives not* a clinking voice ask Lambert he can tell you too. (276: 37–277:2)

Cf. " 'Twas Rank and Fame"

REMARKS: Bloom's earlier skepticism of Richie's statements seems at least partially justified here. When the song is examined closely, it appears that Richie is exaggerating. He remembers the words of the song fairly accurately, varying only line four of stanza one:

> Stanza 1:
> 'Twas rank and fame that tempted thee,
> 'Twas empire charm'd thy heat. . . .
> But love was wealth, the world to me,
> Then, false one, let us part;
> The prize I fondly deem'd my own,
> Another's now may be;
> For ah! with love, life's gladness flown,
> Leaves grief to wed, to wed with me;
> Leaves grief alone to me;
> With love, life's gladness flown,
> Leaves grief alone to me.
>
> Stanza 2:
> Tho' lowly bred, and humbly born,
> No loftier heart than mine;
> Unlov'd by thee my pride would scorn
> To share the crown that's thine;
> I sought no empire save the heart,
> Which mine can never be;
> Then false one, we had better part,
> Since love lives not, lives not in thee;
> Since love lives not in thee;
> Yes! false one, better part,
> Since love lives not in thee.

Richie's ecstasies about Simon's rendition of the song seem overly enthusiastic because the song itself is not a particularly difficult one to sing, and the lines Richie quotes are relatively simple. The ninth line in stanza two, "Since love lives not in thee," contains the highest note in the song, a G natural, which is a minor third lower than the highest note in *"M'appari."* The line "Then false one . . . ," which Richie seems to connect with the note about which he raves, has no outstanding notes in it at all. Through the use of the song, Joyce confirms Bloom's opinion that Richie's statements must be taken with the proverbial grain of salt. "'Twas Rank and Fame" is also a song about a false lover and serves to reenforce further the betrayal and false love motif in the chapter.

Brothers-in-law: relations. We never speak as we pass by. (277: 9)

Cf. "We Never Speak as We Pass By"

Remarks: Simon's disdain for his brother-in-law prompts the allusion from Bloom. The song is a minstrel ballad sung by a cuckolded husband about his fallen "Nell":

Stanza 1:
The spell is past, the dream is o'er,
And tho' we meet, we love no more,
One heart is crush'd to droop and die,
And for relief must heav'nward fly,
The once bright smile has faded, gone,
And given way, to looks forlorn!
Despite her grandeur's wicked flame,
She stoops to blush beneath her shame.

Chorus:
We never speak as we pass by,
Altho' a tear bedims her eye;
I know she thinks of her past life,
When we were loving man and wife.

Stanza 2:
In guileless youth, I sought her side,
And she became my virtuous bride,
Our lot was peace, so fair so bright,
One summer day, no gloomy night,
No life on earth more pure than ours
In that dear home midst field and flow'rs
Until the tempter came to Nell,
It dazzled her, alas! she fell.

We never speak as we pass by, etc.

Stanza 3:
In gilded hall, midst wealth she dwells,
How her heart aches, her sad face falls,
She fain would smile, seem bright and gay,
But conscience steals her peace away,
And when the flatt'rer cast aside,
My fallen and dishonor'd bride,
I'll close her eyes in death, forgive,
And in my heart her name shall live.

The irony of this song, which fits Bloom's situation more closely than any other of the songs in which he symbolically has participated, is that he uses it to describe the Richie-Simon relationship rather than his own relationship with Molly. But music has helped establish such a communality of theme and characters here, that the allusion works on all levels simultaneously.

Rift in the lute I think. Treats him with scorn. See. He admires him all the more. (277:10–11)

Cf. "Rift in the Lute"

REMARKS: Bloom's speculation alludes to the first line of stanza two of Vivien's song to Merlin in Tennyson's *Idylls of the King,* as she tries to quell the fears of the suspicious Merlin:

"In Love, if Love be Love, if Love be ours,
Faith and unfaith can ne'er be equal powers:
Unfaith in aught is want of faith in all.

"It is the little *rift within the lute,* [italics mine]
That by and by will make the music mute,
And ever widening slowly silence all.

"The little rift within the lover's lute,
Or little pitted speck in garner'd fruit,
That rotting inward slowly moulders all.

"It is not worth the keeping: let it go:
But shall it? answer, darling, answer, no.
And trust me not at all or all in all."

Ostensibly Bloom uses the "Rift in the Lute," like the preceding reference to "we never speak . . . ," to refer to the family division of Simon and Richie, but, again like the preceding reference, the connotations of the entire song are vastly more analogous to Bloom's own dilemma than to the one to which Bloom refers. The deceitful Vivien sings this song to her lover-master so that she may learn his secrets, after which she will leave him unconscious, useless, lost, and alone, as Molly-Martha-Zerlina has duped her Leopold-Lionel-Masetto.

Obviously the function of these last two songs is to provide additional musical parallels to the main dilemma of the chapter and the book. The question of whether they represent an unconscious effort of Bloom to see his own situation of unrequited affection in the relationship of Richie and Simon must remain only a tantalizing possibility.

Thou lost one. All songs on that theme. (277:23)

Cf. *"M'appari"*

REMARKS: Bloom at last recognizes the universality of experience as reflected in *"M'appari."* The corollary is that his experiences as lover and cuckold are universal human experiences and that the song is all things to all themes. As Bloom broods on the theme of lost love and the cruelty of it, his thoughts come back inevitably to Molly and his own situation.

Blumenlied I bought for her. The name. (278:32)

Cf. *"Blumenlied"*

REMARKS: Cowley's improvisations at the piano prompt speculation on methods and style of piano playing, beginner's techniques, and the traditional second- or third-year piano solo, which Bloom bought for Milly. It was not, however, the pedagogy of musical instruction which prompted him to buy the music but the coincidence of the name ("The Flower Song") with the family name, as Bloom, like Joyce, begins to pay attention to the significance of life's coincidences and correspondences.

Why do you call me naught? You naughty too? O, Mairy lost the pin of her. Bye for today. Yes, yes, will tell you. Want to. To keep it up. Call me that other. Other world she wrote. My patience are exhaust. To keep it up. You must believe. Believe. The tank. It. Is. True.
Folly am I writing? (279:22–27)

Cf. "O Mary Lost the Pin of Her Drawers"

REMARKS: As Bloom begins his letter to Martha Clifford, with the continued improvisations of Father Cowley in the background, the words of Martha's letter to Bloom recur again to him, and the "naughty" quality recalls the naughty song, which Bloom has previously associated with Martha and the degrading, comic effect of their affair.[13] Martha's subject-verb agreement error ("... patience are ...") couples in Bloom's mind with the pronoun-antecedent agreement error (*it* for *drawers*) in the line "to keep it up" from "O Mary Lost the Pin of Her Drawers," on which he had previously remarked. The ridiculous tenor of Martha's whole letter combines with the cheap bawdiness of the song to bring Bloom momentarily to consider the possible absurdity of his own position ("Folly am I writing?").

> Her ear too is a shell, the peeping lobe there. Been to the seaside. Lovely seaside girls. Skin tanned raw. Should have put on coldcream first make it brown. Buttered toast. O and that lotion mustn't forget. Fever near her mouth. Your head it simply. Hair braided over: shell with seaweed. Why do they hide their ears with seaweed hair? And Turks their mouth, why? Her eyes over the sheet, a yashmak. Find the way in. A cave. No admittance except on business. (281:21–28)

Cf. "Seaside Girls"

REMARKS: The sea and Miss Douce's sunburned skin turn Bloom's thoughts again to "Seaside Girls," their universal qualities, their role as temptress-figures, Boylan, and hence Molly. The line "your head it simply [swirls]" starts a series of literal associations of swirling curls, shells, seaweed, and seaweed hair. The sea reference and universal connotation of the girls' image in the song [14] provide a background for some brief speculation on womanhood in general before Bloom's thoughts return to Molly and her promiscuity ("Her eyes ...").

> —What are the wild waves saying? he asked her, smiled. (281: 34)

Cf. "What Are the Wild Waves Saying?"

REMARKS: The song is a duet, in which a brother and sister listen to the voice of the waves. In the first stanza Paul thinks he hears their "low, lone song." His sister corrects him, "Brother I hear no singing!/'Tis but the rolling wave. ..." But they both agree that it is "the voice of the great Creator ... in that mighty tone." Lidwell is trying to establish a duet with Miss Douce and thinks he hears her siren song in the sound of the waves in the shell, but "charming," Lydia, "sea-smiling," remains "unanswering." If there is a "low, lone song," she is one of the sirens who makes it.

> Bob Cowley's twinkling fingers in the treble played again. The landlord has the prior. A little time. Long John. Big Ben. Lightly

he played a light bright tinkling measure for tripping ladies, arch and smiling, and for their gallants, gentlemen friends. One: one, one, one: two, one, three, four. (282:3–7)

Cf. Minuet from *Don Giovanni*

REMARKS: Frederick Sternfeld has an excellent rendition of Joyce's application of "One: one, one, one: two, one, three, four," to the minute from *Don Giovanni:* [15]

ONE: ONE, ONE; ONE: TWO, ONE, THREE, FOUR

Sternfeld's analysis of the passage has borne the brunt of some uncharitable remarks from Marian Kaplun, who contends:

> One could not even *say* aloud the "one, three, four" in the rhythm of the minuet as he reproduces it at the tempo at which it is usually performed: It would be a verbal, much less a vocal impossibility. What is more, neither the numbers nor the punctuation correspond meaningfully to the time values or natural stresses of the notes as any voice would sing them.[16]

Miss Kaplun has probably confused the minuet with the watusi, a much faster dance. I have no difficulty in performing the "vocal impossibility" of verbally putting the words to the music. Quarter notes and eighth notes in a minuet are far from the sixty-fourth notes of progressive jazz. The minuet is never performed quickly, and there is no reason to suppose that it was in *Don Giovanni*. Further, what Sternfeld fails to mention and what Kaplun does not realize is that the numbers and punctuation of the disputed passage describe the step and motions of the dancers rather than harmonic variations, time values, or stresses in the dance. The narrator is, after all, describing not the music itself so much as the image of dancing couples which the music calls forth.

Bloom recognizes the dance and conjures up his own image of a great ball, which to him demonstrates the disparity in material wealth between classes.

Minuet of *Don Giovanni* he's playing now. Court dresses of all descriptions in castle chambers dancing. Misery. Peasants outside. Green starving faces eating dockleaves. Nice that is. Look: look, look, look, look, look: you look at us. (282:11–14)

Cf. Minuet of *Don Giovanni*

REMARKS: The dancers displaying their pomp and wealth as they dance the minuet seem to Bloom to be calling attention to themselves. Sternfeld again has correlated the music of the minuet to Bloom's mental image:

LOOK, LOOK, LOOK, LOOK, LOOK; YOU LOOK AT US

The effect of the light, tripping major strains of the minuet is to turn Bloom from the melancholy which accompanied Cowley's minor key improvisations:

> That's joyful I can feel. Never have written it. Why? My joy is other joy. But both are joys. Yes, joy it must be. Mere fact of music shows you are. Often thought she was in the dumps till she began to lilt. Then know. (282:15–18)

As Bloom consciously modulates from the sadness of the minor mode to the happiness of the major mode he reflects on former times with Molly, remembering that the music she sang was also a reflection of her mood.

> M'Coy valise. My wife and your wife. Squealing cat. Like tearing silk. When she talks like the clapper of a bellows. They can't manage men's intervals. Gap in their voices too. Fill me. I'm warm, dark, open. Molly in *qui* [sic] *est homo*: Mercadante. My ear against the wall to hear. Want a woman who can deliver the goods. (282:19–24)

Cf. *"Quis est homo?"*

REMARKS: The several aspects of Mrs. M'Coy's voice suggest to Bloom an inability of women to go from one vocal register to another. The lower register of the voice with its sensual connotations ("warm, dark, open") Bloom associates with the lower register notes in *"Quis est homo?"* In the Lotus Eaters episode when Bloom had been thinking of a series of religious works, *"Quis est homo?"* from Rossini's *Stabat Mater* had produced an association with Mercadante's *Seven Last Words* (82:15–17). In the passage presently under consideration, Bloom, his memory inaccurately shaded by the previous association, connects *"Quis est homo?"* with Mercadante again.

Only the goddess Molly may ask or answer such a question. Bloom tries to in the sand at the end of Nausica, but the answer is blank. It is up to Molly in Penelope to unite them all as antecedents of the masculine third-person pronoun and link them all in her mind and syntax to Leopold.

> Jog jig jogged stopped. Dandy tan shoe of dandy Boylan socks skyblue clocks came light to earth.

> O, look we are so! Chamber music. Could make a kind of pun

on that. It is a kind of music I often thought when she. Acoustics
that is. Tinkling. Empty vessels make most noise. Because the
acoustics, the resonance changes according as the weight of the
water is equal to the law of falling water. Like those rhapsodies
of Liszt's Hungarian, gipsyeyed. Pearls. Drops. Rain. Diddle
iddle addle addle oodle oodle. Hiss. Now. Maybe now. Before.
(282:25–34)

Cf. Liszt's Hungarian Rhapsodies
  "Handy Spandy"

REMARKS: The dandy tan shoes of dandy Boylan suggest the lines of the
nursery rhyme "Handy Spandy":

> Handy Spandy Jack o'dandy
> Loves plum cake and sugar candy. . . .

Boylan's light lines are meant to contrast with Bloom's references to the
dark, mysterious music of Liszt. Boylan's music provides a light, tripping,
airy prelude to an afternoon of pleasure, while Bloom's mood and music are
somber and dark, reflecting an underlying despondency. The pun on chamber music is, of course, an old one for Joyce, and tends to bear out the story
of the easy-going widow, Jenny, and her prophetic urination after hearing
the poems.[17] If the darkness of the music is reflected in the urination tones,
certainly the thought of making music by this means is a light one. If drops
falling into a chamber pot sound dark and hollow, there is nothing particularly grim about the method of tone production. Hence we get in theme
or thought a mixture of light and dark as we do in the contrast of the
nursery rhyme and Liszt.

—*Qui sdegno,* Ben, said Father Cowley.
—No, Ben, Tom Kernan interfered, *The Croppy Boy.* Our native Doric. (282:39–41)

Cf. *"Qui sdegno"*
  "The Croppy Boy"

REMARKS: In the bar, Father Cowley's suggestion that *"Qui sdegno"* be
sung is vetoed in favor of "The Croppy Boy," which Tom Kernan calls
"our native Doric." This incident, which might be easily passed over, assumes
considerable significance when one examines in detail the songs in question.
"Qui sdegno" (*"In diesen heil'gen Hallen"*) is from Mozart's *Magic Flute*
and is a song of peace and the banishment of strife:

> Within this hallow'd dwelling
> Revenge and sorrow cease,
> Here, troubled doubts dispelling,
> The weary heart hath peace.

"The Croppy Boy," conversely, is about particularly Irish matters, betrayal, religion, sentimentality, and war. This is the song the boys want to hear and the things about which their lives revolve. *"Qui sdegno,"* a song of peace, is voted down in favor of the inherently militant, emotional "Croppy Boy," as the songs of love which dominate the first half of the chapter give way to songs of war which are central to the latter part. The link between the two basic musical themes of love and war is, of course, betrayal, which plays a great part in each. Attention shifts concomitantly from the love themes of the novel to the patriotic-political-messianic themes which conclude the chapter.

Both Sternfeld and Worthington have done excellent explications of the relationship of "The Croppy Boy" to the text, though neither gives a complete account.[18] The song is heard in the background for the next four pages of *Ulysses*, though only once is the reader given the quoted words as they are sung by Ben Dollard. The rest of the song is paraphrased by the narrator as it is heard and absorbed by Bloom, though the description of the song is not Bloom's but the narrator's. As with the *"M'appari"* passage, we get the words of the song, followed in most passages by the appropriate accompanying thoughts of Bloom. Bloom hears the initial chords of the introduction just as he is about to leave. The music causes him to pause.

For convenience in what follows the narrator's paraphrases of "The Croppy Boy" are placed in the left hand column and on the right actual words of the stanzas. These quotations will be interspersed with Bloom's thoughts where relevant.

The voice of dark age, of unlove, earth's fatigue made grave approach, and painful, come from afar, from hoary mountains, called on good men and true. The priest he sought, with him would he speak a word. (283:16–19)	"Good men and true! in this house who dwell, To a stranger bouchal, I pray you tell Is the priest at home? or may he be seen? I would speak a word with Father Green." (Stanza 1)

Cf. "The Croppy Boy"

REMARKS: As Bloom hears the first strains of the song, his thoughts go first to Dollard's voice production and then to the singer's reduced circumstances, thoughts which the narrator comprehends in his description of Dollard's voice.

The priest's at home. A false priest's servant bade him	"The Priest's at home boy and may be seen,

welcome. Step in. The holy father. Curlycues of chords.
(283:27–28)

'Tis easy speaking with Father
   Green
But you must wait till I go and
   see
If the Holy Father alone may
   be."
(Stanza 2)

Cf. "The Croppy Boy"

REMARKS: Perhaps it is sentiment for the ensuing betrayal of the croppy boy
which prompts Bloom's thoughts, meantime, to turn to the society that
betrays people like Ben and reduces them to poverty. Bloom is moved to
make up a hasty, satric little lullaby about the situation:

Ruin them. Wreck their lives. Then build them
cubicles to end their days in. Hushaby. Lullaby.
Die, dog. Little dog, die. (283:29–30)

The voice of warning, solemn warning, told them the
youth had entered a lonely
hall, told them how solemn
fell his footstep there, told
them the gloomy chamber, the
vested priest sitting to shrive.
(283:31–34)

The youth has enter'd an empty
   hall,
What a lonely sound has his
   light foot-fall!
And the gloomy chamber's chill
   and bare,
With a vested Priest in a lonely
   chair.
(Stanza 3)

Cf. "The Croppy Boy"

REMARKS: Bloom's thoughts are still, however, with Dollard, Ben's present
pastime, and his deep voice.

The voice of penance and of
grief came slow, embellished,
tremulous. Ben's contrite beard
confessed: *in nomine Domini,*
in God's name. He knelt. He
beat his hand upon his breast,
confessing: *mea culpa.* (284:2–
5)

The youth has knelt to tell his
   sins;
"Nomine Dei," the youth begins:
At "mea culpa" he beats his
   breast,
And in broken murmurs he
   speaks the rest.
(Stanza 4)

Cf. "The Croppy Boy"

REMARKS: Here again we have a mistake on Joyce's part in the divergence between the words of a song and the words in the text of *Ulysses*. The disparity of *"nomine Domini"* (which doesn't fit the tune) in the text with "Nomine Dei" in the song cannot be attributed to an error in Bloom's thinking. Since the narrator is given the words, the error is clearly Joyce's.

Bloom's attention is now directed to the song, as the Latin reminds him of the morning mass in All Hallows and the trip to the cemetery. At this point Joyce rearranges stanzas five and six of the song: placing six next in the text.

The sighing voice of sorrow sang. His sins. Since easter he had cursed three times. You bitch's bast. And once at masstime he had gone to play. Once by the churchyard he had passed and for his mother's rest he had not prayed. A boy. A croppy boy. (284:13–17)	"I cursed three times since last Easter day— At masstime once I went to play; I passed the churchyard one day in haste, And forgot to pray for my mother's rest. (Stanza 6)

Cf. "The Croppy Boy"

REMARKS: The paraphrase of the song by the narrator is interrupted by the phrase "You bitch's bast." The phrase has been used twice previously, both times in connection with the blind piano-tuner (250:19 and 263:20). The tap of the tuner's cane as he returns to the Ormond Bar for his tuning fork is heard just before the passage above, so that Joyce blends the blind man's oath with "The Croppy Boy" at the appropriate moment to add still another dimension to the lyrics. The curses of the croppy boy juxtaposed against the blind piano-tuner's oath connect the two, as the themes of betrayal, false fatherhood, and blindness merge.

In this passage we find one of the main points on which Frederick Sternfeld bases his thesis that "The Croppy Boy" is Stephen Dedalus in search of a real father. The croppy boy's failure to pray for his mother's rest is equated with Stephen's refusal "to make his peace both with his mother and with organized religion, even at his dying mother's behest." [19] The parallels between Stephen and the croppy boy provide the major thematic impetus for this long and important song.[20]

Bloom's thoughts following stanza six of "The Croppy Boy" do not seem to be linked thematically with the song. Staring at Miss Douce, he is reminded of the low-cut dress Molly wore the evening the Blooms attended a concert in honor of the Shah of Persia.

Tuning up. Shah of Persia liked that best. Remind him of home sweet home. (284:27–29)

Cf. "Home Sweet Home"

REMARKS: That the tuning up of the orchestra would sound most like music to the Shah evokes in Bloom's mind the comic allusion to "Home, Sweet Home." The song with its attendant line, "Be it ever so humble," conjures up a poor fireside hearth and stresses comically the universality of life for all men. As Bloom comes to the end of this speculation, the narrator goes back to stanza five of "The Croppy Boy."

All gone. All fallen. At the siege of Ross his father, at Gorey all his brothers fell. To Wexford, we are the boys of Wexford, he would. Last of his name and race. (285:1–3)	"At the siege of Ross did my father fall, And at Gorey my loving brothers all, I alone am left of my name and race, I will go to Wexford and take their place." (Stanza 5)

Cf. "The Croppy Boy"
"The Boys of Wexford"

REMARKS: Here Joyce produces an interesting variant in the patriotic pattern as he interjects "we are the boys of Wexford," the first line of the chorus of the previously discussed popular Irish fight song, "The Boys of Wexford." As with the line "you bitch's bast," there is no certainty whether the Wexford reference comes from Bloom's thoughts, or is merely an elaboration on the song text by the narrator. One explanation for the origin of the name "Croppy Boy" was that it was a nickname given to the Wexford rebels because of their close-cropped hair.[21] This makes the croppy boy, by definition, one of the "boys of Wexford." In any event, the introduction of "The Boys of Wexford" in the passage serves to add reenforcement to the warlike atmosphere created by "The Croppy Boy."

The lines of stanza five are especially meaningful to Bloom, whose thoughts of Molly have plunged him back into the gloom of isolation.

> I too, last my race. Milly young student.
> Well, my fault perhaps. No son. Rudy. Too late
> now. Or if not? If not? If still? (285:4–6)

Like the croppy boy, Bloom is the last of his name and race. If there were any issue out of the alliance between Milly and the student, it would not bear Bloom's name. His solitude, the death of Rudy, his only son, and his own failure as a husband to Molly come crushing down on Bloom, only to give way to desperate hopes.

He bore no hate. (285:7)　　"I bear no hate against living
　　　　　　　　　　　　　　thing."
　　　　　　　　　　　　　　(Stanza 7, line 1)

Cf. "The Croppy Boy"

REMARKS: Bloom, tired of the emotional sentimentality of the song and
tired of his own trials and maudlin thoughts, links the above line of the
song to himself: "Hate. Love. Those are names. Rudy. Soon I am old"
(285:8). Here for the first time the song is fused with Bloom and in
consubstantiality he too becomes the croppy boy. Now the narrator's paraphrase of the song becomes mixed with Bloom's stream of consciousness as
he anticipates the next line.

Ireland comes now. My　　"But I love my country above
country above the king. She　　my King."
listens. Who fears to speak of　　(Stanza 7, line 2)
nineteen four? (285:12–13)

Cf. "The Croppy Boy"
　　"The Memory of the Dead"

REMARKS: At this, Bloom glances about at Miss Douce and thinks of still
another Irish war song. Through the song, Ben Dollard is, in effect, speaking of '98 to listening Miss Douce. "The Croppy Boy" is a ballad of the Re-
bellion of 1798, as is "The Memory of the Dead," the first line of which—
"Who fears to speak of Ninety-Eight?"—Bloom alters to make humorously
contemporaneous with his own time. Further, the song, like "The Boys of
Wexford," serves to provide an additional warlike counterpoint to Dollard's
rendition of "The Croppy Boy."

—*Bless me, father,* Dollard　　"Now, Father! bless me, and let
the croppy cried. *Bless me and*　　me go
let me go. (285:15–16)　　To die, if God has ordained
　　　　　　　　　　　　　　it so."
　　　　　　　　　　　　　　(Stanza 7, lines 3, 4)

Cf. "The Croppy Boy"

REMARKS: The words in italics are theoretically a direct quotation, since
they have before them a dash, the mark Joyce uses to indicate quotations.
Here again the words are not only inexact, but do not fit the tune. Since
Dollard could not have sung the words in the text to the "Croppy Boy"
tune, the alteration must be laid to Joyce himself. Again Bloom is identified
with the croppy boy, since he, like the croppy boy, begins to go.

Bloom looked, unblessed to go. Got up to kill: on eighteen bob a week. Fellows shell out the dibs. Want to keep your weathereye open. Those girls, those lovely. By the sad sea waves. Chorusgirl's romance. Letters read out for breach of promise. From Chickabiddy's own Mumpsypum. Laughter in court. Henry. I never signed it. The lovely name you. (285:18–23)

Cf. "Seaside Girls"
    "By the Sad Sea Waves"

REMARKS: Thoughts of Miss Douce bring "Seaside Girls" again to Bloom's mind. ("Those girls, those lovely.") This time the song is accompanied by a second seaside song, "By the Sad Sea Waves," which is a lament about vanished hope and pleasure:

> By the sad sea waves, I listen while they moan
> A lament o'er graves of hope and pleasure gone.
> I was young, I was fair,
> I had once not a care,
> From the rising of the morn to the setting of the sun;
> Yet I pine like a slave
> By the sad sea wave.
> Come again, bright days of hope and pleasure gone,
> Come again, bright days
> Come again, come again.

Bloom's loneliness, brought back into his unconscious by the Boylan theme of the seaside girls, calls forth in his consciousness the image of the second song with its wonderful days that are now memories. The hope that those days will come again combines with the images of those lovely seaside girls, who have now become chorus girls, to produce thoughts of love letters and finally Martha Clifford's letters. The "Seaside Girls" theme acts as a collection of all temptresses. All girls' romances, then specifically those of chorus girls, then his romance with Martha Clifford dominate Bloom's mind. Martha will have "nothing in black and white," for Bloom doesn't sign his letters, and his attempt at recapturing the "bright days" is only a half-hearted one at best. They will never come again and if they could, only Molly could resurrect them.

Low sank the music, air and words. Then hastened. The false priest rustling soldier from his cassock. A yeoman captain. They know it all by heart. The thrill they itch for.

The Priest said nought, but a
    rustling noise
Made the youth look above in
    wild surprise;
The robes were off, and in
    scarlet there

Yeoman cap.	Sat a yeoman captain with
Tap. Tap.	fiery glare.
Thrilled, she listened, bend-	(Stanza 8)
ing in sympathy to hear. (285:	
24–29)	

Cf. "The Croppy Boy"

REMARKS: Bloom, watching the attentive Miss Douce, speculates on her expectation of the climax of the song. Then Miss Douce's anticipation becomes sexual anticipation to Bloom as he digresses on sex and then the similarity between women and musical instruments. The point is that the imminent betrayal takes on sexual overtones and becomes linked with Miss Douce and all temptresses as she tempts Bloom and all men. Juxtaposed against this is the tapping of the blind piano-tuner's cane as he shuffles toward the Ormond to participate in the betrayal motif also.

They want it: not too much polite. That's why he gets them. Gold in your pocket, brass in your face. With look to look: songs without words. Molly that hurdygurdy boy. (285:35–37)

Cf. "Songs without Words"

REMARKS: As the betrayal of the croppy boy begins to impinge upon Bloom's situation, all women take on universal betraying significance and Bloom's betrayal by Boylan and Molly becomes one more drop in the river of countless seductions and unspoken coquettish looks, like Mendelssohn's "Songs without Words."

With hoarse rude fury the	With fiery glare and with fury
yeoman cursed. Swelling in	hoarse,
apoplectic bitch's bastard. A	Instead of blessing, he breathed
good thought, boy, to come.	a curse:
One hour's your time live,	" 'Twas a good thought, boy to
your last. (286:1–3)	come here and shrive,
	For one short hour is your time
	to live."
	(Stanza 9)

Cf. "The Croppy Boy"

REMARKS: The associations of the earlier tapping of the blind piano-tuner's cane are utilized in the narrator's lines describing stanza nine, as the blind man's curse ("bitch's bastard") becomes the curse of the yeoman in the song. Again the universalization of character and theme comes into play as the yeoman captain now takes on also overtones of the blind piano-tuner.

| On yonder river. (286:10) | "Upon yon river three tenders float." |
| | (Stanza 10, line 1) |

Cf. "The Croppy Boy"

But look. The bright stars fade. O rose! Castille. The morn. Ha. Lidwell. For him then not for. Infatuated. I like that? (286:14–15)

Cf. "Goodbye, Sweetheart, Goodbye"
The Rose of Castille

REMARKS: As Miss Douce's bosom heaves, Bloom discovers that it is not Boylan or the croppy boy, but George Lidwell, for whom she has been looking so picturesque and acting so coquettishly. Bloom's discovery of Miss Douce's fickleness brings musical associations of love flown away, as lines from the plaintive "Goodbye, Sweetheart, Goodbye" and *The Rose of Castille* are recalled, both of which are associated with lost love and Molly.

I hold this house. Amen. He gnashed in fury. Traitors swing. (286:27)	"The Priest's in one, if he isn't shot—
	We hold his house for our Lord the King,
	And, Amen, say I, may all traitors swing!"
	(Stanza 10, lines 2,3,4)

Cf. "The Croppy Boy"

REMARKS: The betrayer of the croppy boy finally unmasked, Bloom becomes aware that the end of the song is approaching, and hastens to leave—"Get out before the end" (286:29). Bloom will not waste his time in pity over his own betrayal or the croppy boy's. He has other business to be about.

O'er ryehigh blue. Bloom stood up. (286:34–35)

Cf. "When the Bloom Is on the Rye"

REMARKS: In the best Wagnerian tradition, Bloom exits as he enters, to the strains of his leitmotif. He passes by Pat the waiter as Dollard begins the last verse of "The Croppy Boy."

At Geneva barrack that young man died. At Passage was his body laid. Dolor! O, he dolores! The voice of the mournful chanter called to dolorous prayer. (286:39–41)

At Geneva Barrack that young
 man died,
And at Passage they have his
 body laid.
(Stanza 11, lines 1, 2)

Cf. "The Croppy Boy"
 "The Shade of the Palm"

REMARKS: "The Croppy Boy" becomes the yearning call of a lover to his Dolores to wait for him, as the song merges with "The Shade of the Palm" for Dolores-Douce. But it is not the croppy boy who is leaving, in the "Shade of the Palm" analogy, but Bloom; and the girl for whom Bloom yearns and sorrows is not Miss Douce but Molly.

> By rose, by satiny bosom, by the fondling hand, by slops, by empties, by popped corks, greeting in going, past eyes and maidenhair, bronze and faint gold in deepseashadow, went Bloom, soft Bloom, I feel so lonely Bloom. (287:1–4)

So Joyce combines the motif of love from all of the love songs of the early part of the chapter, particularly "The Shade of the Palm" and its sirens and betrayal associations, with the theme and songs of war and betrayal, particularly "The Croppy Boy," in one vast community of theme and motif, encompassing not only Bloom and Molly's marriage and Bloom and Stephen's union but the general situations of love and war everywhere.

Pray for him, prayed the bass of Dollard. You who hear in peace. Breathe a prayer, drop a tear, good men, good people. He was the croppy boy. (287:6–8)

Good people who live in peace
 and joy,
Breathe a prayer and a tear for
 the Croppy boy.
(Stanza 11, lines 3, 4)

Cf. "The Croppy Boy"

REMARKS: Part of the tears shed for the croppy boy in the last stanza should also be shed for Bloom, who now, in his martyrdom, has become identified with the croppy boy, again tying together all the situations into one grand communal package.

Scaring eavesdropping boots croppy bootsboy Bloom in the Ormond hallway heard growls and roars of bravo . . . (287:9–10)

Cf. "The Croppy Boy"

REMARKS: The communality theme is now so all-encompassing that even the cleanup boy is included, which provides an opportunity to recapitulate the major themes and significance of "The Croppy Boy." First, the whole false-father motif of the song is reflected in Stephen's view of his own father. The trusting boy comes to make his confession to a false father, a betraying yeoman captain who links the "Croppy Boy" to the overall betrayal theme of the novel. Second, the croppy boy's sins are few and far between, but the connection with Stephen is obvious through the croppy boy's sin of forgetting to pray for his mother's rest, a parallel to Stephen's sins regarding his mother's death and Stephen's agenbite of inwit. Having been betrayed by the false father, the croppy boy is led off to be executed as Stephen is symbolically by Privates Carr and Compton in Circe.

The third element entering into the "Croppy Boy" situation is the blind piano-tuner, who becomes in Sirens another croppy-boy surrogate as he comes tapping his way into the Ormond Bar. His "bitch's bastard" echoes through the narrator's rendition of Dollard's song linking him with the young hero. His entering the "lonely Ormond Hall" at the end of Sirens puts him directly in the croppy boy's place. That Stephen is directly related also to the blind piano-tuner is apparent first in Proteus, where to escape the "ineluctable modality of the visible," Stephen taps with his ash plant in the same fashion as the piano-tuner. It is Bloom who helps the piano-tuner across the street, who tries to achieve unity with him by feeling the hairs on his belly and around his ears, and who finally performs the same task for the fallen Stephen-piano-tuner-croppy boy in Circe. Thus Stephen as the croppy boy is in search of a true father, because in his present state he is able only to grope through the world of the visible, the here and now. His link with mankind through the father must be reestablished. He is blind to material things around him and only a spiritual union with a true father will put him right. Bloom will provide that function for Stephen as he has for the piano-tuner and the croppy-boy existence with all of its guilt about the mother's rest will be alleviated.

Finally, betrayal ties in "The Croppy Boy" and the theme of war, which predominates the last part of Sirens, with love which is dominant in the first half of the episode. Through the betrayal theme Bloom is again united with the croppy boy as the connotations of the song reach out through "The Shade of the Palm" to encompass the love motives of the earlier references. Eventually everyone can be linked with the croppy boy, even the bar boy in the hall, as the song, like other major musical works in this chapter, takes on overtones of being both the means and the end of the universalizing process.

Yes, her lips said more loudly, Mr Dollard. He sang that song lovely, murmured Mina. And *The last rose of summer* was a lovely song. Mina loved that song. Tankard loved the song that Mina.

'Tis the last rose of summer Dollard left Bloom felt wind wound round inside. (288:4–9)

Cf. "'Tis The Last Rose of Summer"

REMARKS: "'Tis The Last Rose of Summer," which will be heard twice more in the next two pages, is the song which Lady Harriet (Martha) sings to her love-smitten Lionel in Flotow's *Martha*. Its theme runs throughout the opera as Martha's leitmotif and the central melody of their love:

> 'Tis the last rose of summer,
> Left blooming alone;
> All her lovely companions
> Are faded and gone;
> No flow'r of her kindred,
> No rose bud is nigh,
> To reflect back her blushes
> Or give sigh for sigh.

The song serves the function at this late point in the chapter of reemphasizing the plight of Bloom, his loneliness and sorrow, by reiterating the *Martha* parallels from earlier sections of the chapter.

Bloom is linked once more to the opera *Martha*, when he is referred to as "Lionelleopold" in a subsequent paragraph which attempts to bring together several aspects of the story in a brief recapitulation:

> Up the quay went Lionelleopold, naughty Henry with letter for Mady, with sweets of sin with frillies for Raoul with met him pike hoses went Poldy on. (288:17–19)

All a kind of attempt to talk. Unpleasant when it stops because you never know exac. Organ in Gardiner street. Old Glynn fifty quid a year. Queer up there in the cockloft alone with stops and locks and keys. Seated all day at the organ. Maunder on for hours, talking to himself or the other fellow blowing the bellows. (288:28–33)

Cf. "The Lost Chord"

REMARKS: Bloom's speculations on "Old Glynn" lead to his slight variation of the first line of "The Lost Chord" ("Seated *all* day . . ." for "Seated *one* day . . ."). The picture of Glynn's solitary figure in the organ loft is identified by Bloom with the organist who sits idly playing in the song:

> Seated one day at the organ,
> I was weary and ill at ease,
> And my fingers wandered idly
> Over the noisy keys.

> I knew not what I was playing,
> Or what I was dreaming then,
> But I struck one chord of music,
> Like the sound of a great Amen,
> Like the sound of a great Amen.

The organist's fingers wandering idly over the noisy keys are the basis of a pun by Bloom. ("Maunder on for hours.") John Henry Maunder was, of course, a contemporary organist and choir director during Bloom's time who was very well known for his oratorios. The *Oxford Companion to Music* sums up the quality of his works with characteristic succinctness:

> Of his compositions the apparently inextinguishable cantatas, *Penitence, Pardon, and Peace,* and *From Olivet to Calvary* long enjoyed popularity and still aid the devotions of undemanding congregations in less sophisticated areas.[22]

In linking Maunder with Glynn's idling over the keyboard, Bloom's musical taste and knowledge prove themselves here to be a bit more sophisticated than some of his earlier remarks might have indicated.

Tap. Tap. Tap. Tap.
—The wife has a fine voice. Or had. What? Lidwell asked.
—O, that must be the tuner, Lydia said to Simonlionel first I saw, forgot it when he was here. (288:41–289:2)

Cf. *"M'appari"*

REMARKS: At this stage of the chapter Joyce has established so many motifs musical and otherwise that he is able to orchestrate them in various combinations, as they all blend musically into one. This passage ties together the piano tuner (Stephen by extension), Molly, Simon, and Lionel, and thus the plot of the opera *Martha.* As the motifs are used in combination with other motifs they become almost interchangeable, finally creating the desired universal effect.

—Very, Mr Dedalus said, staring hard at a headless sardine.
Under the sandwichbell lay on a bier of bread one last, one lonely, last sardine of summer. Bloom alone. (289:11–13)

Cf. " 'Tis The Last Rose of Summer"

REMARKS: The effect of the reference, beside its comic intent, is to allude musically, again through a theme from *Martha,* to Bloom's plight and position.
As he passes the blind piano-tuner in front of Daly's window, Bloom begins a recapitulation of the major songs in the chapter, embellishing them

with references to several others. The last two pages of the chapter (289–91), containing sixteen references to eleven songs, constitute a sort of musical finale to the episode.

Four o'clock's all's well! Sleep! All is lost now. Drum? Pompedy. Wait, I know. Towncrier, bumbailiff. Long John. Waken the dead. (289:36–39)

Cf. *"Tutto è sciolto"*
   "Pomp and Circumstance"
   "John Peel"

REMARKS: The lover's meeting is accompanied by the theme from Bellini, with all of the accompanying connotations derived during the chapter. The plaintive aria gives way to a drum roll and the suggestion of the somber processional "Pomp and Circumstance." But the music shifts in tempo and demeanor as Bloom considers waking the dead with "John Peel," an old rousing English hunting song. The association of the crier's "all's well!" with Peel's "View hal-loo" produces the allusion to the song ("Long John, Waken the Dead"). When we consider the words to "John Peel," we see that, like Bloom's lost love, the croppy boy, and Dignam, Peel is gone, never to return again:

   Stanza 1:
   D'ye ken John Peel, with his coat so gay,
   D'ye ken John Peel at the break o' the day,
   D'ye ken John Peel when he's far, far away,
   With his hounds and his horn in the morning?
   For the sound of his horn brought me from my bed,
   And the cry of his hounds which he oft-times led,
   Peel's "View hal-loo" would awaken the dead,
   Or the fox from his lair in the morning.

   Stanza 4:
   D'ye ken John Peel, with his coat so gay?
   He lived at Troutbeck once on a day;
   Now he has gone far, far away,
   We shall ne'er hear his voice in the morning.
   For the sound of his horn, etc.

All is lost for Peel as it seems for the lovesick Bloom. But that Bloom can put it in those terms of the rousing hunting song shows that all is indeed not lost for him and that his common sense will conquer.

Pom. Dignam. Poor little *nominedomine.* Pom. It is music, I mean of course it's all pom pom pom very much what they call *da capo*. Still you can hear. As we march we march along, march along. Pom. (289:39–42)

Cf. "Pomp and Circumstance"
    "The Croppy Boy"

REMARKS: With a little drumroll ("Pom") and another suggestion of "Pomp and Circumstance" we march on past Dignam and the croppy boy ("Poor little *nominedomine*. Pom"), right to the end of the paragraph. *Da capo*, the term directing a musician to go back to the beginning and start again, is probably used by Bloom to refer to the life cycle and its connection with Dignam, the croppy boy, and, by extension, mankind in general. Bloom seems to picture existence as a continual march. When you come to the end you go back and start again. His statement above represents a variation in musical terms on the metempsychosis theme, which he has been thinking about throughout the book.

I must really. Fff. Now if I did that at a banquet. Just a question of custom shah of Persia. Breathe a prayer, drop a tear. All the same he must have been a bit of a natural not to see it was a yeoman cap. Muffled up. Wonder who was that chap at the grave in the brown mackin. (290:1–5)

Cf. "The Croppy Boy"

REMARKS: The tempo changes as Bloom breaks wind, but even this is associated with the croppy boy ("Breathe a prayer, drop a tear," from stanza eleven). The credibility of the song worrying him, Bloom searches for an excuse for the croppy boy's stupidity in not recognizing the yeoman captain. Bloom's decision that the captain must have been muffled up reminds him of the man muffled in the brown mackintosh.

A frowsy whore with black straw sailor hat askew came glazily in the day along the quay towards Mr Bloom. When first he saw that form endearing. Yes, it is. I feel so lonely. (290:7–9)

Cf. "*M'appari*"

REMARKS: Here Bloom provides still another, humorous, variation on the theme of lost love. The opera *Martha* has a further analogy in the scene with the frowsy whore. Lionel's line about when first he saw "that form endearing" now becomes Leopold's as he remembers the first time he saw the whore, and the appointment they made but never kept.

Wet night in the lane. Horn. Who had the? Heehaw. Shesaw. Off her beat here. What is she? Hope she. Psst! Any chance of your

wash. Knew Molly. Had me decked. Stout lady does be with you
in the brown costume. Put you off your stroke. That appointment
we made. Knowing we'd never, well hardly ever. Too dear too
near to home sweet home. (290:10–15)

Cf. "I Am the Captain of the Pinafore"
   "Home Sweet Home"

REMARKS: Bloom uses references to two songs in describing why an assignation he had planned was never completed. "Knowing we'd never, well hardly
ever" is from the captain's song in *HMS Pinafore*:

> *Captain:* I am never known to quail
>   At the fury of a gale,
>   And I'm never, never sick at sea.
> *Crew:* What, never?
> *Captain:* No, never!
> *Crew:* What, never?
> *Captain:* Hardly ever.

Bloom, indirectly through the song, compares his meeting the prostitute with
whom he had made the appointment, with being seasick. But their union
was never consummated because the girl knew Molly, and the meeting would
have been "too dear too near to home sweet home." Here again the words to
the song "Home Sweet Home" have a humorous kind of irony to them when
seen against the context of the passage under consideration:

> 'Mid pleasures and palaces though we may roam,
>   Be it ever so humble, there's no place like home!

Bloom's "pleasures" in the "palace" of the frowsy prostitute are "too dear,"
and "too near" Bloom's "home sweet home."

Near bronze from anear near gold from afar they chinked their
clinking glasses all, brighteyed and gallant, before bronze Lydia's
tempting last rose of summer, rose of Castille. (290:27–29)

Cf. "The Thirty-Two Counties"
   " 'Tis The Last Rose of Summer"
   The Rose of Castille

REMARKS: As Bloom walks along the street, the last calls of the Sirens in
the form of songs from the episode pursue the fleeing Ulysses-Leopold. Again
Joyce juxtaposes musical theme on musical theme in a sort of chord-making
effort. The chinking of the glasses comes from the patriotic boozy thirty-two
counties song, in which all the counties are toasted successively. The chorus
refers to the clinking glasses:

> So chink your glasses chink,
> 'Tis a toast we all must drink,
> And let ev'rybody join in the chorus,

> Old Ireland is our home, and no matter where we roam,
> We'll be true to the dear land that bore us.

So all the patriotism and sacrifice and betrayal have come to little more than the drunken crowd in the Ormond singing songs of former glories and swilling down patriotic toasts, a theme to be elaborated on in Barney Kiernan's in the next episode. The "gallant" heroes of the Ormond are far from the sacrifice of the "gallant pictured hero" behind the glass of Lionel Mark's window, Robert Emmet, whose words close the chapter. Bloom's sardine image under the sandwich bowl, similarly related to Miss Douce's rose and *The Rose of Castille,* also helps close this scene with a combination of sadness, temptation, and martyrdom.

Tap. A youth entered a lonely Ormond hall. (290:32)

Cf. "The Croppy Boy"

REMARKS: Here Joyce goes out of his way to be sure that we do not miss the association between the croppy boy and the blind piano-tuner. His link here is unmistakable as the piano-tuner enters the Ormond, a Stephen Dedalus about to submit himself to the wiles of a false father and his friends.

Bloom viewed a gallant pictured hero in Lionel Marks's window. Robert Emmet's last words. Seven last words. Of Meyerbeer that is. (290:33–35)

Cf. *The Seven Last Words of Christ*

REMARKS: Here we have one of the most obvious associative patterns in the novel, as Bloom goes from Emmet's last words, to Christ's seven last words, to Meyerbeer's oratorio. The nobility of the last words of Emmet-Christ, however, emerge slightly tarnished, since Bloom, while reading them, breaks wind under cover of the sound of a passing trolley.

This last musical reference is part of Joyce's over-all tendency in the chapter to build up a seemingly serious situation or state of mind and then ruthlessly but comically destroy the illusion. Emmet's last words, preceded by the solitary figure of Ireland's martyred croppy boy and associated with Christ's martyrdom, are, in the text, juxtaposed with the present-day Irish heroes, Simon Dedalus and company, who are tipping a few in memory of the dead, as Bloom provides the final degrading air of accompaniment to Emmet's noble sentiments with a blast of burgundy-generated gas.

> —True men like you men.
> —Ay, ay, Ben.
> —Will lift your glass with us.

They lifted.

Tschink. Tschunk. (290:36–40)

Cf. "The Memory of the Dead"

    "The Thirty-Two Counties"

REMARKS: The last "tschinking" and tschunking" of the glasses in the bar accompanies words quoted directly from stanza one of "The Memory of the Dead." The song urges that the glories of Ireland's history be celebrated with alcohol:

> Who fears to speak of Ninety-Eight?
>   Who blushes at the name?
> When cowards mock the patriot's fate,
>   Who hangs his head for shame?
> He's all a knave, or half a slave,
>   Who slights his country thus;
> But a *true* man, like you, man,
>   Will fill your glass with us . . .

The reference to "The Memory of the Dead" provides a fitting combination of nostalgic militancy and strong drink as a last characterization of the assembled music-lovers in the Ormond Bar. The other patriotic drinking song of thirty-two boozy salutes completes the round of toasting with its appropriate glass chinking.

Tip. An unseeing stripling stood in the door. (290:41)

Cf. "The Croppy Boy"

REMARKS: Though there are no words from the song which match these, the waiting youth is analogous to the croppy boy. Both are awaiting their betrayal by the false father, while the true father has left the scene. The idea of seeing more when one is blind, developed by Stephen in Proteus and later refuted by Bloom, and the betrayal idea of the croppy boy fit Meyerbeer's oratorio and the words of Christ, "Father why have you forsaken me?" Hence the croppy boy, Stephen, and Bloom (the last two associated directly in the episode with the croppy boy) are all ultimately Christ figures. This image of all three consubstantial with Christ prefigures this same identification later in Circe.

12. Cyclops

—Circumcised! says Joe.

—Ay, says I. A bit off the top. (292:22–23)

Cf. "A Little Bit Off the Top Will Do for Me"

REMARKS: This allusion is the first example of many cliché song references used to characterize the speech of the habitués of Barney Kiernan's. This reference to a popular comic music-hall song is given in comment on the barfly's own mention of the name Moses Herzog. "Each verse of the song describes a different situation and provides a different meaning for the chorus, which begins, 'Carve a little bit off the top for me, For me!'"[1] While many of the titles used by the characters in the chapter seem apt and funny, it is partly because we are not as familiar with the songs as was the Dublin audience of 1904. Many of the songs were household words then and their use as metaphors less striking than trite.

So we turned into Barney Kiernan's and there sure enough was the citizen up in the corner having a great confab with himself and that bloody mangy mongrel, Garryowen, and he waiting for what the sky would drop in the way of drink. (295:11–14)

Cf. "Garryowen"

REMARKS: The dog is mentioned several times in the chapter; his hostility to the world and especially his hatred of Bloom, culminating in his chasing the fleeing Ulysses down the street, is discussed at length. Garryowen as Joseph Prescott suggests, is appropriately named:

> Joyce's point in calling the mangy, vicious mongrel Garryowen becomes fully clear only when we consider that the name fittingly combines the title of a popular Irish roistering song—to go with the nationalist context—and the filthy associations of Garryowen, the suburb of Limerick which the song celebrates.[2]

"Garry Owen" is a song of riot and drunken debauchery:

Stanza 1:
Let Bacchus' sons be not dismayed,
But join with me each jovial blade;
Come drink and sing and lend your aid,
To help me with the chorus.

Stanza 2:
We'll beat the bailiffs out of fun,
We'll make the Mayors and Sheriffs run;
We are the boys no man dares dun,
If he regards a whole skin.

Chorus:
Instead of Spa we'll drink down Ale,
And pay the reck'ning on the nail;

No man for debt shall go to jail,
From Garry Owen in Glory,
We are the boys that take delight,
In smashing the Lim'rick lights when lighting,
Through the streets like sporters fighting,
And tearing all before us.

The dog becomes, through his actions and the associations of the song, the sullen, drunken, brawling, prejudiced, self-righteous symbol of his master.

—There he is, says I, in his gloryhole, with his cruiskeen lawn and his load of papers, working for the cause. (295:15-16)

Cf. "The Cruiskeen Lawn"

REMARKS: The musical reference is to a traditional Scotch and Irish song, the translation of which is literally "my full little jug." The metaphor is not quite apt, for the citizen is waiting for someone to buy him a drink with a thirst on him he "wouldn't sell for half a crown" (295:36).

Doing the rapparee and Rory of the hill. (295:27)

Cf. "The Irish Rapparrees"
    "Rory of the Hill"

REMARKS: The barfly's description of the citizen indicates that he has heard the citizen's political invective before, since both the song allusion that he uses to describe his activities have a carping, nationalistic quality about them. The Rapparrees were Irish soldiers who stayed behind to badger the British army after the defeat of James II. Also Rory's boys are mentioned several times in the song: "For Rory's boys are in the wood . . ./ And never had poor Ireland more loyal hearts than these. . . ." [3] "Rory of the Hill," which celebrates a fighter for Irish independence, is based on Captain Rory of the Hill, who, under the authority of the Irish Land League,[4] used to harass landlords, evictors, and the tenants who paid them. So the citizen is depicted as a superpatriot by the barfly.

The eyes in which a tear and a smile strove ever for the mastery were of the dimensions of a goodsized cauliflower. (296:17-19)

Cf. "Erin, The Tear and the Smile in Thine Eyes"

REMARKS: The tear and smile are a reference to Thomas Moore's song. The import of the song serves to raise the citizen to even greater heights by literally making him the personification of Ireland. The full text of the song compounds the satire:

Erin! the tear and the smile in thine eyes
Blend like the rainbow that hangs in the skies;
Shining through sorrow's stream,
Sad'ning through pleasure's beam,
Thy suns, with doubtful gleam,
Weep while they rise!

Erin! thy silent tear never shall cease,
Erin! thy languid smile ne'er shall increase,
Till, like the rainbow's light,
Thy various tints, unite.
And form in heaven's sight
One arch of peace!

From his girdle hung a row of seastones which dangled at every movement of his portentous frame and on these were graven with rude yet striking art the tribal images of many Irish heroes and heroines of antiquity . . . the Rose of Castille, the Man for Galway. The Man that Broke the Bank at Monte Carlo, . . . Savourneen Deelish, . . . the Bride of Lammermoor, . . . Dark Rosaleen, . . . Tristan and Isolde, . . . the Bold Soldier Boy, Arrah na Pogue, . . . the Colleen Bawn, . . . The Lily of Killarney. . . . (296:32–297:18)

Cf. *The Rose of Castille* . .
   "The Man for Galway"
   "The Man Who Broke the Bank at Monte Carlo"
   "Savourneen Deelish"
   Lucia di Lammermoor
   "My Dark Rosaleen"
   Tristan und Isolde
   "The Bowld Sojer Boy"
   "Arrah-na-Pogue"
   "The Colleen Bawn"
   The Lily of Killarney

REMARKS: The list of those likenesses on the seastones around the citizen's waist begins with legitimate Irish heroes and is expanded to include a long and incongruous array of characters, much like the lists which populate passages of *Finnegans Wake*. The number and disparity of the names as well as the dissimilarities of their stories provide some of the more hilarious overtones of the giganticizing process. This list includes, as do most character lists, mostly names of very well-known people including the title characters from popular operas and songs. A couple of the names are slightly changed: *Lucia di Lammermoor* becomes Scott's original "Bride of Lammermoor," and

"The Bowld Sojer Boy" becomes "the Bold Soldier Boy." [5] Some nineteen song references are used in this way to swell the ranks of various lists and add to the comic effect of Cyclops.

> —Ah, well, says Joe, handing round the boose. Thanks be to God they had the start of us. (298:23-24)

Cf. "One More Drink for the Four of Us"

REMARKS: After the citizen indignantly begins to tick off the names of English people's deaths in *The Irish Independent,* a paper "founded by Parnell to be the workingman's friend" (298:3-4), Joe makes the calming remark above. The song reference is intended by Joe to provide a transition from thoughts of death to thoughts of whiskey, the business at hand, since it alludes to the chorus of an old drinking song "One More Drink for the Four of Us":

> Glorious, glorious, one more drink for the four of us.
> Sing glory be to God that there are no more of us
> For one of us could kill it all alone.

And it is a tribute to Joe's tact as well as the booze that the citizen is momentarily quieted.

> So of course the citizen was only waiting for the wink of the word and he starts gassing out of him about the invincibles and the old guard and the men of sixtyseven and who fears to speak of ninetyeight . . . (305:10-13)

Cf. "The Memory of the Dead"

REMARKS: The song is an entirely appropriate cliché to describe the citizen since it combines an all-encompassing patriotic zeal with strong drink.[6]

> And the citizen and Bloom having an argument about the point, the brothers Sheares and Wolfe Tone beyond on Arbour Hill and Robert Emmet and die for your country, the Tommy Moore touch about Sara Curran and she's far from the land. (305:33-36)

Cf. "She Is Far from the Land"

REMARKS: The barfly's appositive to Bloom's conversation with the citizen about dying for your country involves a song Thomas Moore presumably wrote for Sara Curran, the daughter of John Philpot Curran, a famous trial lawyer who defended Wolfe Tone, Lord Edward Fitzgerald, and other Irish patriots. Sara was in love with Robert Emmet, who was subsequently executed. The song is a commemoration of her suffering:

> She is far from the land where her young hero sleeps,
> And lovers around her sighing;
> But coldly she turns from their gaze and weeps,
> For her heart in his grave is lying.

Presumably the barfly's comments here are substantive and not mere clichés. The allusion relates directly to Robert Emmet, though the topic is not developed further during the episode.

—The memory of the dead, says the citizen taking up his pint-glass and glaring at Bloom.

—Ay, ay, says Joe.

—You don't grasp my point, says Bloom. What I mean is . . .

—*Sinn Fein!* says the citizen. *Sinn fein amhain!* The friends we love are by our side and the foes we hate before us. (306:17-23)

Cf. "The Memory of the Dead"

  "Sinn Fein"

  "Oh! Where's the Slave, So Lowly"

REMARKS: Since, as we have seen, the song "The Memory of the Dead" is a combination of Irish militancy and drinking,[7] it is doubly appropriate that the citizen should use it here in a patriotic barroom tirade.

The citizen's next reference is possibly to the Irish fighting song *"Sinn Fein"* ("Ourselves Alone"). The chorus will suffice to demonstrate the unwavering aims of both the song and the citizen:

> We'll make our own proposals and for ourselves
>   fight to be FREE
> In ev'ry clime throughout, SHIN FANE! we'll shout in
>   the name of LIBERTY.
> We'll not reduce our claims, our hopes, our aims and
>   our slogan sure will gain
> The freedom for SHIN FANE the glory of SHIN FANE our
>   battlecry will ever be SHIN FANE.

The last lines of the citizen's fervent outburst, "The friends we love are by our side and the foes we hate before us," is a slight alteration of some lines in Thomas Moore's song of fallen Ireland, "Oh! Where's the Slave, So Lowly." Following are the words to the second stanza:

> Less dear the Laurel growing,
> Alive, untouch'd and blowing.
> Than that whose braid
> Is pluck'd to shade

The brows with vict'ry glowing
We tread the land that bore us,
Her green flag o'er us, o'er us,
The friends we've tried
Are by our side,
And the foe we hate before us.
Farewell, Erin! farewell, all,
Who live to weep our fall! [italics mine]

The song references above emphasize not only the antagonistic temper of the citizen, but also his reliance on the stock quotations and changeless clichés which represent a great segment of the inflexible attitude of Irishmen like him. All this is meant to provide a foil for the incongruous logicality of Bloom's attempts to reason with him.

Considerable amusement was caused by the favourite Dublin streetsingers L-n-h-n and M-ll-g-n who sang *The Night before Larry was stretched* in their usual mirth-provoking fashion. (307: 1–4)

Cf. "The Night Before Larry Was Stretched"

REMARKS: To characterize the citizen's last patriotic outburst, the giganticised narration begins with a lengthy description of a military execution (presumably of a patriot) which carries with it implications of the crucifixion in the form of thunderclaps and celestial phenomena. Then there is an indication that the solemn mood will change when the announcement of excursion trains to handle country people is set forth, and the transition to mirth is completed with the reference to "The Night Before Larry Was Stretched."

The song is a curious mixture of pathos, ribaldry, and grisly realism. It was intended to be funny, but at the same time in its description of the last violent jerks of the hanged man, it has a sort of gallows black humor that provides the ideal transition for Joyce from the parody of patriotism and execution to one of lighthearted comedy.

Ali Baba Backsheesh . . . (307:26–27)

Cf. "Baa, Baa Black Sheep"

REMARKS: The blending of Ali Baba with the nursery rhyme is one of a series of comic combinations included in the delegation known as the "Friends of the Emerald Isle." Again the nomenclature is utilized for its humorous effect rather than for deep symbolic meaning.

The hero folded her willowy form in a loving embrace murmuring fondly *Sheila, my own.* (309:32–34)

Cf. "Mona, My Own Love"

REMARKS: The reference may be to a maudlin song of parting in which the persona laments the loss of his departed lover and longs for his own demise. Though the song does not exactly fit the execution context of the passage, the spirit certainly does.

> And one night I went in with a fellow into one of their musical evenings, song and dance about she could get up on a truss of hay she could my Maureen Lay, and there was a fellow with a Ballyhooly blue ribbon badge spiffing out of him in Irish and a lot of colleen bawns going about with temperance beverages and selling medals and oranges and lemonade and a few old dry buns, gob, flahoolagh entertainment, don't be talking. Ireland sober is Ireland free. And then an old fellow starts blowing into his bagpipes and all the gougers shuffling their feet to the tune the old cow died of. (311:6-15)

Cf. "The Low-Backed Car"
   "Ballyhooly"
   "The Colleen Bawn"
   "The Tune the Old Cow Died On"

REMARKS: What the barfly remembers is probably the performance of one of Samuel Lover's "Irish Evenings," since the song and dance about "she could get up on a truss of hay" is from the first stanza of "The Low-Backed Car," a key song reference at the end of Eumaeus. The first lines of the song are,

> When first I saw sweet Peggy,
> 'Twas on a market day.
> A lowback'd car she drove, and sat
> Upon a truss of hay;

Lover wrote the song for his patriotic entertainments. The barfly, to his everlasting chagrin, found himself not only at a patriotic entertainment, but also at a temperance party. The man with the Ballyhooly blue ribbon badge refers to a comic temperance song, "Ballyhooly." A stanza and chorus give a fair representation of the song:

> There's a dashing sort of boy, who is call'd his mother's joy;
> His ructions and his elements they charm me;
> He takes the chief command in a water drinking band,
> Called the Ballyhooly blue ribbon army!
> The ladies all declare he's the pride of every fair,
> And he bears the patriotic name of Dooley;
> When the temperance brigade go out upon parade,
> Faith there's not a sober man in Ballyhooly.

Chorus:
Whilliloo, hi, ho! Let us all enlist you know,
For their principles and elements they charm me;
Sure we don't care what we ate,
If we drink our whisky nate,
In the Ballyhooly blue ribbon army!

The allusion to colleen bawns is of course an allusion to that symbol of young Irish Womanhood in the song "Colleen Bawn," from *The Lily of Killarney.* The song is discussed elsewhere in the text, but the reference is meant here merely to be a satiric allusion to the girls who plead temperance in the Irish name.

The last musical allusion in the passage is a bagpipe song which the barfly compares to the first song old Farmer John sings to his cows in "The Tune the Old Cow Died On." One old cow tries to emulate it, which subsequently causes her death.

So off they started about Irish sport and shoneen games the like of the lawn tennis and about hurley and putting the stone and racy of the soil and building up a nation once again and all of that. . . . the vocalist chairman brought the discussion to a close, in response to repeated requests and hearty plaudits from all parts of a bumper house, by a remarkably noteworthy rendering of the immortal Thomas Osborne Davis' evergreen verses (happily too familiar to need recalling here) *A nation once again* in the execution of which the veteran patriot champion may be said without fear of contradiction to have fairly excelled himself. (316:31–34, 317:17–24)

Cf. "A Nation Once Again"

REMARKS: Even if the barfly did not intend a reference to the song, Joyce surely did not want his readers to miss the allusion. In the giganticized narration the song is unmistakably mentioned. The lyrics appropriately treat of sport as well as patriotism, for they deal with the persona's vision of ancient Greece and Rome, which prompt his concept of a free Ireland "in forum, field, and fane." The song is another instance of allusion used simply to giganticize the action of Cyclops.

—My wife? says Bloom. She's singing, yes. I think it will be a success too. He's an excellent man to organise. Excellent.

Hoho begob, says I to myself, says I. That explains the milk in the cocoanut and absence of hair on the animal's chest. Blazes doing the tootle on the flute. (319:26–30)

Cf. "Said I to Myself, Said I"
    "Phil the Fluter's Ball"

REMARKS: The barfly is not fooled for a second about Blazes' collaboration with Molly. Again he expresses himself in song-oriented clichés. The term, "Said I to Myself, Said I," if not originating in the song from Gilbert and Sullivan's *Iolanthe,* certainly gained popularity by its appearance in the well-known operetta. In *Iolanthe* it is a qualifying statement by the Lord Chancellor to explain his overly pious statements regarding his position in life. It works also as a cliché of incredulity for the barfly. The "tootle on the flute" that Blazes will be playing with Molly is from the chorus of "Phil the Fluter's Ball," which has further possibilities for double entendre:

> With the toot of the flute,
> And the twiddle of the fiddle, O'
> Hopping in the middle, like a herrin' on a griddle, O'
> Up, down, hadns arown'
> Crossin' to the wall,
> Oh, hadn't we the gaiety at Phil the Fluter's Ball!

Again, the barfly, with all his trite utterances, gets to the truth of things.

—There's hair, Joe, says I. (324:25)

Cf. "There's Hair"

REMARKS: As the boys at the bar admire with appropriate comments a smutty picture in the *Police Gazette* the barfly is not to be outdone in the offering of clichés. Again, the song is a popular music-hall song of the day, in which the persona's hair is very much remarked on and admired by girl friends, the Prince of Wales, and finally an old orangutan in the zoo, each remarking "there's hair."

. . . he drank to the undoing of his foes, a race of mighty valorous heroes, rulers of the waves . . . (325:24–25)

Cf. "Rule Britannia"

REMARKS: The allusion is to the song that is still a household word for English imperialism, "Rule, Britannia, Britannia rules the waves!" Its use in the present context is obvious.

So he went over to the biscuit tin Bob Doran left to see if there was anything he could lift on the nod, the old cur after him backing his luck with his mangy snout up. Old mother Hubbard went to the cupboard. (325:41–326:2)

Cf. "Old Mother Hubbard"

REMARKS: This nursery-rhyme allusion seems to be the tritest of all the barfly's clichés; but only because the nursery rhyme referred to is still as familiar to us as all the other references must have been to a turn-of-the-century Dublin audience. I don't think Joyce was trying to make us admire the adroitness of the barfly's metaphor in any of the passages of his description in the episode. Rather the singular dullness of his thought patterns is exemplified by the ringing clichés. As some of the songs and expressions pass out of current usage, they assume an aura of originality which was lacking in 1904. Just how bad they are is much more apparent in a nursery-rhyme triteness such as "Old Mother Hubbard."

Save the trees of Ireland for the future men of Ireland on the fair hills of Eire, O. (326:40–41)

Cf. "The Fair Hills of Eire, O"

REMARKS: The citizen's lament for the once numerous forests of Ireland that are being laid waste includes an allusion to this hymn to the fertility of the Irish soil and her "woods . . . tall and straight, grove rising after grove."

The fashionable international world attended *en masse* this afternoon at the wedding of the chevalier Jean Wyse de Neaulan, . . . Miss Bee Honeysuckle, . . . Miss O. Mimosa San . . . . (327:1–3, 10, 11)
Senhor Enrique Flor . . . played a new and striking arrangement of *Woodman, spare that tree* at the conclusion of the service. (327:27–31)

Cf. "You Are the Honeysuckle, I Am the Bee"
   The Geisha
   "Woodman Spare that Tree"

REMARKS: When Lenehan remarks, "Europe has its eyes on you" (326:42), the third-person narrator begins a lengthy description of a foliaceous wedding attended by all sorts of people whose names have something to do with trees or herbaceous plants, including "Miss Bee Honeysuckle" from the music-hall song "You Are the Honeysuckle, I Am the Bee," and "Miss O. Mimosa San" from the operetta *The Geisha*. Senhor Flor's rendition of "Woodman, Spare that Tree" is a magnificently apt song for the occasion. Its maudlin ecological lyrics begin,

> Woodman, spare that tree!
> Touch not a single bough;
> In youth it sheltered me,
> And I'll protect it now; . . .

—But what about the fighting navy, says Ned, that keeps our foes at bay? (328:36–37)

Cf. "The Lads in Navy Blue"

REMARKS: Ned joins the little band of clichémongers as he refers to the British navy in terms of the well-known song about the invincibility of the English on the sea:

> It is the Navy, the British Navy
> That keeps our foes at bay.
> Our old song, Britannia rules the waves,
> We still can sing to-day.

—That's your glorious British navy, says the citizen, that bosses the earth. The fellows that never will be slaves, with the only hereditary chamber on the face of God's earth and their land in the hands of a dozen gamehogs and cottonball barons. (329:14–18)

Cf. "Rule Britannia"

REMARKS: The quotation is from the song in which Britannia rules the waves, and Britains never will be slaves. The popularity and hence banality of the clichés has already been noted,[8] as well as the triteness of the citizen's speech.

But those that came to the land of the free remember the land of bondage. And they will come again and with a vengeance, no cravens, the sons of Granuaile, the champions of Kathleen ni Houlihan.

—Perfectly true, says Bloom. But my point was . . . (330:4–9)

Cf. "The Star Spangled Banner"

REMARKS: In linking America with the promised land through the reference to the national anthem, and linking Ireland under the British to the Egyptian bondage of the Jews, the citizen has rekindled memories of the Messianic theme so prevalent in Aeolus and the earlier chapters. The motif will form a major part of the significance of Cyclops. The prophet, Moses, or Messiah to lead the Irish out of bondage is none other, of course, than Leopold Bloom, who stands in the citizen's very presence attempting to make a point about universal reaction to discipline. As in Aeolus he is ignored or mocked by the Irish even when all the symbols and the conversation point to his emerging as the leader of the Irish people. Stephen in Skylla and Charybdis, with dreams and bird omens and Mulligan's taunting prophetic jibes pointing the way to Bloom as Stephen's salvation, is just as blind. At the crucial time when Bloom passes out of the library before him, he still is unable to see the meaning and import of Bloom and his presence. Here again the citizen links the nationalistic-patriotic motif with the Messianic pattern, which will conclude the episode with Bloom's ascending to heaven.

—We are a long time waiting for that day, citizen, says Ned. Since the poor old woman told us that the French were on the sea and landed at Killala. (330:10–12)

Cf. "The *Shan Van Vocht*"

REMARKS: Ned paraphrases "The *Shan Van Vocht*" in quoting Irish history ("Since the poor old woman . . ."). The warning of "The *Shan Van Vocht*" ("The Poor Old Woman," *i.e.,* Ireland) in the song recounts the hope of Ireland's liberation by Napoleon's army. The first verse of the song contains the old woman's main promise:

> O the French are on the sea
> Says the Shan Van Vocht,
> O the French are on the sea
> Says the Shan Van Vocht.
> O the French are on the sea,
> They'll be here the break o' day,
> And the Orange will decay
> Says the Shan Van Vocht.

Thus in the song, Ireland recounts its own hope for its freedom from bondage, as Lenehan reiterates the Messianic motif inherent in Irish nationalism and prepares the way for Bloom to emerge at the end of the chapter as that Messianic figure.

. . . and she pulling him by the whiskers and singing him old bits of songs about *Ehren on the Rhine* and come where the boose is cheaper. (330:34–36)

Cf. "Ehren on the Rhine"
  "Come Where My Love Lies Dreaming"

REMARKS: The citizen turns his attention to maligning Queen Victoria, referring to her drunken habits and her conduct with her coachman. "Ehren on the Rhine" is a song of parting between a soldier and his love who promise to meet after the war at Ehren on the Rhine. He dies, his last words being that he won't make the appointment. The second reference is probably a drunken parody of "Come Where My Love Lies Dreaming," another well-known lovesong. The songs seem to have little significance other than being obviously malicious.

The scenes depicted on the emunctory field, showing our ancient duns and raths and cromlechs . . . the vale of Ovoca . . . the glen of Aherlow . . . (332:7-9, 17, 18-19)

Cf. "The Meeting of the Waters"
  "Patrick Sheehan"

REMARKS: As the citizen and Bloom begins to lock horns over the Jewish issue the citizen spits and wipes his face with a handkerchief which is described at great length by the narrator. Especially important are the Irish scenes embroidered upon it, including the vale of Avoca, commemorated in Thomas Moore's beautiful "The Meeting of the Waters" and the Glen of Aherlow so prominent in Kickham's "Patrick Sheehan."

God save Ireland from the likes of that bloody mouseabout. (336: 4-5)

Cf. "God Save Ireland"

REMARKS: Having been told that Bloom has won money on Throwaway, the barfly changes his attitude toward Bloom in the narration. The line is of course the last words in the famous quotation of the Manchester Martyrs. That the barfly quotes it is an ironic commentary on the Dublin citizenry, who condemn their would-be Messiah and his ideas for economic sanctions, etc. for the *Sinn Fein* Movement.

And last, beneath a canopy of cloth of gold came the reverend Father O'Flynn attended by Malachi and Patrick. (340:16-17)

Cf. "Father O'Flynn"

REMARKS: As the citizen calls a benediction on all assembled at the bar, the giganticized narration calls forth what must be the longest ecclesiastical procession in history, all of which precedes Father O'Flynn (fabled in the song bearing his name as the best of all priests). The comic song which gives Father O'Flynn such a high rating is the perfect humorous allusion to conclude the long and funny procession evoked by the citizen's remark.

And all the ragamuffins and sluts of the nation round the door and Martin telling the jarvey to drive ahead and the citizen bawling and Alf and Joe at him to whisht and he on his high horse about the jews and the loafers calling for a speech and Jack Power trying to get him to sit down on the car and hold his bloody jaw and a loafer with a patch over his eye starts singing *If the man in the moon was a jew, jew, jew* . . . (342:14-20)

Cf. "If the Man in the Moon Were a Coon"

REMARKS: The song which the loafer sings is a parody of a music-hall song degrading the Negro by poking fun at his color, image, and habits:

Stanza 1:

Say, Jasper, 'taint no use talking even though you talk from now till noon,
Don't try to tell me, Mister Know-it-all, a coon is up in the moon;
Why! a nigger, with his brown figure, cert'n'y darkens up the silv'ry moon;
Wake up! you're dreaming with your eyes aglare,
You great big foolish coon.

Stanza 2:

Most e'ry one has heard stories that a chicken is a coon's delight,
Just think the dangers to a hen roost with that good old moon out of sight;
'Deed! chicken would be soft pickin' if that man up in the moon were
    black;
Oh, my! the harvest for the darkey with
That big sack on his back.

Chorus:

If the man in the moon were a coon, coon, coon, what would you do?
He would fade with his shade the silv'ry moon, moon, moon, away
    from you;
No roaming 'round the park at night,
No spooning in the bright moonlight,
If the man in the moon were a coon, coon, coon . . .

In the song reference Joyce emphasizes the universal qualities of prejudice and bigotry by the substitution of *jew* for *coon*. The sinister effect of "Garryowen" and its debauchery and the combination of racism and anti-Semitism in the song reference present an extremely disparaging picture of Ireland's "citizens" despite the first-rate comedy which Joyce provides throughout the chapter.

The departing guest was the recipient of a hearty ovation, many of those who were present being visibly moved when the select orchestra of Irish pipes struck up the wellknown strains of *Come back to Erin*, followed immediately by *Rakoczy's March*. (343:8–12)

Cf. "Come Back to Erin"
    "Rákóczy March"

REMARKS: The citizen's send-off of Bloom is orchestrated by a humorously appropriate combination of the sentimental and the martial. The lyrics of the first well-known song are typically maudlin and Irish:

Come back to Erin, Mavourneen, Mavourneen,
Come back Aroon, to the land of thy birth . . .

The stirring military march of Miklos Scholl introduces us to the Hungarian goodbyes which close the paragraph and provide the pomp and ceremonial atmosphere in which the citizen throws the biscuit tin. The linking of Hungary and Ireland in the conjunction of the two songs follows the linking in Griffiths' *The Resurrection of Hungary* of Hungarian history with Ireland's bondage and the birth of the *Sinn Fein* Movement. Francis Rákóczy was a leader in the Hungarian resurrection and the march titled after him became famous after Liszt used it as a part of his recital tour in Hungary in 1838. So it is appropriate that the super patriots of Cylops see their departing savior off to climes with Hungarian titles.

Tarbarrels and bonfires were lighted along the coastline of the four seas on the summits of . . . the mountains of Mourne . . .
(343:12–15)

Cf. "The Mountains of Mourne"

REMARKS: It is not at all certain that Joyce had in mind the song here or merely the mountains which gave it its name. At any rate Percy French's song is a comic, nostalgic comparison between the sights and girls of London and those "where the Mountains of Mourne sweep down to the sea." The music fits the passage perfectly.

13. Nausicaa

But waiting, always waiting to be asked and it was leap year too and would soon be over. (351:35–37)

Cf. "Waiting"

REMARKS: Gerty forms part of her self-image through the use of this song as Molly does.[1] Although the note of anticipation and self-identification as siren in the song imposes some initial link between the romantic aspirations of Molly and Gerty, Joyce would give the same dreams to a majority of women —even Maria in "Clay" is not wholly immune to them. The song acts then as a communal link between Bloom's women and as a universalizing force in the novel.

And she tickled tiny tot's two cheeks to make him forget and played here's the lord mayor, here's his two horses, here's his

gingerbread carriage and here he walks in, chinchopper, chinchopper, chinchopper chin. (353:12–15)

Cf. "Here Sits the Lord Mayor"

REMARKS: Only the obvious appears involved here. Cissy Caffrey placates
Baby Boardman for the loss of his ball by chucking him under the chin and
reciting the traditional nursery rhyme.

With all his faults she loved him still when he sang *Tell me,
Mary, how to woo thee* or *My love and cottage near Rochelle*
and they had stewed cockles and lettuce with Lazenby's salad
dressing for supper and when he sang *The moon hath raised* with
Mr Dignam that died suddenly and was buried, God have mercy
on him, from a stroke. (354:36–42)

Cf. "With All Her Faults I Love Her Still"
   "Tell Me, Mary, How to Woo Thee"
   "My Love and Cottage Near Rochelle"
   "The Moon Hath Raised Her Lamp Above"

REMARKS: The songs that Gerty's father sang on those memorable occasions
were all romantic, sentimental songs, references calculated to reenforce the
sentimental bent of the girl's thoughts. And, indeed, the references with their
sentimentality do come this time indirectly from Gerty's stream of consciousness. The words are almost alike in their sentimental connotations:

> With all her faults I love her still,
> And even though the world should scorn;
> No love like hers my heart can thrill,
> Although she's made that heart forlorn!
>   ("With All Her Faults")

> Tell me, Mary, how to woo thee,
> Teach my bosom to reveal
> All its sorrows sweet unto thee,
> All the love my heart can feel;
>   ("Tell Me, Mary . . .")

> When I beheld the anchor weighed,
> and with the shore thine image fade,
> I deemed each wave a boundless sea
> that bore me still from love and thee.
>   ("My Love and Cottage . . .")

> The moon hath raised her lamp above,
> To light the way to thee my love.
>   ("The Moon Hath Raised . . .") [2]

... and the choir began to sing *Tantum ergo* and she just swung her foot in and out in time as the music rose and fell to the *Tantumer gosa cramen tum*. (360:5–8)

Then they sang the second verse of the *Tantum ergo* . . . (361:27)

Cf. "*Tantum ergo*"

REMARKS: As the mass builds to a climax and the prayers to the Virgin are said and *Tantum ergo* sung, so too does Gerty move to her climax, in an orgasmic parody of the conclusion of chapter four of *Portrait*. Gerty swings her foot in time to the music as the girl in Stephen's scene stirs the water hither and thither with her foot. In both works the Virgin and the ecclesiastical elements are blended. In Stephen's vision, the girl on the beach is Virgin, temptress, and inspiration. Bloom's view is of the virgin Gerty trying her utmost to tempt him. Both blend the sexual climax with ecclesiastical elation and worship. As the strains of the mass chants drift onto the beach and the virgin-temptress-Gerty engages in vicarious intercourse with Bloom, the scene from *Portrait* is repeated, this time not in the fantasized, stream-of-consciousness-surrogate narration of Stephen but in the naturalistically developed thoughts of Gerty and Bloom. The similar situations occur at approximately the same time in each novel and lead to different conclusions (masturbation and aesthetic elevation) only because the characters they represent begin at opposite points and not because the ultimate significance of the scenes is radically different. The obvious consubstantiality of the two scenes is a prime indicator of the communal existence of Bloom and Stephen.

—O my! Puddeny pie! (363:17)

Cf. "Georgie Porgie"

REMARKS: Evidently one of Crissy's prime child-rearing techniques is the use of nursery rhymes. While there is only a rough correspondence between Cissy's expression and "pudding and pie," from the second line of the rhyme, other nursery rhymes used in the same way suggest that the reference is present.

How moving the scene there in the gathering twilight, the last glimpse of Erin, the touching chime of those evening bells and at the same time a bat flew forth from the ivied belfry through the dusk, hither, thither, with a tiny lost cry. (363:30–33)

Cf. "Though the Last Glimpse of Erin"
   "Those Evening Bells"

REMARKS: The allusion to "Though the Last Glimpse of Erin" effectively ties in Gerty with another female principle Joyce is fond of using, the woman as Ireland. The first stanza of the popular song by Thomas Moore makes this explicit:

Tho' the last glimpse of Erin with sorrow I see,
Yet wherever thou art shall seem Erin to me;
In exile thy bosom shall still be my home,
And thine eyes make my climate wherever we roam.

Thus, Gerty is not only virgin and temptress, but also Ireland. Like Stephen's girl at the end of chapter four of *Portrait,* she coalesces all three into one consubstantial whole. Supporting the Gerty-as-Ireland motif, the chimes of the bell at the Star of the Sea church, again through a Thomas Moore song, "Those Evening Bells," become the bells of home and youth and "that sweet time/When last I heard their chime."

If she saw that magic lure in his eyes there would be no holding back for her. Love laughs at locksmiths. She would make the great sacrifice. (364:22–24)

Cf. *Love Laughs at Locksmiths*

REMARKS: Gerty's proverbial phrase about love and locksmiths comes from the title of an 1803 comic opera by George Coleman, which was written in the bawdy comic style of the turn of the nineteenth century, and which gives an unintended ribald counterpoint to her high-blown sentiments of the moment.

Perhaps it was an old flame he was in mourning for from the days beyond recall. She thought she understood. She would try to understand him because men were so different. The old love was waiting, waiting with little white hands stretched out, with blue appealing eyes. Heart of mine! She would follow her dream of love, the dictates of her heart that told her he was her all in all, the only man in all the world for her for love was the master guide. Nothing else mattered. Come what might she would be wild, untrammelled, free.

Canon O'Hanlon put the Blessed Sacrament back into the tabernacle and the choir sang *Laudate Dominum omnes gentes* . . . (364:40–365:8)

Cf. "Love's Old Sweet Song"
   "Waiting"
   "Laudate Dominum omnes gentes"

REMARKS: Here Gerty is closer to home than she thinks, for she inadvertantly uses a reference to the theme song of Molly and Blazes' assignation when she alludes to "Love's Old Sweet Song." Having established the song as a leitmotif which we cannot by this time fail to recognize, Joyce puts an allusion to it in Gerty's mouth, linking it with Bloom's sad countenance and mourning. And if Bloom's countenance is sad it is indeed partly Molly's fault. Gerty again accurately perceives Molly, the "old love . . . waiting, waiting." Having earlier in this episode established the link between Molly and Gerty through the song reference to "Waiting," Joyce builds on the association to make Molly the fantasy and real former lover of Bloom in both Gerty's mind and in the larger context of novel. So in this most important passage in terms of theme in the episode, Gerty resolves to become, like Nausicaa, the means of salvation for her lonely, saddened Ulysses. She will devote herself to him for ever even if it is all vicarious. But we will find out that Bloom has sensed something more than the vicarious about Gerty's attitude toward him, and she provides the stimulation at least for his masturbation, even if it is Molly of whom he thinks while he has his orgasm. Like Stephen, Bloom has found his inspiration figure on Sandymount Strand. Even the use of the words *wild* and *free* echo Stephen's language in the beach scene in *Portrait*. Gerty has been the initial source of inspiration and erection in this upside-down parody of effectuality. Even the choir of celestial singers from The Star of the Sea joins in chorus to celebrate the erection/ resurrection of Bloom with a chorus of *"Laudate Dominum."*

> Thankful for small mercies. Cheap too. Yours for the asking. Because they want it themselves. Their natural craving. Shoals of them every evening poured out of offices. Reserve better. Don't want it they throw it at you. Catch em alive, O. Pity they can't see themselves. A dream of wellfilled hose. (368:21–26)

Cf. "Cockles and Mussels"

REMARKS: Bloom's thoughts, in contrast to Gerty's are on the mundane aspects of love. He and Gerty have just experienced a vicarious sort of sexual experience as the Mirus bazaar fireworks burst overhead. Bloom's aroused mood leads to the speculations of the passage above. "Catch em alive, O" is a reference to "Cockles and Mussels," a traditional Irish song about a fishmonger named Molly Malone. The first verse and chorus contain the popular line, "alive, O!" which runs throughout the song:

> In Dublin's fair city,
> Where the girls are so pretty,
> I first set my eyes on sweet Molly Malone,
> As she wheel'd her wheelbarrow
> Thro' streets broad and narrow,
> Crying, Cockles and mussels! alive, alive, O!

> Chorus:
> Alive, alive, O!
> Alive, alive, O!
> Crying, Cockles and mussels! alive, alive, O!

Molly Malone's huckstering of her fish is associated by Bloom with girls' selling their physical attractions, thoughts of which are ever present in the protagonist's mind. The song provides another consubstantial link between Bloom and Stephen. In Stephen's morning walk along Sandymount, he encounters some cocklepickers whom he mistakes for midwives. He ascribes to them later the sensuality of seventeenth-century bawds through his allusion to the canting songs. Here Stephen's and Bloom's flights of sensual fantasy coalesce with the song about the cocklepickers being used to describe the sex drives of loose women.

Put them all on to take them all off. Molly. Why I bought her the violet garters. Us too: the tie he wore, his lovely socks and turnedup trousers. He wore a pair of gaiters the night that first we met. His lovely shirt was shining beneath his what? of jet. Say a woman loses a charm with every pin she takes out. Pinned together. O Mairy lost the pin of her. Dressed up to the nines for somebody. Fashion part of their charm. (368:32–39)

Cf. "She Wore a Wreath of Roses the Night that First We Met"
 "O, Mary Lost the Pin of Her Drawers"

REMARKS: Bloom's thoughts of Molly's garters lead to men's vanity and Boylan's gaiters as Bloom paraphrases the first two lines of an old ballad, "She Wore a Wreath of Roses." Here the "wreath of roses" from the first line of the song becomes Boylan's "pair of gaiters" ("He wore a pair of gaiters the night that first we met"). If we examine the first stanza of the song we see that Bloom has made other changes in the lyrics:

> She wore a wreath of roses
> The first night that we met,
> Her lovely face was smiling
> Beneath her curls of jet;
> Her footstep had the lightness,
> Her voice the joyous tone,
> The tokens of a youthful heart
> Where sorrow is unknown;
> I saw her but a moment—
> Yet me-thinks I see her now,
> With the wreath of summer flowers
> Upon her snowy brow.

"Her lovely face" in the third line of the song becomes "his [Boylan's] lovely shirt"; "smiling" in the same line becomes "shining"; and "her curls of jet" in the fourth line become "his what? of jet." Bloom's version of the song emphasizes Boylan's vanity and tends to point up the foppery of that characteristic. Bloom is doing fairly well in altering the lyrics of the song to fit

Boylan and Molly's first meeting, until he is stuck with Boylan's shirt shining under curls of jet. Either the preposterousness of this image is too much for even Bloom or he just can't think of another word when he substitutes *what?* for *curls.*

Hodgart and Worthington have incorrectly identified the second line of Bloom's paraphrase ("His lovely hair . . .") as coming from the song "Her Golden Hair Was Hanging Down Her Back," [3] the lyrics of which resemble the words of Bloom's stream of consciousness only in the mention of hair.

Stanzas two and three of "She Wore a Wreath of Roses" see a waning of the girl's beauty and happiness.

> Stanza 2:
> A wreath of orange blossoms
> When next we met she wore;
> Th' expression of her features
> Was more thoughtful than before;
> And standing by her side was one
> Who strove and not in vain,
> To soothe her, leaving that dear home
> She ne'er might view again;
> I saw her but a moment—
> Yet me-thinks I see her now,
> With the wreath of orange blossoms
> Upon her snowy brow.

> Stanza 3:
> And once again I see that brow,
> No bridal wreath is there,
> The widow's sombre cap conceals
> Her once luxuriant hair;
> She weeps in silent solitude,
> And there is no one near,
> To press her hand within his own,
> And wipe away the tear;
> I see her brokenhearted!
> Yet me-thinks I see her now,
> In the pride of youth and beauty,
> With a garland on her brow.

There is perhaps a veiled warning for the errant Molly in the woman who ". . . weeps in silent solitude . . . [with] no one near/To press her hand within his own. . . ." At any rate, the loss of feminine charm in stanzas two and three provides the association for the loss-of-charm reference in the next sentence of Bloom's stream of consciousness ("Say a woman loses a charm with every pin she takes out").

The mention of pins brings Bloom's thinking back again to the song of the two sluts, "O Mary Lost the Pin of Her Drawers." The reference to this melody provides an orchestration of purposeful vulgarity which underscores the low common denominator of the whole passage.

Maiden discovered with pensive bosom. Little sweetheart come and kiss me. Still I feel. The strength it gives a man. That's the secret of it. Good job I let off there behind coming out of Dignam's. Cider that was. Otherwise I couldn't have. Makes you want to sing after. *Lacaus esant taratara.* (370:17-22)

Cf. *"La causa è santa"*

REMARKS: It is not certain whether Bloom is referring in the passage above to the song-producing qualities of breaking wind or of having an orgasm. In either case the pleasant feeling produced is somewhat incongruously associated with "The Sacred Cause" from Meyerbeer's *Les Huguenots.*

Bloom's memory of this sextet is, as we have seen before,[4] fairly accurate. His phraseology of *"La causa è santa"* corresponds to the musical values of the sixteenth and dotted eighths of the corresponding musical passage in the second and fourth staffs (Cosse's and Retz's parts), *Lacaus* making up one sequence of a sixteenth and dotted eighth, *esant* the next sixteenth and dotted eighth, and, switching to the third and fifth staffs, the *taratara* corresponding to Tavannes and Meru's *"De dritti miei"*:

Bloom remembers not one part of the sextet but the continuum of six voices.

The words to *"La causa,"* "Upon a righteous cause relying/To death my enemies defying," have, it is true, a sort of elation and exaltation about them, but there is also the inescapable humor of their delightful inappropriateness for Bloom at this point in his day's activities.

> Didn't look back when she was going down the strand. Wouldn't give that satisfaction. Those girls, those girls, those lovely seaside girls. (371:31-33)

Cf. "Seaside Girls"

REMARKS: This time the mention of the seaside girls song seems devoid of connotations of Boylan. The universality motif embodied in the song is reiterated as again it becomes the theme of all beautiful young girls, Nausicca-like in bringing physical and emotional relief and comfort to the frustrated, strife-torn Ulyssean wanderers of the world.

> For this relief much thanks. In *Hamlet,* that is. Lord! It was all things combined. Excitement. When she leaned back felt an ache at the butt of my tongue. Your head it simply swirls. (372:30-33)

Cf. "Seaside Girls"

REMARKS: Here the universalization process is specifically alluded to ("It was all things combined") and the consubstantial process directly tied in with *Hamlet.* Finally as a major song motif of ultimate unity, the "Seaside Girls" is alluded to with its universal temptresses to tie the universality motif here into one neat package with the Hamlet-Shakespeare consubstantiality theme. In other words, the consubstantiality motifs are also consubstantial.

> But the ball rolled down to her as if it understood. Every bullet has its billet. Course I never could throw anything straight at school. (372:41-373:2)

Cf. "Every Bullet Has Its Billet"

REMARKS: As Bloom thinks about the inevitability of the meeting between himself and Gerty and the unspoken understanding on their encounter, he decides perhaps it was dictated by fate, since the ball he threw back to Cissy Caffrey came to rest in front of Gerty. To emphasize his point about the fatalistic aspects of the course of the ball, Bloom quotes the title of an 1815 sea chanty, "Every Bullet Has Its Billet." The song urges bravery on the basis of the inevitable preordination of death:

I'm a tough, true hearted Sailor,
Careless, and all that, d'ye see;
Never at the times a railer,
What is time or tide to me?
All must die when fate shall will it,
Providence ordains it so;
Ev'ry bullet has its billet,
Man the boat, boys,
Yo, heave ho!
Yo, heave ho!
Yo, heave ho!
Man the boat, boys,
Yo, heave ho!

As "providence ordains" the home of the bullet, so in Bloom's mind has it ordained the path and home of the ball he has thrown.

Sad however because it lasts only a few years till they settle down to potwalloping and papa's pants will soon fit Willy and fullers' earth for the baby when they hold him out to do ah ah. (373:3–6)

Cf. "Looking Through the Knothole"

REMARKS: As the plight of dull marital routine settles upon the once romantic girl of Bloom's thoughts, it is orchestrated to the tune of an American nonsense song, which was popular with children who sang its many variations to the tune of "Reuben, Reuben." One of the two line verses is:

Mama's teeth will soon fit Nelly;
Don't stick pins in the baby's belly.[5]

Bloom's line in the passage above is another of the infinite number of versions of the song. Bloom is piecing together bits of babyhood and childhood experience as he reenforces his brief picture of the mundane trials of raising a family with the reference to the children's song, which concerns itself with such uninspiring activities as diaper changing.

She'd [Gerty] like scent of that kind. Sweet and cheap: soon sour. Why Molly likes opoponax. Suits her with a little jessamine mixed. Her high notes and her low notes. At the dance night she met him, dance of the hours. Heat brought it out. She was wearing her black and it had the perfume of the time before. (374:28–33)

Cf. "Dance of the Hours"

REMARKS: The associations of smell, the bazaar dance, and Ponchielli's "Dance of the Hours" here parallel a strikingly similar passage on page 69.[6]

In the earlier passage the perfumed aroma is Bloom's own as he sits in the jakes reading Philip Beaufoy's column. Boylan's sweet breath odor mentioned in the earlier passage is parallel to Molly's opoponax and jessamine smell in the later reference. We see in the above passage that the "Dance of the Hours" is in Bloom's mind inseparable from the lovers' first meeting.

Dreadful life sailors have too. Big brutes of ocean-going steamers floundering along in the dark, lowing out like seacows. *Faugh a ballagh.* Out of that, bloody curse to you. (378:24–27)

Cf. *"Faugh a Ballagh"*

REMARKS: Not only does the Gaelic resemble the sound of a fog horn for Bloom, but the song is about clearing the way, each stanza and the chorus beginning, "Faugh-a-ballagh—clear the way boys!" A song about the glories and the charges of the Fourth Dragon Guards, its use is obvious here.

Others in vessels, bit of a handkerchief sail, pitched about like snuff at a wake when the stormy winds do blow. Married too. Sometimes away for years at the ends of the earth somewhere. (378:27–30)

Cf. "The Stormy Winds Do Blow"

REMARKS: The second musical reference in the sea sequence equates the Siren-temptress figure with ultimate destruction. This 1840 song of the sea again represents "a fair pretty maid" as being identified with shipwreck and ultimate destruction:

Stanza 1:
One Friday morn when we set sail,
  Not very far from land,
We there did espy a fair pretty maid
  With a comb and a glass in her hand, her hand, her hand,
  With a comb and a glass in her hand.

Stanza 2:
Then up starts the capt'n of our gallant ship,
  And a brave young man was he;
"I've a wife and child in fair Bristol town,
  But a widow I fear she will be."

Stanza 3:
Then up starts the mate of our gallant ship,
  And a bold young man was he;

"Oh, I have a wife in fair Portsmouth town,
    But a widow I fear she will be."

Stanza 4:
Then up starts the cook of our gallant ship,
    And a gruff old soul was he;
"Oh, I have a wife in Plymouth town,
    But a widow I fear she will be."

Stanza 5:
And then spoke the little cabin boy,
    And a pretty little boy was he;
"Oh, I am more grieved for my daddy and my mammy,
    Than you for your wives all three."

Stanza 6:
Then three times round went our gallant ship,
    And three times round went she;
For the want of a life-boat they all went down
    And she sank to the bottom of the sea.

Chorus:
For the raging seas did roar,
And the stormy winds did blow,
While we jolly sailor-boys were up unto the top,
And the land-lubbers lying down below, below, below,
And the land-lubbers lying down below.

The reference to the marital status of the crew in the song helps provide the association which sparks Bloom's subsequent thoughts of marriage. These last two songs, then, furnish the link between Bloom's predominantly asexual thoughts of the sea and sailors and his underlying preoccupation in the chapter with sex and the female temptress. All of this establishes Bloom more firmly than ever as a Ulysses figure. The subtlety of the association of the sea song, women, and sex, though it renders their connection no less real, has the effect of temporarily relegating sensuality largely to the level of Bloom's subconscious rather than to that of his conscious mind.

Wife in every port they say. She has a good job if she minds it till Johnny comes marching home again. If ever he does. Smelling the tail end of ports. (378:31–33)

Cf. "When Johnny Comes Marching Home Again"
REMARKS: Bloom uses the title of the patriotic song to cast aspersions on

the chastity of sailors and their waiting wives. The words to the spirited song become tinged with irony in the situations Bloom envisions:

> When Johnny comes marching home again,
> Hurrah, hurrah!
> We'll give him a hearty welcome then,
> Hurrah, hurrah!
> The men will cheer, the boys will shout,
> The ladies they will all turn out,
> And we'll all feel gay,
> When Johnny comes marching home.

How can they like the sea? Yet they do. The anchor's weighed. Off he sails with a scapular or a medal on him for luck. (378:33–35)

Cf. "The Anchor's Weighed"

REMARKS: Having considered a sailor's triumphant return, Bloom next ponders his parting, again using a musical reference to provide the tie between his conscious thoughts of the sea and his unconscious thoughts of love and women. The song is about the parting between a sailor and his downcast lover:

> Stanza 1:
> The tear fell gently from her eye
> When last we parted on the shore;
> My bosom heav'd with many a sigh,
> To think I ne'er might see her more,
> To think I ne'er might see her more.
>
> "Dear youth," she cried, "and canst thou haste away?
> My heart will break, a little moment stay;
> Alas, I cannot, I cannot part from thee."
> "The anchor's weigh'd, the anchor's weigh'd,
>   farewell! farewell! remember me."
>
> Stanza 2:
> "Weep not, my love," I trembling cried,
> "Doubt not a constant heart like mine;
> I ne'er can meet another maid
> Whose charms can fix that heart like thine,
> Whose charms can fix that heart like thine!"
>
> "Go, then," she cried, "but let thy constant mind
> Oft think of her you leave in tears behind."
> "Dear maid, this last embrace my pledge shall be!

The anchor's weigh'd, the anchor's weigh'd,
farewell! farewell! remember me."

Here the lyrics fit exactly the context of Bloom's stream of consciousness as stanza two completes the other half of the fidelity cycle originating with Bloom's earlier imputations on the chastity of sailors' wives. In stanza two of this song Bloom musically alludes to the virtue of the male with the wandering sailor's promise to his lover to be faithful. The parallel between the wandering sailors and the wandering Odysseus-Bloom is not difficult to draw. Bloom is sure of the sailors' wives' infidelity, just as he is sure of Molly's. On the other hand, whether the promise of the departing sailor to remain chaste will be kept is with Bloom a matter of some ambiguity. He says of the sailors, "Wife in every port they say" (378:31), but makes no further mention of their unfaithfulness. In his own situation he works at his illicit relationships, but so far has had little return for his effort. Whether or not his affair with Martha will ever come to illicit intercourse is as dubious as the sailors' continuing chastity in foreign ports. The "Anchor's Weighed" completes the maritime group of musical references which serve the purpose of providing an undercurrent of amour to Bloom's speculations on the sea.

From house to house, giving his everwelcome double knock, went the nine o'clock postman, the glowworm's lamp at his belt gleaming here and there through the laurel hedges. (379:10-13)

Cf. "The Young May Moon"

REMARKS: This passage, a part of the narrative linking the hour with romance and love-making, has been immediately preceded by the bursting of a rocket which we have already seen is equated to an orgasm. The phrase and song have phallic connotations in their earlier associations with Molly and Blazes.[7] Joyce makes use of these earlier developed connotations here to provide another indirect reference to love-making at this the violet hour of the evening.

Don't know what death is at that age. And then their stomachs clean. But being lost they fear. When we hid behind the tree at Crumlin. I didn't want to. Mamma! Mamma! Babes in the wood. Frightening them with masks too. Throwing them up in the air to catch them. I'll murder you. Is it only half fun? Or children playing battle. Whole earnest. How can people aim guns at each other? Sometimes they go off. Poor kids. (379:32-39)

Cf. "Babes in the Wood"

REMARKS: The reference to "Babes in the Wood" is a recollection of an English nursery tale and the song which celebrates it. The song relates the story of two lost children who perish in the woods:

> My dear do you know a long time ago,
> Two little children whose names I don't know
> Were stolen away on a bright sunny day,
> And were left in the woods, as I've heard people say.
>
> And when the night came on, so sad was their plight,
> The sun had gone down and the moon gave no light.
> The poor little children they sobbed and they cried,
> And all in the darkness they laid down and died.
>
> And when they were dead the robin so red
> Took strawberry leaves and over them spread,
> And all the day long this was their song—
> "O don't you remember the babes in the wood?"

The serious consequences of the song provide a transitional element to turn Bloom's thinking to the more serious aspects of life which justify children's fear.

Too late for *Leah, Lily of Killarney*. (380:20)

Cf. *The Lily of Killarney*

REMARKS: As Bloom reviews his day including all the things he didn't do as well as those he did, his failure to see either of the entertainments playing in Dublin comes to mind. The reference is obvious.

Three cheers for the sister-in-law he hawked about, three fangs in her mouth. Same style of beauty. Particularly nice old party for a cup of tea. The sister of the wife of the wild man of Borneo has just come to town. Imagine that in the early morning at close range. (380:30–34)

Cf. "The Wild Man from Borneo Has Just Come to Town"

REMARKS: One of Bloom's references to the citizen's sister-in-law: "The sister of the wife . . ." introduces the music-hall song, which seems to have little significance other than supplying Bloom with an appropriate title for the citizen.

14. Oxen of the Sun

. . . praying for the intentions of the sovereign pontiff, he gave them for a pledge the vicar of Christ which also as he said is vicar of Bray. (391:6–8)

Cf. "The Vicar of Bray"

REMARKS: The song is a seventeenth-century ballad to which additions have been made over the years to fit evolving historical situations. The ballad is about the unscrupulous Vicar of Bray who swears allegiance to whatever king, church, or party is in power, vowing in the refrain:

> And this is law I will maintain,
> Until my dying day, Sir,
> That whatsoever King may reign,
> Still I'll be the Vicar of Bray, Sir.

As the power shifts from Catholic to Protestant, from Tory to Whig, so the Vicar of Bray denounces all those out of power and swears allegiance to all those in power. The allusion and Stephen's demeanor is antipope and anticlerical; at the same time in the passage he is playing the role of priest.

. . . or she knew him not and then stands she in the one denial or ignorancy with Peter Piscator who lives in the house that Jack built and with Joseph the Joiner patron of the happy demise of all unhappy marriages . . . (391:34–38)

Cf. "The House that Jack Built"
  "Ballad of Joking Jesus"

REMARKS: Stephen's blasphemy here deals with the conception of Jesus, punning on the word *know* as meaning both carnal knowledge and Peter's professed ignorance. The reference to the nursery rhyme is interesting if puzzling. Perhaps the cumulative succession of events, people, and animals in the rhyme indicates that things are merely part of some inevitable long succession. Peter, by living in the house that Jack built, the church, like Mary and Joseph follows an inevitable course in the long preordained succession of ecclesiastical events. "Joseph the Joiner" is of course from Mulligan's bawdy parody of Christianity and fits well Stephen's sarcastic mood and tone.

Hereupon Punch Costello dinged with his fist upon the board and would sing a bawdy catch *Staboo Stabella* about a wench that was put in pod of a jolly swashbuckler in Almany which he did

now attack: *The first three months she was not well, Staboo* . . .
(392:4–8)

Cf. "Staboo Stabella"

REMARKS: The song appears to be about pregnancy. Like many bawdy songs, it appeared only rarely, if ever, in print. I have not been able to locate it, though R. M. Adams says the song was Gogarty's.[1]

. . . on a bridebed while clerks sung kyries and the anthem *Ut novetur sexus omnis corporis mysterium* till she was there unmaided. (392:42–393:2)

Cf. *"Kyrie eleison"*
"Ut novetur sexus omnis corporis mysterium"

REMARKS: The *Kyrie,* "Lord, have mercy," is a remnant of Greek that remains in the Latin Mass. It occurs early in the mass and in a number of other prayers and hymns. Thornton translates the anthem title, "That the whole mystery of physical sexuality be known."[2] No one has been able to locate this anthem which probably is just a figment of Stephen's imagination.

He gave them then a much admirable hymen minim by those delicate poets Master John Fletcher and Master Francis Beaumont that is in their *Maid's Tragedy* that was writ for a like twining of lovers: *To bed, to bed,* was the burden of it to be played with accompanable concent upon the virginals. An exquisite dulcet epithalame of most mollificative suadency for juveniles amatory whom the odoriferous flambeaus of the paranymphs have escorted to the quadrupedal proscenium of connubial communion. (393:2–11)

Cf. "To Bed, to Bed"

REMARKS: The most interesting thing about Stephen's reference is that the union in the song is never consummated. Thus, the girl calls, "To bed, to bed/And never ceaseth," yet the persona goes to bed to think about her in his pain, his supposition being that she has called for separate sleeping accommodations. At any rate, it is another contribution to the bawdy lyrics which characterize the party, and the reference is typical of Stephen's erudite, allusive reference pattern and his self-proclaimed celibate priest role.

Remember, Erin, thy generations and thy days of old, how thou settedst little by me and by my word and broughtest in a stranger to my gates to commit fornication in my sight and to wax fat and kick like Jeshurum. (393:25–28)

Cf. "Let Erin Remember the Days of Old"

REMARKS: As the biblical narration begins, the voice of God intones its warnings to the Irish as it once did to the errant tribes of Israel, linking once again the Jewish nation with the Irish, a prime political association in the novel. Besides a purely biblical parody there is an allusion to the Thomas Moore song. The second line of the song, "Ere her faithless sons betrayed her," continues the theme of betrayal which looms so large in Stephen's mind throughout the first chapter. The betrayers, the Mulligans and Shawns of the world, are still, in Stephen's mind, betraying not only their country but her savior Stephen-Christ-God-Dedalus. The above allusion continues the pattern and theme for Stephen, since the entire sequence casts Stephen and by extension Bloom in the role of God.

But one evening, says Mr Dixon, when the lord Harry was cleaning his royal pelt to go to dinner . . . (400:39–40)

Cf. "The Finding of Moses"

REMARKS: The ballad contains the allusion to the "royal pelt" in the first stanza:

> In Agypts land, contaygious to the Nile,
> Old Pharo's daughter went to bathe in style,
> She tuk her dip and came unto the land,
> And for to dry her royal pelt she ran along the strand. . . .

The allusion seems to have little significance beyond heaping more sarcasm on Henry VIII.

. . . gave three times three, let the bullgine run, pushed off in their bumboat and put to sea to recover the main of America. (401:25–26)

Cf. "Let the Bullgine Run"

REMARKS: Cecil Sharp tells us that *Bullgine* is black dialect for *engine*.[3] Perhaps phallic in its connotations here, it provides a fitting end in contemporary dialect of this lengthy story about bulls of all sorts.

> —Pope Peter's but a pissabed.
> A man's a man for a' that. (401:29–30)

Cf. "A Man's a Man for a' That"

REMARKS: This parody of Robert Burns' song tends to sum up the hilarity and pave the way for the entrance of the great blasphemer, Mulligan, who enters at that moment.

> . . . the agnatia of certain chinless Chinamen . . . (410:32–33)

Cf. "Chin Chin Chinaman"

REMARKS: The allusion is used by Mulligan because it ingeniously combines an hereditary, physical characteristic with an exceptionally well-known phrase from a popular opera, *The Geisha*.

> And, lo, wonder of metempsychosis, it is she, the everlasting bride, harbinger of the daystar, the bride, ever virgin. It is she, Martha, thou lost one, Millicent, the young, the dear, the radiant. How serene does she now arise, a queen among the Pleiades, in the penultimate antelucan hour, shod in sandals of bright gold, coifed with a veil of what do you call it gossamer! It floats, it flows about her starborn flesh and loose it streams emerald, sapphire, mauve and heliotrope, sustained on currents of cold interstellar wind, winding, coiling, simply swirling, writhing in the skies a mysterious writing till after a myriad metamorphoses of symbol, it blazes, Alpha, a ruby and triangled sign upon the forehead of Taurus. (414:29–41)

Cf. "M'appari"
"Seaside Girls"

REMARKS: In one of the most obvious of all the consubstantiality passages in the novel, an allusion to parallax ("Parallax stalks behind and goads them . . ." [414:16–17]) gives way to the "wonder of metempsychosis," the eternal female figure. The description of this eternal figure as "Martha, thou lost one, Millicent, the young, the dear, the radiant," has brought about a combination of the predominant female images of Bloom's day and life. The recollection of "M'appari" comprehends, as we have seen in the Sirens chapter,[4] not only the image of Martha Clifford, to whom Bloom was writing as Simon Dedalus sang the song in the Ormond Bar, but Molly, the Martha of the song, lost to her pining Lionel-Leopold at that four o'clock hour of assignation. The song carries with it, then, a twofold association to its namesake, Martha Clifford, and its real heroine, Molly. Both are subsumed into the image of Milly, the female image of the future.

Since the next appositive in the combination of the eternal female figure, "Millicent the young . . . ," equates Milly with the image, it remains only to include the other female light of Bloom's day, Gerty MacDowell. This is done indirectly with another musical reference, "simply swirling," this time to the song "Seaside Girls," originally introduced by Milly and with which Bloom, in the Nausicaa chapter, had recently equated Gerty in particular and womankind in general. Its connotations of Blazes Boylan further link the seaside girls song to *"M'appari"* in Bloom's associative pattern. So the major motifs of female consubstantiation, *"M'appari"* and "Seaside Girls," combine in one metempsychic whole to illuminate the process of universal unity which permeates the novel.

These references to what are perhaps the main musical themes in the novel tie together in a few sentences most of the love interests of the protagonist and one of the major themes of the novel. This reverie of Bloom's picturing the ideal or composite of all females is, both in its rhetoric and its recapitulatory aspects, suggestive of the visions and hallucinations to come in the Circe chapter.

. . . the dark horse Throwaway drew level, reached, outstripped her. All was lost now. (415:26–27)

Cf. *"Tutto è sciolto"*

REMARKS: The reference is used in a humorous way, to draw upon some of the passion of its connotations in Sirens to lend satire to the Ascot Gold Cup report.

The sweet creature turned all colours in her confusion, feigning to reprove a slight disorder in her dress: a slip of underwood clung there for the very trees adore her. (416:14–16)

Cf. "Delight in Disorder"

REMARKS: The disorder in her dress is reminiscent of Robert Herrick's song,

> A sweet disorder in the dress
> Kindles in clothes a wantonness. . . .

Vincent and his girl are surprised in their love-making by Father Conmee, a scene we have already heard about in Wandering Rocks. The sensual connotations of the song reenforce that tone in the passage, but the song seems to have little significance beyond that.

Dost envy Darby Dullman there with his Joan? (423:35)

Cf. "Darby and Joan"

REMARKS: The song alluded to is about a couple who have been together for fifty years and the trials they have faced. The "Dullman" part of the reference stems from the chorus lines,

> Always the same, Darby my own,
> Always the same to your old wife Joan.[5]

At any rate, the conjunction between Darby and Joan and Purefoy is well taken.

> Burke's! Thence they advanced five parasangs. Slattery's mounted foot where's that bleeding awfur? (424:30–32)

Cf. "Slattery's Mounted Foot"

REMARKS: "Slattery's Mounted Foot" is a comic song about a group of drinkers organized under "Slattery's eldest son," who hie themselves to a shebeen (an illegal pub), are refused service for lack of payment, then are accosted by the police before they flee back into the hills. Slattery's Foot is probably habitually mounted upon some bar rail thus providing double entendre of the song title. The allusion fits exactly the spirit of the rowdy exodus to Burke's.

> Proceed to nearest canteen and there annex liquor stores. March! Tramp, tramp the boys are (attitudes!) parching. Beer, beef, business, bibles, bulldogs, battleships, buggery and bishops. *Whether on the scaffold high.* Beerbeef trample the bibles. *When for Irelandear.* Trample the trampellers. Thunderation! Keep the durned millingtary step. *We fall.* (424:39–425:3) [italics mine]

Cf. "Tramp, Tramp, Tramp, the Boys Are Marching"
　　"God Save Ireland"

REMARKS: The military tone of the American Civil War song leads in this passage to pure patriotism with the allusion (referential words appear in italics in quotation) to "God Save Ireland." The interesting thing here is that the transition between the references and in the narration hinges on the phenomena of the two song references both having the same music. I have already glossed the fact that "God Save Ireland" is set to the tune of "Tramp, Tramp, Tramp," so that once the tune has been established with the first reference, Joyce uses it as a bridge to the second. The tramping military is, typically, mixed with boozy patriotism here in the musical parallel to the other mixtures of nationalism and alcohol in Aeolus and Cyclops.

> You, sir? Ginger cordial. Chase me, the cabby's caudle. Stimulate the caloric. Winding of his ticker. Stopped short never to go again when the old. (425:9–12)

Cf. "My Grandfather's Clock"

REMARKS: The watch reference is an allusion to the chorus of the song:

> Ninety years without slumbering (tick, tock, tick, tock),
> His life-seconds numbering (tick, tock, tick, tock),
> It stopped short never to go again
> When the old man died.

Bloom's pulling out of his watch here is reminiscent of the same act in Davy Byrne's recalling Nosey Flynn's remark, "If you ask him to have a drink first thing he does he outs with the watch to see what he ought to imbibe" (178:8–10). His fiddling with his watch now would seem to indicate that there is something to Flynn's remarks.

Lovey lovekin. None of your lean kine, not much. Pull down the blind, love. (425:18–20)

Cf. "Pull Down the Blind"
   "Oh, My Love"

REMARKS: As Dixon begins to discourse on Bloom's history for the other medical students he inevitably gets around to Molly and the equally inevitable description of her profile. The description is enhanced by an allusion to one of two comic songs of the time, "Oh! My Love," or "Pull Down the Blind." The first, listed by Hodgart and Worthington, has a chorus as follows:

> Oh! my love won't you please pull down the curtain
> Oh! my love can't you see I'm madly flirtin'
> Oh! my love won't you please put out that light
> I can look at you for an hour or two
> But I can't stay up all night.

The peeping-Tom attitude of the song is perfectly reflected by Dixon's subsequent narration of Molly's physical attributes. Thornton has discussed a second song, "Pull Down the Blind," which has the words "pull down the blind, love, come don't be unkind." [6] Either song would work to foreshadow Molly's appearance in the upper-story window during the penumbra urination of Bloom and Stephen.

Womanbody after going on the straw? Stand and deliver. Password. There's hair. Ours the white death and ruddy birth. Hi! Spit in your own eye, boss. Mummer's wire. (425:28–31)

Cf. "There's Hair Like Wire Coming Out of the Empire"

REMARKS: The drinking salutation which we have seen before in Barney Kiernan's seems to contain a reference this time not so much to the song

"There's Hair" as to another music-hall song of the period, "There's Hair
Like Wire Coming Out of the Empire." Though I have not been able to
locate the text or music to the song, the subsequent reference to "mummer's
wire" seems not only to indicate the umbilical cord of birth but to utilize
the song to tie in the drinking salutation with the umbilical-cord theme
which has been prevalent since the Martello tower was called the omphalos
in the first episode and since Stephen's first thoughts of the universal umbilical cord and its link with the father-son and consubstantiality motifs.
Molly's not having a son has just been discussed. Stephen then thinks of the
telegram he sent to Mulligan ("Mummer's wire") with a quotation "cribbed
out of Meredith" (425:31). The song allusion could act as a sublimal connection between the drinking expression and the wire, because Stephen's
Oedipal desire for his mother, reenforced by the association of Molly's
motherhood and her sensuality, stirs in him subconscious memories of desire
for his own mother. Hence the reference to the umbilical cord and the wire
to Mulligan. I do not mean to suggest that this perhaps overly ingenious
interpretation indicates beyond doubt that the song reference bears the brunt
of tying all of these strands together; however, it is another possible indication that the whole Oedipal motif is somehow tied in with Molly as a central
mother figure.

Here, Jock braw Hielentman's your barleybree. (425:35)
We are nae fou. We're nae tha fou. (426:11–12)

Cf. "Willie Brew'd a Peck o' Maut"
    "A Highland Lad My Love Was Born"

REMARKS: The words are allusions to a combination of two Robert Burns
songs. The first is a Bacchanalian drinking song:

> We are na fou, we're no that fou,
> But just a wee drap in our e'e;
> The cock may craw, the day may daw,
> But aye we'll taste the barely bree.

The chorus of the Highlandman song begins, "Sing hey my braw John
Highlandman." Coming as the references do in the welter of accents and
allusions to other languages, the allusions play a two-fold role: to underscore the drinking and debauchery of the occasion and to flavor the narration with a Scottish dialect.

Every cove to his gentry mort. (425:39–40)

Cf. "The Rogue's Delight in Praise of His Stroling Mort"

REMARKS: As the conversation includes sex in a plethora of dialects and
perhaps an allusion to Milly, it is only fitting that the canting songs again

appear, this time in the narrator's vocabulary as well as Stephen's. The quotation translated, "Every Doe to his silken Girl," seems to prefigure Bloom's hermaphrodite tendencies in Circe. At any rate, the allusion does fulfill in general the criteria of bawdiness and dialect which seem to pervade the passage.

On the road to Malahide. Me? If she who seduced me had left but the name. What do you want for ninepence? Machree, Macruiskeen. (425:42–426:2)

Cf. "On the Road to Mandalay"
"The Bridal of Malahide"
"When He Who Adores Thee"
"The Cruiskeen Lawn"

REMARKS: The first allusion is to the song derived from Kipling's "Mandalay," "On the Road to Mandalay." While the song is not bawdy it is nevertheless about a girl who has tempted a British sailor from the callow housemaids he knows in Britain back to the "Old Moulmein Pagoda" and a sensual life of bliss. The corruption of the title with the substitution of Malahide for Mandalay suggests the comparison between the first song and the lost sensuality of a marriage never consummated in the song "The Bridal of Malahide." [7] The reference to Moore's song, "When he who adores thee," contains altered words (bracketed) to the first two lines which change them from beautiful melancholy to bawdy:

When he [she] who adores [seduced] thee has left but the name
Of his fault and his sorrow behind. . . .

The brackets in the first line represent Joyce's alteration of the line. The song is a well-known ballad and the line change and parody would have been immediately apparent to Joyce's contemporary audience.

In answer to what is wanted for ninepence (presumably in the way of another drink) the answer, "Machree, Macruiskeen," is a reference to the first line of the refrain of "The Cruiskeen Lawn," "Little Full Jug," with all its bibulous connotations.

Smutty Moll for a mattress jig. And a pull alltogether. (426:2–3)

Cf. "Eton Boating Song"

REMARKS: The words to the chorus, "All pull together,/With your back between your knees," carries in the present narrative circumstance (Molly's prowess on the mattress is tied in by the previous line) of Oxen of the Sun a double entendre. Also there are several bawdy parodies which capitalize on the gross connotations of the chorus. [8]

Mowsing nowt but claretwine. (426:14) [9]

Cf. "The Rakes of Mallow"

REMARKS: The reference here is to another boisterous drinking song. The rakes of the title, like the revelers in Burke's, spend their time in drunken boisterousness:

> Beauing, belleing, dancing, drinking,
> Breaking windows, damning, sinking
> Ever raking, never thinking
> Live the rakes of Mallow.

The reference in the passage under consideration is to the first line of the third stanza, "One time nought but claret drinking," which Joyce has transformed to fit his penchant for dialect approximations here at the end of Oxen of the Sun.

With a railway bloke. How come you so? Opera he'd like? Rose of Castille. Rows of cast. (426:16–17)

Cf. *The Rose of Castille*

REMARKS: Bantam Lyons comes in, presumably drunk and with somebody from a railroad. This triggers this reference to Lenehan's riddle, "What opera is like a railway line? (134:16). Joyce employs a sort of stream-of-conscious association pattern in his narrative here, an uncommon device for the narrator and one which seems to have no other reasons for being except the former association of *The Rose of Castille* with Lenehan's riddle and the fact that Lyons shows up with a railroad man. The same association will be made in Circe (455:26–27, 491:13–14).

The colleen bawn, my colleen bawn. (426:19–20)

Cf. "The Colleen Bawn"

REMARKS: Bantam, who is deep in his cups ("Tight. I shee you, shir. Bantam . . ." [426:13–14]), begins to sing "The Colleen Bawn," which seems to bear little significance beyond the obvious in the present context.

The ruffin cly the nab of Stephen. (426:21–22)
Land him in chokeechokee if the harman beck copped the game. (426:26–27)

Cf. "The Ruffin Cly the Nab of Harmanbeck"

REMARKS: This reference to the seventeenth-century canting song is still another boisterous drinking allusion. Head translates the title "The devil take the constable's head," [10] and the passage seems to deal with illegally steaming open a telegram with a tip on the Ascot Gold Cup in it.[11] Presumably the act would have landed the malefactor in jail had the police known about it. At any rate the allusion provides still another outlandish dialect variation as well as another ribald song for the conclusion of Oxen of the Sun.

Landlord, landlord, have you good wine, staboo? Hoots, mon, wee drap to pree. (426:42–427:1)

Cf. "Staboo, Stabella"
"Willy Brew'd a Peck o' Maut"

REMARKS: As the drinking continues the atmosphere of ribaldry and wild drinking is underscored by two more musical allusions to drunken debauchery. Hodgart and Worthington cite the first line as a reference to "Staboo, Stabella," a bawdy catch with many variants, but, as I have earlier admitted, I have not located it. The second sentence in the quotation refers to Burns's "Willy Brew'd a Peck o' Maut," which has already been alluded to on the previous page as a scene-setting device. The reference is to line two of the chorus, "But just a wee drap in our e'e." [12]

Bonsoir la compagnie. (427:6)

Cf. *"Vive L'amour"*

REMARKS: As closing time comes to Burke's the roisterers are ushered out to the strains of *"Bonsoir la compagnie,"* probably a corruption of *"Vive la compagnie"* the last line of the well-known, *"Vive L'amour.*

Who wander through the world. (427:15–16)

Cf. "We May Roam Through This World"

REMARKS: Some concern has been voiced for Stephen, who is without a key or a "plais whear to lay crown off his hed 2 night" (427:10–11). As the bartender calls, "Time," the concern and benediction is again voiced, "Who wander through the world." The reference here is perhaps to Thomas Moore's song which extols the virtues of Ireland and home as compared to the far-flung climes visited by the would-be traveller. The implications of the song may lie in linking Molly to the woman of the chorus:

> Then remember whenever your goblet is crowned,
> Thro' this world, whether eastward or westward you roam,
> When a cup to the smile of dear woman goes round,
> Oh, remember the smile which adorns her at home.

Home for Stephen, if Bloom has his way, will be 7 Eccles St. and Molly the attraction and unifying force. If Joyce had the Moore melody in mind it would constitute a foreshadowing of Bloom's proposing this to Stephen and Bloom's attempt to use Molly as the attraction for Stephen to keep him there and in Ireland.

> Golly, whatten tunket's yon guy in the mackintosh? Dusty Rhodes. Peep at his wearables. By mighty! What's he got? Jubilee mutton. Bovril, by James. Wants it real bad. D'ye ken bare socks? Seedy cuss in the Richmond? Rawthere! Thought he had a deposit of lead in his penis. Trumpery insanity. Bartle the Bread we calls him. That, sir, was once a prosperous cit. Man all tattered and torn that married a maiden all forlorn. Slung her hook, she did. Here see lost love. Walking Mackintosh of lonely canyon. (427:17–25)

Cf. "John Peel"
    "The House that Jack Built"

REMARKS: The two musical references do little to throw any light on the identity of Mackintosh in this longest passage dealing with him in the novel. The first allusion is to "John Peel," "D'ye ken bare socks?" The reference to either his socklessness or shoelessness is one of the indications that he should indeed be an inmate in the Richmond. The reference is ironic, for the gay coat is, of course, a brown mackintosh.

In the second song reference we learn that the once prosperous citizen was a "man all tattered and torn that married a maiden all forlorn." The reference to "The House that Jack Built" is significant in so far as the nursery rhyme has a priest "all shaven and shorn" marry "the man all tattered and torn," who only "kissed the maid all forlorn." Tattered Mackintosh's marriage to the maiden is therefore underscored and a great piece added to the puzzle of who he is. It rules out Mr. Duffy, since the dead woman of whom we have had previous mention ("The man in the brown mackintosh loves a lady who is dead" [333:32–33]) is now presumably identified as his wife.

> We're nae tha fou. (427:39)

Cf. "Willy Brew'd a Peck o' Maut"

REMARKS: The ejection of the rowdy crew from the bar is completed though they continue to object, this time in terms of the first refrain line of Robert Burns's ballad, "Willie Brew'd a Peck o' Maut." As in the previous reference to this ballad the boisterousness is underscored, and by now the line and complaint that they are still not that drunk becomes a refrain which echoes through the entire closing scene in Burke's.

Mona, my thrue love. Yook. Mona, my own love. Ook. (427:41–42)

Cf. "Mona, My Own Love"

REMARKS: This song of parting has been referred to before in Cyclops.[13] The song fits here in two senses. It is a song of parting, as the group is about to break up, and it involves love, the purchase of which is Stephen and Lynch's aim as they head for the brothel district.

Whisper, who the sooty hell's the johnny in the black duds? Hush! Sinned against the light and even now that day is at hand when he shall come to judge the world by fire. Pflaap! *Ut implerentur scripturae.* Strike up a ballad. Then outspake medical Dick to his comrade medical Davy. Christicle, who's this excrement yellow gospeller on the Merrion hall? Elijah is coming washed in the Blood of the Lamb. (428:8–15)

Cf. "Medical Dick and Medical Davy"
   "Washed in the Blood of the Lamb"

REMARKS: The object of speculation in the above passage, Bloom, the prophet of doom come to save Stephen from himself, is again identified with Elijah as he was in the conclusion of Cyclops. The degraded state into which Israel, i.e., Stephen, has fallen is evidenced by not only his drunkenness, but also Mulligan's bawdy ballad "Medical Dick and Medical Davy," a rendition of which Stephen now joins. Bloom, come to cleanse his prospective ward, blends in with the figure of Elijah and Dowie, setting the stage for the lively evangelistic oratory at the end of the episode. This again unmistakably indicates Bloom's prophetic and Messianic roles, now as guide to the only partially created creator of the uncreated conscience of his race.

15. Circe

I gave it to Molly
Because she was jolly,
The leg of the duck
The leg of the duck. (430:17–20)

I gave it to Nelly
To stick in her belly
The leg of the duck
The leg of the duck. (430:29–32)

> She has it, she got it,
> Wherever she put it
> The leg of the duck. (431:7–9)

Cf. "The Leg of the Duck"

REMARKS: Though Cissy had formerly belonged to a "Bloom section," Nausicaa, her presence here cannot be accounted an hallucination of Bloom; rather Cissy and the bawdy song she sings are a part of the general introduction to the chapter. The introduction (pp. 429–431) is a collection of debased images designed to cast an aura of filth, squalor, and degradation upon the scene and set the predominant mood of the chapter, a panorama of the seamy, corrupt aspects of human behavior and thought. Cissy Caffrey and her song, then, are part of the window dressing, the preamble to the unrestrained Nighttown scenes to follow. The words to "The Leg of the Duck" present the prevailing gross motif of the introduction, which prepares the way for the bawdy action which follows in the chapter.

> (*Stephen, flourishing the ashplant in his left hand, chants with joy the* introit *for paschal time. . . .*) (431:10–11)
> *Vidi aquam egredientem de templo a latere dextro. Alleluia.* (431:15)
> *Et omnes ad quos pervenit aqua ista.* (431:22)
> *Salvi facti i sunt.* (432:10)

Cf. "*Aspergus Mei*"

REMARKS: The chant may be translated as follows: "I saw a stream of water welling forth from the right of the temple, Alleluia: bringing salvation to all those who stood in its course." [1] The *Aspergus Mei* is a prayer preliminary to the mass. The allusion is incorrectly labeled "The Introit" by Hodgart and Worthington. However, the *Aspergus* does serve in Circe to introduce a second motif, the mass. As "The Leg of the Duck" is juxtaposed to the *Aspergus,* so is blatant sex mixed with religion all through the episode, culminating in the celebration of a black mass. Indeed, if the salvation promised in Stephen's chant does come about, religion will have played a part in the libidinous freedom from the fetters of the superego and its agenbite of inwit.

> *Aurora borealis* or a steel foundry? Ah, the brigade, of course. South side anyhow. Big blaze. Might be his house. Beggar's bush. We're safe. (*He hums cheerfully.*) London's burning, London's burning! On fire, on fire! (434:27–30)

Cf. "Scotland's Burning"

REMARKS: The thought that the fire might be at Blazes Boylan's house occasions some lightheartedness for Bloom as it prompts him to hum the round:

> Scotland's burning! Scotland's burning!
> Look out! look out!
> Fire! fire! fire! fire!
> Pour on water, pour on water

Though the words in the quotation are incorrect, it is possible that zealous Irish school boys converted *Scotland* to *London,* a natural thing in a country which does not hold England in deathless admiration. In any case, the round cheerfully attests to the pleasure with which Bloom would greet a fire in the Boylan residence.

A VOICE

(*Sharply.*) Poldy!

BLOOM

Who? (*He ducks and wards off a blow clumsily.*) At your service.

> (*He looks up. Beside her mirage of datepalms a handsome woman in Turkish costume stands before him. Opulent curves fill out her scarlet trousers and jacket slashed with gold. A wide yellow cummerbund girdles her. A white yashmak violet in the night, covers her face, leaving free only her large dark eyes and raven hair.*) (439:3-13)

Cf. "The Shade of the Palm"

REMARKS: That Bloom sees his wife beside palm trees and dressed in a costume of the Near East is in keeping with his constant association of Molly and the mysterious East. There is also in this image the unmistakable suggestion of Molly as "the queen of the Eastern sea" in "The Shade of the Palm." Bloom's mental association of Molly with Idolores, the girl waiting in the song, which was so prominent in the Sirens chapter,[2] recurs here in Circe. Though the song was for the most part associated with Miss Douce in Sirens, our assumption there that Molly is identified as the queen of the Eastern Sea is justified by this later mental association by Bloom.

MARION

(*Softly.*) Poldy!

BLOOM

Yes, ma'am?

MARION

Ti trema un poco il cuore?

(*In disdain she saunters away, plump as a pampered pouter pigeon, humming the duet from* Don Giovanni.)

BLOOM

Are you sure about that *Voglio?* I mean the pronunciati . . .
(441:3–12)

Cf. "*Là ci darem*"

REMARKS: In the Circe version of the passage from the duet it is Molly-Zerlina who asks of Leopold-Giovanni, "Does your heart tremble a little?" instead of the correct words in the opera, "*Mi trema un poco il cor*" (My heart trembles a little). Vernon Hall points out that Joyce's use of "*cuore*" instead of the poetical *cor(e)* in the opera text indicates that the lines from the duet were probably given by the author from memory.[3] Here we see the first signs of Bloom's masochistic, feminine tendencies which play such a large role later in the chapter. Again Joyce builds on a musical image already created as he brings the whole *Don Giovanni* motif back into play. Hall notes this in his explanation of the passage:

> Joyce can by this time depend on our knowledge of the ways he has hitherto employed the Don Giovanni theme. So, when he wants to illustrate Bloom's consciousness of Molly's sadism and her desire to play the role of a man, and Bloom's masochism and desire to be a woman, he is able to do it merely by the substitution of a word. . . . It is the "new womanly man" [493:30] . . . Bloom whose heart should flutter in fear, not the Molly who holds the whip hand. Bloom is Zerlina. The only shred of self-respect Bloom can seize upon at this point is once again to ask about the pronunciation of that "voglio" that is not even in the text. This time, though, he is not able to finish. His voice trails off, "pronunciati. . ."[4]

There's someone in the house with Dina
There's someone in the house, I know,

There's someone in the house with Dina
Playing on the old banjo. (443:29–32)

Cf. "Someone's in the Kitchen with Dinah"

REMARKS: The minstrel singer confuses the words slightly.[5] Instead of "there's someone in the house. . . ." the words to the song are, "Someone's in the kitchen. . . ." Here the mistake in the lyrics is significant, for Bloom, projecting the hallucinations, has drawn the parallel between Dina and Molly, and the relevant activities of Boylan's visit presumably occur in the bedroom rather than the kitchen. The associations between *"Là ci darem"* (entry above) and cuckoldry have given rise to Bloom's thoughts of Molly's liking for Negro servants and the song, which is nothing other than an associative restatement of the Boylan-Molly assignation. The relatively harmless kitchen flirtations of Dina in the song are replaced by the more ominous doings in the house.

For old sake'sake. I only meant a square party, a mixed marriage mingling of our different little conjugials. You know I had a soft corner for you. (*Gloomily.*) 'Twas I sent you that valentine of the dear gazelle. (444:11–14)

Cf. "I Never Nursed a Dear Gazelle"

REMARKS: Bloom's mention of the "dear gazelle" Hodgart and Worthington cite as a reference to the Thomas Moore song from *Lalla Rookh*. Although there is another Moore poem, "The Gazelle," which has the words "dear gazelle" in it, Bloom quotes later in the chapter from the *Lalla Rookh* song and the predominantly disheartened mood of the song fits Bloom's wistful thoughts in the present passage. The lyrics of "I Never Nursed . . ." tell of one whose hopes, plans, and loves never come to happiness:

> Oh! ever thus, from childhood's hour,
>   I've seen my fondest hopes decay;
> I never lov'd a tree or flow'r,
>   But 'twas the first to fade away.
>
> I never nurs'd a dear gazelle,
>   To glad me with its soft black eye,
> But when it came to know me well,
>   And love me, it was sure to die!
>
> Now too—the joy most like divine
>   Of all I ever dreamt or knew,
> To see thee, hear thee, call thee mine,—
>   O misery! must I lose *that* too?

The song might well be Bloom's. Underlying the words "dear gazelle" and the whole scene, the song is yet another association with the lost Molly, whom even in his subconscious Bloom struggles to forget.

Ladies and gentlemen, I give you Ireland, home and beauty. (445:5)

Cf. "The Death of Nelson"

REMARKS: The ludicrousness of Bloom's position is emphasized by the in-appropriateness of his toast. "Ireland, home and beauty," is a variation of "for England, home and beauty" from Nelson's last speech in this song of English patriotism, a portion of which follows:

> "Now long enough I've lived!
> In honor's cause my life was pass'd,
> In honor's cause I fall at last,
> For England, home, and beauty,
> For England, home, and beauty."
> Thus ending life as he began,
> England confess'd that ev'ry man
> That day had done his duty,
> That day had done his duty.

Whether Bloom was aware of the incongruity of his toasting Ireland in terms that can only be associated with England or whether the toast is a Joycean irony is uncertain, though the song reference in Mrs. Breen's next line can only be construed as ironical.

The dear dead days beyond recall. Love's old sweet song. (445:7)

Cf. "Love's Old Sweet Song"

REMARKS: The "dear dead days" are of course from "Love's Old Sweet Song," which again is Molly's theme song. The irony here lies in the fact that Mrs. Breen, Bloom's mental salvation from the depths of despair to which he has fallen, should bring up the very song which he associates so closely with Molly. Bloom, even in his pleasantest triumphal mental projec-tions, is unable to rid himself of thoughts of his wife. This recurring com-bination of pathos and incongruity form a prominent aspect of Bloom's character.

BLOOM

(*Wearing a purple Napoleon hat with an amber halfmoon, his fingers and thumbs passing slowly down to her soft moist meaty palm which she surrenders gently.*) The witching hour of night. I took the splinter out of this hand, carefully, slowly. (*Tenderly, as he slips on her finger a ruby ring.*) Là ci darem la mano.

MRS BREEN

(*In a onepiece evening frock executed in moonlight blue, a tinsel sylph's diadem on her brow with her dancecard fallen beside her moonblue satin slipper, curves her palm softly, breathing quickly.*) Voglio e non. You're hot! You're scalding! The left hand nearest the heart. (445:18–30)

Cf. *"Là ci darem"*

REMARKS: The reference to *"Là ci darem"* is used in a parallel situation in the Lotus Eaters chapter (p. 77) when Bloom picks up Martha Clifford's letter at the post office, assumes the role of Don Giovanni, and walks away humming the lines from the song.[6] Hall points out that in the present passage we can expect *voglio* (I want to) from Mrs. Breen and not *vorrei* (I'd like to), for after all it is Bloom's hallucination, and Zerlina-Mrs. Breen should be wholeheartedly in favor of Don Bloom's attentions instead of merely being inclined toward him.

THE NAVVY

(*Shouts.*)

We are the boys. Of Wexford.

PRIVATE COMPTON

Say! What price the sergeantmajor?

PRIVATE CARR

Bennett? He's my pal. I love old Bennett.

THE NAVVY

(*Shouts.*)
The galling chain.
And free our native land. (451:15–25)

Cf. "The Boys of Wexford"

REMARKS: The two British soldiers pass accompanied by a navvy who is shouting the lyrics to this Irish patriotic song mentioned in Aeolus (p. 129), Lestrygonians (p. 163), and Sirens (p. 285). The soldiers, Private Carr and Compton, evidently have no idea of the nature of the song, for they prove to be quite belligerent later in this chapter about those who appear to deride their king and country. Here they seem to pay little attention to the navvy's shouts, which would constitute an insult to them if they knew the context of the words from the chorus,

> We are the boys of Wexford,
> Who fought with heart and hand,
> To burst in twain the galling chain,
> And free our native land.

You know that old joke, rose of Castille. Bloom. The change of name Virag. (455:26–27)

Cf. *The Rose of Castille*

REMARKS: Bloom tries to divert the attention of the watch from the Bloom-Flower name change with a pun on the title *The Rose of Castille*. Here again Bloom presumably refers to the pun ("Rows of cast steel") appearing earlier in Aeolus (134:19) and Calypso (426:17). The whole hallucination is the product of Bloom's guilt feelings, in this case for his liaison with Martha Clifford.

THE DARK MERCURY

The Castle is looking for him. He was drummed out of the army.

MARTHA

(*Thickveiled, a crimson halter round her neck, a copy of the* Irish Times *in her hand, in tone of reproach, pointing.*) Henry! Leopold! Leopold! Lionel, thou lost one! Clear my name. (456:7–14)

Cf. "M'appari"

REMARKS: As Martha demands that her name be cleared, she addresses Bloom not only by his assumed name, Henry, and his real name, but also by Lionel, his name in his role in Flotow's *Martha*. Martha's next words, in apposition to Lionel, are, "thou lost one," the words used in Simon Dedalus's Sirens chapter version of *"M'appari."* In the Sirens episode, both Martha Clifford and Molly were identified with Martha in the song and the opera, and, while it is Martha Clifford who seems to be the Martha in the present passage, the connotations of Molly-Martha and Lionel-Leopold, so strong in the Sirens chapter, lie just beneath the surface in Circe.

BLOOM

(*His hand on the shoulder of the first watch.*) My old dad too was a J. P. I'm as staunch a Britisher as you are, sir. I fought with the colours for king and country in the absentminded war under General Gough in the park and was disabled at Spion Kop Bloemfontein, was mentioned in dispatches. I did all a white man could. (*With quiet feeling.*) Jim Bludso. Hold her nozzle again the bank. (457:27–458:3)

Cf. "The Absent-minded Beggar"
  "Jim Bludso"

REMARKS: "The Absent-minded Beggar" has been alluded to [7] as a plea for those who fought in the Boer war. Bloom attempts to ingratiate himself by enlisting the same sympathies, through Kipling's allusion as well as his own supposed service. His recital of his deeds crescendoes to a comparison of himself with the hero of the ballad "Jim Bludso," who gave up his life holding his riverboat against the bank so that his passengers could escape the burning ship.

He was down and out but, though branded as a black sheep, if he might say so, he meant to reform, to retrieve the memory of the past in a purely sisterly way and return to nature as a purely domestic animal. (461:27–462:1)

Cf. "There Is a Flower that Bloometh"

REMARKS: ". . . the memory of the past" is the concluding line of *"There Is a Flower that Bloometh"* (again a musical pun reference, this time to the Henry Flower-Leopold Bloom name change), which admonishes the listener to recapture the memories of better, warmer time:

There is a flow'r that bloometh
When autumn leaves are shed,
With the silent moon it weepeth,
The spring and summer fled.
The early frost of winter
Scarce its brow hath overcast,
Oh! pluck it ere it wither,
'Tis the mem'ry of the past,
Oh! pluck it ere it wither,
'Tis the mem'ry, the mem'ry of the past.

It wafteth perfume o'er us,
Which few can e'er forget,
Of the bright scenes gone before us,
Of sweet though sad regret
Let no heart brave its power
By guilty thoughts o'ercast,
For then a poison'd flower
Is the mem'ry of the past,
For then a poison'd flower
Is the mem'ry, the mem'ry of the past.

The message of the song, a bit overdrawn and overly sentimentalized, complements the exaggeration of the court-plea parody in Bloom's mind and adds to the humor of the passage.

He said that he had seen from the gods my peerless globes as I sat in a box of the *Theatre Royal* at a command performance of *La Cigale*. (465:25–27)

Cf. *La Cigale et la Fourmi*

Remarks: Mrs. Barry refers to Henri Chivot, Alfred Duru, and Edmond Audran's opera based on the popular fable of the grasshopper and the ant by Fontaine.

Dignam's voice, muffled, is heard baying under ground: Dignam's dead and gone below. (474:17–18)

Cf. "Old Roger Is Dead and Gone to His Grave"

Remarks: In this singing game with many variants, a number define how Roger or Billy or Tommy, depending on the version, dead and gone to his grave, jumps out of the grave and hits an old woman picking ripe apples from the grave. The song is central to the resurrection motif of Dignam and the story of Reuben J. Dodd's son, which is alluded to immediately following.

Reuben J. A florin I find him. (*He fixes the manhole with a resolute stare.*) My turn now on. Follow me up to Carlow.

(*He executes a daredevil salmon leap in the air and is engulfed in the coalhole. . . .*) (474:22–26)

Cf. "Follow Me Up to Carlow"

REMARKS: The sources of Tom's speech and action are two earlier stories: one of Bloom's about a boatman who saved Reuben J's son and was rewarded by the father with a florin (pp. 94–95) and Lenehan's story of Rochford going down into a gas-choked manhole to rescue a man (pp. 232–233). In the present passage, Rochford's last statement as he goes down the coal hole after Dignam, "Follow me up to Carlow," is the title of an Irish nationalistic song about a leader urging his men to battle:

> Lift, MacCahir Oge, your face,
> Brooding o'er the old disgrace,
> That black Fitzwilliam stormed your place,
> And drove you to the fern!
> Grey said victory was sure—
> Soon the Firebrand he'd secure;
> Until he met at Glenmalure
>   Feagh MacHugh O'Byrne!
>
> Chorus:
> Curse and swear, Lord Kildare!
> Feagh will do what Feagh will dare;
> Now Fitzwilliam, have a care—
>   Fallen is your star, low!
> Up with halbert, out with sword,
> On we go; for by the Lord
> Feagh MacHugh has given the word:
>   Follow me up to Carlow.

The song seems to have little hidden meaning for the passage and serves merely to stress Rochford's heroism in Bloom's thoughts by equating Tom with Irish war heroes in his use of their battle cry.

BLOOM

Is this Mrs Mack's?

ZOE

No, eightyone. Mrs Cohen's. You might go farther and fare worse. Mother Slipperslapper. (*Familiarly.*) She's on the job herself tonight with the vet, her tipster, that gives her all the winners and pays for her son in Oxford. (475:15–21)

Cf. "The Fox"

REMARKS: Mother Slipperslapper, to whom Zoe refers, is a character in a popular folk ballad about a fox who sets out to steal some poultry:

> Stanza 1:
> A fox went out on a moonlight night
> And he begged the moon to give him light,
> For he'd a long way to go that night
> Before he could reach his den-oh!
>   Den-oh! den-oh!
>   He'd a long way to go that night
>   Before he could reach his den-oh!
>
> Stanza 3:
> He seized the grey goose by the sleeve—
> Says he, "Madam Goose, and by your leave,
> I'll carry you off without reprieve
> And take your home to my den-oh!"
>   Den-oh, den-oh,
>   I'll carry you off without reprieve
>   And take you home to my den-oh!
>
> Stanza 4:
> Then old mother slipperslapper jumped out of bed
> And out of the window popped her head.
> Crying, "John, John, John the grey goose is gone
> And the fox is away to his den-oh!"
>   Den-oh, den-oh,
>   Oh! John! John! John! the grey goose is gone
>   And the fox is away to his den-oh!

Zoe's telling Bloom that he might go farther and fare worse resembles the length of the prospective journey of the fox in the first stanza of the song. Her equation of Bella Cohen with Mother Slipperslapper suggests that Bella, like Mother Slipperslapper, might have just the fine goose (whore) that Bloom (the fox) is looking for.

ZOE

You'll know me the next time.

BLOOM

(*Forlornly.*) I never loved a dear gazelle but it was sure to . . .

(*Gazelles are leaping, feeding on the mountains. Near are lakes. Round their shores file shadows black of cedargroves. Aroma rises, a strong hairgrowth of resin. It burns, the orient, a sky of sapphire, cleft by the bronze flight of eagles. Under it lies the womancity, nude, white, still, cool, in luxury. A fountain murmurs among damask roses. Mammoth roses murmur of scarlet winegrapes. A wine of shame, lust, blood exudes, strangely murmuring.*)

ZOE

(*Murmuring singsong with the music, her odalisk lips lusciously smeared with salve of swinefat and rosewater.*)

Schorach ani wenowach, benoith Hierushaloim. (476:24–477:14)

Cf. "I Never Nursed a Dear Gazelle"
     "Song of Solomon"

REMARKS: Bloom again quotes from the Moore song, slightly altering the words of the second stanza, "I never nurs'd a dear gazelle," [8] to "I never loved. . . ."

Bloom is referring here to his propensity for sadness and disappointment which has its ultimate roots in Molly's infidelity. This time, however, the line triggers a brief hallucination in which the dismal truth is enveloped in the soft music of the orient, the exotic Eden where things are different, intriguing, and romantic. The song, which is from *Lalla Rookh*, a poem about the Middle East, furthers the Eastern motif which runs through Bloom's thoughts. As the hallucination proceeds this exotic spirit is infused in Zoe, whose words, *"Schorach ani wenowach, benoith Hierushaloim"* (I am black yet comely, O ye daughters of Jerusalem), are from the "Song of Songs" (I:5). Zoe, described as having odalisk lips, is singing the words from the bride's apology and song to her lover. In the biblical passage Israel is the bride confessing her own unworthiness, her sins, and the anger of her brothers and sisters. As the scene shifts back to reality, Bloom, blending the hallucination with Zoe's previous speech, says, "I thought you were of good stock by your accent" (477:16). When the real Zoe breathes her "stale garlic" breath at Bloom the roses of his oriental vision part to *"disclose a sepulchre of the gold of kings and their mouldering bones"* (477:21–22), all that is left of Bloom's vision of Israel, his promised land of the East.

> But our buccaneering Vanderdeckens in their phantom ship of finance . . . (478:23–25)
> These flying Dutchmen or lying Dutchmen as they recline in their upholstered poop, casting dice, what reck they? (479:19–21)

Cf. *The Flying Dutchman*

REMARKS: Bloom's reference to Vanderdecken, the Flying Dutchman, is to the legend celebrated in both song and opera. Wagner's *Der Fliegende Hollander* is alluded to later in Eumaeus. All musical versions are based on the tale of the seagoing, wandering Jew archetype, who can't go home until judgment day unless he finds a woman who would love him faithfully until death. While the context of the story would fit excellently the plot of *Ulysses* and Bloom's plight, the present allusion does not seem to lend itself to those connotations. Bloom's condemnation of the captains of commerce or the moneyed class who bilk the poor, in the context of the wandering Jew might even be construed as an anti-Semitic reference, and it is certainly more prosaic than the romanticism of the legend.

> The poor man starves while they are grassing their royal mountain stags or shooting peasants and phartridges in their purblind pomp of pelf and power. But their reign is rover for rever and ever and ev . . . (479:25–28)

Cf. "Hallelujah Chorus"

REMARKS: The last sentence in Bloom's speech suggests the closing lines of the "Hallelujah Chorus" from Handel's *Messiah:*

> . . . and he shall reign for ever and ever,
> for ever and ever . . .

Bloom in the word *rover* is announcing the end of the exploitation of the masses in the new Bloomusalem. The "Hallelujah Chorus" is, in the popular mind, perhaps the epitome of thunderous, triumphal music, and it serves in the present situation to introduce a long, magnificent, comic procession, including the Cameron Highlanders, the Welsh fusiliers, and the pillar of the cloud.

> *A fife and drum band is heard in the distance playing the Kol Nidre.* (480:5–6)

Cf. *"Kol Nidre"*

REMARKS: This prayer is sometimes sung for the eve of Yom Kippur. The prayer is a renunciation of all evil things for the coming year and is a high point of the beginning Yom Kippur celebration. The use of a fife-and-drum band to orchestrate the prayer-song here further adds to the incongruity of Bloom's solemn resolutions and declarations and augments the general hoopla of the occasion.

(*. . . Bloom's boys run amid the bystanders with branches of hawthorn and wrenbushes.*)

BLOOM'S BOYS

The wren, the wren,
The king of all birds,
Saint Stephen's his day,
Was caught in the furze. (481:8–15)

Cf. "The Wren, the Wren, the King of All Birds"

REMARKS: The reference to Bloom's boys has its historical antecedents in the wren-boys, who sang the same song that Bloom's boys do in Circe. The following note is attached to the song in F. W. Horncastle's *Music of Ireland, pt. iii.* (London, 1844):

On the anniversary of St. Stephen's Day groups of young villagers carry about a holly bush adorned with ribbons and with several wrens depending from it. This is conveyed from house to house with much ceremony, the wren-boys chanting several verses, the burthen of which may be collected from the lines of the song. Contributions are, of course, levied and the evening spent in merriment.

The full text of the song is as follows:

The wren, the wren, the king of all birds,
Saint Stephen's Day was caught in a furze,
Although he is little, his family's great;
I pray you, good landlady, give us a treat.
Sing hey! sing ho!
Sing holly, sing holly!
A drop just to drink, it would cure melancholy.
Sing hey! sing ho!
Sing holly, sing holly!
A drop just to drink, it would cure melancholy.

My box would speak if it had but a tongue,[9]
And two or three shillings would do it no wrong,

So show us some pity in order that we
May drink you good health for your kind charity.
Sing hey!, etc.

And if you draw it of the best,
I hope in heaven your soul it may rest,
But if you draw it of the small,
It won't agree with the wren-boys at all!
Sing hey!, etc.

The song creates a parallel between Bloom and St. Stephen, the first Christian martyr, adding one more hero to the list that Bloom represents and foreshadowing his eventual hallucinatory martyrdom. Also it provides another link of consubstantiation with Stephen Dedalus.

Joybells ring in Christ church, Saint Patrick's, George's and gay Malahide. (428:27–28)

Cf. "The Bridal of Malahide"

REMARKS: This passage includes snatches of the first stanza of a song celebrating another famous event, "The Bridal of Malahide." The beginning of the wedding festivities is described in that first stanza:

The joy-bells are ringing
In gay Malahide,
The fresh wind is singing
Along the sea-side:
The maids are assembling
With garlands of flowers,
And the harpstrings are trembling
In all the glad bowers.

As we explained earlier,[10] the song goes on to relate how the wedding festivities are interrupted by an invading enemy and how the bridegroom assumes immediate command, dons his armor, and is off to war. The effect of the song is first to add to the significance and pomp of the spectacle surrounding Bloom and second to provide a link to the new hallucinatory image of Bloom as an Irish hero.

Half a league onward! They charge! All is lost now! Do we yield? No! We drive them headlong! Lo! We charge! (484:4–6)

Cf. *"Tutto è sciolto"*

REMARKS: Bloom assumes leadership of the fight for Irish independence and delivers a series of battle clichés. As the fearless leader of his own hallucination Bloom quotes the Anglicized version of the song *"Tutto è sciolto"* ("All Is Lost Now"). The scene strikes a sharp contrast to the situation in which the song appeared in the Sirens chapter. There Bloom thinks of the song in connection with his being cuckolded and concludes, "As easy stop the sea. Yes: all is lost" (273:4).[11] In the present situation, however, Bloom, the magnificent, the undismayed, rallies his forces to turn defeat to victory. The enemy's charge, to the words of Tennyson's "Charge of the Light Brigade," is repulsed, and, overcoming despair, Bloom's forces vanquish all in a grand sweep. The song reference in the present passage can easily be projected as the focal point of a desire for the strength to reverse the defeat in his marital situation.

BLOOM

My beloved subjects, a new era is about to dawn. I, Bloom, tell you verily it is even now at hand. Yea, on the word of a Bloom, ye shall ere long enter into the golden city, which is to be, the new Bloomusalem in the Nova Hibernia of the future.

(*Thirtytwo workmen wearing rosettes, from all the counties of Ireland, under the guidance of Derwan the builder, construct the new Bloomusalem. It is a colossal edifice, with crystal roof, built in the shape of a huge pork kidney, containing forty thousand rooms. . . .*) (484:19–28)

Cf. "The Holy City"

REMARKS: At the height of Bloom's hallucination, he becomes not only the saviour and political-social leader of Ireland, but also the Messiah coming to save Stephen, Dublin, and, by extension of the microcosm, Ireland and the world. Bloom will be the new Messiah and Dublin the holy city. This then is the logical outcome of all the Messianic references in the book: Bloom the Moses of Taylor's speech in Aeolus, overcoming all with humanity and equanimity, leading her artists out of bondage, freeing her people from the superstitions of the citizen in Cyclops, and bringing humanity and understanding. The last net over which Stephen must fly is only hinted at in *Portrait* and only imprecisely revealed to him in *Ulysses.* The agenbite of inwit goes far beyond his mother's death and his role in her last hours, even beyond anything Oedipal: it extends to his basic lack of humanity and understanding of just what humanity means. Nor is the problem exclusively Stephen's: it is the Theban disease of spirit which permeates the city and country, a malady which only Bloom-Messiah may cure. The conversion of the city and its people can come only through the suffering of its Messiah. Joyce orchestrates and informs the great conversion in this epical vision of Bloom with F. E. Weatherly's "The Holy City." The song tells of a three-part dream in which Jerusalem undergoes a change to darkness after the Crucifixion and becomes the city of promise after the Resurrection:

Last night I lay a-sleeping,
There came a dream so fair:
I stood in old Jerusalem,
Beside the temple there;
I heard the children singing,
And ever as they sang,
Me-thought the voice of Angels,
From Heav'n in answer rang;
Me-thought the voice of Angels
From Heav'n in answer rang
"Jerusalem! Jerusalem!
Lift up your gates and sing,
Hosanna in the highest,
Hosanna to your King."

And then methought my dream was chang'd,
The streets no longer rang,
Hushed were the glad Hosannas
The little children sang;
The sun grew dark with mystery,
The morn was cold and chill,
As the shadow of a cross arose
Upon a lonely hill,
As the shadow of a cross arose
Upon a lonely hill.
Jerusalem! Jerusalem!
Hark! how the Angels sing:
"Hosanna in the highest,
Hosanna to your King!"

And once again the scene was changed,
New earth there seem'd to be,
I saw the Holy City
Beside the tideless sea;
The light of God was on its streets,
The gates were open wide,
And all who would might enter,
And no one was denied.
No need of moon or stars by night,
Or sun to shine by day,
It was the new Jerusalem
That would not pass away,

It was the new Jerusalem
That would not pass away.
Jerusalem! Jerusalem!
Sing for the night is o'er!
Hosanna in the highest,
Hosanna for evermore!
Hosanna in the highest,
Hosanna for evermore!

The miraculous conversion of Ireland-Jerusalem will, however, not be as quickly achieved as it is in the song vision, at least insofar as it concerns the artist, Stephen. As we have seen in the later stages of *Portrait* and in a more pronounced way in *Ulysses,* Stephen's reality is conditioned by a world of literary and ecclesiastical allusion which inform and give meaning to anything perceived by the senses. This body of literary and liturgical patterns, which his life had begun to assume as the ultimate truths, render the "ineluctable modality of the visible" distorted by any number of mythic and symbolic patterns which Stephen confuses with reality. So his search for a father figure or a strong figure to bring him out of the childish selfcenteredness becomes real to him only in terms of Shakespeare, who must be father and son both, and the unity of the consubstantial God and the Trinity. But Stephen's paradise lies with a source nearly inconceivable to the young aesthete: old, literal Bloom is the sought-after father figure, living through experiences which are curiously similar to or parodies of Stephen's experiences. Their consubstantiality by definition equates the parts, father and son, with the whole, so that Stephen wants and needs the father figure for consubstantial completion.

> Clap clap hands till Poldy comes home,
> Cakes in his pocket for Leo alone. (486:11–12)

Cf. "Clap Hands"

REMARKS: There are a number of variations to this nursery rhyme, one of which runs as follows:

> Clap hands, clap hands,
>   Till father comes home;
> For father's got money,
>   But mother's got none.

Several other variants mention "cakes for baby." The nursery rhyme is the beginning of a series of children's games which the benevolent Bloom plays with adoring youngsters.

(He plays pussy fourcorners with ragged boys and girls.) Peep! Bopeep! *(He wheels twins in a perambulator.)* (486:20–21)

Cf. "Little Bo Peep"

REMARKS: Bloom uses the nursery rhyme to further his subconscious image as a great benevolent figure even unto the children, the least of all. The Bo Peep rhyme, with its connotations of the shepherd tending her lost flock, re-enforces the image of Bloom as a Messianic figure to Ireland and more particularly in this episode to Stephen.

Give us a tune, Bloom. One of the old sweet songs. (491:2)

Cf. "Love's Old Sweet Song"

REMARKS: As we have seen (p. 63), this is one of the two songs Molly is to sing on her tour, through which the song has become inextricably linked to her and Boylan throughout the book. In response to Flynn's petition Bloom sings the following improvised lines:

(*With rollicking humour.*)

> I vowed that I never would leave her,
> She turned out a cruel deceiver.
> With my tooraloom tooraloom tooraloom tooraloom.
> (491:4–7)

Bloom's song takes on additional significance in the light of the reference to "Love's Old Sweet Song," for it is Molly about whom Bloom sings. As Flynn's request demonstrates, Molly is still in the back of Bloom's mind. Flynn's reference triggers the second song, the lyrics of which bring her once more to the center of Bloom's thoughts.

What railway opera is like a tramline in Gibraltar? The Rows of Casteele. (*Laughter.*) (491:13–14)

Cf. *The Rose of Castille*

REMARKS: We have heard a slightly different version of the joke before in the newspaper office from Lenehan, who now rises up to condemn Bloom for stealing his joke: "Plagiarist! Down with Bloom!" (491:16). This is a good example of references which have occurred earlier in Stephen's presence appearing subsequently in Bloom's hallucinations. According to a number of critics Joyce has been guilty of these "errors" by having events that have occurred in Bloom's day occur in Stephen's hallucinations and vice versa. Actually the critics may well be wrong and Joyce perfectly justified. These seeming errors occur so often in Circe simply because the main thrust of the novel is that Bloom and Stephen are living each others' lives, that their experiences are coincidental, and that by Circe they can draw on each other's experiences and collective subconscious to give meaning and substance to their hallucinatory passages. At any rate, *The Rose of Castille* is another of Molly's leitmotifs, since she throughout the novel has been identified with the heroine and title role of the opera.

As these images of Molly arise one after the other, Bloom's concomitant weakness becomes more apparent and his rule begins to crumble. He makes every mental effort to save his hallucinatory leader-image from his own weakness by testimonials to his prowess from "The Veiled Sibyl" and other women.

In the world of the subconscious, however, there are the inevitable feelings of inferiority despite whatever facades may be erected. Bloom's efforts at building his own image fail and he goes into a long, cataclysmic decline and fall from power.

A HOLLYBUSH

And in the devil's glen? (496:16-17)

Cf. "The Cock Crew"
   "Pretty Molly Brannigan"

REMARKS: The hollybush here of course links Sephen's riddle and all his guilt from the agenbite of inwit with Bloom's guilt at his shortcomings in marriage.[12] Bloom's failure is exemplified by the excerpt from "Pretty Molly Brannigan."

The relevant words from the song are,

> Since Molly's gone and left me here alone to die,
> The place where my heart was you'd aisy rowl a turnip in,
> 'Tis as large as all Dublin, and from Dublin to the Divil's glen.

Bloom's guilt, associated with sexual failure and Molly's promiscuity and desertion of the marital bonds, parallels Stephen's guilt and failure in his Oedipal relationship with his mother.

(Bloom with asses' ears seats himself in the pillory with crossed arms, his feet protruding. He whistles Don Giovanni, a cenar teco. Artane orphans, joining hands, caper round him. Girls of the Prison Gate Mission, joining hands, caper round in the opposite direction.) (496:24-28)

Cf. Commendatore's lines, *Don Giovanni*, V, iii

REMARKS: Vernon Hall claims that Bloom's whistling the lines of the Commendatore's ghost from *Don Giovanni* ("Don Giovanni, a cenar teco") is an attempt to keep up his spirits.[13] However, Hall fails to take into consideration the music involved. The line is sung at an extremely slow tempo, in a sort of dirge-like setting accompanied by claps of thunder. The passage, marked andante, is hardly one which Bloom or anyone else would whistle to cheer his spirits. Rather he puts himself in the Don's place as his past misdeeds are recounted, and like the Don he is about to atone for them. The line Bloom whistles is the one the Commendatore sings as he enters to lead the Don to hell for his transgressions, which like Bloom's have dealt mostly with sex. Bloom-Giovanni is meeting his just reward.

Music without Words, pray for us. (498:30)

Cf. "Songs without Words"

REMARKS: Appearing in the litany to Bloom, this phrase, like all the other appellations in the litany, signifies his symbolic or noteworthy role in preceding episodes. In this particular address, however, Bloom's role is extraordinarily unclear. Here Joyce is stressing the dependence upon music rather than the words of Sirens for the significance of the episode and Bloom's role in it, exemplified by the line "but Bloom sang dumb." (276:35)

A choir of six hundred voices, conducted by Mr Vincent O'Brien, sings the Alleluia chorus, accompanied on the organ by Joseph Glynn. (499:4–6)

Cf. "Hallelujah Chorus"

REMARKS: This chorus is sung in Handel's *Messiah* after the resurrection of Christ in the latter or Easter portion of the work. The chorus completes the image of Bloom's elevation and eventual Christ-like martyrdom which began nineteen pages before.

(*She holds his hand which is feeling for her nipple.*) I say, Tommy Tittlemouse. Stop that and begin worse. (500:6–7)

Cf. "Little Tommy Tittlemouse"

REMARKS: The words to this well-known nursery rhyme might easily under the circumstances take on a double entendre:

> Little Tommy Tittlemouse
> Lived in a little house;
> He caught fishes
> In other men's ditches.

Thus, Zoe, either in a derisive or complimentary manner, proposes intercourse.

(*Outside the gramophone begins to blare* The Holy City.)

STEPHEN

(*Abruptly.*) What went forth to the ends of the world to traverse not itself. God, the sun, Shakespeare, a commercial traveller, having itself traversed in reality itself, becomes that self. Wait a moment. Wait a second. Damn that fellow's noise in the street. Self which it itself was ineluctably preconditioned to become. *Ecco!* (504:31–505:7)

Cf. "The Holy City"

REMARKS: When the signs which he seeks are at hand Stephen rejects them, as he has done all through the novel. Nowhere is this more apparent than the passage in which Stephen hears the gramophone playing "The Holy City." He is in the midst of his usual symbolic tirade, when the sound of the song intrudes upon his consciousness. Bloom, the saviour of the new Jerusalem, is at hand. The omens are present; the music is blaring the announcement; but Stephen, caught up in his own symbology, shutting out the external world and the external symbols of the novel as well as his one genuine chance at salvation, hears "The Holy City" not as a song which has meaning for him but merely as a noise in the street. Just as he has rejected God as a shout in the street, so does he now reject the announcement of Bloom's coming and the metamorphosis Stephen has so desperately longed for, as he damns "that fellow's noise in the street." The rejection of the symbolic meaning which is intruded so persistently on Stephen's consciousness prefigures his rejection in literal terms of his personal Messiah, Bloom, in the Ithaca episode. But by Ithaca the matter is out of Stephen's hands. He has been affected by his meeting with Bloom and for better or worse their consubstantiation is sealed in Circe.

THE GRAMOPHONE

Jerusalem!
Open your gates and sing
Hosanna . . .

(*A rocket rushes up the sky and bursts. A white star falls from it, proclaiming the consummation of all things and second coming of Elijah. Along an infinite invisible tightrope taut from zenith to nadir the End of the World, a twoheaded octopus in gillie's kilts, busby and tartan filibegs, whirls through the murk, head over heels, in the form of the Three Legs of Man*). (507: 4–14)

Cf. "The Holy City"

REMARKS: Back at Bella Cohen's, Florry has just announced that according to the papers the end of the world is about to occur that summer. This time the song is used to herald the coming of the antichrist, Reuben J. Dodd, who together with his son forms a separate but equal consubstantial father-son variation on Stephen's ecclesiastical theme. Elijah, proclaiming the end of the world, exhorts all present "to sense that cosmic force" (507:33) through which they all can be identified with Christ. Stephen, of course, has been doing this ever since the opening of *Portrait,* when he identified himself with both Christ and Satan. The theme, transformed in *Ulysses* into a cosmic force of unity, allows all symbol patterns and experience to be expanded to include variations embracing all characters. Symbol patterns shift, evolve, transmogrify, and explain in different situations varied but related experiences so that all characters could at one point, as Elijah says, become Christ, Elijah, or anybody else. The variant upon the father-son motif here at the variation crossroads of the book brings in Dodd and son as a part of the Hamlet-Christ motif and stresses the simultaneous operation of all symbol patterns in the episode. So Elijah, described with overtones of the old mystic, A.E., arrives to reenforce the announcement of the mystical conversion of all Jerusalem-Dublin to the New Bloomusalem. "The Holy City" provides the background motif for this transubstantiation and that is the reason the song appears so prominently in the chapter. "The Holy City," in detailing the transformation of Jerusalem, deals on a metaphoric level with the metamorphosis of the New Bloomusalem, the amalgamation of Bloom's and Stephen's worlds as well as the salvation of the city of Dublin through the exhortations of Ben Bloom, Elijah, A.E., and the high priest and smith forging the Uncreated Conscience of his Race, Stephen Dedalus.

THE END OF THE WORLD

(*With a Scotch accent.*) Wha'll dance the keel row, the keel row, the keel row? (507:15–17)

Cf. "Weel May the Keel Row"

REMARKS: The End of the World, first alluded to by A.E. in Lestrygonians, was connected by him with a Scotch accent in a conversation partially overheard by Bloom. The well-known Scottish song provides the end of the world with something Scottish to say and the additional incongruity of his dancing and inviting the others to join. The dance also parodies the consubstantiality theme. It is an eightsome reel. First the principal individual moves in the center of the ring dancing. Then he chooses his partner and is later joined one after another by the others, until all are involved in the identical dance.

Tell mother you'll be there. (507:27–28)

Cf. "Tell Mother I'll Be There"

REMARKS: As Elijah urges the assemblage to repentance and Jesus, one of his entreaties takes the form of this sentimental ballad of an oft erring son who entreats the angels, now that his mother is dead, to inform her that he will be along also. The maudlin quality of the song reenforces the comic overtones in its use here by the old evangelist, Elijah, and foreshadows the anguish of May's apparition as she warns of hell-fire.

Now then our glory song. All join heartily in the singing. En-core! (*He sings.*) Jeru . . .

THE GRAMOPHONE

(*Drowning his voice.*) Whorusalaminyourhighhohhhh . . . (*The disc rasps gratingly against the needle.*) (508:13–17)

Cf. "The Holy City"

REMARKS: In the conclusion of this song sequence, all the characters in the room, exhorted to consubstantiality by Elijah, are asked to sing of the new millennium, but the song is interrupted unceremoniously by the malfunction-ing machine, and the song of the three whores is not of the glories of the rejuvenated city but gutteral sounds of anguish: "Ahhkkk!" (508:19). Bella Cohen's is an unlikely place for a golden age to dawn.

BLOOM

(*An elbow resting in a hand, a forefinger against his cheek.*) She seems sad.

VIRAG

(*Cynically, his weasel teeth bared yellow, draws down his left eye with a finger and barks hoarsely.*) Hoax! Beware of the flapper and bogus mournful. Lily of the alley. All possess bachelor's button discovered by Rualdus Colombus. Tumble her. Columble her. Chameleon. (*More genially.*) Well then, permit me to draw your attention to item number three. There is plenty of her visible to the naked eye. Observe the mass of oxygenated vegetable matter on her skull. What ho, she bumps! The ugly duckling of the party, longcasted and deep in keel. (512:24–513:5)

Cf. "Lily of the Valley"
  "Sally in Our Alley"
  Ophelia's Song, *Hamlet*, IV, v, 63–64
  "What Ho, She Bumps!"

REMARKS: Virag's reply contains reference to no less than four songs. His first reference, "Lily of the Alley," is a combination of two songs: "Lily of the Valley" and "Sally in Our Alley." The first of these, a popular comic song of the late nineteenth century, contains a lighthearted proposition:

> Lily Lily of the Valley
> Dearie, dearie, let's be pally
> Sweetie, You're the nicest flower of the lot
> Be my Lily, Oh! Be my Lily,
> I'll be your Forget me not.

"Sally in Our Alley" extols the qualities of Sally, a young lower-class girl:

> Of all the girls that are so smart,
> There's none like pretty Sally;
> She is the darling of my heart,
> And lives in our alley:
> There is no lady in the land
> That's half so sweet as Sally;
> She is the darling of my heart,
> And lives in our alley.

Together the two songs add up to the seduction of a lower-class girl, the point that Virag is trying to make as he extols the delights of the uncomplicated flesh.

As Virag proceeds in the same vein, his words "Tumble her. Columble her" suggest stanza four of one of Ophelia's songs in the fourth act of *Hamlet*:

> Quoth she, "Before you tumbled me,
>   You promis'd me to wed."
> "So would I ha' done, by yonder sun,
>   An thou hadst not come to my bed."

What appears to be a weak musical identification hinging entirely on the word *tumble* is reenforced in William Schutte's *Joyce and Shakespeare* [14] by a whole series of other identifications from *Hamlet*. Virag uses the bawdy aspects of Ophelia's song in his Mephistophelian urging that everything is ultimately concerned with the sensual.

The last song reference in the passage is to "What ho, she bumps!" an 1899 music-hall song about an inane popular saying which the boys mouthed on various occasions in which girls were present. The first stanza is typical of the rest:

> Have you noticed in your travels, at the seaside or in town,
> They're sure to have a saying now-a-days;
> "Now we shan't be long," and "Let 'em all come," have had their fling,
> So I will sing to you the latest phrase.
> Last summer, down at Margate, two young ladies in a boat,
> Were pulling for the shore without a doubt;
> The water it was very rough, it bump'd them up and down,
> When from the shore some boys began to shout:
>
> Chorus:
> What ho, she bumps! what ho, she bumps!
> It seem'd to give the ladies all the mumps! yes, all the mumps!
> Those pretty little misses were feeding all the fishes,
> And the boys were shouting out, what ho, she bumps!

The words of the boys on the beach are really only the same sort of catcall of derision at the propriety of womankind that Virag is giving.

VIRAG

We can do you all brands, mild, medium and strong. Pay your money, take your choice. How happy could you be either . . .

BLOOM

With? . . . (513:8–13)

Cf. "How Happy Could I Be With Either"

REMARKS: The last part of Virag's statement is a paraphrase of the musical complaint of a man who suffers from the presence of two lovers:

> How happy could I be with either,
> Were t'other dear charmer away;
> But while you thus tease me together,
> To neither a word will I say.
> Ri tol de rol lol de rol li do.
>
> How happy could I be with either
> Dear, dear maids so beauteous and gay;
> And with thee my heart it would ever
> Its love and affection convey.
> Ri tol, etc.

How happy I could be with either
To charm me by night and by day;
To be to each one a fond lover,
And pass hours of pleasure away.
Ri tol, etc.

Virag has meant the song to be merely another off-color allusion, but Bloom for a moment reads more into the song, asking "with? . . ." as he thinks of Molly and Martha.

That suits your book, eh? Fleshhotpots of Egypt to hanker after. Wallow in it. Lycopodium. (*His throat twitches*.) Slapbang! There he goes again. (513:27–29)

Cf. "Slap! Bang! Here We Are Again, Boys!"

REMARKS: Virag's "slapbang . . ." is from another rousing song which the rakes of the turn of the century sang in their robust manliness. One stanza of the twenty-four in the song will demonstrate the primitive qualities the lyrics espouse:

When you feel blue and worried too,
And things are not just right,
Throw out your chest and try your best
To sing with all your might:

Chorus:
Slap! Bang! Here we are again!
Here we are again, boys, here we are again!
Slap! Bang! Here we are again,
A jolly bunch (gang) are we!

Like the song, Virag's urging has by this time become worn and banal.

Stop twirling your thumbs and have a good old thunk. See, you have forgotten. Exercise your mnemotechnic. *La causa è santa.* Tara. Tara. (*Aside.*) He will surely remember. (514:16–19)

Cf. *"La causa è santa"*

REMARKS: Virag's mention of *"La causa"* is accompanied by the "Tara Tara" of the sextet as it had been in earlier references (pp. 168, 370) and is preceded by an allusion to *The Huguenots* ("Not for sale. Hire only. Huguenot" [514:5–6]) as it was in the reference in the Lestrygonians episode. *"La causa è santa"* (the cause is sacred), a sextet from Meyerbeer's *The Huguenots,* appears here to be only an aptly ironic phrase to urge Bloom to remember his grandfather's lessons, presumably in sex.

Jocular. With my eyeglass in my ocular. (516:13–14)

Cf. "And That's What I Shall Say"

REMARKS: The song is from Gilbert and Sullivan's *Patience,* in which Bunthorne and Jane discuss what he will say to Grosvenor, who, because he is so serious, sincere, and pure, has taken all of Bunthorne's female admirers. Bunthorne will admonish the other to be less serious: "I'll tell him that unless he will consent to be more jocular—/ . . . To cut his curly hair, and stick an eyeglass in his ocular . . ." Virag by using the first person transfers to himself the happy-go-lucky mood Bunthorne would have Grosvenor assume, the image Virag has fostered throughout Circe.

HENRY

(In a low dulcet voice, touching the strings of his guitar.) There is a flower that bloometh. (517:26–28)

Cf. "There Is a Flower that Bloometh"

REMARKS: The song has its obvious connection to the passage by its combination of the names, Flower and Bloom. If we examine the lyrics of the song (they appear in an earlier gloss in Circe, p. 262) there is also another connection to Bloom's hallucinatory pattern. The flower, the memory of the past, can, according to the song, be either a treasure or a curse, depending on whether or not guilt feelings accompany the individual who does the remembering. Bloom's memories of his love scene with Molly in the rhododendrons are a far cry from his hallucinations in the Circe episode, which are, as stanza two suggests, "By guilty thoughts o'ercast." Bloom has in the past also been beset by pangs of conscience in his adulterous role of Henry Flower. This role and the degrading innermost thoughts of his subconscious, objectified in Circe, are the "poisoned flowers" of his mind.

Sing us something. Love's old sweet song. (518:11)

Cf. "Love's Old Sweet Song"

REMARKS: Bloom's softness, embodied in Henry Flower, manifests itself most poignantly in his memories of past glories on Howth. But as Florry calls immediately afterward for Stephen to sing "Love's Old Sweet Song," we are abruptly reminded of the grim realities of the present in which the memories of the past have fast become the old sweet song of love of Molly and Blazes.

If I could only find out about octaves. Reduplication of personality. Who was it told me his name? *(His lawnmower begins to purr.)* Aha, yes. *Zoe mou sas agapo.* (518:28–519:1)

Cf. *"Maid of Athens"*

REMARKS: Stephen refers to the refrain line of Byron's lyrics in the poem "Maid of Athens," which was set almost immediately after Byron wrote it to the music of this subsequently very popular ballad. Byron's translation, "My life, I love you!" here is used ironically by Stephen, who is talking about musical reproduction of notes in the octave and about the reproduction of personality. The Byronic reference from Philip Drunk is an attempt by Stephen to identify that part of his personality at least with Byron, an identification he has been trying to establish at least since chapter two of *Portrait.* The problem of reduplication is also inherent in the consubstantiality motive.

(*Ben Jumbo Dollard, rubicund, musclebound, hairy-nostrilled, hugebearded, cabbageeared, shaggychested, shockmaned, fatpapped, stands forth, his loins and genitals tightened into a pair of black bathing bagslops.*)

BEN DOLLARD

(*Nakkering castanet bones in his huge padded paws, yodels jovially in base barreltone.*) When love absorbs my ardent soul.

(*The virgins, Nurse Callan and Nurse Quigley, burst through the ringkeepers and the ropes and mob him with open arms.*) (521:26–522:6)

Cf. "Love and War"

REMARKS: It will be recalled that Ben's rendition of the song in the Sirens chapter prompted Bloom's stream-of-consciousness passage about the size of Ben's genitals the night he borrowed an undersized dress suit from Leopold and Molly. Bloom's comment in the Sirens passage, "Well, of course, that's what gives him the base barreltone," (270:38–39) was the product of Bloom's reflections on Ben's parts and the low notes of "Love and War," which Ben was singing at the time. The present reference is an externalized reflection and distortion of Bloom's stream of consciousness from the earlier passage.

HENRY

(*Caressing on his breast a severed female head, murmurs.*) Thine heart, mine love. (*He plucks his lutestrings.*) When first I saw . . . (522:13–16)

Cf. *"M'appari"*

REMARKS: Bloom's desire to emulate Ben is expressed in Henry's plucking the lute and starting to sing *"M'appari."* The song is, however, for a tenor, not a bass, and relegates Henry to the role of the plaintive lover, Lionel. The song can do little more than recall the pining of Lionel-Leopold for his Martha-Molly which occupied such a prominent position in the Sirens chapter. The song reconfirms the anguish about his lost wife that lies just beneath the surface of all Bloom's hallucinations.

(Henry Flower combs his moustache and beard rapidly with a pocketcomb and gives a cow's lick to his hair. Steered by his rapier, he glides to the door, his wild harp slung behind him. . . .) (522:23–26)

Cf. "The Minstrel Boy"

REMARKS: The last line of this description is from line four of the first stanza of Moore's popular ballad, "The Minstrel Boy":

> The Minstrel Boy to the war is gone,
> In the ranks of death you'll find him;
> His father's sword he hath girded on,
> And his wild harp slung behind him . . .

If Dollard is a man's man with his bass barreltone, Leopold-Henry is little more than a man's minstrel boy with his songs of lost love. This is reflected in his failure to assert himself and the general acquiescence of his next line.

All is lost now. (523:4)

Cf. *"Tutto è sciolto"*

REMARKS: This is Bloom's theme song of resignation and despondency in the Sirens chapter. It shows up here again as another despondent tenor aria in contrast to Dollard's manly bass.

> O, the poor little fellow
> Hi-hi-hi-hi-his legs they were yellow
> He was plump, fat and heavy and brisk as a snake
> But some bloody savage
> To graize his white cabbage
> He murdered Nell Flaherty's duckloving drake. (524:18–23)

Cf. "Nell Flaherty's Drake"

REMARKS: This rollicking comic song meant to demonstrate the bawdy, jovial aspect of Stephen's personality, even in his capacity as would-be cardinal and Roman Catholic primate of all Ireland, is a logical extension of Stephen's scene with the director of studies at Belvedere when Stephen shuns the priesthood because the priest's mirthless face is incapable of the joy and humor of the lively concertina and the singing young men in the street. The song in Stephen's fantasy here depicts the incompatibility of this comic-bawdy aspect of his personality with his former aspirations for the priesthood. Thus, when Florry asks him if he is a spoiled priest, he thinks, "Cardinal sin. Monks of the screw," (523:24), which prompts the hallucination of himself as cardinal.

> Shall carry my heart to thee,
> Shall carry my heart to thee,
> And the breath of the balmy night
> Shall carry my heart to thee. (525:3–6)

Cf. "Winds that Blow from the South"

REMARKS: I have not been able to locate this song cited by Hodgart and Worthington.

> *She is dressed in a threequarter ivory gown, fringed round the hem with tasselled selvedge, and cools herself, flirting a black horn fan like Minnie Hauck in* Carmen. (527:2–4)

Cf. *Carmen*

REMARKS: The reference to the opera used in describing Bella's entrance is the first indication of the role which she is to play in Bloom's hallucinations. Carmen in the opera is a coquettish gipsy girl who completely dominates the luckless Don José until her death in the last act. She is a *La Belle Dame* figure whose rule over José brings about his gradual degeneration and eventual ruin. Bella's dominance over Bloom, though it will be far more masculine than Carmen's, will degrade Bloom just as much as Carmen's dominance degraded José.

> To be a shoefitter in Mansfield's was my love's young dream, the darling joys of sweet buttonhooking, to lace up crisscrossed to kneelength the dressy kid footwear satinlined, so incredibly small, of Clyde Road ladies. (529:23–26)

Cf. "Love's Young Dream"

REMARKS: The song to which Bloom alludes in the first sentence is a Thomas Moore song of the exuberant anticipation of youth:

Oh! the days are gone when Beauty bright
My heart's chain wove;
When my dream of life, from morn till night,
Was love, still love.
Now hope may bloom,
And days may come
Of milder, calmer beam,
But there's nothing half so sweet in life
As love's young dream;
No, there's nothing half so sweet in life
As love's young dream.

The song with its romanticism emphasizes the irony of Bloom's banal ambition.

(*He throws a leg astride and, pressing with horseman's knees, calls in a hard voice.*) Gee up! A cockhorse to Banbury cross. I'll ride him for the Eclipse stakes. . . . The lady goes a pace a pace and the coachman goes a trot a trot and the gentleman goes a gallop a gallop a gallop a gallop. (534:19–26)

Cf. "Ride a Cock Horse"
"This Is the Way the Ladies Ride"

REMARKS: Bella becomes a man, Bello, and Bloom a woman subjected to a series of indignities by Bello, who sits on Bloom's back and rides him around chanting parts of the nursery rhymes. Since Bloom's penchant for role reversal in Freudian terms goes back to preadolescent desires, it is only natural that the actual vision of the switch should include nursery rhymes.

Take that! (*He recorks himself.*) Yes, by Jingo, sixteen three quarters. (535:6–7)

Cf. "We Don't Want to Fight"

REMARKS: Though the phrase seems merely to be an old cliché, Thornton relates the following:

. . . "By Jingo" took on a new meaning in 1877 when it was used in a music hall song entitled "We Don't Want to Fight," by G. W. Hunt, the chorus of which said "We don't want to fight, but by Jingo if we do,/ We've got the ships, we've got the men, and got the money, too./We've fought the Bear before, and while we're Britons true,/The Russians shall not have Constantinople." [15]

The militancy of the anti-Russian Crimean War song may indeed add to Bello's bellicose stance.

. . . Signor Laci Daremo, the robust tenor . . . (536:25–26)

Cf. *"Là ci darem"*

REMARKS: Bloom's desire to be violated by a procession of lovers including Signor Laci Daremo indicates that the song has always had masochistic connotations for Bloom. Ever since the song has been identified with Blazes and Molly there has been a certain vicarious satisfaction in it for the cuckold. That masochism reveals itself in the satisfactions of being violated by a gentleman whose name is an anagram of the song title in this role-reversal sequence.

The sawdust is there in the corner for you. I gave you strict instructions, didn't I? Do it standing, sir! I'll teach you to behave like a jinkleman! If I catch a trace on your swaddles. Aha! By the ass of the Dorans you'll find I'm a martinet. The sins of your past are rising against you. Many. Hundreds. (537:12–17)

Cf. "Doran's Ass"

REMARKS: As if determined to reach the lowest possible common denominator in Bloom's degraded id, Joyce has Bello augment the already unsavory hallucination with a reference to "Doran's Ass," a ballad which relates the story of Paddy Doyle's brief affair with a jackass. Doyle, drunk, mistakes a jackass for his girl, spends the night making love with the animal, and finally weds his girl two days later. The song, in keeping with the spirit of the passage, provides fitting accompaniment to Bloom's degradation as the sins of his past rise up to confront him.

Learn the smooth mincing walk on four inch Louis XV heels, the Grecian bend with provoking croup, the thighs fluescent, knees modestly kissing. (540:25–28)

Cf. "The Grecian Bend"

REMARKS: Bello, in describing the wiles of females to the feminine Bloom, uses the title of a song made famous by William H. Lingard, a female impersonator of the 1860s. The chorus, describing the graceful Grecian bend, is as follows:

> The Grecian bend, as I now show,
> You must admit is all the go;
> The head well forward, and the body you extend,
> To be perfect in the Grecian Bend.

(*Milly Bloom, fairhaired, greenvested, slimsandalled, her blue scarf in the seawind simply swirling, breaks from the arms of her lover and calls, her young eyes wonderwide.*) (542:17-19)

Cf. "Seaside Girls"

REMARKS: The *"seawind simply swirling"* links Molly to "Seaside Girls" which has since the Calypso episode expanded in connotation to embrace all of womankind. As part of the degradation of Bloom, the possibility of an incestuous relationship looms in his subconscious.

THE CIRCUMCISED

(*In a dark guttural chant as they cast dead sea fruit upon him, no flowers.*) Shema Israel Adonai Elohenu Adonai Echad. (544:24-26)

Cf. "*Shema Israel*"

REMARKS: The chant of the Circumcised (Hear Oh Israel, the Lord Our God, the Lord is One) is the most common prayer in Judaism. Every Jew is supposed to repeat the prayer before he dies. The chant is sung at all services including the burial and three times a day in prayer at home. The reference demonstrates again that Bloom in his mind is inevitably bound, even in death, to his Semitic background.

I was precocious. Youth. The fauns. I sacrificed to the god of the forest. The flowers that bloom in the spring. It was pairing time. Capillary attraction is a natural phenomenon. (549:16-18)

Cf. "The Flowers that Bloom in the Spring"

REMARKS: The passage refers to a song from Gilbert and Sullivan's *Mikado*. The song, mirroring Bloom's life, shows the difference between the dreams of youth in stanza one, in which Bloom pleasantly revels, and the truth of the situation in stanza two, which Bloom recognizes in his next speech:

> Stanza 1:
> The flowers that bloom in the spring,
> Tra la,
> Breathe promise of merry sunshine,
> As we merrily dance and we sing,
> Tra la,
> We welcome the hope that they bring,
> Tra la,
> Of a summer of roses and wine,
> Of a summer of roses and wine,
> And that's what we mean when we say that a thing

Is welcome as flowers that bloom in the spring,
Tra la, etc.

Stanza 2:
The flowers that bloom in the spring,
Tra la,
Have nothing to do with the case.
I've got to take under my wing,
Tra la,
A most unattractive old thing,
Tra la,
With a caricature of a face,
With a caricature of a face,
And that's what I mean when I say or I sing,
"Oh, bother the flowers that bloom in the spring!"
Tra la, etc.

The shifting of gears in the song from fancy to reality between stanzas one and two is analogous to Bloom's mental shift from the youthful blade of the preceding passage to the rejected would-be lover of the following:

(*With pathos.*) No girl would when I went girling.
Too ugly. They wouldn't play . . . (550:2-3)

O Leopold lost the pin of his drawers
He didn't know what to do,
To keep it up,
To keep it up. (553:2-5)

Cf. "O Mary Lost the Pin of Her Drawers"

REMARKS: Bloom starts to get up and his back trousers button snaps. The two sluts of the Coombe who originally sang "O Mary Lost the Pin of Her Drawers" for Bloom appear to sing a new version of the song.

BELLA

(*Turns to the piano.*) Which of you was playing the dead march from *Saul?* (555:1-3)

Cf. "Dead March" from Handel's *Saul*

REMARKS: Either the remark is facetious on Bella's part, or Stephen was actually playing the "March" in his morbid, death-in-life frame of mind. Zoe, who answers, "Me," probably was not playing it, since it fits more closely the grisly state of Stephen's mentality which subsequently produces the ghoul-like image of his mother.

ZOE

Give a thing and take it back
God'll ask you where is that
You'll say you don't know
God'll send you down below. (555:18–22)

Cf. "Give a thing and take it back"

REMARKS: On the simplest level the rhyme represents no more than Zoe coquettishly teasing Bloom by refusing to return the potato. The heirloom is, however, associated with Bloom's mother and does represent a fetish of Bloom's childhood, so the rhyme listed by the Opies [16] as a swapping or giv-ing rhyme is entirely appropriate to this journey through libidinous memory.

STEPHEN

The fox crew, the cocks flew,
The bells in heaven
Were striking eleven.
'Tis time for her poor soul
To get out of heaven. (558:1–6)

Cf. "The Cock Crew"

REMARKS: Here Stephen alters his riddle of the Nester episode:

> *The cock crew*
> *The sky was blue:*
> *The bells in heaven*
> *Were striking eleven.*
> *'Tis time for this poor soul*
> *To go to heaven.* (26:33–38)

Stephen's fox in Circe is doing the crowing, the time has been altered to eleven p.m. and the soul is leaving heaven instead of going there. The asso-ciation with Stephen's mother is fairly obvious. The riddle has been part of the agenbite-of-inwit motif since the Telemachea. It is resurrected now first because Stephen hears mention of eleven o'clock after all are gathered around the table upon which the money has been placed for the girls. The payment for the girls and the ensuing scene prompts in Stephen's mind the riddle and the foreshadowing of Stephen's hallucination of the return of his mother's ghost. The point has been made [17] that Stephen's guilt is not merely ecclesiastical, but is also Oedipal. The roots of this go all the way back to the gradual blending of the maternal and virgin-mother images of his boyhood with the romance and finally flesh of Stephen's adolescence and eventual manhood. As I have noted, his attempt to bury the guilt of the Oedipal complex manifests itself in the riddle of the holly bush and Stephen-fox's endeavors to bury his mother-grandmother under it. But Circe represents the resurrection of just those things Bloom and Stephen have buried in the id. Stephen realizes this and sensing the resurrection of the guilt in his consciousness heralds its coming with another rendition of his riddle.

STEPHEN

How is that? *Le distrait* or absentminded beggar. (*He fumbles again in his pocket and draws out a handful of coins. . . .*) (558: 20–22)

Cf. "The Absent-Minded Beggar"

REMARKS: Stephen has already associated the song with *Hamlet* (187:22) through the French title to the play. As we have seen in the earlier reference,[18] the song deals with a collection for the families of men who went to fight in the Boer War, each of whom, "doing his country's work," is fondly referred to as "The Absent-Minded Beggar." In Circe, Stephen's overpayment to Bella is refunded by Bloom as this time the song triggers Stephen's association of himself wiith Hamlet. He drops his matches which Bloom returns as Stephen continues his symbolic associations: "Lucifer" (558:27). Though Stephen most probably refers to himself in the *Hamlet* reference, it is prompted by Bloom and the association between Bloom's attending him and the helping persona of the song. Stephen, the beggar, and Bloom are thus linked in a foreshadowing of the key mirror image when both are identified with Shakespeare.

STEPHEN

Why striking eleven? Proparoxyton. Moment before the next Lessing says. Thirsty fox. (*He laughs loudly.*) Burying his grandmother. Probably he killed her. (559:9–12)

Cf. "The Cock Crew"

REMARKS: Bloom's immediately preceding count of the change with the eleven shilling total triggers the association which is buried just beneath the surface of Stephen's consciousness. Eleven is the penultimate number with its stress on the next to last syllable, bringing to mind Lessing's dicta on time and its relationship to art, and thus Stephen's art, the riddle, with its relationship to the parts and the time and action of the fox burying his grandmother. Stephen identifies himself as the fox in his descriptiin of the fox as "thirsty." Stephen's guilt over his part in his mother's death is at least tacitly admitted through the riddle symbology, "Probably he killed her."

STEPHEN

(*Extends his hand to her smiling and chants to the air of the bloodoath in the* Dusk of the Gods.)

>   Hangende Hunger,
>   Fragende Frau,
>   Macht uns alle kaput. (560:25–30)

Cf. *Die Götterdämmerung*

REMARKS: Stephen's phrase "unfulfilled longing, a questioning wife, ruin us everyone" [19] is as straightforward a response as Stephen can muster to Zoe's question, "Is he hungry?" (560:24). His chanting the response to the music of the bloodoath from Wagner's opera, however, brings in all of the overtones of betrayal which prompt Siegfried to swear the oath with Gunther. Whether Stephen is worried about betrayal by Bloom (who has originally initiated the question of food) as he later demonstrates in the "Ballad of Little Harry Hughes" which he sings in the Ithaca episode, or whether the remarks are addressed to Zoe, the "fragende Frau," is not clear. At any rate, Stephen serves notice that he is on guard against unsolicited offers of assistance and foreshadows the rejection of Bloom's offer of hospitality in Ithaca.

ZOE

What day were you born?

STEPHEN

Thursday. Today.

ZOE

Thursday's child has far to go. (562:5–10)

Cf. "Monday's Child Is Fair of Face"

REMARKS: Again nursery rhymes provide a return to preadolescence as Zoe quotes from a rhyme about the children associated with the days of the week. In this case Zoe's description of Stephen as traveller fits his role as exile.

I am twentytwo too. Sixteen years ago I twentytwo tumbled, twentytwo years ago he sixteen fell off his hobbyhorse. (563: 17–19)

Cf. Ophelia's Song in *Hamlet*, IV, v, 63–64

REMARKS: The tumbling in this speech has regularly been interpreted as a reference to Ophelia's Song in *Hamlet*, but it is probably less oblique than that. Bloom has just told us he hurt his hand twenty-two years previously in a fall from a horse. Stephen immediately makes the connection between himself and Bloom through the incident and its related mathematics. Stephen is twenty-two: sixteen years before he fell on the cinder path at Clongowes and in the ensuing events had his hand hurt by Father Dolan. Don John Conmee has referred to the event on the page immediately preceding in Circe: "Now, Father Dolan! Now. I'm sure that Stephen is a very good little boy" (561:24–25). So the *tumble* is an event in Bloom-Stephen's life rather than a primary allusion to Ophelia's song. Stephen at last begins to put together the facts of his consubstantial existence with Bloom.

MARION

He ought to feel himself highly honoured. (*She plops splashing out of the water.*) Raoul, darling, come and dry me. I'm in my pelt. (565:19–22)

Cf. "The Finding of Moses"

REMARKS: Ellmann points out that *Venus im Pelz* is the primary source for the pelt reference.[20] The present allusion might also be to the comic song about the discovery of Moses by the Pharaoh's daughter, who had gone to bathe and was running along the bank drying "her royal pelt." In that case the allusion furthers the Near Eastern motif as well as the idea of Molly as the discoverer and inspiration figure behind Moses-Bloom-Stephen.

LYDIA DOUCE

(*Her mouth opening.*) Yumyum. O, he's carrying her round the room doing it! Ride a cock horse. (566:24–26)

Cf. "Ride a Cock Horse"

REMARKS: Again the nursery rhyme is used to further a thought from the depths of the subconscious memory in a blend of subliminal desire and childhood libido.

MRS CUNNINGHAM

(*Sings.*)
　　　　And they call me the jewel of Asia. (569:1–3)

Cf. "The Jewel of Asia"

REMARKS: Mrs. Cunningham's exhibitions have already been discussed in Hades. Her representation of herself as the glamorous geisha may have been intended to parallel Molly's image in the Eastern motif, the link in this passage being through Martin Cunningham's resemblance to Shakespeare and, through the *Hamlet* motif, to Bloom.

A stout fox drawn from covert, brush pointed, having buried his grandmother, runs swift for the open, brighteyed, seeking badger earth, under the leaves. (572:21–23)

Cf. "The Cock Crew"

REMARKS: The fox's pursuit by the hounds unleashed by Simon Dedalus is Stephen's symbolic interpretation of the guilt of his Oedipal complex, with the father the potential avenger.

His nag, stumbling on whitegaitered feet, jogs along the rocky road. (573:20–21)

Cf. "The Rocky Road to Dublin"

REMARKS: Stephen has already tried to denigrate Deasy's Irish pretensions with the song association (p. 31). This reference advances the same cause, associating Deasy sarcastically with the North and the Orangemen.

　　　　Yet I've a sort a
　　　　Yorkshire relish for . . . (574:10–11)

Cf. "My Girl's a Yorkshire Girl"

REMARKS: Initial remarks of Privates Carr and Compton and Cissy Caffrey link them to the action and symbology of the Yorkshire girl, though they are at the time of the passage quoted outside Bella Cohen's while the song will be played on the pianola inside. Their initial identification with the song provides the introduction to this important song reference.

(*The pianola, with changing lights, plays in waltz time the prelude to* My Girl's a Yorkshire Girl. (574:10-11) [21]

Two young fellows were talking about their girls, girls, girls,
Sweethearts they'd left behind . . . (576:2-3)

"My little shy little lass has a waist. (576:26)

Best, best of all,
Baraabum! (577:28-29)

My girl's a Yorkshire girl. (578:9)

Yorkshire through and through. (578:11)

Though she's a factory lass
And wears no fancy clothes. (578:26-27)

Baraabum! (578:29)

. . . *through and through, Baraabum!* (579:10)

Gum, he's a champion. (579:13)

. . . *Dilly with snowcake no fancy clothes* (579:15-16)

. . . *sort of viceroy and reine relish for tublumber bumpshire rose.*
Baraabum! (579:17-18)

Cf. "My Girl's a Yorkshire Girl"

REMARKS: We have already seen the betrayal relationship of the song and the Molly-Boylan liaison, with Molly identified as the Yorkshire girl.[22] In his Oedipal preoccupation, Stephen, perhaps through the Yorkshire girl's name, Rose (also one of the Virgin's names in the litany) identifies his mother with the Yorkshire girl and himself with the young lover in the song. Like the young men he is brought up short by the irate husband, Simon, who admonishes him, "Think of your mother's people!" (579:4). The song and the wild dancing of the company at Bella Cohen's becomes for Stephen, in his own words, a "Dance of death" (579:6). He is then immediately confronted by the apparition of his dead mother and a choir of virgins and confessors hymning to the Virgin.

Arabesquing wearily, they weave a pattern on the floor, weaving, unweaving, curtseying, twisting, simply swirling.) (577:13–14)

Cf. "Seaside Girls"

REMARKS: The dance of Stephen and Zoe told in the language of the seaside girls is probably no more than Joyce using an already established musical cliché in what seems an appropriate description.

. . . blind coddoubled bicyclers . . . (579:15)

Cf. "Johnny I Hardly Knew Ye"

REMARKS: The entire passage including the song is an amalgamation of previous events, most of which occur in Wandering Rocks. The reference to the poster Bloom has seen (86:19) advertising the college bicycle races seems to be an allusion to the war-maimed veteran of the song, "Johnny I Hardly Knew Ye." [23] But the individual allusions in the passage as a whole (579:7–18) are not so important as the things-happening-all-at-once narrative technique, which here in Circe has been applied to the simultaneously operative ids of Bloom and Stephen with additional descriptive material by the author. The impression that all things are literally happening at once, conveyed on a realistic level in Wandering Rocks as we traced the intertwining paths of the Dublin citizens through a few minutes of their day, is duplicated on the subconscious level in Circe, by the interacting ids of Bloom and Stephen.

More women than men in the world. You too. Time will come. (580:24–25)

Cf. "Three Women to Every Man"

REMARKS: Though the conversation has been about death here, the introduction of this line from the song brings in marital considerations. On the elementary level there are more women than men in the world because the men are dying off. On another level we have to consider the rest of the song, the subtitle of which is "Why Can't Every Man Have Three Wives?" The song is a treatise on marriage, in which "some girls are single all their lives" and others, more fortunate, shouldn't try to be "boss of the show." May might here be predicting that Stephen will someday be married.

You sang that song to me. *Love's bitter mystery.* (581:2–3)

Cf. "Who Goes with Fergus?"

REMARKS: Stephen's song of retreating to the woods with one of Ireland's great heroes is easily translated into a love song for his mother. As we have seen, Stephen identifies with the poet-hero, and Fergus's call becomes a sirensong for his mother. In these passages of expunging himself of his guilt, his mother's reference to the song and particularly to the love part, to which she had alluded during the last days of her illness, shows how Oedipal the memory is to him and the hold over him which the reference has assumed.

> *Nothung!*
> (*He lifts his ashplant high with both hands and smashes the chandelier. . . .*) (583:2–4)

Cf. *Siegfried*

REMARKS: Stephen places himself here in the disposition of Siegfried when Siegfried ends the old order and power of the gods by breaking Woton's spear. He brings an end to the dominance of the old order of guilt and the imposition of the past. But Woton's spear is made of ash as is Stephen's divination rod. Woton's spear represents the unbreakable treaties, runes, and symbols with which he wields power over the universe, as Stephen's ashplant is his symbol of the divination of the symbols and allusions which govern his world. He has, in effect, through the creation of a damning set of symbols for the events of his own existence also constructed a hell of the agenbite of inwit which has plagued him throughout the book. Stephen, by assuming the Siegfried role, attempts desperately to liberate himself from the tyranny of his self-imposed old-order hell, symbolized by Woton's spear, i.e., the chandelier which Stephen-Siegfried feels he breaks. But though the old order is destroyed in the toppling masonry and the "ruin of all space" (583:5), yet Stephen has done the destroying with his own ashplant, i.e., with his own symbols and rationalizations, and the symbology and agenbite of inwit which he has striven so hard to vanquish are still really intact. Only by accepting his consubstantiality with Bloom and hence the human race will the tyranny of the old symbols with their conscience pangs be broken and the new Bloomusalem be at hand.

> . . . *woman's slipperslappers* . . . (586:16)

Cf. "Old Mother Slipperslapper" or "The Fox"

REMARKS: Though Hodgart and Worthington cite this song reference, the passage is probably not a direct reference to the song but merely to the footwear which bears a coincidental title.

The bold soldier boy. (588:24)

Cf. "The Bowld Sojer Boy"

REMARKS: As Cissy Caffrey protests to the onlookers that she is with her soldier friend, Stephen's very polite and humble answer, the most civil he has given anybody during the novel, is "why not?" followed by the reference to Lover's song which extols the virtues and the amiability of soldiers. The allusion is meant to be most cordial and the reference to soldiers complimentary, if typically obtuse. But Stephen has difficulty in communication even when he wishes to communicate.

DOLLY GRAY

(*From her balcony waves her handkerchief, giving the sign of the heroine of Jericho.*) Rahab. Cook's son, goodbye. Safe home to Dolly. Dream of the girl you left behind and she will dream of you. (589:6–10)

Cf. "Goodbye Dolly Gray"
   "The Girl I Left Behind Me"
   "The Absent-Minded Beggar"

REMARKS: Dolly Gray is a classic girl-left-behind-by-the-soldier-boyfriend. She is referred to in the well-known chorus:

   Good-bye, Dolly I must leave you, tho' it breaks my heart to go;
   Something tells me I am needed at the front to fight the foe;
   See the soldier boys are marching, and I can no longer stay;
   Hark I hear the bugle calling; good-bye to Dolly Gray.

"Cook's son" is a part of the "fifty thousand horse and foot [soldiers] going to Table Bay" in "The Absent-Minded Beggar," the second song in this trio about departing soldiers. "Dream of the girl you left behind," a reference to "The Girl I Left Behind Me," a song about a soldier's thoughts of his stay-at-home sweetheart, completes the theme. The technique, seen in Oxen of the Sun and Circe, is to juxtapose several similar references with a given motif or individual for exaggerated, comic effect.

. . . *with the halo of Joking Jesus* . . . (591:16–17)

My methods are new and are causing surprise,
To make the blind see I throw dust in their eyes. (591:18–19)

Cf. "Ballad of Joking Jesus" or "The Song of the Cheerful (but slightly sarcastic) Jesus"

REMARKS: The lines are from stanza three of Gogarty's song which becomes in *Ulysses* Mulligan's "Ballad of Joking Jesus." Stanza three:

> My methods are new and are causing surprise:
> To make the blind see I throw dust in their eyes
> To signify merely there must be a cod
> If the Commons will enter the Kingdom of God.[24]

The deification of Edward through Mulligan's ballad tends to throw a little comic cold water on Stephen's seriously intended remarks about how his country should die for him rather than him dying for the country.

THE VIRAGO

Green above the red, says he. Wolfe Tone.

THE BAWD

The red's as good as the green, and better. (593:3–6)

Cf. "The Green Above the Red"

REMARKS: The metonymical names for England and Ireland may or may not be a direct reference to the ballad here. The song is, of course, just what its name suggests, a song of Irish patriotism, and the bawd's inverted use of it here to glorify England accentuates the difference of opinion between herself and the virago.

THE CROPPY BOY

(*The rope noose round his neck, gripes in his issuing bowels with both hands.*)

I bear no hate to a living thing,
But love my country beyond the king. (593:18–22)

Cf. "The Croppy Boy"

REMARKS: We have already seen in Sirens Stephen's identification with the croppy boy. Here his altercation with the soldiers is comically expanded into the martyrdom of the croppy boy. The great love of the croppy boy for his country comments satirically on Stephen's idea that the country should die for him.

. . . the croppy boy's tongue protrudes violently.)

THE CROPPY BOY

Horhot ho hray ho rhother's hest. (594:2–5)

Cf. "The Croppy Boy"

REMARKS: Here the identification between Stephen and the croppy boy is further cemented as Stephen's guilt over his mother, his religious refusals, and his Oedipal complex is subliminally punished and the confession rung from him still another time in the croppy-boy episode with Privates Carr and Compton.

EDWARD THE SEVENTH

(Dances slowly, solemnly, rattling his bucket and sings with soft contentment.)

> On coronation day, on coronation day,
> O, won't we have a merry time,
> Drinking whiskey, beer and wine! (594:18–23)

Cf. "De Golden Wedding"

REMARKS: The song further degrades the picture of King Edward and makes Private Carr's righteous defense of him appear the more ludicrous.

OLD GUMMY GRANNY

(Rocking to and fro.) Ireland's sweetheart, the king of Spain's daughter, alanna. Strangers in my house, bad manners to them! *(She keens with banshee woe.)* Ochone! Ochone! Silk of the kine! *(She wails.)* You met with poor old Ireland and how does she stand? (595:13–18)

Cf. "The Shan Van Vocht"
  "I Had a Little Nut Tree"
  "The Wearing of the Green"

REMARKS: Old Gummy Granny is a degraded parody of the old woman, the traditional name for Ireland, derived from the "Shan Van Vocht." [25] The "king of Spain's daughter" refers to "I Had a Little Nut Tree," a nursery rhyme which tells of a nut tree, so miraculous that it prompts a visitation by the king of Spain's daughter. In this parody of Irish history, the nut tree is something which prompts the visitation by the English, i.e., Carr and Compton, and their staying as strangers in the house of Ireland. "You met with poor old Ireland" refers to the patriotic song about the usurpation of Ireland by the British, another in this series of anti-British references which bear satirically on the developing altercation between Stephen and the soldiers.

Soggarth Aroon? (595:21)

Cf. *"Soggarth Aroon"*

REMARKS: Stephen, addressing Old Gummy Granny, the detested figure of Ireland, asks not how she stands but how he stands her, satirically comparing the Holy Ghost with *Soggarth Aroon* (Dear Priest). The song is a patriotic one pledging the persona to fight on for Ireland side by side with the dear priest who seems in the song to be the backbone of Irish life. Thus the patriotic motif is blended by Stephen with the religious motif, both anathema to Stephen.

THE CITIZEN

Erin go bragh! (596:4-5)

Cf. "Erin *go Bragh*" ("Ireland Forever")

REMARKS: Though this line is put in the citizen's mouth only because it is such a well-known cliché, part of its popularity may have come from an anonymous song with that title. Thornton has located the words to the chorus, which could easily be a description of the citizen himself:

> Oh, then his shillelah he flourishes gaily,
> With rattle 'em, battle 'em, crack and see-saw
> Och, liberty cheers him, each foe, too, it fears him,
> While he roars out the chorus of Erin-go-Bragh.[26]

Major Tweedy, moustached like Turko the terrible, in bearskin cap . . . (596:21-22)

Cf. *Turko the Terrible*

REMARKS: Bloom has previously made the association between Turko and Tweedy. Tweedy's service to the crown in Gibraltar is close enough to the Near East to reenforce the Turko association, and he is pictured here as an example of the great services the Irish performed for the crown.

(*Massed bands blare* Garryowen *and* God save the king.)
(597:6)

Cf. "Garryowen"
  "God Save the King"

REMARKS: We have already seen in Cyclops hiw "Garryowen" acts as a
sort of degraded Irish national anthem [27] and how "God Save the King"
has been taken down a peg by Bloom in Lestrygonians as he pictures Edward sucking candy on his throne.[28] Both combine here as background
martial music for the coming comic epic battle between the forces of Ireland
(Stephen) and the forces of England (Carr).

The brave and the fair. (597:10)

Cf. "Alexander's Feast"

REMARKS: The lyrics from Handel's chorus conclude in martial splendor,
"None but the brave deserve the fair." The song title provides a comic aggrandizement of a titanic struggle between Stephen and Carr (the brave)
over Cissy Caffrey (the fair).

White thy fambles, red thy gan
And thy quarrons dainty is. (598:6–7)

Cf. "The Rogue's Delight in Praise of His Stroling Mort"

REMARKS: Stephen's problem is one of communication. All the way through
the episode with Cissy and the soldiers Stephen's usual opaqueness of speech
has prevented anyone from really understanding a word he was saying. If
anything, it speaks volumes not only about his lack of humanity but also
about his alienation from the human condition and communication. The
quotation from the canting song addressed to Cissy is translated by Head.[29]
  My own paraphrase is:

> Thy hand is white and red thy lip,
> And thy body is dainty.

Stephen has obviously intended a compliment to Cissy, but in a language
Cissy could not hope to understand.

Dublin's burning! Dublin's burning! On fire, on fire! (598:11)

Cf. "Scotland's Burning"

REMARKS: The distant voices chant still another parody [30] of the nursery
rhyme round to present a cataclysmic hellfire background to herald the black
mass.

Factory lasses with fancy clothes toss redhot Yorkshire baraa-bombs. (598:29-30)

Cf. "My Girl's a Yorkshire Girl"

REMARKS: As the black mass begins, the inverted character of everything is intensified. We have already seen the Yorkshire girl as surrogate for Molly, mother, virgin, Cissy Caffrey etc. So the song with its multiplicity of referents is used to swell the crowd and increase the enormity of the events in the last-day festivities.

FATHER MALACHI O'FLYNN (599:20, 24)

Cf. "Father O'Flynn"

REMARKS: A combination of Mulligan, the irreverent priest who opened the novel with the introit to God, and the nearly perfect Father O'Flynn of the song now intones the introit to the devil to herald the opening of the black mass of Circe. Malachi Mulligan, the most blasphemous of men, and Father O'Flynn, whose priestly activities put all the other clerics to shame, form the proper blend of satanic and saintly to officiate at the devil's mass.

(In strident discord peasants and townsmen of Orange and Green factions sing Kick the Pope *and* Daily, daily sing to Mary.*)* (600:8-10)

Cf. "Kick the Pope"
   "Daily, daily sing to Mary"

REMARKS: The songs are just what they would be expected to be, a comic antipapist song and a well-known Roman Catholic hymn. They represent the poles of anticlerical and religious feeling.

OLD GUMMY GRANNY

(Thrusts a dagger towards Stephen's hand.) Remove him, acushla. At 8:35 a.m. you will be in heaven and Ireland will be free. *(She prays.)* O good God, take him! (600:15-18)

Cf. "The Shan Van Vocht"

REMARKS: The last line of the quotation is from stanza five of the song.

> Will old Ireland then be free?
> Says the Shan Van Vocht.

Old Ireland shall be free
From the centre to the sea,
Then hurrah! for Liberty,
Says the Shan Van Vocht.

The quotation completes the identification between Old Gummy Granny and the Shan Van Vocht. Moreover, the rest of the old woman's speech with its threat of death and promise of heaven sounds a great deal like the threat of Stephen's mother in Bella Cohen's. Stephen's old-woman-as-Ireland motif, started in Telemachus, is tied in with the agenbite of inwit motif, because Stephen has deserted both mother and Ireland and the connection between the two lies just under the surface, the "Shan Van Vocht" being one of the main links.

Who . . . drive . . . Fergus now.
And pierce . . . wood's woven shade? . . . (608:26–27)

. . . shadows . . . the woods.
. . . white breast . . . dim . . . (609:3–4)

Cf. "Who Goes with Fergus?"

REMARKS: Stephen's incoherent rendition of Fergus's song represents his subconscious effort to escape. We have seen how the phrase "love's bitter mystery" links the song with Stephen's Oedipal fixation. But another line that keeps haunting Stephen, "And no more turn aside and brood," represents his efforts to flee the unpleasant aspects of the "bitter mystery" of love which haunts him as well as the rest of the guilt he has felt in his desertion of his mother-country-church. So even in near unconsciousness Stephen yearns for the peace of mind which other connotations of that same song deny him.

In the shady wood. The deep white breast. Ferguson, I think I caught. A girl. Some girl. Best thing could happen him . . . (609: 11–13)

Cf. "Who Goes with Fergus?"

REMARKS: Bloom, in the form now of a father image, has the potential to provide Stephen with two sorely needed remedies for his psychological plight: to bring to the younger man the equanimity and humanity Stephen lacks and to provide a reconciliation with the father image and an end to the Oedipal problems plaguing him. Bloom inadvertently alludes to some of Stephen's difficulty when he says, "Face reminds me of his poor mother," and intuits that Stephen's thoughts are with "a girl. Some girl." But he is sadly off base when he concludes, "Best thing could happen him."

16. Eumaeus

Between this point and the high, at present unlit, warehouses of
Beresford Place Stephen thought to think of Ibsen, associated
with Baird's, the stonecutter's, in his mind somehow in Talbot
Place, first turning on the right, while the other, who was acting
as his *fidus Achates* inhaled with internal satisfaction the smell
of James Rourke's city bakery, situated quite close to where they
were, the very palatable odour indeed of our daily bread, of all
commodities of the public the primary and most indispensable.
Bread, the staff of life, earn your bread, O tell me where is fancy
bread? At Rourke's the baker's, it is said. (614:18–28)

Cf. "Tell Me Where is Fancy Bred"

REMARKS: The first musical reference in the chapter is to a Shakespearean
song, sung by Bassanio in *The Merchant of Venice* (III, ii, 63–71). Schutte
attributes the last passage beginning, "Bread, the staff . . ." to Bloom's
stream of consciousness,[1] perhaps because of the advertisement quality of the
rhyme. This attribution is doubtful since the narration is in a slightly in-
flated, half humorous style in keeping with the line, and up to this point in
the chapter nothing has been heard from Bloom's stream of consciousness.
"Tell Me Where is Fancy Bred" is, however, quite common both as a
popular cliché and as a song set to music in the eighteenth century by
T. Augustine Arne. The pun is of course on the words *fancy* and *bred* with
the second line of the song altered in *Ulysses*. The Shakespearean lyrics are
as follows:

> Tell me where is fancy bred,
> Or in the heart or in the head?
> How begot, how nourished?
>   Reply, reply,
> It is engend'red in the eyes,
> With gazing fed, and fancy dies
> In the cradle where it lies.
>   Let us all ring fancy's knell.
>   I'll begin it,—Ding, dong, bell.
>   Ding, dong, bell.

The song, posing a philosophical question about love, seems to have little
textual significance other than the pun on *bread* derived from its title.

Mr Bloom, availing himself of the right of free speech, he having just a bowing acquaintance with the language in dispute

though, to be sure, rather in a quandary over *voglio* . . . (622:
14–16)

Cf. *"Là ci darem"*

REMARKS: Bloom's quandary over *voglio* has already been noted in this
study.[2] The *voglio-vorrei-Là ci darem*-Boylan-Molly adultery association is
never out of Bloom's mind for long, as he demonstrates here.

My little woman's down there. She's waiting for me, I know. *For
England, home and beauty.* She's my own true wife I haven't
seen for seven years now, sailing about. (624:19–22)

Cf. "The Death of Nelson"

REMARKS: We have already heard the one-legged sailor of Wandering
Rocks chant this song as he begs through the streets. The song seems to be a
fairly standard cliché for sailors to express their concept of duty and the
deprivations they must endure.

Quite a number of stories there were on that particular Alice Ben
Bolt topic, Enoch Arden and Rip van Winkle and does anybody
hereabouts remember Caoc O'Leary, a favourite and most trying
declamation piece, by the way, of poor John Casey and a bit of
perfect poetry in its own small way? Never about the runaway
wife coming back, however much devoted to the absentee. (624:
26–32)

Cf. "Ben Bolt"

REMARKS: The "Alice Ben Bolt" reference is to the song which relates the
story of a sailor's return to find his wife dead and conditions mightily
changed:

> Oh: don't you remember sweet Alice, Ben Bolt—
> Sweet Alice whose hair was so brown,
> She wept with delight, when you gave her a smile,
> And trembled with fear at your frown.
> In the old church yard, in the valley, Ben Bolt,
> In a corner obscure and alone,
> They have fitted a slab of the granite so gray,
> And sweet Alice lies under the stone,
> They have fitted a slab of the granite so gray,
> And sweet Alice lies under the stone.

Bloom rightly thinks of the song as representative of such stories of husband's
absence and eventual return as *Enoch Arden* and *Rip Van Winkle*.

You little expected me but I've come to stay and make a fresh start. There she sits, a grass widow, at the selfsame fireside. Believes me dead. Rocked in the cradle of the deep. (624:35–38)

Cf. "Rocked in the Cradle of the Deep"

REMARKS: Bloom's description of the supposedly dead sailor's being "Rocked in the Cradle of the Deep" refers to the very popular nineteenth-century song by Mrs. Emma Willard. The song has the ring of a church hymn as it describes the peaceful quality that a watery grave holds for a believer:

> Rock'd in the cradle of the deep
> I lay me down in peace to sleep;
> Secure I rest upon the wave,
> For thou O! Lord, hast pow'r to save.
> I know thou wilt not slight my call,
> For thou dost mark the sparrow's fall!
> And calm and peaceful is my sleep,
> Rock'd in the cradle of the deep,
> And calm and peaceful is my sleep,
> Rock'd in the cradle of the deep.

The song seems to have no particular religious significance in the passage beyond demonstrating the piety of Bloom's imaginary wife. The reference is merely a musical way of alluding to a sailor's death.

Though not an implicit believer in the lurid story narrated (or the egg-sniping transaction for that matter despite William Tell and the Lazarillo-Don Cesar de Bazan incident depicted in *Maritana* on which occasion the former's ball passed through the latter's hat), having detected a discrepancy between his name (assuming he was the person he represented himself to be and not sailing under false colours after having boxed the compass on the strict q. t. somewhere) and the fictitious addressee of the missive which made him nourish some suspicions of our friend's *bona fides* . . . (626:17–27)

Cf. *William Tell*
    Maritana

REMARKS: The reference to William Tell concerns itself with the story of Tell's skill in shooting the apple from his son's head. The lagend predates both Schiller's play and Rossini's opera, though Bloom may have had the opera in mind since the next reference is to *Maritana,* an opera by William Vincent Wallace. The references to both *William Tell* and *Maritana* are made in connection with the sailor's story of Simon Dedalus's marksmanship. The allusion to William Tell's unerring aim is correct but the second allusion to *Maritana* is not so accurate. The narrator has his facts slightly confused, for in *Maritana*, Lazarillo, in order to foil the execution of Don César, removes the cartridges from the guns of the firing squad and Don César merely pretends to die. There is no placing of a ball through Don César's hat in the opera. Whether the mistake is Bloom's or the narrator's here is a question of point of view. The narrator is describing Bloom's thoughts at this point, but whether the parenthetical error in the passage is Bloom's or Joyce's is impossible to determine.

> Suffice it to say that, as a casual glance at the map revealed, it covered fully three fourths of it and he fully realised accordingly what it meant, to rule the waves. (630:8–11)

Cf. "Rule Britannia"

REMARKS: Bloom turns and is impressed with Britain's power and responsibility. The expression "rule the waves" is handed down from Thomson and Arnes's stirring anthem of the 1740s, already dealt with in this study.[3] The use of the allusion here seems obvious.

> . . . the public at large . . . should extend its gratitude also to the harbourmasters and coastguard service who had to man the rigging and push off and out amid the elements, whatever the season, when duty called *Ireland expects that every man* and so on . . . (630:30–35)

Cf. "The Death of Nelson"

REMARKS: The patriotism of the previous song is transferred from England to Ireland as it was in Mulligan's original allusion (15:32–33). Bloom thinks about the heroism of the sailors who answer their country's call. In several earlier allusions to the song, sailors particularly provide the frame of reference. Thus this allusion draws upon the earlier connotations of humor and the sea for part of its force.

The Skibbereen father . . . (631:12)

Cf. "Old Skibbereen"

REMARKS: The skibbereen reference fits another Joycean double entendre. The song deals with a conversation between a father and a son as to why the elder left the town of Skibbereen in Cork. The application to the sailor and his son, Danny, is obvious. A scib is also a boat, from which the town name derives, and a skibber the skipper. So the song fits both the sailor's occupation and his father role.

> As bad as old Antonio,
> For he left me on my ownio. (632:10–11)

Cf. "Has Anybody Here Seen Kelly?"

REMARKS: This song has already been discussed as a sort of comic relief from thoughts of death.[4] The present allusion operates in much the same way. After the discussion of Antonio the tattoo maker who was supposedly eaten by sharks, the sailor is reminded of appropriate lyrics from the song.

> On the other hand he might be only bluffing, a pardonable weakness, because meeting unmistakable mugs, Dublin residents, like those jarvies waiting news from abroad, would tempt any ancient mariner who sailed the ocean seas to draw the long bow about the schooner *Hesperus* and etcetera. (636:14–18)

Cf. "The Wreck of the Hesperus"

REMARKS: The saga of the Hesperus to which Bloom refers is best known through Longfellow's poem which became a popular sea song. The initial words of the song closely resemble the words "sailed the ocean seas . . . the schooner *Hesperus*," which appear in the text. The first two lines of the song are as follows:

> It was the schooner Hesperus
> That sail'd in the wint'ry sea . . .

"The Wreck" relates the tale of a frozen captain and his little daughter who perished on "the reef of Norman's Woe." The tale is a typical sentimental sea ballad and is viewed by Bloom as being representative of its kind and a typical sailor's tale.

> However, reverting to friend Sinbad and his horrifying adventures (who reminded him a bit of Ludwig, *alias* Ledwidge, when he occupied the boards of the Gaiety when Michael Gunn was identified with the management in the *Flying Dutchman,* a stupendous success, and his host of admirers came in large numbers, everyone simply flocking to hear him though ships of any sort, phantom or the reverse, on the stage usually fell a bit flat as also did trains) . . . (636:33–40)

Cf. *Sinbad the Sailor*
   The Flying Dutchman

REMARKS: Sinbad in the passage above refers to the pantomine *Sinbad the Sailor,* which is discussed at some length by the narrator in the Ithaca episode (678:26–38). This theatrical association triggers the reference to Ledwidge, a baritone, who played the Dutch sea captain in Wagner's opera *The Flying Dutchman,* which seems to have drawn a remarkable crowd for Dublin, a city supposed to have favored Italian opera.[5]

All are washed in the blood of the sun. (637:27–28)

Cf. "Washed in the Blood of the Lamb"

REMARKS: Bloom comically turns the song and sermon reference around to fit his theory of the increased sensual aspects of Eastern women who live nearer the sun. The pun on sun and son fits the religious as well as voluptuous aspect of the allusion.

> —*The biscuits was as hard as brass,*
> *And the beef as salt as Lot's wife's arse.*
> *O Johnny Lever!*
> *Johnny Lever, O!* (640:6–9)

Cf. "Leave Her, Johnny"

REMARKS: In response to Skin-the-goat's accusation of ship scuttling by a Captain John Lever of the Lever line, the sailor is reminded of a sea chantey with similar sounding words and proceeds to sing a stanza. The sailor's version is a good deal stronger than the popular version in which stanza two, the one alluded to in the *Ulysses* rendition, says merely, "The bread is hard and the beef is salt."[6]

. . . the coal seam of the sister island would be played out . . . (641:30)

Cf. "Harp or Lion"

REMARKS: The term "sister Ireland" may or may not be from stanza three of Sullivan's Irish patriotic song. England is personified satirically in this violently anti-British song, as Bloom assesses the weaknesses and strengths of Britain and the Irish bias connected with such evaluations.

In any case that was very ancient history by now and as for our friend, the pseudo Skin-the-etcetera, he had transparently outlived his welcome. He ought to have either died naturally or on the scaffold high. (642:28–31)

Cf. "God Save Ireland"

REMARKS: Bloom speculates on Skin-the-goat Fitzharris, proprietor of the shelter and one of the Invincibles who participated in the Phoenix Park murders in 1882. Now, twenty-two years later, Fitzharris's way, reflects Bloom, has faded into antiquity. The last phrase of the passage is a line from the chorus of "God Save Ireland." The line, "Whether on the scaffold high/Or the Battle fields we die," has occurred to Bloom earlier in the day.[7] Bloom associates the song, dealing with the execution of the Manchester Martyrs, with the bygone era of intense fervor and rash patriotic deeds in which Fitzharris took an active part, but for which he has never atoned.

> So similarly he had a very shrewd suspicion that Mr Johnny Lever got rid of some £. s. d. in the course of his perambulations round the docks in the congenial atmosphere of the *Old Ireland* tavern, come back to Erin and so on. Then as for the others, he had heard not so long before the same identical lingo, as he told Stephen how he simply but effectually silenced the offender. (642:35–41)

Cf. "Leave Her Johnny"
   "Come Back to Erin"

REMARKS: The Johnny Lever to whom Bloom refers in this passage was charged by another of Fitzharris's patrons earlier in the conversation with being the captain who, in the pay of the crown, purposely let his ship sink in Galway Bay.[8] Captain John has become Johnny in Bloom's mind because of the sailor's song sung a moment before. Lever's money will be spent, reflects Bloom, in an Irish tavern as Lever sings songs like "Come Back to Erin." The song to which Bloom refers is an old nostalgic ballad urging Mavourneen's return to the old sod:

> Come back to Erin, Mavourneen, Mavourneen,
> Come back, Aroon, to the land of thy birth;
> Come with the shamrocks and springtime, Mavourneen,
> And its Killarney shall ring with our mirth.
> Sure, when you left us, our beautiful darling,
> Little we thought of the lone winter days,
> Little we tho't of the hush of the starshine
> Over the mountain the bluffs and the brays! . . .

Bloom is like Stephen in his contempt for those vocal exponents of the glories of Ireland whose actions do not match their words.

> It is hard to lay down any hard and fast rules as to right and wrong but room for improvement all round there certainly is though every country, they say, our own distressful included, has the government it deserves. (643:15–19)

Cf. "The Wearing of the Green"

REMARKS: The reference to "every country . . . our own distressful included" suggests part of the lyrics of stanza one of this patriotic song, alluded to previously in *Ulysses*. The song, very popular at the turn of the century, was undoubtedly known to both Bloom and Stephen and serves as a brief but sufficient allusion to convey the history of Ireland's oppression, so often discussed that it can be boiled down to a cliché like the present reference.

> To improve the shining hour he wondered whether he might meet with anything approaching the same luck as Mr Philip Beaufoy if taken down in writing. Suppose he were to pen something out of the common groove (as he fully intended doing) at the rate of one guinea per column, *My Experiences,* let us say, *in a Cabman's Shelter.* (647:2–7)

Cf. "How Doth the Little Busy Bee"

REMARKS: Bloom's industry in writing his experiences for publication is compared indirectly to that of the "little busy bee" in the song from Isaac Watts's poem. The phrase "To improve the shining hour" is from stanza one of the song:

> How doth the little busy bee
> Improve each shining hour,
> And gather honey all the day
> From every opening flower!

Whether or not the reference is to the poem or the song is uncertain, but the effect is to provide a half humorous twist to Bloom's literary aspirations and perhaps to his cuckolding.

> Of course nobody being acquainted with his movements even before, there was absolutely no clue as to his whereabouts which were decidedly of the *Alice, where art thou* order even prior to his starting to go under several aliases such as Fox and Stewart, so the remark which emanated from friend cabby might be within the bounds of possibility. (649:26–32)

Cf. "Alice Where Art Thou"

REMARKS: Bloom's description of Parnell's whereabouts as being of the "*Alice, where art thou* order" is a reference to the song which relates the quest of a forlorn lover for his mate:

> The birds sleeping gently,
> Sweet Lyra gleameth bright,

Her rays tinge the forest,
And all seems glad tonight.
The wind sighing by me,
Cooling my fever'd brow;
The stream flows as ever,
Yet, Alice, where art thou?
One year back this even,
And thou were by my side,
And thou were by my side,
Vowing to love me;
One year past this even,
And thou wert by my side,
Vowing to love me,
Alice, whate'er might betide.

The silver rain falling
Just as it falleth now;
And all things sleep gently!
Ah! Alice, where art thou?
I've sought thee by lakelet,
I've sought thee on the hill,
And in the pleasant wildwood,
When winds blew cold and chill;
I've sought thee in forest;
I'm looking heav'nward now,
I'm looking heav'nward now;
Oh! there 'mid starshine,
I've sought thee in forest,
I'm looking heav'nward now.
Oh! there amid the starshine,
Alice, I know, art thou.

The answer to the question in the song is, of course, that Alice is dead. In his use of the "Alice Where Art Thou" reference Bloom implies that since Parnell has let it be thought in the past that he was dead, the possibility still exists that again Parnell may just have dropped from sight letting people think he is dead.

A magnificent specimen of manhood he was truly, augmented obviously by gifts of a high order as compared with the other military supernumerary, that is (who was just the usual everyday *farewell, my gallant captain* kind of an individual in the light dragoons, the 18th hussars to be accurate) . . . (651:23–28)

Cf. "Farewell, My Gallant Captain"

REMARKS: Bloom's description of Kitty's husband as a *"farewell, my gallant captain* kind of an individual" refers to the finale to Act I of Wallace's *Maritana*. In the opera Don César befriends a poor apprentice who is about to be arrested by an officious, pitiless captain of the guard. During a quarrel, César challenges the captain (who has promised to teach César a lesson) to a duel. Later as César returns to the stage, after presumably having beaten the captain, he sings:

> Farewell, my gallant Captain!
> I told you how 'twould be; . . .
> You'll not forget the lesson due to me . . .

In comparing Kitty's husband with the Captain in *Maritana*, Bloom draws an uncomplimentary picture of the former and implies that both got their just deserts.

—Just bears out what I was saying, he with glowing bosom said to Stephen. And, if I don't greatly mistake, she was Spanish too.

—The king of Spain's daughter, Stephen answered, adding something or other rather muddled about farewell and adieu to you Spanish onions and the first land called the Deadman and from Ramhead to Scilly was so and so many . . .

—Was she? Bloom ejaculated surprised, though not astonished by any means. I never heard that rumour before. Possible, especially there it was, as she lived there. So, Spain. (652:9–18)

Cf. "I Had a Little Nut Tree"
   "Farewell to You, Ye Fine Spanish Ladies"

REMARKS: Bloom continues his reflections on the Parnell-O'Shea affair, mistakenly speculating on what he thinks is her passionate Spanish blood. Actually Kitty O'Shea was not Spanish. This is another case of Bloom's identifying Molly (who has Spanish blood) with an adulteress.[9] He ventures the information that Kitty is Spanish to Stephen, who replies rather flippantly with quotations from the nursery rhyme and sea song.

"The king of Spain's daughter" is a reference to the nursery rhyme "I had a little nut tree," which has been alluded to previously in one of Stephen's hallucinations in the Circe episode (595:14–15). The nursery rhyme probably depicts the visit of Juana of Castille to Henry VII's court in 1506: [10]

> I had a little nut tree,
>   Nothing would it bear
> But a silver nutmeg
>   And a golden pear;

> The king of Spain's daughter
> Came to visit me,
> And all for the sake
> Of my little nut tree.

The use of the nursery rhyme indicates Stephen's opinion of the conversation, which he sees reduced to little more than the canting of children, and his contempt for Bloom's belief in such nonsense. Stephen's association is superficial here, since he merely picks up the word *Spanish* and links it with the phrase from the rhyme.

In the passage above Stephen continues his musical associations on things Spanish as he gives a garbled version of the seasong "Farewell to You, Ye Fine Spanish Ladies." The phrase "The first land called the Deadman" is from stanza four, and though Stephen's "Ramhead" reference also appears in stanza four, "Scilly" is back in the second stanza:

Stanza 1
Now farewell to you, ye fine Spanish ladies,
   Now farewell to you, ye ladies of Spain,
For we've received orders to sail for old England,
   And perhaps we may never more see you again.

Stanza 2
We'll range and we'll rove like true British sailors;
   We'll range and we'll rove all on the salt seas;
Until we strike soundings on the Channel of England,
   From Ushant to Scilly is thirty-five leagues.

Stanza 4
The first land we made, it is called the Dead-man,
   Next, Ram Head off Plymouth, Start, Portland, and Wight.
We sailed by Beachy, by Fairly, and Dungeness,
   And then bore away for the South Foreland Light.

Though Stephen's quotations are derisive and purposely off the topic, Bloom, failing to understand their origin, does not take the hint and makes himself appear even more asinine in Stephen's eyes by taking the remarks at face value. The effect of the entire passage with its song references is to demonstrate both Stephen's contempt for Bloom's conversation and Bloom's naive credulity.

. . . on the rest of which was *In old Madrid,* a ballad, pretty in its way, which was then all the vogue. (652:31–33)

Cf. "In Old Madrid"

REMARKS: This song will be one of Molly's major solos in Penelope. Bloom has already associated her with the song in Sirens (275:27) because of her

Spanish eyes and background. It is apparent that the picture to which the above quotation refers is the origin of that association. When Spain is mentioned here Bloom immediately produces his wife's picture together with the song title.

Thank you, sir though in a very different tone of voice from the ornament of the legal profession whose headgear Bloom also set to rights earlier in the course of the day, history repeating itself with a difference; after the burial of a mutual friend when they had left him alone in his glory after the grim task of having committed his remains to the grave. (655:10–16)

Cf. "The Burial of Sir John Moore"

REMARKS: The incident at Dignam's funeral referred to in the passage occurred when Bloom pointed out to John Henry Menton that the latter's hat was crushed (115:24). The phrase "left him alone in his glory" is from the last stanza of the song set to Clark Wolfe's poem which relates the last hurried rites accorded the British leader by his vanquished and retreating army:

> Slowly and sadly we laid him down,
>   From the field of his fame fresh and gory—
> We carved not a line, we raised not a stone,
>   But we left him alone with his glory!

When the origin of the words is known, Bloom's irony in linking Dignam and Moore becomes apparent. The association producing the reference is not limited strictly to Dignam's burial, however. The song of the British chief fallen and hastily buried by his defeated followers may have been prompted in Bloom's thoughts by the somewhat analogous situation of Parnell's defeat and death.

Since "Grace," hats have played a large role in certifying the respectability of various characters. Hats are the outward signs of decorum and community standing. When Kernan's hat was knocked off onto the men's room floor at the beginning of "Grace," its restoration became a metaphor of his salvation during the story. The propriety of the hats of the congregation at the Gardiner Street Mass were an outward, if satiric, indication of Kernan's being finally numbered among the righteous. There have been allusions to the same motif in *Ulysses,* notably in connection with "The Hat Me Father Wore." [11] Bloom restores Parnell's hat and outward dignity in this present, remembered context, but Bloom senses that the hat is not as important as the natural dignity of Parnell's answer on that occasion, unlike the outwardly dignified but really boorish Menton's. Thus, for Bloom the outward signs of decorum mean nothing. Real heroism and worth are something else. This is of course what the song is all about. No monuments or commemorative lines need mark the occasion of glory if it is honest and real.

But something substantial he certainly ought to eat, were it only an eggflip made on unadulterated maternal nutriment or, failing that, the homely Humpty Dumpty boiled. (656:22–25)

Cf. "Humpty Dumpty"

REMARKS: The reference to the egg as a "Humpty Dumpty" is of course an allusion to the well-known nursery rhyme:

> Humpty Dumpty sat on a wall
> Humpty Dumpty had a great fall;
> All the King's horses and all the King's men,
> Couldn't put Humpty together again.

Opie tells us that the rhyme originally was a riddle. The reason that the king's men could not put Humpty together is that he is an egg.[12] Humpty Dumpty in the *Ulysses* passage relates to the original riddle and is probably part of the banal style of the chapter rather than purely a figment of Bloom's stream of consciousness.

A move had to be made because that merry old soul, the grass-widower in question who appeared to be glued to the spot, didn't appear in any particular hurry to wend his way home to his dearly beloved Queenstown and it was highly likely some sponger's bawdyhouse of retired beauties off Sheriff street lower would be the best clue to that equivocal character's whereabouts for a few days to come . . . (658:5–11)

Cf. "Old King Cole"

REMARKS: The description of the sailor as "that merry old soul" is a reference to the nursery rhyme:

> Old King Cole
> Was a merry old soul,
> And a merry old soul was he;
> He called for his pipe,
> And he called for his bowl,
> And he called for his fiddlers three.

Besides the incongruity of describing the gruff sailor in terms of Old King Cole, his prospective merriment in Dublin's bawdy houses seems to be the only connection between the rhyme as a whole and the old salt to whom the ironical reference is made. Again there is a question whether the terminology involving the nursery rhyme reference is Bloom's or the narrator's, though the humor of the phrase remains the same either way.

So they passed on to chatting about music, a form of art for which Bloom, as a pure amateur, possessed the greatest love, as they made tracks arm-in-arm across Beresford place. Wagnerian music, though confessedly grand in its way, was a bit too heavy for Bloom and hard to follow at the first go-off but the music of Mercadante's *Huguenots,* Meyerbeer's *Seven Last Words on the Cross,* and Mozart's *Twelfth Mass,* he simply revelled in, the *Gloria* in that being to his mind the acme of first class music as such, literally knocking everything else into a cocked hat. (661: 3-12).

Cf. *The Huguenots*
    Seven Last Words of Christ
    "Gloria" from *Twelfth Mass* of Mozart

REMARKS: Bloom suggests that Stephen come home with him and subsequently leads him out of the shelter toward Eccles Street. As their conversation turns to music, they at last hit an area of common interest. It is significant that even though their tastes are diametrically opposed, and though it seemed through the tedious and often embarrassing scene at the cabman's shelter that the overtures of friendliness would always be one-sided, here in music there is finally a common ground on which to establish a relationship. Even in this conversation, however, Bloom shows up to the greatest possible disadvantage.

Bloom's taste in music, while it cannot be condemned for being completely insipid, reflects nevertheless a sort of Victorian dilettantism and appreciation of the popular musical works of his day rather than the great ones. Bloom's musical views are further devaluated by the fact that he muddles in some way his references to most of the works he cites as his favorites. He attributes the *Huguenots* to Mercadante and the *Seven Last Words* to Meyerbeer instead of the other way around. These mistakes are interesting here, since he has correctly identified the composers with the songs in previous episodes (*Huguenots,* p. 168; *Seven Last Words,* p. 82), though he did identify Meyerbeer with the *Seven Last Words* at the end of the Sirens chapter (p. 290). His next reference is to Mozart's *Gloria,* which Bloom has attributed to the *Twelfth Mass* and which we have seen[13] was not really a part of the *Twelfth Mass* but merely ascribed to the *Twelfth Mass* in the Novello Publishing Company edition. The true *Twelfth Mass* of Mozart (K. 262) is seldom performed and is infinitely less popular than the *Gloria* Bloom attributes to it. Bloom's assertion, therefore, that he reveled in the *Twelfth Mass* has more braggadocio than truth in it.

He infinitely preferred the sacred music of the catholic church to anything the opposite shop could offer in that line such as those

Moody and Sankey hymns or *Bid me to live and I will live thy protestant to be.* He also yielded to none in his admiration of Rossini's *Stabat Mater,* a work simply abounding in immortal numbers, in which his wife, Madam Marion Tweedy, made a hit, a veritable sensation, he might safely say greatly adding to her other laurels and putting the others totally in the shade in the jesuit fathers' church in Upper Gardiner street, the sacred edifice being thronged to the doors to hear her with virtuosos, or *virtuosi* rather. (661:12–22)

Cf. "Bid Me to Live"
   Stabat Mater

REMARKS: As Bloom charges on into the aesthetics of liturgical music he becomes more deeply mired in the rut of his own musical ignorance. His singling out "Bid Me to Live" as a Protestant hymn or anthem is erroneous. The early seventeenth-century song by Henry Lawes is based on Robert Herrick's poem "To Anthea." Usually only the first three stanzas of Herrick's poem are included in the song:

TO ANTHEA,
Who May Command Him Anything

Bid me to live, and I will live
  Thy protestant to be;
Or bid me love, and I will give
  A loving heart to thee.

A heart as soft, a heart as kind,
  A heart as sound and free,
As in the whole world thou canst find,
  That heart I'll give to thee.

Bid that heart stay and it will stay,
  To honor thy decree:
Or bid it languish quite away,
  And 't shall do so for thee.

Bloom's confusion of the song with a hymn arises from the word *protestant* to which he gives sectarian connotations.

It is not until we come to Rossini's *Stabat Mater* that Bloom makes an error-free citation. He associates the work as he did in the Lotus Eaters episode (p. 82) with Molly's solos. His familiarity with the oratorio is probably the result of Molly's connection with it.

There was the unanimous opinion that there was none to come up to her and, suffice it to say in a place of worship for music of a sacred character, there was a generally voiced desire for an encore. On the whole, though favouring preferably light opera of the *Don Giovanni* description, and *Martha,* a gem in its line, he had a *penchant,* though with only a surface knowledge, for the severe classical school such as Mendelssohn. And talking of that, taking it for granted he knew all about the old favourites, he mentioned *par excellence* Lionel's air in *Martha, M'appari,* which, curiously enough, he heard, or overheard, to be more accurate, on yesterday, a privilege he keenly appreciated, from the lips of Stephen's respected father, sung to perfection, a study of the number, in fact, which made all the others take a back seat. (661:22–36)

Cf. *Don Giovanni*
   Martha
   "*M'appari*"

REMARKS: Once Molly is back in Bloom's stream of consciousness, it is inevitable that the next musical associations that he makes are to *Don Giovanni* and *Martha.* It is significant that Bloom is able to quote so extensively from *Don Giovanni* and seem to be so familiar with that opera and with *Martha* on one hand while he is so mistaken about other equally well-known composers on the other. His familiarity with the two operas goes to prove the identification which Bloom feels himself with the works. In the passage under consideration the references serve to juxtapose his extensive knowledge of the two operas with his mistake of placing Mendelssohn in "the severe classical school." Mendelssohn, who is regarded with Chopin and Schumann as being among the early nineteenth-century romanticists, has been criticized as writing charming and beautiful music which is seldom very deep and is "occasionally facile and commonplace,"[14] a description hardly representing Mendelssohn's works as severely classical.

In six of the seven musical allusions Bloom makes in his brief discussion of musical tastes with Stephen we have a sort of musical recapitulation or musical microcosm of many of the major themes of the novel as Bloom fires the scatter-shot of his musical knowledge at Stephen.

Exquisite variations he was now describing on an air *Youth here has End* by Jans Pieter Sweelinck, a Dutchman of Amsterdam where the frows come from. (663:12–14)

Cf. "*Mein junges Leben hat ein End*"

REMARKS: Stephen does not seem to be offended or aware of Bloom's errors, but begins a statement of his own musical preferences with allusions to the

Shakespearean songs which characterize many of the musical references in his segments of the novel. As he grows more animated he brings up the Sweelinck song. Stanley Sultan points out, "The hymn is sung by a dying youth, a fact obscured by Joyce's translation of its title." [15] Sultan goes on to say that the song signals Stephen's knowledge that his old life has ended and that he has now come to "know God," Leopold Bloom.[16] While I cannot subscribe to Sultan's theory of the discovery of God, there is little question that Stephen has reached a turning point in his life. He has accepted the invitation of another man to accompany him, and Stephen has "felt a strange kind of flesh of a different man approach him" (660:33–34). There has been a union affected between the two men and music has been an agent of that bond.

Even more he liked an old German song of *Johannes Jeep* about the clear sea and the voices of sirens, sweet murderers of men, which boggled Bloom a bit:

> *Von der Sirenen Listigkeit*
> *Tun die Poeten dichten.*

These opening bars he sang and translated *extempore*. Bloom, nodding, said he perfectly understood and begged him to go on by all means, which he did. (663:14–22)

. . . Stephen singing more boldly, but not loudly, the end of the ballad:

> *Und alle Schiffe brücken* (665:15–17)

Cf. *"Dulcia dum loquitur cogitat insidias"*

REMARKS: Richard Bass identifies the song [17] Stephen sings and tells us that Stephen's idea of what it is all about ("sirens, sweet murderers of men") is indeed what the song discusses. Bass then speculates that these sirens are the betraying women mentioned in Eumaeus: Kitty O'Shea, diseased prostitutes, etc. who Stephen feels are eager to entrap. More likely, however, the song prefigures Ithaca and the ballad of Little Harry Hughes in which both Bloom and Stephen are victimized. Bass goes on to say that stanza three, which the reader does not hear but Bloom presumably does, "warns against the 'arrant cunning' the 'insidias' of honeyed words," linking the admonition of the stanza with Bloom's warning Stephen about Mulligan. I have taken the liberty of translating Bass's German version: "Atrides and Achilles have experienced this. Many a hero has gone mad who has trusted in this kind of thing, and has had to end his life in great heartbreak when he allowed himself to be deceived by false friends." It may be that Stephen, so wary of betrayal and usurpation, is already preparing himself for the rejection of Bloom's overtures and enunciating the message of the Harry Hughes ballad.

The driver never said a word, good, bad or indifferent. He merely watched the two figures, as he sat on his lowbacked car, both black—one full, one lean—walk towards the railway bridge, *to be married by Father Maher.* As they walked, they at times stopped and walked again, continuing their *tête-à-tête* (which of course he was utterly out of), about sirens, enemies of man's reason, mingled with a number of other topics of the same category, usurpers, historical cases of the kind while the man in the sweeper car or you might as well call it in the sleeper car who in any case couldn't possibly hear because they were too far simply sat in his seat near the end of lower Gardiner street *and looked after their lowbacked car.* (665:18–29)

Cf. "The Low-Backed Car"

REMARKS: The references to the lowbacked car and the phrases *"to be married by Father Maher"* and *"and looked after their lowbacked car"* are from Samuel Lover's song about sweet Peggy. The words, alluded to previously,[18] are worth quoting in full:

> When first I saw sweet Peggy,
>   'Twas on a market day,
> A low-backed car she drove, and sat
>   Upon a truss of hay;
> But when that hay was blooming grass,
>   And decked with flowers of Spring,
> No flow'r was there that could compare,
>   With the blooming girl I sing!
> As she sat in the low-back'd car—
> The man at the turnpike bar,
>   Never asked for the toll,
>   But just rubbed his owld poll
> And looked after the low-back'd car.
>
> In battle's wild commotion,
>   The proud and mighty Mars,
> With hostile scythes, demands his tithes
>   Of death—in warlike cars;
> But Peggy, peaceful goddess,
>   Has darts in her bright eye,
> That knock men down, in the market town,
>   As right and left they fly!
> While she sits in her low-back'd car,
> Than battle more dangerous far—
>   For the doctor's art
>   Cannot cure the heart,
> That is hit from the low-back'd car.

Sweet Peggy, round her car, sir,
  Has strings of ducks and geese,
But the scores of hearts she slaughters
  By far out-number these;
While she among her poultry sits,
  Just like a turtle dove,
Well worth the cage, I do engage,
  Of the blooming god of love!
While she sits in her low-backed car,
The lovers come near and far,
  And envy the chicken
  That Peggy is pickin',
As she sits in the low-backed car.

I'd rather own that car, sir,
  With Peggy by my side,
Than coach-and-four and gold *galore,*
  And a lady for my bride;
For the lady would sit forninst me,
  On a cushion made with taste,—
While Peggy would be beside me,
  With my arm around her waist.
As we drove in a low-backed car,
To be married by Father Maher,
  Oh, my heart would beat high,
  At her glance and her sigh—
Though it beat in a low-backed car.

As Bloom and Stephen pass the turnpike bar they are by now fairly engrossed with one another. The song reference emphasizes humorously the bond that has been created between the two men. As this bond has been established through music, it is best described in music.[19]

17. Ithaca

What had prevented him from completing a topical song (music by R. G. Johnston) on the events of the past, or fixtures for the actual years, entitled *If Brian Boru could but come back and see old Dublin now,* commissioned by Michael Gunn, lessee of the Gaiety Theatre, 46, 47, 48, 49 South King street, and to be introduced into the sixth scene, the valley of diamonds, of the second edition (30 January 1893) of the grand annual Christmas pantomime *Sinbad the Sailor* (written by Greenleaf Whittier, scenery by George A. Jackson and Cecil Hicks, costumes by Mrs and Miss Whelan, produced by R. Shelton 26 December 1892 under the personal supervision of Mrs Michael Gunn, ballets by Jessie Noir, harlequinade by Thomas Otto) and sung by Nelly Bouverist principal girl? (678:26–38)

Cf. "If Brian Boru"

REMARKS: Brian Boru, about whom Bloom's song was to have been written, was the early Irish hero who defeated the Scandinavian invaders at Clontarf in 1014, in a decisive battle which brought an end to their raids on Ireland.[1] Like much of the matter of the Ithaca episode, the *Sinbad* reference seems to have little bearing, directly or indirectly, upon the narrative.

What fragments of verse from the ancient Hebrew and ancient Irish languages were cited with modulations of voice and translation of texts by guest to host and by host to guest?

By Stephen: *suil, suil, suil arun, suil go siocair agus, suil go cuin* (walk, walk, walk your way, walk in safety, walk with care).

By Bloom: *Kifeloch, harimon rakatejch m'baad l'zamatejch* (thy temple amid thy hair is as a slice of pomegranate). (687:36–688:7)

Cf. *"Shule Aroon"*
  Song of Solomon

REMARKS: After having been made consubstantial through the image of Shakespeare in Bella Cohen's and having been retransubstantiated with the ritual cocoa, Blephen and Stoom seek again some common ground on a more mundane level, returning once more to music. The fragment which Stephen sings is from the Irish ballad *"Shule Aroon,"* which dates at least from the eighteenth century. The words which Bloom quotes are part of the description of the bride's beauty in the *Song of Solomon* (IV:iii). The reference is part of a series of Semitic references in the general description of Bloom's background and the comparison of the backgrounds of Bloom and Stephen, as they seek ethnic evidence of their consubstantiality.

What anthem did Bloom chant partially in anticipation of that multiple, ethnically irreductible consummation?

> *Kolod balejwaw pnimah*
> *Nefesch, jehudi, homijah.*

Why was the chant arrested at the conclusion of this first distich? In consequence of defective mnemtechnic. (689:3–9)

Cf. *"Hatikvah"*

REMARKS: In the quest for a common identity, Bloom and Stephen write down and compare Gaelic and Hebrew characters in what appears to be an effort to discover bonds of similarity between the Irish and Hebrew languages. Then they move to a comparison of the history of the Jews and the Irish, the indignities suffered by the two peoples, and their chances of eventual independence. Bloom is stirred by the conversation to chant the well-known Jewish song of hope. His lines are the first two of the song which is now the Israeli national anthem. Following is a free translation of the song:

> While yet within the heart-inwardly
> The soul of the Jew yearns,
> And towards the vistas of the East-eastwards
> An eye to Zion looks.
> 'Tis not yet lost, our hope,
> The hope of two thousand years,
> To be a free people in our land
> In the land of Zion and Jerusalem.

In combining the aspirations of the Irish with those of the Jews, there is to Bloom a hope of combining his future and Stephen's. As Bloom has throughout the novel thought of the East as being an escape from his problems, here he again, this time through music, looks to the East for salvation. He sees himself united vicariously with Stephen through their tentatively established similarities in background. The song becomes the expression of Bloom's hope of being the father figure for whom the younger man has been searching. He is already Stephen's link to the past:

What was Stephen's auditive sensation?
He heard in a profound ancient male unfamiliar melody the accumulation of the past. (689:21–23)

Stephen will be Bloom's means to immortality, the salvation to his frustrating, futile existence:

What was Bloom's visual sensation?
He saw in a quick young male familiar form the predestination of a future. (689:24–26)

Recite the first (major) part of this chanted legend?

> *Little Harry Hughes and his schoolfellows all*
> *Went out for to play ball . . . .*
> *And the very first ball little Harry Hughes played*
> *He drove it o'er the jew's garden wall.*
> *And the very second ball little Harry Hughes played*
> *He broke the jew's windows all.*

How did the son of Rudolph receive this first part?

With unmixed feeling. Smiling, a jew, he heard with pleasure and saw the unbroken kitchen window.

Recite the second part (minor) of the legend.

> *Then out there came the jew's daughter*
> *And she all dressed in green.*
> *'Come back, come back, you pretty little boy,*
> *And play your ball again.'*

> *'I can't come back and I won't come back*
> *Without my schoolfellows all,*
> *For if my master he did hear*
> *He'd make it a sorry ball.'*

> *She took him by the lilywhite hand*
> *And led him along the hall*
> *Until she led him to a room*
> *Where none could hear him call.*

> *She took a penknife out of her pocket*
> *And cut off his little head,*
> *And now he'll play his ball no more*
> *For he lies among the dead. . . .*

How did the father of Millicent receive this second part?

With mixed feelings. Unsmiling, he heard and saw with wonder a jew's daughter, all dressed in green.

Condense Stephen's commentary.

One of all, the least of all, is the victim predestined. Once by inadvertence, twice by design he challenges his destiny. It comes when he is abandoned and challenges him reluctant and, as an apparition of hope and youth holds him unresisting. It leads him to a strange habitation, to a secret infidel apartment, and there, implacable, immolates him, consenting.

Why was the host (victim predestined) sad?

He wished that a tale of a deed should be told of a deed not by him should by him not be told. (690:16–692:10)

Cf. "Little Harry Hughes"

REMARKS: Now that Bloom's Semitic background has been compared with Stephen's Celtic origins and their mutual identity has been tentatively established both in prose and song and now that Bloom's hopes for the future have been specifically recounted, Joyce has prepared us for one of the most important musical references of the novel, Stephen's rendition of the ballad "Little Harry Hughes." This ballad is more than just an anti-Semitic ballad; the parallels are too close to the present situation to be passed over so lightly. In the complete version of the ballad, collected by Cecil T. Sharp, we see how little Harry, like Stephen, is lured into the Jew's house with the promise of goodies:

> Stanza 3:
> The first that came out was a Jew's daughter
> Was dressed all in green:
> Come in, come in, my little Sir Hugh,
> You shall have your ball again.
>
> Stanza 4:
> O no, O no, I dare not acome
> Without my playmates too;
> For if my mother should be at the door
> She would cause my poor heart to rue.
>
> Stanza 5:
> The first she offer'd him was a fig,
> The next a finer thing,
> The third a cherry as red as blood,
> And that enticed him in.
>
> Stanza 6:
> She set him up in a gilty chair,
> She gave him sugar sweet.
> She laid him out on a dresser board
> And stabb'd him like a sheep.

Unlike Harry, Stephen will not be seduced with seeming kindness and cocoa. Bloom understands early that he is somehow part of the action of the song when he glances at his own kitchen window, though he wishes, as the last sentence in the passage indicates, to be dissociated from the song. He is, however, doubly implicated in the song, as the next few lines of the text prove:

> Why was the host (victim predestined) sad?
> He wished that a tale of a deed should be told of a deed not by him should by him not be told.

Why was the host (reluctant, unresisting) still?
In accordance with the law of the conservation of energy.

Why was the host (secret infidel) silent?
He weighed the possible evidences for and against ritual murder. . . .
(692:8-15)

We see that Bloom, the host, becomes the "victim predestined." He is further described as "reluctant, unresisting," and as being a "secret infidel." Bloom's role as the murdering Jew in Stephen's ballad changes in the "victim predestined" description. Bloom is predestined to be victimized by Stephen, the "apparition of hope and youth," who accepts Bloom's good offices and is about to leave, denying Bloom the fatherhood he longs for. We realize further that Bloom, though "reluctant" to see Stephen leave, will be "unresisting" and not press him to stay. But there are other ways in which Bloom and Stephen have played a consubstantial role as victim. The Jew's daughter who does little Harry in is, of course, analogous Milly, who has already been identified as having a communal identity with her mother. Stephen, if he is lured into Bloom's house, might easily become a son-in-law to Bloom, a prospect alluded to shortly after the Hughes ballad is sung (p. 695). If so Milly would be victimizing Stephen who is not about to be "immolated" by such traps.

But Molly and Milly are consubstantial and Bloom has been victimized by his wife's infidelity and in his consubstantial role with Simon by May's Oedipal infidelity with Stephen, who, also in the Oedipal triangle, has become a victim of his mother's temptations. When everyone is everyone else, there is plenty of victimization to go around. But victim or not, Bloom is still Stephen's "secret infidel" host as the cycle is completed. Stephen's ballad, by alluding to the victimization of both himself and Bloom, confirms his interchangeability with Bloom and emphasizes the real consubstantial bonds existing between the two men.

Though Bloom still offers Stephen a place to sleep, the younger man refuses and leaves shortly after singing his ballad. Stephen wishes to create no additional nets like those over which he has had to fly in his past.

Why might these several provisional contingencies between a guest and a hostess not necessarily preclude or be precluded by a permanent eventuality of reconciliatory union between a schoolfellow and a jew's daughter?

Because the way to daughter led through mother, the way to mother through daughter. (695:13-18)

Cf. "Little Harry Hughes"

REMARKS: The result of addressing the possibility of an eventual marriage between Stephen and Milly in terms of their counterparts ("schoolfellow and jew's daughter") from the Hughes ballad is an additional indication that the ties which would bind Stephen to the Bloom clan are to be considered an "immolation" which would spell his doom. It is interesting that the consubstantiality motif enters this reference in connection with the simultaneous identity of Molly and Milly: have one of them and you've had them both.

> . . . the monthly recurrence known as the new moon with the old moon in her arms . . . (700:34–35)

Cf. "Sir Patrick Spens"
REMARKS: The near cliché about the new moon appears in nearly all versions of this medieval ballad. It is a part of a sailor's omen of disaster:

> "Late, late yestreen I saw the new moone,
>   Wi the auld moon in hir arme,
> And I feir, I feir, my deir master,
>   That we will cum to harme."

Thus it is appropriate in this consideration of the significance of various celestial phenomena.

> What occupied the position originally occupied by the sideboard?
> A vertical piano (Cadby) with exposed keyboard, its closed coffin supporting a pair of long yellow ladies' gloves and an emerald ashtray containing four consumed matches, a partly consumed cigarette and two discoloured ends of cigarettes, its musicrest supporting the music in the key of G natural for voice and piano of *Love's Old Sweet Song*. . . . (706:19–26)

Cf. "Love's Old Sweet Song"
REMARKS: The piano, the cigarette butts and "Love's Old Sweet Song," with all its adulterous connotations, serve again as mute reminders of the afternoon's activities. Bloom has come back from the projected hopeful land of the future to the realities of his own life.

> Were there testimonials?
> Numerous. From clergyman, British naval officer, wellknown author, city man, hospital nurse, lady, mother of five, absentminded beggar.

How did absentminded beggar's concluding testimonial conclude?

What a pity the government did not supply our men with wonderworkers during the South African campaign! What a relief it would have been! (722:12–20)

Cf. "The Absent-Minded Beggar"

REMARKS: The chronical of testimonial signers sounds a great deal like the "duke's son, cook's son, son of a hundred kings" from the opening of the chorus. The absentminded beggar of the song was himself engaged in the South African campaign and his pleas for wonderworkers for the boys at the front in the Boer War would naturally follow from the plea in the song for assistance for the soldier who has "left a lot o' little things behind him."

. . . the music in the Ormond Hotel (Shira Shirim) . . . (729:4)

Cf. *Song of Songs*

REMARKS: Bloom eventually retires, thinking of the events of the day and defining each one with a word connoting a rite or with some other appropriate parenthetical appellation. *Shira Shirim* means "Song of Songs," an apt description of the Sirens episode, an extended medley consisting of no less than forty-seven songs.

What selfevident enigma pondered with desultory constancy during 30 years did Bloom now, having effected natural obscurity by the extinction of artificial light, silently suddenly comprehend?

Where was Moses when the candle went out? (729:24–28)

Cf. "Where Was Moses When the Light Went Out?"

REMARKS: S. Spaeth quotes the words and music to the song, telling us that one answer to the question was "down the cellar, eating sauerkraut." [2] Thornton sees Bloom's answer as being "in the dark," a logical conclusion. The interesting thing here is the living through an identical experience by Bloom and Moses, who have already been identified on several occasions as being consubstantial.

18. Penelope

. . . the night Boylan gave my hand a great squeeze going along by the Tolka in my hand there steals another I just pressed the back of his like that with my thumb to squeeze back singing the young May Moon shes beaming love because he has an idea about him and me . . . (740:9–13)

Cf. "The Young May Moon"

REMARKS: Like Bloom, Molly remembers fairly accurately the night she, her husband, and Blazes took their all important first walk. The scene is set in Molly's mind as it was in her husband's with her rendition of "The Young May Moon." [1]

Of the various motifs identified with the Molly-Boylan assignation this is one of the most prevalent. The song, promising good things for the aspiring lover ("'Tis never too late for delight, my dear . . ."), constitutes Molly's sirensong for her potential lover, Blazes. This is, of course, just what the about-to-be-cuckolded Bloom suspects. As the first song in Molly's finale to the book it also marks her first confession of infidelity. Before Molly proceeds through a whole list of deviations from her marriage vows, she anticipates memories of misconduct with her musical seductress motif, "The Young May Moon."

. . . O Sweetheart May wouldnt a thing like that simply bore you stiff to extinction actually too stupid even to take his boots off . . . (744:21–23)

Cf. "Sweetheart May"

REMARKS: Molly's use of the song to describe Denis Breen, the husband of the former Josie Powell, who was at one time interested romantically in Bloom, has connotations beyond those suggested by the title. The song tells the story of the love of a little girl of eight for a man to whom she declares, "I love you, and when I grow big,/Now promise to marry your May!" When the girl grows up, the man with "years on his head" longs to see her. The opening of the chorus outlines the pitfalls of the long wait:

> Sweetheart May, when you grow up one day
> You may marry another and my love betray . . .

So the song is an appropriate theme for the Molly-Josie-Bloom triangle and the early romance of Bloom and Josie before each "betrayed" the other with their marriages.

. . . Bartell dArcy too that he used to make fun of when he commenced kissing me on the choir stairs after I sang Gounods *Ave Maria* what are we waiting for O my heart kiss me straight on the brow and part which is my brown part . . . (745:31–35)

Cf. *"Ave Maria"*

"Good-Bye!"

REMARKS: In this incongruous memory we have a rather amusing liaison that acts as a summary for all of Bloom's memories of Molly's angelic, religious solos. Molly's hymn to the Immaculate Virgin casts Molly momentarily by association in a role similar to Mary's. This holiness she quickly dispels, however, with her reference to Tosti's "Good-bye!" The lines to which she alludes are "What are we waiting for? Oh! my heart! Kiss me straight on the brows! and part!" Her transformation of the lines is hardly the work of the Virgin Mary. So, Molly's role as virgin-inspiration figure in the novel is ludicrously blended here with her temptress-fertility role, as the dying strains of the well-known prayer to the Virgin and Molly's double entendre produce the overture to Molly's choir-staircase copulation.

. . . when I threw the penny to that lame sailor for England home and beauty when I was whistling there is a charming girl I love and I hadnt even put on my clean shift or powdered myself or a thing . . . (747:34–37)

Cf. "The Death of Nelson"

"It Is a Charming Girl I Love"

REMARKS: The lame sailor, as we have learned in the Wandering Rocks, was singing the lines "For England home and beauty," when Molly threw him a coin from her window that afternoon. Molly of course had little on her mind except the impending rendezvous with Boylan. The words to the chorus of stanzas one and two of "The Death of Nelson" add another humorous overtone to the tardy Boylan's visit:

> England expects that every man
> This day will do his duty . . .

We learn at the end of the song ". . . that every man/That day [like Boylan] had done his duty." Molly, waiting at her window, whistles still another sirensong, "It Is a Charming Girl I Love" from *The Lily of Killarney*, as she waits for her lover. Clearly throughout her soliloquy Molly sees herself as a siren figure leading men to passion only to cast them away. The chorus of the song is about unrequited love:

> Botheration! botheration!
> Her likeness I never shall see;
> There is but one Colleen Bawn
> And she does not love me.

. . . a good job he was able to open the carriage door with his knife or theyd have taken us on to Cork . . . (748:13–15)

Cf. "O Mr. Porter"

REMARKS: The song reference is to the chorus of a very popular music-hall song of the day:

> Oh, Mr. Porter what shall I do?
> I want to go to Birmingham and they're taking me on to Crewe . . .

Like Simon Dedalus, Molly has a habit of using appropriate quotations from songs to enliven her sometimes tedious thinking.

> . . . little chits of missies they have now singing Kathleen Kearney and her like on account of father being in the army and my singing the absentminded beggar and wearing a brooch for lord Roberts when I had the map of it all and Poldy not Irish enough . . . (748:27-31)

Cf. "The Absent-Minded Beggar"

REMARKS: Molly realizes that she and Poldy have never been wholly accepted in the really "proper" Irish society of Dublin. We know from Joyce's story "A Mother" that Kathleen Kearney was in the Gaelic League—Irish revival crowd, who superficially at least were all for anything Irish and disdained anything English. Of course Molly's father, old Major Tweedy, was in the pay of the British and thus his daughter was suspect, especially when she sang songs like "The Absent-Minded Beggar," which as we previously have seen [2] is a song of patriotism about the poor British soldiers on active duty, a tune not calculated to win widespread sympathy in occupied Ireland.

> . . . was it him managed it this time I wouldnt put it past him like he got me on to sing in the *Stabat Mater* by going around saying he was putting Lead Kindly Light to music I put him up to that till the jesuits found out he was a freemason thumping the piano lead Thou me on copied from some old opera . . . (748: 31-36)

Cf. *Stabat Mater*
   "Lead Kindly Light"

REMARKS: Bloom's memories of Molly singing gloriously in the *Stabat Mater* are partially the result of his own ingenuity. The lyrics to "Lead Kindly Light" were written by John Henry Newman and thus perfectly acceptable to the Catholic church, although the well-known tune by Protestant John B. Dykes in 1865 was not, leaving the door open for Bloom's plagiarized version. The memory is still another example of the magnificent twists of Bloom's mind.

. . . all invention made up about he drinking the champagne out of her slipper after the ball was over . . . (752:1–3)

Cf. "After the Ball"

REMARKS: The reference seems little more than Molly's use of another musical cliché to describe what she considers to be male chauvinist stories of deeds that really do nothing for the females involved.

frseeeeeeeefronnnng train somewhere whistling the strength those engines have in them like big giants and the water rolling all over and out of them all sides like the end of Loves old sweet sonnnng . . . (754:38–41)

Cf. "Love's Old Sweet Song"

REMARKS: As Molly's thoughts return unerringly to the sex act and her lovers, the first of her major love motifs is heard again. We have heard the song throughout the novel as a primary motif in Bloom's mind for the Molly-Boylan liaison. Significantly it occurs in Penelope just after Molly's long reminiscence over her vigorous afternoon of lovemaking with Boylan. With the sound of a train whistle in the distance, her thoughts assume a tone of reverie, reflecting on time and the nature of love. The onomatopoetic device of the engine's whistle is employed here to imitate the sustained notes in the conclusion of the song. The strength of the engines fascinates Molly, and they assume phallic proportions as "Love's Old Sweet Song" becomes in Penelope a song of love for more than Boylan; instead it is a love motif for all of Molly's former loves and the days that are lost and gone forever.

. . . the smell of the rainwater in those tanks watching the sun all the time weltering down on you faded all that lovely frock fathers friend Mrs Stanhope sent me from the B Marche Paris . . . (755:13–15)

Cf. " 'Tis the Last Rose of Summer"

REMARKS: Molly's memories are not entirely of sex. Her memories of older days often involve her girlhood with her father's regiment on Gibraltar. In the phrase, "faded all that lovely," Molly has perhaps subconsciously admitted to herself that the days of her youth are just about over. The phrase approximates the early part of stanza one of " 'Tis the Last Rose of Summer":

> 'Tis the last rose of summer
> Left blooming alone,
> All her lovely companions
> Are faded and gone!

The song reference suggests that Molly sees her own plight and youth as faded though she would not consciously admit this to herself. It is ironic that Joyce also used the song in the Sirens chapter to describe the sad and cuckolded Bloom. However, neither one will admit that youth is just about fled. Bloom keeps up the semblances of virility with Martha Clifford and Molly displays her continuing sexual vigor with Boylan. If, as the song suggests, they are in the stage of the last rose of summer, Mr. and Mrs. Bloom are still blooming separately, if not alone.

> . . . wd give anything to back in Gib and hear you sing in old Madrid or Waiting . . . (755:20–21)

Cf. "In Old Madrid"

"Waiting"

REMARKS: Throughout the rest of the chapter the two songs recur as sirensong symbols of the ever-pervading, all-encompassing female. Both are songs of a patient girl awaiting her lover's return, and both are pictures of fulfillment suspended until the return of the absent lover.[3] Though Molly was waiting for Boylan at the four o'clock assignation hour and though her thoughts of her current sexual activities still deal chiefly with Boylan, it is Bloom who is the Ulysses of the novel, who has been away on his trip around Dublin and whose wife is the Penelope. Molly has not exactly been weaving tapestries during Bloom's absence; however, it is to Bloom that her thoughts constantly return and him for whom her final "yes" is voiced.

> . . . waiting always waiting to guiiiide him toooo me waiting nor speeeed his flying feet . . . (757:6–7)

Cf. "Waiting"

REMARKS: The "waiting" motif occurs again shortly after as Molly's thoughts go back to her girlhood as Major Tweedy's daughter. As a girl she remembers, she was on the verge of running away to find her ideal lover. This reference serves to set up the image of Molly's dreams of what she desires in life. Once again the perpetually expectant girl merges with the siren figure as the song pictures a girl in similar anticipation. The wheat field of stanza one of the song gives way to Ben Howth rhododendrons as the concluding act of love in the novel is anticipated by the imminent appearance of the lover in stanza three from which Molly sings. Following are the first and third stanzas as quoted by Thornton:

> The stars shine on his pathway, the trees bend back their leaves
> To guide them to the meadow among the golden sheaves,
> Where stand I, longing, loving, and listening as I wait,
> To the nightingale's wild singing, singing, sweet singing to its mate.

I hear his foot-fall's music, I feel his presence near,
All my soul, responsive, answers and tells me he is here;
O, stars, shine out your brightest, O, nightingale, sing sweet,
To guide him to me, waiting, and speed his flying feet.[4]

The realization of these dreams ocurred one day with Bloom amid the Ben Howth rhododendrons. It is Molly's understanding of this that forms the conclusion of the book—her affirmation of life and relationship with Mulvey, who is subsumed by Bloom in the scene on Howth.

> . . . O thanks be to the great God I got somebody to give me what I badly wanted to put some heart up into me youve no chances at all in this place like you used *long ago* I wish somebody would write me a loveletter his wasnt much and I told him he could write what he liked yours ever Hugh Boylan *in Old Madrid* silly women believe *love is sighing I am dying* still if he wrote it I suppose thered be some truth in it . . . (758:27–34) [italics mine]

Cf. "In Old Madrid"

REMARKS: The motif of eternal expectation is amplified in the references to "In Old Madrid." For a few minutes in her long monologue Molly becomes completely honest with herself about her relations with Boylan. The italicized lines are from the first stanza, quoted previously [5] and the chorus, "Come my love the stars are shining,/Time is flying,/Love is sighing;/Come for thee a heart is pining,/Here alone I wait for thee!" The words alluded to indicate that Molly sees herself as the expectant lover waiting to be fulfilled by her ideal. That Molly demands a letter of affection shows she wants more than mere sexual gratification. Boylan, who signs his letters "yours ever" and whose lovemaking lacks tenderness, is unable to fulfill Molly's demands for the ideal. She is destined to wait a little longer behind her lattice in old Madrid.

> . . . I never thought hed write making an appointment I had it inside my petticoat bodice all day reading it up in every hole and corner while father was up at the drill instructing to find out by the handwriting or the language of stamps singing I remember shall I wear a white rose . . . (759:24–28)

Cf. "Shall I Wear a White Rose or Shall I Wear a Red?

REMARKS: Molly's perpetual anticipation of the ideal love begins early with Mulvey's note proposing a meeting: The song she sang is a fourth theme of anticipation to rank along with "Waiting," "In Old Madrid," and "The

Young May Moon." Once the appointment has been made the anticipation becomes focused on what should be worn:

> Shall I wear a white rose,
> Shall I wear a red?
> Will he look for garlands?
> What shall wreathe my head?
> Will a riband charm him
> Fair upon my breast?
> Scare I can remember
> How he loves me best.
>
> I must look my fairest
> When tomorrow's here;
> He will come to claim me!
> Shall I still be dear?
> I must look my brightest
> On that happy day,
> As his fancy drew me
> When so far away.
>
> I shall need no roses
> If his heart be true,
> Not a single wreathlet,
> Red or white or blue,
> In tomorrow's twilight,
> When my soul's at rest:
> Then I need not ask him
> How he loves me best.

In this song the anticipation becomes near surety as the wedding seems only a day or so off and the girl's hopes are about to be realized. Perhaps it is just the persona's wishing for the consummation that makes it seem so sure, but Molly, in holding Mulvey's letter, has more than mere idle wishes to indicate that a meeting will take place.

> . . . and I wanted to put on the old stupid clock to near the time he was the first man kissed me under the Moorish wall my sweetheart when a boy . . . (759:28–31)

Cf. "My Sweetheart, When a Boy"

REMARKS: Thornton claims the words which he found to this song are by James Lyman Malloy,[6] but they are the same words as those in the song by Frederick Enoch and Wilford Morgan. The persona of the song is a man remembering a girl from his youth. This is made clear in the last lines of the song:

When I remember her again,
My sweetheart, when a boy.

Molly changes the gender of the persona by making Mulvey the boy she is thinking about, but the sentiments of the song remain:

'Tho' many gentle hearts I've known,
And many a pretty face,
Where love sat gaily on his throne, in beauty and in grace,
Yet never was in my heart enthrall'd
With such enchanted joy,
As by the darling whom I call'd
My sweetheart, when a boy.

. . . what did I tell him I was engaged for fun to the son of a Spanish nobleman named Don Miguel de la Flora and he believed that I was to be married to him in 3 years time theres many a true word spoken in jest there is a flower that bloometh . . . (759:33–37)

Cf. "There Is a Flower That Bloometh"

REMARKS: The song has previously been identified with Bloom,[7] and the name of Molly's would-be fiancé has, as she thinks, the quality of a premonition about it. The conclusion of the first stanza, "Oh! pluck it ere it wither,/ 'Tis the mem'ry, the mem'ry of the past," identifies Molly's thoughts of Bloom as memories of the past, as, in the present context, are Molly's thoughts about Mulvey. But the thrust of Mulvey's sections both here and at the end of Molly's thoughts is that like all the lovers' he will become a part of the great pronoun *he*, Leopold Bloom. So Mulvey's first love scene under the Moorish wall becomes Bloom's scene on Howth and Bloom incorporates all of Molly's lovers into one consubstantial being.

. . . Molly darling he called me . . . (761:2)
. . . Harry Molly Darling I was thinking of him on the sea all the time . . . (762:12–13)

Cf. "Mollie Darling"

REMARKS: The name that Mulvey calls Molly is quite possibly an allusion to a popular nineteenth-century song by Will S. Hays. The persona of the song, deeply enamoured of Molly, inquires constantly if she loves him. The chorus is as follows:

Mollie fairest, sweetest, dearest,
Look up, darling, tell me this;

> Do you love me, Mollie Darling?
> Let your answer be a kiss.

Mulvey's use of the song reference is intended to be an unqualified confession of love.

> . . . I can see his face clean shaven Frseeeeeeeeeeeeeeeeeeeeeeefrong that train again weeping tone once in the dear deaead days beyond recall close my eyes breath my lips forward kiss sad look eyes open piano ere oer the world the mists began I hate that istsbeg comes loves sweet ssooooooong . . . (762:23–28)

Cf. "Love's Old Sweet Song"

REMARKS: The references are to stanza one of the song:

> Once in the dear dead days beyond recall,
> When on the world the mist began to fall.

Molly has perhaps unknowingly been futilely trying with Boylan to recapture the dear dead days of her youth. If the song is hers and Boylan's, it is also Mulvey's. But even the dear dead days of Mulvey seem to have been climaxed by Molly's memory of something less than eternal bliss: "how did we finish it off yes O yes I pulled him off into my handkerchief" (760:35–36).

In both the above passages involving "Love's Old Sweet Song," the music allusion has been triggered by the sound of the train whistle, further suggesting remoteness and places long ago in its melancholy sound. Clearly much of Molly's chapter consists at least in part of wishful thinking, and previous and potential assignations receive a glamour in her mind which is often far from reality. In contrast to this, however, her detailed recollections of her day of bliss with Bloom high on Ben Howth rhododendrons is exactly in detail how he remembers the situation. But even this is blended with memories of Mulvey under the Moorish wall. The reality with which she closes the novel is a composite of consubstantiality of all her lovers, which looks strangely like Leopold Bloom.

> . . . I could have been a prima donna only I married him comes looooves old . . . (763:8–9)

Cf. "Love's Old Sweet Song"

REMARKS: In the present context, Molly's song of fanciful bliss in the inaccurately remembered "dear dead days beyond recall," is extended to cover all that she would have been had she not married Bloom.

. . . My Ladys Bower is too long for an encore about the moated grange at twilight and vaulted rooms . . . (763:10–11)

Cf. "My Lady's Bower"

REMARKS: The song that Molly rejects is about "the courtly days of yore" and its effect on young lovers:

> 'Thro the moated grange at twilight,
> My love and I we went,
> By empty rooms and lonely stairs,
> In lover's sweet content,
> And round the old and broken casement,
> We watch'd the roses flow'r,
> But the place we lov'd the best of all,
> Was call'd "My Lady's Bow'r."
>
> And with beating hearts we enter'd
> And stood and whisper'd low,
> Of the sweet and lovely lady
> Who liv'd there years ago!
> And the moon shone in upon us
> Across the dusty floor,
> Where her little feet had wander'd
> In the courtly days of yore
> And it touch'd the faded arras
> And again we seem'd to see
> The lovely lady sitting there,
> Her lover at her knee,
> And we saw him kiss her fair white hand
> And Oh! we heard him say
> "I shall love thee love forever,
> Tho' the years may pass away!" . . .
>
> But then they vanish'd in a moment,
> And we knew 'twas but a dream!
> It was not they who sat there
> In the silver moonlight gleam!
> Ah! no, 'twas we, we two together
> Who had found our golden hour.
> And told the old, old story
> With "My Lady's Bow'r;" . . .

Although Molly is right about the song being long, there might have been another, subliminal, reason for her rejecting it. She would probably have been identified with the lady of the bower and the classic love affair that had taken place in "days of yore," but rejected the idea that those days of love are gone forever and that someone else and her lover would take their place. There is a subtle superannuation of old lovers for new here, even if the old love is revered, it is only a nostalgic memory and "too long [and too late] for an encore," as Molly informs us.

> . . . yes Ill sing Winds that blow from the south that he gave after the choirstairs performance . . . (763:12–13)

Cf. "Winds That Blow From the South"

REMARKS: I have not been able to locate this song.

> . . . I wish hed sleep in some bed by himself with his cold feet on me give us room even to let a fart God or do the least thing better yes hold them like that a bit on my side piano quietly sweeeee theres that train far away pianissimo eeeeeeee one more song . . . (763:19–23)

Cf. "Love's Old Sweet Song"

REMARKS: The end of Molly's reverie about times remote and exotic is punctuated significantly and paradoxically by her breaking wind to the dying pianissimo notes of "Love's Old Sweet Song." Like the appropriateness of Bloom's wind breaking to the strains of Robert Emmet's and Christ's last words at the conclusion of the Sirens chapter, there is a deliciously appropriate irony to Molly's fart in the concluding reference to "Love's Old Sweet Song." For all the hoopla surrounding her general infidelity and her assignation with Boylan, Bloom's equanimity has conquered all. As he lies asleep, aware of Molly's activities, but not spurred to any great action regarding them, Molly's song of love dies out lower (piano) and lower (pianissimo), accompanied as it is by the degrading but necessary fart. Fantasy is at last stripped aside and only the essentials of life remain. As Bloom says, "Life goes on," and Molly's fart smells no sweeter than Penelope's, Gerty Mac-Dowell's, Martha Clifford's or Cissy Caffrey's.

> . . . I hate those ruck of Mary Ann coalboxes out for the day . . . (764:33–34)

Cf. "McGilligan's Daughter, Mary Ann"

REMARKS: This remark is puzzling, but in the light of the song it may be a disparagement of heavy-set peasant women who go on day outings whenever there is a suitable holiday. The second stanza and chorus of the song particularly describe Mary Ann's physical attributes:

> Sure 'tis aisy to be seen that she is no beauty queen,
> And her double chin is steam rolled every day.

An her eye-brows they are shifted and her face is being lifted,
Though who is goin' to lift it I can't say.
She's a darlin' she's a daisy and she's set the city crazy,
Though in build, and talk, and manner, like a man . . .

. . . sending me that long strool of a song out of the Huguenots
to sing in French to be more classy O beau pays de la Touraine
that I never even sang once . . . (771:18–21)

Cf. *The Huguenots*
    "O beau pays de la Touraine"

REMARKS: Molly's prospective solo would indeed add class to her repertoire,
because it is the song of Queen Margaret of Valois, whose noble effort to
unite the Protestants and Catholics in France is doomed to failure. At the
beginning of Act II of *Les Huguenots* when the solo occurs, however, the
scene is still tranquil and her rich lovely melody extolling the virtues of
Touraine provides a moment of calm before the storms so soon to break.

. . . and he goes about whistling every time were on the run
again his huguenots or the frogs march pretending to help the
men with our 4 sticks of furniture . . . (772:11–14)

Cf. *The Huguenots*

REMARKS: It is not certain exactly which song Molly has in mind when she
mentions "the frogs march," though I suspect that its juxtaposition with *The
Huguenots* connotes a slang reference to a march from the opera about the
French. The allusion is probably to the "Soldiers' Chorus," in which the chorus
maintains a drum-like "rat-a-plan, rat-a-plan, rat-a-plan-plan-plan" against a
sustained melody.

. . . and her or her son waiting Bill Bailey wont you please come
home . . . (774:4–5)

Cf. "Bill Bailey, Won't You Please Come Home"

REMARKS: The song, as its title implies, is about a distraught woman waiting
for her man to return:

> Won't you come home, Bill Bailey, won't you come home?
>   She moans de whole day long;
> I'll do de cooking, darling, I'll pay de rent,
>   I knows I've done you wrong.
> 'Member dat rainy eve dat I drove you out
>   Wid nothing but a fine tooth comb.
> I know I'se to blame, well ain't dat a shame?
>   Bill Bailey, won't you please come home?

Dignam's absences for prolonged drinking bouts, do not, so far as we are told in *Ulysses,* seem to be his wife's fault. Molly has probably used the song merely as a cliché for the nightly searches for the absent Dignam.

> . . . Simon Dedalus too he was always turning up half screwed singing the second verse first the old love is the new was one of his so sweetly sang the maiden on the hawthorn bough . . . (774: 14–17)

Cf. "The Old Love and the New Love"
"So Sweetly Sang the Maiden on the Hawthorn Bough"

REMARKS: Molly in her recalling Simon Dedalus's error in the lyrics of the song probably made a mistake herself in the title of "The Old Love and The New Love." The song is about the old love for a woman and the "new" one for Ireland, and how the persona must abandon the first for the second. If Simon did start with the second verse he began the story *in medias res* with the soldier already about to set off to join "the brave United men." The second allusion, to "So Sweetly . . . ," presumably deals with Simon's misquoted version, which makes the song exceptionally difficult to locate. I have not been able to identify it at any rate.

> . . . he was always on for flirtyfying too when I sang Maritana with him at Freddy Mayers private opera . . . (774:17–18)

Cf. *Maritana*

REMARKS: See remarks for following *Maritana* allusion.[8]

> . . . he had a delicious glorious voice Phoebe dearest . . . (774: 18–19)

Cf. "Phoebe Dearest, Tell O Tell Me"

REMARKS: The song is again about a suitor kept in doubt and anguish by a desired female:

> Phoebe, dearest, tell, o tell me,
> May I hope that you'll be mine?
> Oh, let no cold frown repel me,
> Leave me not with grief to pine.

A woman's position of dominance over her lover is a leitmotif which runs through a large number of Molly's song allusions as well as her soliloquy generally. This song of Simon's, especially in the present context of his singing with her, is another hint of his bondage to the ever-present symbol of fertility and femininity, Molly Bloom.

. . . goodbye *sweet*heart he always sang it not like Bartell dArcy
sweet *tart* goodbye . . . (774:19–20)

Cf. "Goodbye, Sweetheart, Goodbye"

REMARKS: There seems little more to this reference than Dedalus's exhibiting
less male chauvinism in his pronunciation of the lyrics than D'Arcy, and
Molly appreciates the more sentimental version rather than the one characteristic of men like Boylan.

. . . O Maritana wildwood flower we sang splendidly though it
was a bit too high for my register even transposed and he was
married at the time to May Goulding . . . (774:22–25)

Cf. "Oh Maritana"

REMARKS: The song Molly refers to is a duet between Don César and Maritana in Act III of the opera. In the duet Don César returns to find his wife,
Maritana, who has been manipulated in the schemes of Don José, still faithful
to him. There is some clarification of identities and finally husband is reunited with wife. The duet involves Don César's error in charging his wife
with infidelity:

> Don César:
> Oh, Maritana! wildwood flow'r,
> Did they but give thee a prouder name
> To place thee in a kingly bower
> And deck thee with gilded shame!
>
> Maritana:
> No! Maritana though in this bow'r,
> Lips the most pure, shall never blame;
> A captive in a stranger's power,
> Shall perish ere she yield to shame.
>
> But who art thou my conduct thus to scan? . . .
>
> Don César:
> I am thy husband, Don César de Bazan.
>
> Maritana:
> My husband! . . .
>
> Don César:
> Thy husband! . . .
>
> Both:
> Nevermore to part,

Thine forever is this faithful heart.
Thine forever, etc.

The marital relation between the two characters in the opera provides the stimulus for Molly's next observation that Simon was married to May Goulding when he sang the duet with Molly. The faithfulness of Maritana is a satirical allusion to the unfaithfulness of Molly. Simon's role in this as the questioning husband is again a crisscrossing of the jumbled themes and situations of the novel. As Simon and Bloom are consubstantial in their husband role to Molly, so it was Simon who became consubstantial with Bloom by singing Lionel's role in *"M'appari"* in the Sirens episode. But Simon's wife is May, whose faithfulness Simon might question in her Oedipal affair with Stephen. To add a final thread of incongruity to the theme, Stephen's liaison with Molly is projected by Bloom in the hope that Stephen will become a part of the Bloom household. So this song from *Maritana* provides the loom to weave together the whole tapestry of intertwining marital infidelity threads. Finally, Molly may be talking of her own marriage when she asserts that the whole faithfulness testimonial of the song is "a bit too high for my register even transposed."

. . . they all write about some woman in their poetry well I suppose he wont find many like me *where softly sighs of love the light guitar* where poetry is in the air the blue sea and the moon shining so beautifully coming back on the nightboat from Tarifa the lighthouse at Europa point the guitar that fellow played was so expressive will I never go back there again all new faces *two glancing eyes a lattice hid* Ill sing that for him theyre my eyes if hes anything of a poet *two eyes as darkly bright as loves own star* arent those beautiful words as loves young star . . . (775:22–31) [italics mine]

Cf. "In Old Madrid"

REMARKS: Molly's realization of Boylan's inadequacies does not dampen her ardour in her search for the ideal and her fulfillment. She contemplates an assignation with Stephen, who will become her salvation from the boredom of the waiting, ever-unfulfilled woman. The italicized words in the quotation are from "In Old Madrid." Molly has once again become the ever-waiting lover in the window whose lover will appear on the scene and spirit her off to a life of bliss. Perhaps the fulfillment will come from the poet and Molly will live in eternal bliss and immortality through Stephen's poems. And so Molly joins Stephen and Bloom in seeing herself as a symbolic character. Each of the three principals does this in a unique way. Stephen through the *Portrait* sees himself largely in symbolic terms and carries this tendency right over into *Ulysses*. While Bloom's thoughts of himself as a symbolic figure are confined largely to his subconscious, they are explicitly manifested in the Circe episode and in such conscious song references as those to *Don Giovanni* and *Martha*. Now Molly manifests her own projection as a symbol. She will be Stephen's "dark lady," his earthy Beatrice, as she so richly deserves. Through the Penelope episode the principal leitmotifs suggesting this theme of coquettish love goddess are "The Young May Moon," "Love's Old Sweet Song," and "In Old Madrid."

. . . for the love of Mike listen to him the winds that waft my sighs to thee so well he may sleep and sigh the great Suggester Don Poldo de la Flora if he knew how he came out on the cards this morning hed have something to sigh for . . . (778:5–9)

Cf. "Winds That Waft My Sighs to Thee"

REMARKS: Bloom's sighs in his sleep suggest his wife's satiric allusion to the gentle, precious "Winds That Waft My Sighs to Thee." Even in sleep Bloom, the degraded, lies in bondage to his goddess-wife.

. . . Ill go about rather gay not too much singing a bit now and then mi fa pietà Masetto then Ill start dressing myself to go out presto non son più forte Ill put on my best shift and drawers let him have a good eyeful out of that to make his Micky stand for him Ill let him know if thats what he wanted that his wife is fucked yes and damn well fucked too up to my neck nearly not by him 5 or 6 times . . . (780:17–23)

Cf. *"Mi fa pietà Masetto"*
　　"Presto non son più forte"

REMARKS: If Bloom sees himself as some kind of Don Giovanni who demands his breakfast in bed the following morning, Molly will have her revenge on him. For her Bloom is no Don Giovanni but only a cuckolded Masetto and she will let him know it in no uncertain terms. Molly will let her husband know that he is a cuckold in the same way she first indicated to Boylan her romantic intentions toward him, through music. Both she and Bloom know *Don Giovanni* so well that he can't mistake her message when she hums it, and neither by this time can the reader. The reference serves to complete the cycle of *Don Giovanni* references and particularly those surrounding *"Là ci darem."* In the scene in which the duet is sung the Don's attempts to seduce Zerlina are at first met with hesitation (*"vorrei e non vorrei"*). Suspecting that the Don might be fooling her, Zerlina sings, *"Mi fa pietà Masetto"* (I feel sorry for Masetto) to which the handsome cavalier replies, *"Io cangierò tua sorte"* (I will change your lot). Persuaded, Zerlina yields, *"Presto non son più forte"* (Suddenly I am no longer strong).

Molly's intent here is to cripple her husband's role as dominant figure in the household, but of course that is impossible. Bloom already knows what has happened, has gone over every detail to his own chagrin and masochistic satisfaction, and has already conquered all with his ultimate weapon, equanimity.

. . . whatll I wear shall I wear a white rose . . . (781:32–33)

Cf. "Shall I Wear a White Rose or Shall I Wear a Red?"

REMARKS: We have already seen this song as an indication of a girl's anxious anticipation of the coming of her lover. Here Molly's preparations are for Stephen's anticipated visit, and Molly is the transformed and rejuvenated young girl of the song.

. . . handsome Moors all in white and turbans like kings asking you to sit down in their little bit of a shop and Ronda with the old windows of the posadas glancing eyes a lattice hid for her lover to kiss the iron . . . (782:38–41)

Cf. "In Old Madrid"

REMARKS: As Molly concludes her soliloquy with a blend of reminiscences of handsome Moors, her first kiss, the affair with Lt. Mulvey, and Poldy on Howth, she sings her last sirensong. As the scene of her liaison with Mulvey and the promise of the Near East blend in with the scene on Howth, all lovers become one and Molly more than ever the perpetually waiting girl who dreams perpetually of fulfillment.

. . . Gibraltar as a girl where I was a Flower of the mountain yes when I put the rose in my hair like the Andalusian girls used or shall I wear a red yes . . . (783:6–8)

Cf. "Shall I Wear a White Rose or Shall I Wear a Red?"

REMARKS: This final reference in Molly's soliloquy reenforces the image of eternal anticipation. As all the lovers, historical and prospective, blend into one consubstantial being, the song Molly sang a few moments before becomes her song of eternal expectation for Mulvey and by extension all her lovers and every man.

NOTES

Introduction

1. "Joyce and Music," *Chesterian* 17 (July–August 1936): 166.
2. "On the Twelve-Note Road," trans. Deryck Cook, *Music Survey* 4 (October 1951): 324.
3. *Music and James Joyce* (Chicago: Folcroft for Argus Book Shop, 1936), p. 6.
4. *James Joyce Quarterly* 2, 4 (Summer 1965): 247–254.
5. *Sound and Poetry,* ed. Northrop Frye (New York: Columbia University Press, 1957), pp. 16–54.
6. *James Joyce Quarterly* 3, 1 (Fall 1965): 12–24.
7. (New York: New Directions, 1941), pp. 98–105.
8. *University of Kansas City Review* 26 (Winter 1959):83–92.
9. *James Joyce Review* 3, 1–2 (1959): 51–53.
10. New York: Oxford University Press, 1961.
11. (New York: Pellegrini and Cudahy, 1951), Chapter 3.
12. *Literary Monographs,* Vol. I, ed. Eric Rothstein and Thomas K. Dunseath (Madison: University of Wisconsin Press, 1967), pp. 245–98, 319–20.
13. *Essays and Studies by Members of the English Association* 31 (1945): 95–106.
14. *PMLA* 68 (1953): 1223–28.
15. *MLQ* 13 (1952): 149–162.
16. *Society and Self in the Novel,* ed. Mark Schorer (New York: Columbia University Press, 1956), pp. 78–116.
17. *PMLA* 71 (1956): 321–339.
18. *PMLA* 72 (1957): 286–295.
19. (New Haven: Yale University Press, 1957). Quotations from this book are reprinted with permission of the author and Yale University Press, copyright 1957.
20. *PMLA* 66 (1951): 78–84. Quotations from this article are reprinted with permission of the author.
21. Ph.D. dissertation, University of North Carolina, 1969. Quotations from this work reprinted by permission of the author.
22. (New York: Columbia University Press, 1959).
23. (Chapel Hill: University of North Carolina Press, 1968). Quotations from this volume in the text are reprinted by permission of the author and the University of North Carolina Press.

Poetry

1. Zack Bowen, "Goldenhair: Joyce's Archetypal Female," *Literature and Psychology* 17, 4 (1967): 219–228. Hereafter cited as "Goldenhair."
2. "Goldenhair," p. 221.
3. "Goldenhair," p. 222.
4. William York Tindall (ed.), *Chamber Music* (New York: Columbia University Press, 1954), p. 83.
5. "Goldenhair," p. 223.

Exiles

1. "Two Unnoted Musical Allusions," *James Joyce Quarterly* 9 (Fall 1971): 140–142.

Dubliners

1. Cf., Zack Bowen, "After the Race," *James Joyce's DUBLINERS: Critical Essays,* ed. Clive Hart (New York: Viking Press, 1969), p. 60.
2. "Maria's Song in Joyce's 'Clay,'" *Studies in Short Fiction* 1, 2 (Winter 1964): 153–54.
3. "'The Lass of Aughrim' or the Betrayal of James Joyce," *The Celtic Master: Contributions to the First James Joyce Symposium Held in Dublin, 1967,* ed. Maurice Harmon (Dublin: Dolmen Press, 1969), pp. 17–25.
4. *Ibid.,* p. 20.
5. *Ibid.,* p. 22.

Stephen Hero

1. John V. Hagopian, "The Epiphany in Joyce's 'Counterparts,'" *Studies in Short Fiction* 1, 4 (Summer 1964): 274.
2. (New York: New Directions, 1963), p. 93.
3. *A Portrait of the Artist as a Young Man* (New York: Viking Press, 1968), p. 252.
4. *Chambers's Biographical Dictionary,* rev. ed., ed. J. O. Thorne (New York: St. Martin's Press, 1968), p. 410.
5. See discussion, p. 26.

A Portrait of the Artist as a Young Man

1. Marguerite Harkness suggested this interpretation.
2. Mabel Worthington, "Gilbert and Sullivan Songs in the Works of James

Joyce," *Hartford Studies in Literature* 1, 3 (1969): 211–12.

3. *Penguin Book of Latin Verse,* ed. Frederick Brittain (Baltimore: Penguin Books, 1962), p. 123.

4. Richard Ellmann, *James Joyce* (New York: Oxford University Press, 1959), pp. 53, 162.

5. Cf. also Robert Cantwell, "Brightness Falls from the Air," *The New Republic* 87, 1131 (5 August 1936): 375–377; and J. H. Friend, "Joyce and The Elizabethans," *The New Republic* 88, 1136 (9 September 1936): 131.

6. In a lecture at SUNY Binghamton, November 1971.

Ulysses Introduction

1. The most comprehensive and ingenius effort thus far to connect the Sirens episode with the fugue is Lawrence Levin's "The Sirens Episode as Music: Joyce's Experiment in Prose Polyphony," *James Joyce Quarterly* 3, 1 (Fall 1965): 12–24; see also David Cole, "Fugal Structure in the Sirens Episode of *Ulysses,*" *Modern Fiction Studies* 19 (Summer 1973): 221–226.

2. Willi Apel, *Harvard Dictionary of Music* (Cambridge, Mass.: Harvard University Press, 1961), p. 112.

3. Stuart Gilbert, *James Joyce's ULYSSES: A Study* (New York: Vintage, 1952), pp. 252–253.

4. Harry Levin, *James Joyce,* p. 99; Horst Petri, *Literatur und Musik* (Gottingen: Sachse and Pohl, 1964), pp. 35–43. Petri's arguments regarding the fugal aspects of the chapter are not unlike some of those presented in this study; however, his conclusion that the structure of the chapter is based on the sonata form is just as indefensible as the fugal structure idea. I am indebted to Calvin Brown for calling Petri's work to my attention.

5. Litz, *James Joyce* (New York: Twayne Publishers, 1966), p. 70.

6. Stanley Sultan, "The Sirens at the Ormand Bar: *Ulysses,*" p. 91.

7. Most of the musical references used in this study are derived from the allusion list published by Matthew Hodgart and Mabel Worthington.

8. Francis Bulhof in her note, "Agendath Again," *James Joyce Quarterly* 7, 4 (Summer, 1970): 326–332, deals with the community-of-existence theme in *Ulysses.* Bulhof begins with the proposition that the minds of Stephen, Bloom, and Molly are completely separable experiences, then proceeds to describe the range of things they share in common. "However sharply the characters of Stephen and Bloom may have been delineated by Joyce, it did not escape his commentators that occasionally the separate consciousness and expression systems of the individuals yield to a supra-individual unity" (p. 329). The conclusion in this note is that because the characters live in a similar environment, the similarity of the objects of their thought "is naturally to be expected." However, this does not take into account thoughts both conscious and subconscious that are nearly identical as well as merely similar.

9. T. S. Eliot, "Tradition and the Individual Talent," in *Selected Essays of T. S. Eliot* (New York: Harcourt, Brace and World, 1964), p. 4.

10. Roderick Davis, "The Fourfold Moses in *Ulysses,*" *James Joyce Quarterly* 7, 2 (Winter 1969–70): 121.

Telemachus

1. W. B. Yeats, "Who Goes with Fergus," in *The Countess Cathleen, The Variorum Edition of the Plays of W. B. Yeats* (New York: Macmillan, 1966), I, ii, 220–225, 231–236.
2. Thornton, *Allusions,* p. 16.
3. *Ibid.,* p. 17.
4. Smith, "Musical Allusions," p. 95.
5. Richard Ellmann, *James Joyce* (New York: Oxford University Press, 1959), pp. 213–14.

Nestor

1. As quoted in Thornton, *Allusions,* p. 30.
2. *Ibid.*
3. John Webster, *The White Devil,* ed. John Russell Brown (Cambridge: Harvard University Press, 1960), Act V, scene iv, ll. 103–104.
4. T. S. Eliot, "The Waste Land," *The Complete Poems and Plays* (New York: Harcourt, Brace and World, Inc., 1962), ll. 74–75.
5. The entire ballad is reprinted in Thornton, *Allusions,* p. 35.

Proteus

1. Thornton, *Allusions,* p. 46.
2. Cf. Smith, "Musical Allusions," p. 54.
3. Error in 1961 edition: should be "di."
4. Cf. also Smith, "Musical Allusions," pp. 39–43.
5. (London, 1673), pp. 19–20.
6. As quoted in Schutte, *Joyce and Shakespeare,* pp. 60–61.
7. Thornton, *Allusions,* p. 62.
8. William Blake, "The Gates of Paradise," *The Complete Poetry and Selected Prose of John Donne and The Complete Poetry of William Blake* (New York: Modern Library, 1941), pp. 1020–1022, ll. 97–98.
9. See discussion, p. 80.
10. See discussion, pp. 72–73.
11. See discussion, p. 67.
12. See discussion, p. 68.
13. See discussion, p. 62.
14. See discussion, p. 80.
15. See also discussion, p. 70.

Calypso

1. See discussion, p. 67.
2. Song not cited in Hodgart and Worthington.
3. James Joyce, *Finnegans Wake* (New York: Viking Press, 1957), p. 12:9.
4. Thornton, *Allusions*, p. 73.
5. Hall, "Joyce's Use of Da Ponte . . . ," p. 80.
6. *Ibid.*, pp. 79–80.
7. See discussion, pp. 85–86.
8. Hall, "Joyce's Use of Da Ponte . . . ," p. 80.
9. I am indebted to Mr. Wayne D. Shirley, Reference Librarian, Music Division, Library of Congress, for providing the words and music to "Seaside Girls," a song we had given up hope of finding.
10. Marguerite Harkness suggested this.
11. *Kobbe's Complete Opera Book*, as cited in Thornton, *Allusions*, p. 76.

Lotus Eaters

1. Thornton, *Allusions*, p. 78.
2. See discussion, pp. 87–88.
3. Iona and Peter Opie, *The Oxford Dictionary of Nursery Rhymes* (Oxford: Oxford University Press, 1952), p. 211.
4. Hodgart and Worthington, *Song in the Works*, p. 207.
5. For complete words and explanation of the Joyce scholarship of the song see Victory Pomeranz, "When M'Carthy Took the Floor," *James Joyce Quarterly* 11, 1 (Fall 1973): 52–54.

Hades

1. For a fuller discussion of "The Croppy Boy," see pp. 194–204.
2. Smith, "Musical Allusions," p. 135.
3. Hall, "Joyce's Use of Da Ponte . . . ," p. 80. Also see my discussion, pp. 87–88.
4. Thornton lists, as do Worthington and Hodgart, "Has Anybody Here Seen Kelly?" which does not have the words, "He's as bad as old Antonio. He left me on my ownio." Thornton goes on to explain that the words were altered to fit an American context from an earlier song, "Oh, Oh, Antonio." He did not have access to the earlier song. *Allusions*, pp. 94–95. The "Has Anybody . . ." song is fairly well known, and the Antonio song appears in *Frances and Day's Album of Famous Old Songs, No. 9*. Not only the words were altered from the Antonio song to the Kelly song, but also the music in "Kelly" bears no resemblance to the Antonio music. A third song, "Kelly from the Isle of Man," which I have not seen, presumably provides the transition between the two. Also C. W. Murphy is listed as cowriter and composer of "Antonio" and "Has Anybody . . ." but in collaboration with Dan Lipton

in the first and Will Leters in the second. I will hazard a guess that Murphy's muse failed to heed the second call and that he lifted some of the lyrics from the first instance and put them in the "Kelly from the Isle of Man" song, which was later adapted by William J. McKenna into the popular "Has Anybody Here Seen Kelly?" Hence the similarities in situations and words.

5. Thornton, *Allusions,* p. 96.
6. See discussion, p. 109.
7. See discussion, pp. 90–91.
8. Thornton, *Allusions,* p. 95.
9. From the song cover of the Pigott & Co. edition (n. d.).

Aeolus

1. See discussion, pp. 86–87.
2. Hall, "Joyce's Use of Da Ponte . . . ," p. 81.
3. *The Oxford Dictionary of Nursery Rhymes* mentions the possible connection between the two songs:

> It has been presumed that the original of "The House that Jack Built" is a Hebrew chant, "Had Gadyo," which was first printed in 1590 in a Prague edition of the *Hagadah.* The chant, a fine early example of the cumulative story, bears comparison with an English folktale, "The Old Woman and her Pig," but a stretch of the imagination is needed to connect the subject-matter (kid, cat, dog, staff, fire, water, ox, butcher, angel of death) with the nuptials of the tattered man and forlorn milkmaid. This is not to disprove the antiquity of the English rhyme which, as JOH points out, "is probably very old, as may be inferred from the mention of the priest all shaven and shorn." More substantial evidence of its age, however, is shown by the equivalents to the rhyme in European languages. (p. 231)

4. *Hagadah of Passover,* trans. Abraham Regelson (New York: Shulsinger Bros., 1944), p. 64.
5. Roderick Davis, "The Fourfold Moses," 120–31.
6. Thornton, *Allusions,* p. 111.
7. Smith, "Musical Allusions," pp. 137–40.
8. *Ibid.,* p. 140.
9. See discussion, pp. 80–81.
10. Poem XXXI.
11. See discussion, p. 80.
12. Hyde's version is quoted on p. 81.
13. Dante, *The Inferno,* trans. John Ciardi (New York: Mentor, 1954), Canto V, ll. 97–104.
14. Prescott, "Local Allusions," p. 1228.
15. *Down by the Liffeyside,* Topic Records, London.

Lestrygonians

1. Smith, "Musical Allusions," pp. 54–55.
2. Thornton, *Allusions,* p. 136.
3. See discussion, pp. 121–122.
4. Patrick Galvin, *Irish Songs of Resistance* (New York, n. d.), p. 50.
5. Zack Bowen, "Lizzie Twigg: Gone But Not Forgotten," *James Joyce Quarterly* 6, 2 (Spring 1969): 138–139.
6. See pp. 57–58.
7. See discussion, pp. 127–128.
8. Hall, "Joyce's Use of Da Ponte . . . ," p. 81.
9. See discussion, p. 85.
10. Hall, "Joyce's Use of Da Ponte . . . ," p. 81.
11. See discussion, pp. 89–90.

Skylla and Charybdis

1. Thornton, *Allusions,* p. 158.
2. See discussion, p. 79.
3. See also discussion, p. 79.
4. Schutte, *Joyce and Shakespeare,* pp. 62–63.
5. *Ibid.,* pp. 65–66.
6. Opie, *The Oxford Dictionary of Nursery Rhymes,* pp. 63–64.
7. As quoted in Schutte, *Joyce and Shakespeare,* p. 61.
8. Hall, "Joyce's Use of Da Ponte . . . ," p. 81.
9. In *English Romantic Writers,* ed. David Perkins (New York: Harcourt, Brace and World, 1967), p. 1003.
10. Thornton, *Allusions,* p. 213.

Wandering Rocks

1. See discussion, p. 157.
2. Thornton, *Allusions,* pp. 228–29.

Sirens

1. For a discussion of the overture to Sirens see the introductory essay on *Ulysses,* p. 53.
2. The order of the entries for "Goodbye Sweetheart Goodbye" is a modification of the order of other entries; all of the references to the song will be cited in chronological order, occasionally leaving out musical references to other songs until I have finished citing all the segments of "Goodbye Sweetheart Goodbye."
3. Smith, "Musical Allusions," pp. 137–140.

4. See discussion, p. 123.

5. See discussion, p. 162 for words.

6. Hodgart and Worthington, *Song in the Works*, p. 69.

7. Thornton, *Allusions*, p. 244.

8. Hodgart and Worthington, *Song in the Works*, p. 194.

9. I am indebted to Mabel Worthington for sharing her discovery of Jeffreys's version of *"M'appari"* with me.

10. For an especially comprehensive treatment see Stanley Sultan, "The Sirens at the Ormond Bar: *Ulysses.*"

11. See discussion, pp. 85–86, 88, 89–90, 141.

12. I am indebted to Joseph Prescott for pointing out to me the methodology by which Joyce arrived at the combination name, "Siopold." Following is the pertinent documentation which Professor Prescott was kind enough to abstract from an as-yet-unpublished section of his dessertation, "James Joyce's ULYSSES as a Work in Progress" (Harvard, 1944), pp. 223–24:

> In the margin of a proofsheet now at Harvard appear the following notations:
>
> Lionel
>   Leopold
>   Simon
>   Richie
>   ~~Richsiopold~~
>   Siopold
>
> Here is a complete record of the progress by which Joyce composed the verbal chord "Siopold!"

13. See discussion, p. 96.

14. See discussion, pp. 90–91.

15. Sternfeld, "Poetry and Music," p. 24.

16. Marian Kaplun, " 'The Song the Sirens Sang,' " p. 52.

17. Ellmann, *James Joyce*, p. 160.

18. Sternfeld, "Poetry and Music," pp. 27–31; Mabel Worthington, "Irish Folksongs in Joyce's *Ulysses*," *PMLA* 71 (1956): 325–28.

19. Sternfeld, "Poetry and Music," p. 30.

20. See discussion, pp. oo–oo for a complete explication of the themes.

21. Kathleen Hoagland, ed., *1000 Years of Irish Poetry* (New York: Grosset & Dunlap, 1962), p. 540.

22. Percy A. Scholes, *The Oxford Companion to Music* (New York: Oxford University Press, 1970), p. 608.

Cyclops

1. Thornton, *Allusions*, p. 256.

2. Prescott, "Local Allusions," p. 1226.

3. Thornton, *Allusions*, p. 259.

4. *Ibid.*

5. The 1934 edition of *Ulysses* read "the bald Soldier Boy," which was a lot funnier.

6. See discussion p. 211 for words.

7. See discussion, p. 211.
8. See discussion, p. 220.

Nausicaa

1. See discussion, pp. 184–185, 334–335.
2. Thornton, *Allusions,* pp. 309–10.
3. Hodgart and Worthington, *Song in the Works,* p. 75.
4. See discussion, p. 138.
5. I am indebted to Thomas E. Connolly for his reminiscence from his boyhood.
6. See discussion, pp. 92–93. Reference not cited in Hodgart and Worthington.
7. See discussion, p. 136.

Oxen of the Sun

1. *Surface and Symbol* (New York: Oxford University Press, 1962), p. 209.
2. Thornton, *Allusions,* p. 331.
3. Cecil Sharp, *English Folk-Chanteys,* p. 68. As cited in Thornton, *Allusions,* p. 338.
4. See discussion, pp. 178–187.
5. Thornton, *Allusions,* p. 347.
6. *Ibid.,* p. 350.
7. See discussion, p. 155.
8. See Alfred MacLochlainn, *Analyst* 10 (March 1956): 16.
9. There probably is a misprint in the new 1961 edition when *Bowsing* from the early edition becomes *Mousing* in the new. *Bowsing* is much more like *bousing* (the modern *boozing*) that Burns uses in "Tam O'Shanter" (Stanza 1, line 5).
10. Richard Head, *The Canting Academy* (London, 1673), p. 14.
11. For a detailed analysis of the scholarship and ramifications of the passage see Thornton, *Allusions,* pp. 352–53.
12. See also Thornton, *Allusions,* p. 354.
13. See discussion, p. 218.

Circe

1. Thornton, *Allusions,* p. 359.
2. See discussion, pp. 160, 162, 167, 168, 170, 184–185, 203, 204.
3. Hall, "Joyce's Use of Da Ponte . . . ," footnote 11, p. 82.
4. *Ibid.,* pp. 82–83.
5. Hodgart and Worthington also fall into the trap calling the song, "Someone's in the House with Dina," p. 77.
6. See discussion, p. 95.

7. See discussion, p. 144.

8. For full text of the song, see p. 257.

9. Although obvious to English readers, it might be well to note Thomas Connolly's remarks to me: "In England and in Ireland, 26 December (the feast of St. Stephen) is called Boxing Day. It is the day that gifts (in boxes) are given to the servants of the household. This fact explains the reference to 'box' in the song."

10. See discussion, p. 155.

11. See discussion, pp. 175–177.

12. See discussion, pp. 72–73.

13. Hall, "Joyce's Use of Da Ponte . . . ," p. 83.

14. Schutte, *Joyce and Shakespeare,* p. 124.

15. Thornton, *Allusions,* p. 403.

16. Iona and Peter Opie, *Lore and Language of School Children* (Oxford: Clarendon Press, 1961), p. 133.

17. See discussion, pp. 72–73.

18. See discussion, p. 144.

19. Thornton, *Allusions,* p. 411.

20. Ellmann, *James Joyce,* p. 380.

21. Again it makes sense here to place a number of references to a song in one entry rather than to list them in separate, strict chronological order.

22. See discussion and words to the song, p. 243.

23. See discussion, pp. 100–101.

24. Ellmann, *James Joyce,* p. 213.

25. See discussion, p. 70.

26. Thornton, *Allusions,* p. 424.

27. See discussion, pp. 212, 225.

28. See discussion, p. 127.

29. See Schutte, *Joyce and Shakespeare,* p. 61.

30. See discussion, pp. 254–255.

Eumaeus

1. Schutte, *Joyce and Shakespeare,* p. 187.

2. See discussion, pp. 87–88.

3. See discussion, pp. 220, 222.

4. See discussion, pp. 48, 50, 108, 115, and footnote 3 Hades.

5. Thornton gives details of both performances, *Allusions,* pp. 439–40.

6. *Ibid.,* p. 443.

7. See discussion, pp. 132–133.

8. *Ulysses,* 639:28–35.

9. Kitty was the daughter of Emma Caroline Mitchell Wood and Sir John Page Wood.

10. Opie, *Oxford Dictionary of Nursery Rhymes,* pp. 330–31.

11. See discussion, p. 104.

12. Opie, *Oxford Dictionary of Nursery Rhymes,* p. 215.

13. See discussion, pp. 99–100.

14. Scholes, *Oxford Companion to Music,* p. 633.

15. Stanley Sultan, *The Argument of ULYSSES* (Columbus: Ohio State University Press, 1964), p. 380–81.

16. *Ibid.,* p. 381.
17. *Explicator* 24, 6 (February 1966): item 55.
18. See discussion, p. 218.
19. Vernon Hall, Jr. sees the episode in quite a different light ("Joyce's *Ulysses* XVI," *Explicator* 12 [February 1954]: item 25). He acknowledges the existence of a legitimate version of the song but bases his interpretation on an obscene version which he says is largely unprintable. He does give us the significant passage, however:

> As she lay on her lowbacked car,
> The man at the turnpike bar,
> Never asked for the toll,
> But just jerked his old pole
> And looked after the lowbacked car.

Hall's explication of the passage in Eumaeus is as follows:

> The major symbolism of these paragraphs is embodied in the crude pun of the ballad's chorus. It echoes the "Nausicaä" experience of Bloom and reminds us not to delude ourselves into thinking that a son has been found. Bloom is incapable of becoming a father.

Evidently Hall did not have access to the original, clean version of the song (printed in the present discussion). If one has the predilection, the double entendre of "rubbed his owld poll" in the legitimate version can be interpreted as being as gross as "jerked his old pole." As Mabel Worthington points out in a later article ("Joyce's *Ulysses* XVI," *Explicator* 13 [December 1954]: item 20), Hall has overlooked another line from the song, "To be married by Father Maher." This line is, of course, from the clean version (Stanza IV, line 10) and would seem to indicate that the obscene version of the song and consequently Hall's interpretation (which **is** strained even when buttressed by the bawdy version) are not the ones that Joyce intended.

Ithaca

1. Galvin, *Irish Songs of Resistance,* pp. 9–10.
2. As cited in Thornton, *Allusions,* pp. 482–83.

Penelope

1. See discussion, pp. 135–136.
2. See discussion, pp. 143–144.
3. See complete text of words in next reference.
4. Thornton, *Allusions,* p. 247.
5. See discussion, pp. 184–185.
6. Thornton, *Allusions,* p. 493.
7. See discussion, pp. 261–262, 281.
8. Pp. 343–344. See also discussion, pp. 140, 306–307, 313.

BIBLIOGRAPHY

Adams, Robert Martin. *Surface and Symbol: The Consistency of James Joyce's ULYSSES.* New York: Oxford University Press, 1962.

Apel, Willi. *Harvard Dictionary of Music.* Cambridge, Mass.: Harvard University Press, 1960.

Bass, Richard. "Joyce's *Ulysses.*" *Explicator* 24, 6 (February 1966): item 55.

Bauerle, Ruth. "Two Unnoted Musical Allusions," *James Joyce Quarterly* 9 (Fall 1971): 140–142.

Blake, William. "The Gates of Paradise." In *The Complete Poetry and Selected Prose of John Donne and The Complete Poetry of William Blake,* pp. 1020–1022. New York: Modern Library, 1941.

Bowen, Zack. "After the Race." In *James Joyce's DUBLINERS: Critical Essays,* edited by Clive Hart, pp. 53–61. New York: Viking Press, 1969.

————. "The Bronzegold Sirensong: A Musical Analysis of the Sirens Episode in Joyce's *Ulysses,*" *Literary Monographs,* Vol. I, ed. Eric Rothstein and Thomas K. Dunseath, pp. 245–298, 319–320. Madison: University of Wisconsin Press, 1967.

————. "Goldenhair: Joyce's Archetypal Female." *Literature and Psychology* 17 (1967): 219–228.

————. "Lizzie Twigg: Gone But Not Forgotten." *James Joyce Quarterly* 6 (Summer 1969): 368–370.

Boyle, Robert, S. J. "*Ulysses* as Frustrated Sonata Form." *James Joyce Quarterly* 2 (Summer 1965): 247–254.

Breit, Harvey. "Footnote." *New York Times Book Review,* 20 January 1957, p. 8.

Brittain, Frederick, ed. *Penguin Book of Latin Verse.* Baltimore: Penguin Books, 1962.

Budgen, Frank Spencer Curtis. *James Joyce and the Making of ULYSSES.* Bloomington: Indiana University Press, 1934.

Bulhof, Francis. "Agendath Again." *James Joyce Quarterly* 4 (Summer 1970): 326–332.

Cantwell, Robert. "Brightness Falls from the Air." *The New Republic* 87 (5 August 1936): 375–377.

Cardus, Neville. "Passages from James Joyce in Music: Matyas Seiber's *Ulysses.*" *Manchester Guardian,* 13 December 1957, p. 7.

Chambers's Biographical Dictionary. Rev. ed. Ed. J. O. Thorne. New York: St. Martins Press, 1968.

Cope, Jackson I. "Rhythmic Gesture: Image and Aesthetic in Joyce's *Ulysses.*" *ELH* 29 (1962): 67–89.

Dallapiccola, Luigi. "On the Twelve-Note Road," trans. Deryck Cook. *Music Survey* 4 (October 1951): 323–325.

Dante, Alighieri. *The Inferno,* trans. John Ciardi. New York: Mentor, 1954.

358

Davies, Phillips George. "Maria's Song in Joyce's 'Clay.'" *Studies in Short Fiction* 1 (Winter 1964): 153–154.

Davis, Roderick. "The Fourfold Moses in *Ulysses.*" *James Joyce Quarterly* 7 (Winter 1969): 120–131.

Duncan, Joseph E. "The Modality of the Audible in Joyce's *Ulysses.*" *PMLA* 72 (1957): 286–295.

Eliot, Thomas Sterns. "Tradition and the Individual Talent." In *Selected Essays of T. S. Eliot,* pp. 3–11. New York: Harcourt, Brace, and World, 1964.

———. "The Waste Land." In *The Complete Poems and Plays,* pp. 37–47. New York: Harcourt, Brace, and World, 1962.

Ellmann, Richard. *James Joyce.* New York: Oxford University Press, 1959.

Epstein, E. L. "The Jewel of Asia." *James Joyce Review* 3 (1959): 47–49.

Friend, J. H. "Joyce and the Elizabethans." *The New Republic* 88 (9 September 1936), p. 131.

Galvin, Patrick. *Irish Songs of Resistance.* New York: Folklore Press, n.d.

Gilbert, Stuart. *James Joyce's ULYSSES: A Study.* New York: Vintage Books, 1955.

Gogarty, Oliver St. John. "Joyce as a Friend of Music." *Tomorrow* (December 1949): 42–45.

Greenway, John. "A Guide Through James Joyce's *Ulysses.*" *College English* 17 (November 1955): 67–78.

Hagadah of Passover, trans. Abraham Regelson. New York: Shulsinger Bros., 1944.

Hagopian, John V. "The Epiphany in Joyce's 'Counterparts.'" *Studies in Short Fiction* 1 (Summer 1964): 272–276.

Hall, Vernon, Jr. "Joyce's *Ulysses* XVI." *Explicator* 12 (February 1954): item 25.

———. "Joyce's Use of Da Ponte and Mozart's *Don Giovanni.*" *PMLA* 66 (1951): 78–84.

Hoagland, Kathleen, ed. *1000 Years of Irish Poetry.* New York: Grosset and Dunlap, 1962.

Hodgart, Matthew John Caldwell and Mabel P. Worthington. *Song in the Works of James Joyce.* New York: Columbia University Press, 1959.

Hughes, Herbert, ed. *The Joyce Book.* London: Sylvan Press, 1933.

Joyce, James. *Chamber Music.* Ed. William York Tindall. New York: Columbia University Press, 1954.

———. *Collected Poems.* New York: Viking Press, 1963.

———. *Dubliners.* New York: Viking Press, 1970.

———. *Exiles.* New York: Viking Press, 1970.

———. *Finnegans Wake.* New York: Viking Press, 1957.

———. *A Portrait of the Artist as a Young Man.* New York: Viking Press, 1968.

———. *Stephen Hero.* New York: New Directions, 1963.

———. *Ulysses.* New York: Random House, 1961.

Joyce, Stanislaus. *Recollections of James Joyce.* New York: James Joyce Society, 1950.

Kain, Richard Morgan. *Fabulous Voyager: James Joyce's ULYSSES.* Chicago: University of Chicago Press, 1947.

Kaplun, Marian H. "The Search for 'The Song the Sirens Sang.'" *James Joyce Review* 3 (1959): 51–53.

Korg, Jacob. "A Possible Source of the 'Circe' Chapter of Joyce's *Ulysses*." *Modern Language Notes* 71 (February 1956): 96–98.

Kranidas, Thomas. "Mr. Duffy and the Song of Songs." *James Joyce Quarterly* 3 (Spring 1966): 220.

Levin, Harry. *James Joyce: A Critical Introduction*. Norfolk, Conn.: New Directions Books, 1960.

Levin, Lawrence L. "The Sirens Episode as Music: Joyce's Experiment in Prose Polyphony." *James Joyce Quarterly* 3 (Fall 1965): 12–24.

Litz, A. Walton. *The Art of James Joyce: Method and Design in ULYSSES and FINNEGANS WAKE*. New York: Oxford University Press, 1961.

Livermore, Ann. "Carmen and *Ulysses*." *Music Review* 28 (1967): 300–310.

MacDonagh, Donagh. "'The Lass of Aughrim' or the Betrayal of James Joyce." In *The Celtic Master: Contributions to the First James Joyce Symposium Held in Dublin, 1967,* edited by Maurice Harmon, pp. 17–25. Dublin: Dolman Press, 1969.

MacLochlainn, Alfred. *Analyst* 10 (March 1956): 16.

Magalaner, Marvin. "The Anti-Semitic Limerick Incidents and Joyce's Bloomsday." *PMLA* 68 (1953): 1219–1223.

——— and Richard M. Kain. *James Joyce: The Man, the Work and the Reputation*. New York: New York University Press, 1956.

McHugh, Roger. "James Joyce's Synge-Song." *Envoy* 3 (November 1950): 12–17.

McNelly, Willis E. "The Use of Catholic Elements as an Artistic Source in James Joyce's *Ulysses*." *Dissertation Abstracts* 17 (1957): 3020.

Mercier, Vivien. "James Joyce and an Irish Tradition." In *Society and Self in the Novel,* edited by Mark Schorer, pp. 78–116. New York: Columbia University Press, 1956.

Opie, Iona (Archibald) and Peter. *The Lore and Language of School Children*. Oxford: Clarendon Press, 1961.

———, eds. *The Oxford Dictionary of Nursery Rhymes*. Oxford: Clarendon Press, 1952.

———. *The Oxford Nursery Rhyme Book*. New York: Oxford University Press, 1955.

Peradotto, J. J. "Liturgical Pattern in *Ulysses*." *Modern Language Notes* 75 (1960): 321–326.

Perkins, David, ed. *English Romantic Writers*. New York: Harcourt, Brace, and World, 1967.

Petri, Horst. *Literatur und Musik*. Gottingen: Sachse and Pohl, 1964.

Pomeranz, Victory. "When M'Carthy Took the Floor." *James Joyce Quarterly* 11, 1 (Fall 1973): 52–54.

Prescott, Joseph. *Exploring James Joyce*. Carbondale: Southern Illinois University Press, 1964.

———. "Local Allusions in Joyce's *Ulysses*." *PMLA* 68 (1953): 1223–1228.

———. "Notes on Joyce's *Ulysses*." *Modern Language Quarterly* 13 (June 1952): 149–162.

———. "A Song in Joyce's *Ulysses*." *Notes and Queries* 197 (1952): 15–16.

Ross, Martin. *Music and James Joyce*. Chicago: Folcroft for Argus Book Shop, 1936.

Scholes, Percy Alfred. *The Oxford Companion to Music*. New York: Oxford University Press, 1970.

Schutte, William M. *Joyce and Shakespeare: A Study in the Meaning of ULYSSES*. New Haven: Yale University Press, 1957.

Seiber, Matyas. "A Note on *Ulysses*." *Music Survey* 3 (June 1951): 263–270.

Shakespeare, William. *Hamlet*. In *The Complete Plays and Poems of William Shakespeare,* edited by William Allan Neilson and Charles Jarvis Hill, pp. 1047–1092. Cambridge, Mass.: Riverside Press, 1942.

Smith, James Penny. "Musical Allusions in James Joyce's *Ulysses*." Ph.D. dissertation, University of North Carolina, 1969.

Steinberg, Erwin Ray. "The Stream of Consciousness Technique in James Joyce's *Ulysses*." *Dissertation Abstracts* 18 (1958): 237–238.

Sternfeld, Frederick. "Poetry and Music—Joyce's *Ulysses*." In *Sound and Poetry,* edited by Northrop Frye, pp. 16–54. New York: Columbia University Press, 1957.

Strong, Leonard Alfred George. "James Joyce and Vocal Music." *Essays and Studies by Members of the English Association* 31 (1945): 95–106.

———. *The Sacred River: An Approach to James Joyce*. New York: Methuen, 1949.

Sultan, Stanley. *The Argument of ULYSSES*. Columbus: Ohio State University Press, 1964.

———. "The Sirens at the Ormond Bar: *Ulysses*." *University of Kansas City Review* 26 (Winter 1959): 83–92.

Thornton, Weldon. "An Allusion List for James Joyce's *Ulysses*." *James Joyce Quarterly* 1 (1963): 17–25.

———. *Allusions in ULYSSES*. North Carolina: University of North Carolina Press, 1968.

Tindall, William York. *James Joyce: His Way of Interpreting the Modern World*. New York: Scribner, 1950.

Webster, John. *The White Devil,* ed. John Russell Brown. Cambridge: Harvard University Press, 1960.

White, Terrence, "Joyce and Music." *Chesterian* 17 (July–August 1936): 163–167.

Worthington, Mabel P. "Gilbert and Sullivan Songs in the Works of James Joyce." *Hartford Studies in Literature* 1 (1969): 211–212.

———. "Irish Folksongs in Joyce's *Ulysses*." *PMLA* 71 (1956): 321–339.

———. "Joyce's *Ulysses*: XVI." *Explicator* 13 (1954): item 20.

———. "Nursery Rhymes in *Finnegans Wake*." *Journal of American Folklore* 70 (January 1957): 37–48.

Yeats, William Butler. "Who Goes with Fergus." In *The Countess Cathleen, The Variorum Edition of the Plays of W. B. Yeats,* pp. 52, 54, 56. New York: Macmillan, 1966.

Zabel, Morton D. "The Lyrics of James Joyce." *Poetry* 36 (July 1930): 206–213.

GENERAL INDEX

SONG INDEX